P9-DFY-929

WINNING AT NEW PRODUCTS

ALSO BY ROBERT G. COOPER

Product Leadership: Creating and Launching Superior New Products

Portfolio Management for New Products
(coauthors, Scott J. Edgett and Elko J. Kleinschmidt)

Product Development for the Service Sector
(coauthor, Scott J. Edgett)

WINNING
at
NEW PRODUCTS

Creating Value through Innovation

FOURTH EDITION

Robert G. Cooper

BASIC BOOKS
A MEMBER OF THE PERSEUS BOOKS GROUP
New York

Copyright © 1988, 1993, 2001, 2011 by Robert G. Cooper

Many of the designations used by manufacturers and sellers to distinguish their products are claimed as trademarks. Where those designations appear in this book and Basic Books was aware of a trademark claim, the designations have been printed in initial capital letters.

Published by Basic Books,
A Member of the Perseus Books Group

All rights reserved. Printed in the United States of America. No part of this book may be reproduced in any manner whatsoever without written permission except in the case of brief quotations embodied in critical articles and reviews. For information, address Basic Books, 387 Park Avenue South, New York, NY 10016-8810.

Books published by Basic Books are available at special discounts for bulk purchases in the United States by corporations, institutions, and other organizations. For more information, please contact the Special Markets Department at the Perseus Books Group, 2300 Chestnut Street, Suite 200, Philadelphia, PA 19103, or call (800) 810-4145, ext. 5000, or e-mail special.markets@perseusbooks.com.

Library of Congress Cataloging-in-Publication Data
Cooper, Robert G. (Robert Gravlin), 1943-
  Winning at new products : creating value through innovation / Robert G. Cooper. — 4th ed.
    p. cm.
  Includes bibliographical references and index.
  ISBN 978-0-465-02578-7 (pbk. : alk. paper) — ISBN 978-0-465-02584-8 (e-book : alk. paper) 1. New products. I. Title.
  HF5415.153.C65 2011
  658.5'75—dc22
                              2011011230

10 9 8 7 6 5 4 3

To the three ladies in my life:
my wife, Linda, and my two daughters, Barbara and Heather

CONTENTS

CHAPTER 3
DRIVERS OF SUCCESS—WHY THE BEST INNOVATORS EXCEL 56

CHAPTER 4
THE *STAGE-GATE*® IDEA-TO-LAUNCH SYSTEM 83

CHAPTER 5
NEXT-GENERATION *STAGE-GATE*®—HOW COMPANIES HAVE EVOLVED AND ACCELERATED THE SYSTEM 120

CHAPTER 6
DISCOVERY—THE QUEST FOR BREAKTHROUGH IDEAS 156

CHAPTER 7
THE FRONT-END WORK—FROM DISCOVERY TO DEVELOPMENT 192

PREFACE

Stage-Gate® has become the most widely used method for conceiving, developing, and launching new products in industry today. *Stage-Gate* is much more than a business process, however. The model was originally conceived by observing successful product developers as they drove bold and major innovations to market. Those early observations led to the conclusion that there was a "better way"— that some innovation teams and project leaders had intuitively figured it out. I tried to capture their *secrets to success* on paper, and so was born the *Stage-Gate* system. Thus, *Stage-Gate* is an idea-to-launch process, but one that encompasses a body of knowledge and best practices. Those best practices embedded within today's *Stage-Gate* are now based on studies of thousands of successful new-product developments and hundreds of companies, and reveal what the winners do differently from the rest.

The emphasis in this fourth edition of *Winning at New Products* is on *bold innovation*. I've watched as companies, a few industries excepted, have shifted their innovation efforts from true innovations and major projects to much smaller and less ambitious attempts over the last decade or so. It's somewhat disheartening to see what these companies are calling "innovation," versus what it should be. In some firms, product development has been totally trivialized—it's "renovation" rather than innovation. I hope this fourth edition does sound a wake-up call, telling you that *true innovation* and *bold product development* is within your grasp. So let's get back to basics and to what made companies great in the first place: The success drivers outlined in the first few chapters and the *Stage-Gate* system are all based on bolder innovation—let's use them!

The first edition of this book was published in 1986, before I had even begun to use the term "stage-gate." That first book reported the results of a number of research studies that colleagues and I had undertaken on new-product success and failure. And it proposed the use of a systematic idea-to-launch business process for the first time. To my surprise, the book had a profound impact on the way many companies approached product development, and firms such as P&G, DuPont, and Exxon Chemicals immediately embraced the concept of my stage-and-gate system.

But those were the early days of management of the innovation process. More research was undertaken, including some that focused on these early adopters of *Stage-Gate*. More success factors were uncovered in our NewProd research series and in our major benchmarking studies that followed; and more experiences were gained with the use of *Stage-Gate* methods (I first used the term "*Stage-Gate*" in an article that appeared in the *Journal of Marketing Management* in 1988). And so the second edition was published in 1993. It went on to become the bible for those businesses trying to overhaul their new-product process and implement *Stage-Gate*. And the third edition in 2001 continued the tradition, but with an emphasis on accelerating idea-to-launch.

This current edition is more than a simple updating of the third edition, however. There is much that is new in it. Some years have passed since I wrote the previous edition, and much more has been learned. Colleagues and I have undertaken major benchmarking studies to uncover and validate best practices in product innovation methods, portfolio management, strategy development, and idea generation. Some practices were well known and our work served to validate them and quantify their effects; but others are new. These new research avenues and their findings have been incorporated into this current book. Additionally, we now have much more experience and insight into the installation of *Stage-Gate* in leading firms worldwide. And these new insights have also been built into the current edition.

But there's another reason for this new book: *Stage-Gate* itself has evolved and morphed . . . it's an evergreen process, not because of my colleagues and me and our research, but because of the many users globally! In other words, inputs from many people and firms—open innovation—have helped to redefine *Stage-Gate*. With thousands of users globally, it's inevitable that new twists, approaches, and methods are uncovered, tested, proven, and incorporated into their idea-to-launch systems. *Stage-Gate* is now faster and more streamlined: Many firms have borrowed the concepts of lean manufacturing and built these into *Stage-Gate*. The next-generation *Stage-Gate* process, or elements of it, has been implemented by a number of firms. Portfolio management has been integrated with gating methods, and the concepts of "lean gates" and "gates with teeth" have been fashioned into the system in order to make sharper and more effective investment decisions. And *Stage-Gate* approaches have even been extended to other types of projects, including technology developments. And there's more: *Stage-Gate* has been made more adaptive, agile, and flexible; it's been modified to suit the new world of *open innovation;* and it's been automated. So much that's new makes today's *Stage-Gate* hardly recognizable to early adopters of the original process!

A number of people have provided insights, guidance, content, and encouragement in the writing of this new book. A close colleague is Scott Edgett. Scott is recognized as a leading researcher in the field of innovation management and was a co-researcher and coauthor of the series of research studies, reports, and articles on the topic of portfolio management and benchmarking best practices.

He is also a director and CEO of the Product Development Institute Inc. Elko J. Kleinschmidt is both a longtime colleague and friend. He and I have undertaken many research studies over the years, and many are referenced in this edition. The folks at Stage-Gate International, who are the professionals who implement *Stage-Gate* in firms globally, are a constant source of new thinking and validation of concepts. In particular, I thank Michelle Jones, vice president at Stage-Gate International, for insights and materials regarding implementation.

Several other people merit special attention. Jens Arleth in Denmark is managing director of Innovation Management U3 in Copenhagen, a consulting firm that specializes in *Stage-Gate* and portfolio management. He has introduced these concepts into Scandinavia, where they are now employed at leading firms throughout the region. He is also the co-developer of the ProBE diagnostic tool, the predecessor to Benchmarker™ (in Appendix A). Angelika Dreher and Peter Fuerst, managing partners at Five I's Innovation Management in Austria, have taken up the challenge of implementing *Stage-Gate* in German-speaking countries and have provided insights and examples that have found their way into this book. Gerard Ryan, managing director of Prodex Systems in Australia, implements *Stage-Gate* and automation software for the system in Australia and New Zealand, and also provided many useful insights and experiences.

Direct assistance was provided by several people: I would also like to thank my publisher, John Sherer of Basic Books (Perseus Books), who provided encouragement and adeptly steered the progress of this book from inception to launch. And thanks to Michelle Welsh-Horst, senior project editor, Perseus Books Group, for ensuring that this book came to press so efficiently and effectively. And I especially thank Michele Wynn, copy editor, who suffered through my writing and helped craft this fine finished product . . . a great job!

Robert G. Cooper
2011

1

THE
INNOVATION
CHALLENGE

Innovation is the specific instrument of entrepreneurship . . . the act that endows resources with a new capacity to create wealth.
—Peter Drucker, *Innovation and Entrepreneurship,* 1985

THE CHALLENGE: HOW TO REALLY INNOVATE

Most companies have ambitious growth goals. The problem is that there are only so many sources of growth. Four of these—market growth, market share increases, new markets, and acquisitions—are proving difficult or expensive. Markets in many industrialized countries and industries are mature and increasingly commoditized; gains in market shares are expensive; and acquisitions often don't work . . . witness share price declines after mergers are announced. New markets—India and China, for example—pose special problems; moreover, those firms that have entered Asia have already realized many of the benefits. Even traditional product development—for most companies, this means line extensions, improvements, and product modifications—seems depleted, and only serves to maintain market share.[1]

The dilemma is this: Shareholders and executives want a steady stream of profitable and high-profile new products; but management practices and the competitive and financial environments are steering companies in a different direction . . . toward smaller, less risky, and less ambitious initiatives. Part of the cause is a preoccupation with short-term profitability, driven in part by the financial community: It's difficult to create highly profitable new products yet maximize short-term results; the goal of "faster, better, cheaper" is elusive.[2] A second cause is that, even with a longer-term focus, it's really difficult to create that game-changing innovation these days—many markets and sectors simply appear barren!

We see exceptional innovations and exceptional companies everywhere today. Let's learn their secrets to success—the approaches, behaviors, and practices that make them the best innovators.

There is hope, and that's what this book is about! We see exceptional innovations and exceptional companies everywhere today. The trouble is, they are the exception—a minority of new products and companies. Odds are, you're not one of them. But these companies and big new products do provide a model, and by studying them, we learn *their secrets to success.* In the next few pages, you'll see some remarkable examples of big winners and gain insights into the approaches, behaviors, and practices that make them so successful. And the rest of the book drills down into the details of these best practices—how to come up with big ideas, pick the winners, and drive them to market—so that you and your company, too, can be a best-in-class innovator. But there are challenges . . .

Is True Innovation Dead?

Developing and launching truly differentiated new products is rare these days for most firms. Research shows that one of the foremost keys to profitability in new-product development is developing and launching *a unique superior product with a compelling value proposition.*[3] However, this is easier said than done: Markets are mature and increasingly commoditized, and hence it's difficult to create that "breakthrough" or game-changing new product. Examples are the food industry, consumer packaged goods in general, chemicals and plastics, and the engineered-products and heavy-equipment industries—huge industries where it is difficult to find true innovations. And disruptive technologies, the source of much product innovation, are also scarce in most industries—those radical technologies that characterized so many industries, from plastics to automotive to home appliances, throughout much of the twentieth century.

Even today's high-tech industries struggle for the "next great innovation." New technologies do emerge and dramatically generate new sales and profits. Examples are cell phones, digital cameras, software, and laptop computers. However, as these markets mature, users' needs change quickly and competitors launch new product after new product, thus it's difficult to sustain product competitive advantage in this leapfrog world.

One result of this dearth in true innovation is a drop in productivity in research-and-development (R&D) spending in the United States. Over a decade, cycle times in product development have reduced from 41.7 months to 24 months, according to a Product Development and Management Association (PDMA) study.[4] This is an astounding 42 percent decrease in time-to-market in ten years! Why? Could it be that U.S. industry has become that much more time efficient in a decade?

**Figure 1.1: Breakdown of Development Portfolios by Project Type—
Then and Now**

% of Projects in the Average Development Portfolio

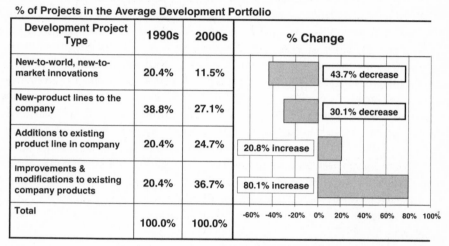

Development Project Type	1990s	2000s	% Change
New-to-world, new-to-market innovations	20.4%	11.5%	43.7% decrease
New-product lines to the company	38.8%	27.1%	30.1% decrease
Additions to existing product line in company	20.4%	24.7%	20.8% increase
Improvements & modifications to existing company products	20.4%	36.7%	80.1% increase
Total	100.0%	100.0%	

Sources: Adams & Boike, endnote 4; Cooper, endnote 2.

Not really, when one looks at the rest of the facts. R&D spending has remained constant in the United States (as a percent of companies' sales), but sales derived from new products are down from 32.6 percent of businesses' sales to 28.0 percent during roughly the same period, a shocking 15 percent drop![5] So time-to-market is down, but so is productivity, measured by the sales-to-R&D ratio. What's happening?

The decreases in productivity and time-to-market are measurable performance outcomes of what's wrong with innovation: Simply stated, managements in most companies, facing mature markets, tough competition, commoditization, and shareholder demands for short-term profits, not surprisingly have opted to focus on fast, low-risk, simple development projects—"low-hanging fruit" initiatives. Consider the portfolio breakdowns in Figure 1.1—a comparison of this century's portfolio with the breakdown in the mid-1990s:

- New-to-the-world products (true innovations) are down by almost half, to 11 percent of the typical development portfolio.
- By contrast, improvements and modifications to existing company products— the least innovative category of developments—have almost doubled and now represent almost 40 percent of the typical development portfolio.

Innovative initiatives are missing, so it's little wonder that sales and productivity from new-product development are down.

THE SOLUTION

The answer is *true innovation*—breakthrough products, services, and solutions that create growth engines for the future. That is, in contrast to the "same old new-product efforts"—extensions, modifications, upgrades, and tweaks, which swamp the majority of companies' portfolios—industry needs some break-through, game-changing, bolder product-innovation initiatives in the development pipeline. This means larger-scope and more systems-oriented solutions and service packages. Examples, such as Apple's iPod, are often cited but seem out of reach for most corporations. But a more careful examination of the iPod's success reveals no magic here, but simply true innovation at work.[6] Note that Apple did not invent the MP3 player; nor was this opportunity in a Blue Ocean;* in fact there were forty-three competitors selling MP3 players when Apple launched! What Apple did was first to identify an attractive strategic arena (MP3s) where it could leverage its strength to advantage and then develop a solution that solved users' problems: an easy-to-use, easy-to-download MP3 system, which also happens to be "cool."

There are dozens of similar examples of true innovation—not as well known as the iPod—in which a company created "big concepts" and bold innovations, and won:

Green Mountain Coffee Roasters

The company began humbly as a small café in rural Vermont in 1981 and was soon doing its own coffee roasting, selling to local hotels and restaurants. Management saw the consumer need, however: an inexpensive and convenient single-serving coffeemaker at home. Green Mountain created the K-Cup and Keurig system, then signed up other well-known coffee companies (Tully's in Seattle, Newman's Own, Timothy's in Canada, and others). The machine itself was simple (unlike some of the European machines imported by major food companies into the United States) and relatively inexpensive. The business model was similar to Gillette's razor-and-blade model, namely, sell the machine cheaply and make money on the K-Cups. The company has been enormously successful, achieving 2010 sales of $1.35 billion, and has been able to win against corporate giants like Kraft and Nestlé.

Procter & Gamble's Olay Skin-Care Business

Once almost given up by P&G (Oil of Olay was cynically referred to as "Oil of Old Lady"), the business was rejuvenated based on the "one big concept" of preventing signs of aging in women's faces.[7] The company searched for and found

---

* An open area in which there are no competitors, as opposed to a Red Ocean, where many competitors exist.

the needed technology (outside of P&G) and has relaunched the business with multiple new products focused on keeping women's faces young looking: Regenerist, Definity, Professional, and others. Olay now does over $2 billion in sales annually.

Corning Glass: LCD Displays and Flat-Screen TVs

In the late 1990s, Corning Glass was growing and profiting, driven by the boom in fiber-optic communications. Then came the crash of 2000, and overnight, the firm's sales plummeted, and share prices plunged from over $100 to about $1. Ten years later, Corning is thriving again. How? Corning's senior management developed a bold product innovation and technology strategy for the company, and provided the needed leadership and direction.[8] They concluded that the "repeatable keys" to Corning's success were: a leadership commitment, a clear understanding of the company's capabilities, a strong connection to the customer and a deep understanding of major customer problems, and a willingness to take big, but well-understood, risks. A number of new opportunities and strategic arenas were identified, assessed, and exploited. The biggest growth engine came from a manufacturing process developed originally in the 1960s for automotive windshields, but which Corning leveraged to create a glass substrate used for the flat LCD displays (for cell phones, initially; then for laptops and desktop monitors; now for LCD TVs and larger displays). Major innovations were developed in each of Corning's businesses over the decade, including creation of four new business platforms and exploitation of three major market adjacencies. New-product sales have now rocketed to 70 percent of annual sales, and profits have moved from minus $500 million to plus $2 billion after taxes.

Sanifair in Germany

This German company developed a systems solution to a problem we all face when traveling on the highway— finding a clean and well-equipped restroom. The company conceived and operates *a chain of public restrooms*, especially at service centers along the highways (they are in almost every service center on autobahns in Germany). The

> Find big problems. Then create big, bold solutions.

facilities are clean, open, friendly, and modern. The restrooms charge 70 cents per use, but the system is this: The user gets a voucher for the shop in the service center, thus up-selling the restroom visitor to spend much more and to buy goods in the service center. As one observer noted, "The travelers probably use the voucher to buy coffee or beer in the service-center restaurant, so they need to visit the restroom again!"

There is a pattern here: finding *major problems* (or opportunities), and developing *bold solutions*. This is the type of *true innovation* that industry needs, and this is what will generate the growth desired by so many firms.

Figure 1.2: Four Vectors Drive Successful Innovation—the Innovation Diamond

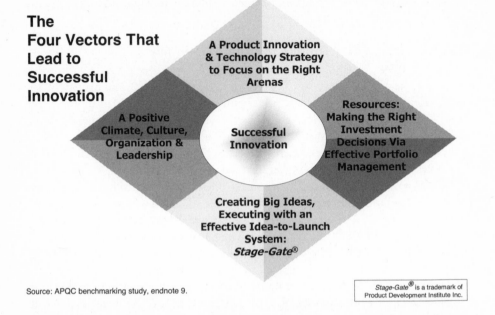

The
Four Vectors That
Lead to
Successful
Innovation

A Product Innovation
& Technology Strategy
to Focus on the Right
Arenas

A Positive
Climate, Culture,
Organization &
Leadership

Successful
Innovation

Resources:
Making the Right
Investment
Decisions Via
Effective Portfolio
Management

Creating Big Ideas,
Executing with an
Effective Idea-to-Launch
System:
Stage-Gate®

Source: APQC benchmarking study, endnote 9.

Stage-Gate® is a trademark of
Product Development Institute Inc.

THE FOUR INNOVATION VECTORS—THE INNOVATION DIAMOND

Four vectors must be in place to undertake this different type of innovation to yield bolder and imaginative projects and products, according to our* benchmarking studies of hundreds of firms (see box for the research basis).[9] The Innovation Diamond in Figure 1.2 portrays these four vectors or drivers of innovation success.

Vector I: Develop a bold innovation strategy that focuses your business on the right strategic arenas that will be your engines of growth.[10]

Most businesses focus their new-product development efforts in the wrong areas—on flat markets, mature technologies, and tired product categories. It's necessary to break out of this box and redirect R&D efforts to more fertile strategic arenas with extreme opportunities. Thus, to succeed in bigger, bolder innovation, your business needs a *product innovation and technology strategy*—a strategy that focuses your business's R&D efforts on the most attractive arenas. Corning's de-

---

* In "our research," I include the work of colleagues and coworkers Elko Kleinschmidt, McMaster University, Canada; and Scott Edgett, formerly at McMaster University, now CEO of the Product Development Institute Inc.

THE RESEARCH UNDERLYING THE BOOK

This book and its prescriptions are very much fact based. Since the 1970s, my colleagues and I have investigated over 2,000 new-product launches and hundreds of companies. The goal: to uncover what winners do differently from losers; what the common denominators of successful new products and businesses are; and what distinguishes the top performing businesses.

NewProd Studies: Some of our studies have focused on *individual new-product projects*—over 2,000 projects, both successes and failures. Multiple gauges of product performance—profitability, market share, meeting objectives, and so on—were measured. Similarly, many characteristics of the project—from the nature of the market through how well the project team executed key activities—were captured. These were then correlated with success in order to identify those factors that distinguish the big new-product winners.

Benchmarking Studies: Other studies looked at the business unit or company rather than individual projects and asked the broader question: Why are some businesses so much better at new products than others? In one of these—the APQC (American Productivity & Quality Center) study, which I often refer to—the top performing businesses in terms of product innovation were identified, and their practices were compared to the rest of firms. The drivers of new-product performance were thus identified. Many of the bar charts in this and chapters to follow come from this APQC study.

Depending on the type of study—at the project level, or a study of businesses—the success factors uncovered are somewhat different. However, regardless of the study, the fundamental question was always the same: What makes for a winner?

cision to focus an existing capability on an embryonic market, namely, flat-panel screens, is an excellent example. And Apple's choice of the new and growing MP3 market (by an outsider firm) is another excellent case of a clever but bold strategic move. But where was Sony, which owned the portable music business in 2000? Sadly, the great majority of firms lack a clearly defined, robust, and well-communicated innovation strategy; they have no focus, or their focus is on arenas that will not yield the growth engines of tomorrow. But once you've decided on your strategic arenas, they become your "hunting grounds" in the search for breakthrough ideas, big concepts, and imaginative solutions.

Vector II: Foster a climate, culture, and organization that promote bolder innovation.

Having the right climate and culture for innovation, an appetite to invest in innovative and more risky projects, and the right leadership from the top is the number one factor that distinguishes top innovation companies, according to our extensive study of innovation results. Those businesses that create a positive climate for innovation, support innovation at every opportunity, reward and recognize innovators and successful development teams, and welcome ideas from all employees do much better at product innovation. Similarly, having the right senior leadership—men and women who drive and support the innovation effort with words as well as through actions—is vital to success. But most businesses lack the needed climate, culture, and leadership for innovation.

Vector III: Create "big ideas" for bold product-service solutions. Then drive these "big concepts" to market quickly via an idea-to-launch system designed for major innovations.

Big ideas lead to big concepts and big solutions. Larger-scope and more imaginative development projects begin with *creating game-changing and blockbuster ideas*. In our benchmarking studies, we have identified over twenty-five proven ways to create big innovation ideas.[11] But many firms rely on but few of these methods and instead look to traditional, somewhat depleted sources for their next breakthroughs—and of course, there are no breakthroughs as a result. Game-changing new-product ideas are the necessary feedstock for an innovative product development effort.

Generating great ideas is half the battle; the other half is getting from the concept stage through to development and into the marketplace . . . through the corporate equivalent of the "valley of death."* That's where *an effective yet rapid idea-to-launch system* is needed. Without such a system, your "great ideas" and "big concepts" are like unpicked grapes on a vine—they'll wither and die. Driving bold innovations to market means installing an effective and efficient idea-to-launch process or system that is designed to handle these major, "big concept" ideas and projects. Just because these projects are imaginative and bold is no reason to throw discipline out the window: The goal is "entrepreneurship but with discipline and due diligence," which is quite different than "shooting from the hip." Another issue is that most businesses' stage-and-gate systems are de-

---

* The "valley of death" describes the gap between conception or invention, versus moving that concept or invention through to a commercialized product—the gap where so many projects die.

signed for small projects, modifications, and product improvements—sustaining innovation—and fail to cope with big, innovative projects and technology platform developments.

Vector IV: Pick the winners via effective portfolio management.

Many businesses have lots of good new-product ideas. But they *lack the appetite to invest* in these larger-scope and more risky projects, in spite of the fact that they promise to be tomorrow's growth engines. Part of the problem is culture (above), but a major part is the *lack of a solid business case*: I can't count the number of times I've heard from executives, "Show me a good business case, and I'm only too happy to invest!" These "big concept" projects are innovative and risky, and it's often difficult to get the right data needed to construct a solid, fact-based business case to convince senior management to make the investment. Thus, it's essential to do the front-end homework, or *due diligence*, and to build a compelling business case if the needed investment is to be made.

Next, senior management often lacks the right methods to make the riskier decisions on "big concept" innovations: For example, they *rely too much on financial tools and return-on-investment methods* to make the Go/Kill decisions, methods that work well for smaller, less innovative projects but invariably lead to the wrong decisions when it comes to larger-scope, riskier innovation projects. And so the company retreats from these potential game-changing projects and ends up doing the same old product improvements and modifications, with little real prospect for growth.

The next chapters delve into the details of the Innovation Diamond in Figure 1.2—the keys to being successful at bold product innovation—and how to implement them in your business. But first, let's step back and look at the vital role that innovation should play in your business and its impact on corporate prosperity and growth, and let's examine why executives need to spend more time thinking about how to become more proficient innovators.

NEW PRODUCTS: THE KEY TO CORPORATE PROSPERITY

New-product development is one of the riskiest, yet most important, endeavors of the modern corporation. Certainly the risks are high: You and your colleagues have all seen large amounts of money spent on new-product disasters in your own firm or industry. But then, so too are the rewards.

Today, new products account for *a staggering 28 percent of company sales*, on average.[12] That is, more than one-fourth of the revenues of corporations are coming from products they did not sell three short years ago. In some dynamic industries, the figure is 100 percent! (Here a "new product" is defined as "new" if it has been on the market by that firm for three years or less, and includes extensions and significant improvements as well.) As might be expected, profits follow closely, with 28.3 percent of company profits derived from new products three years old or newer. The message is simple: Either innovate or die!

Countless corporations owe their meteoric rise and current fortunes to product innovation. For example:

- Apple, beset with problems in computers and its PalmPilot in the 1990s, surged ahead with the iPod in 2001. Apple sold its 250 millionth unit of iPod in 2010, less than ten years after launch, which makes it the most successful product in history. And then followed the formidable iPhone, which caught cell-phone market leaders by surprise; and more recently the iPad—all innovative products that customers lined up for hours to purchase.
- Procter & Gamble, regarded for years as the world's best marketer, in the last decade has rocketed to new prominence as the world's best innovator in its product categories, with many exciting new products. The company now boasts twenty-two brands with sales in excess of $1 billion each, and global sales of $79 billion.[13] Big new products over the last decade include Prilosec OTC (for heartburn relief), Crest Whitestrips (for teeth whitening), Crest Spinbrush (a low-cost throwaway electric toothbrush), and Gillette Fusion (the latest entry into the high-tech world of shaving). The company is now leveraging its brands into the *service sector* with Tide Dry Cleaners and Mr. Clean Car Wash franchises.
- Since its early days as a sandpaper (abrasives) supplier, 3M has looked to a steady stream of innovations to propel the company to greatness (the letters MMM or 3M stand for Minnesota Mining and Manufacturing Company). 3M's first true innovation in the early 1920s was waterproof sandpaper, which reduced airborne dusts during automotive manufacturing. A second major innovation occurred in 1925 when a young lab assistant invented masking tape, the first of many Scotch-brand pressure-sensitive tapes. And it's been nonstop ever since. 3M's strong internal culture of creativity with formal incentives and tangible support for innovation results in a high success rate in turning ideas in the health care, industrial, and other sectors into profitable new products.

The Best Really Shine

Huge differences exist in product innovation performance between the Best and Worst firms. But why? What distinguishes the Best Innovators?

The percentages cited above—that more than one dollar in four comes from new products—are only averages, and thus understate the true impact and potential of product innovation. What CEO wants to be average? A handful of companies do far better than average, according to our extensive benchmarking studies,[14] and thus become the benchmark firms—see Figure 1.3. The top 20 percent of businesses—the *Best*

Figure 1.3: How The Best Businesses Perform in Product Innovation Versus the Rest

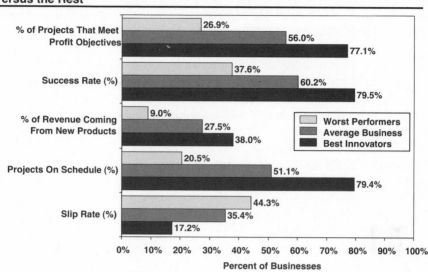

Slip Rate = <u>Actual Time – Scheduled Time</u>
                    Scheduled Time

Source: APQC benchmarking study, endnote 9.

Innovators—are compared to the worst performers (the bottom 20 percent). The Best:

- have 38.0 percent of sales derived from new products launched in the previous three years, versus only 9.0 percent for the Worst, a four-times difference in performance!
- have a commercial success rate of 79.5 percent of initiated development projects (compared to a low of 37.6 percent for the Worst businesses).
- and see the great majority—77.1 percent—of new products they launch meet or exceed their target profit levels (targets set in the business case on which the project was approved). The Worst firms witness only 26.9 percent of new products hitting profit targets—about one in four.

The point is that stellar performance is attainable in product innovation: These Best Innovators show the way. And the differences don't stop here. Most performance metrics in product innovation boil down to time and money, so besides the profit and sales data, also consider the time-metrics results in Figure 1.3:

- On average, about half of new-product development projects are launched on schedule. But the Best Innovators again really shine, with almost 80 percent of their new products launched on schedule. By contrast, the Worst performers see only one in five products getting to market on time.

- The "slip rate" is a useful time metric, capturing the slippage between scheduled time-to-market (usually stated in the project's business case) and the actual time. High slip rates are bad. Note that the Best firms in Figure 1.3 have a slip rate of only 17.2 percent, meaning that if the project was forecast to take 12 months, it actually took 14 months; that is, 2 months late—not bad. By comparison, the Worst businesses have a slip rate of 44.3 percent, meaning that a 12-month time-to-market forecast in reality became 17.3 months!

Suggestion: Time to take stock and conduct a *current state assessment* of your performance in new products:

1. Take a hard look at your performance results in comparison to those in Figure 1.3. Are your results close to the Best companies? If so, well done! But if they're only "average" or worse, the time is ripe to determine why and what can be done.

2. Be sure to look not only at the popular "percentage of revenue from new products" but at other metrics such as "percentage of products hitting profit targets," "success rates," and the two time metrics in Figure 1.3.

New-Product Productivity

Many businesses now use metrics that can be used to gauge *productivity* from R&D spending. The concept of productivity is simple: It is *output over input,* or "the most bang for the buck." More specifically, in the field of product innovation, productivity is defined as output (measured as new-product sales or profits) divided by input (measured as R&D or new-product development costs and time). For example:[15]

$$\text{NPD Productivity} = \frac{\text{Sales (or Profits) from New Products}}{\text{R\&D Spending}}$$

Although one might argue that executives should be most concerned about *profits* from new products rather than just sales, *sales* is the usual metric simply because it is "cleaner"—less complex to determine or calculate, and a more reliable number.

Huge differences in product development productivities exist between the Best and Worst firms, according to a major global study—see Figure 1.4.[16] Productivity was measured as "five years' sales from new products," versus "R&D spending by the company." Both metrics are taken as a percentage of company annual sales to adjust for company size. Consider the results in Figure 1.4:

Figure 1.4: New-Product Development Productivity Metrics—Best versus Worst Companies by Industry

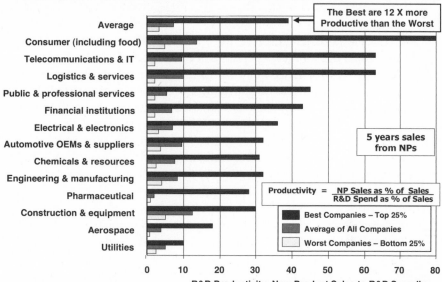

Source of data: A.D. Little Innovation Excellence Study, endnote 16.

R&D Productivity: New-Product Sales to R&D Spending

- The Best firms (defined as the top 25 percent) have *twelve times the productivity* in new-product development of the Worst. That is, the average firm realizes $7.25 in new-product sales for every $1 spent on R&D. But the Best see a huge $39 in sales per R&D dollar, while the 25 percent Worst firms achieve only $3.30 sales dollars.

The data are also broken down by industry:

- The most productive industry is consumer packaged goods, including food. Every $1 spent on R&D here results in $13.64 in new-product sales on average. But compare the Best and the Worst consumer firms: $80 in sales, versus only $4.80 for every R&D dollar, a *stunning 16.7 times difference!*
- A look at the least productive industry—pharmaceutical—reveals similar differences. For every R&D dollar, the pharmaceutical industry generates $1.95 sales dollars over the first five years on the market (but their profit margins are large, and new products usually last many years on the market, thus compensating for the lower new-product sales to R&D ratio). But the most productive firms in this industry see $28 in sales for every R&D dollar spent, while the Worst receive a paltry

> Huge new-product productivity differences exist between the Best and Worst firms, with the Best twelve times more productive than the Worst.

90 cents—again a huge difference: The top 25 percent of pharmaceutical firms are *31 times more productive* in product development than the bottom 25 percent.

I make three important points based on these Best-versus-Worst data in Figures 1.3 and 1.4. First, huge differences exist between the Best and Worst businesses—these are not a few percentage points difference in performance, but order-of-magnitude differences. These huge performance differences beg the question: Why? Why is it that some firms seem to be so successful at product innovation, whereas the majority pale by comparison? What are the secrets to such high-productivity or superb new-product results? Our research shows that it is not just "a few good years" or a couple of lucky new-product winners; rather there are clear, measurable, sustainable, and consistent behaviors, approaches, and methods that the Best companies embrace, and that the rest do not: the "best practices in innovation."

Second, the average business does fairly poorly in comparison to the Best. Odds are that your business is closer to the average than the Best, so your performance probably resembles the rather mediocre results achieved by average firms. The point is that most businesses have much room for improvement, so likely you have missed many of the pivotal best practices in innovation.

The final point is that the Best firms do model the way: They prove that these results are not some mythical or theoretical result but are achievable and realistic. That is, these common denominators or best practices that separate the Best from the rest are both tangible and actionable, and within your grasp.

Suggestion: When you look at innovation performance in your own industry, do you see big differences? Why is it that some businesses are so successful? And when you analyze successes and failures in your own company, are there some patterns? What can you learn here about what it takes to be a best performer in product innovation? As this book unfolds, we lower the microscope on these and other results, and probe the factors that separate the winners from the losers—their best practices and their secrets of success.

HUGE AMOUNTS AT STAKE

Industry spends enormous resources in the quest for new products. Thus, not only are the potential upside rewards substantial, but there is much downside risk, too. R&D expenditures are one metric that captures the magnitude of investments in product innovation. The figures are impressive: Globally, R&D expenditures approach $1 trillion annually, while global spending by U.S. companies amounts to $330 billion (2008)—that's 3.01 percent of these firms' global sales.[17] (Spending on R&D in the United States amounted to $283 billion, or 2.62 percent of gross domestic product [GDP] in 2008.)[18] And in 2008 alone, R&D spending grew by a whopping 5.2 percent in the United States!

Note that R&D spending is not the entire picture. It's estimated that for every $1 spent on new-product R&D, another $2 are spent on "other things" associated with the development and launch of the product—on marketing, capital equipment, and management costs.[19,*]

Certain industries, noted for their growth and profitability in recent decades, spend heavily on R&D. For example, the semiconductor and electronic components industry spends 15.0 percent of annual revenues on R&D; pharmaceuticals is next, averaging 13.1 percent of sales on R&D; the software industry is close behind at 11.1 percent (see Table 1.1 for an industry breakdown of R&D spending).

WHY SO MUCH INNOVATION TODAY?

New products are clearly the key to corporate prosperity. They drive corporate revenues, market shares, bottom lines, and even share prices. But why is new-product development speeding up so much globally, and why is so much more emphasis being placed on product innovation results? Here are four innovation drivers:

- *Technology advances:* The world's base of technology and know-how increases at an exponential rate, making possible solutions and products not even dreamed of a decade or so ago. What was science fiction in *Star Trek* in the 1960s—for example, handheld computers, curing disease through DNA modification, or flip-top portable video communicators—is suddenly a technological reality today.
- *Changing customer needs:* Marketplaces are also in turmoil, with market needs and wants, and customer preferences changing regularly. The company that seemed omnipotent only a few years ago suddenly falls from favor with the consumer. And witness the number of mergers and acquisitions, as major corporations scramble to keep pace with fluid marketplaces. In other markets, customers have come to expect new products with significant improvements: We consumers have become like "kids in a candy shop"—we see what is possible, and we want it.
- *Shortening product life cycles:* One result of the increasing pace of technological change coupled with changing market demands has been shorter product life cycles: Product life cycles have been cut by a factor of about four over the last fifty years.[20] Your new product no longer has a life of five to ten years, but within a few years, sometimes even months, it is superseded by a competitive entry, rendering yours obsolete and necessitating a new product. This has placed much pressure on businesses and their management teams: For example, in one leading electronics firm in the United

---

* Although, not all R&D spending goes to new products; an estimated half goes to process (as opposed to product) development.

TABLE 1.1: R&D SPENDING BY INDUSTRY, 2008 (USD)*

	Global Sales ($ million)	Global R&D ($ million)	R&D as % of Sales
Manufacturing			
Food	$463,794	$4,000	0.86%
Beverage & tobacco	$195,840	$1,157	0.59%
Textiles, leather & apparel	$169,571	$1,239	0.73%
Wood products	$42,717	$266	0.62%
Chemicals – all	$1,243,526	$79,968	6.43%
- Pharmaceutical/medicines	$529,601	$69,516	13.13%
- Other chemicals	$713,926	$10,452	1.46%
Plastics & rubber products	$264,378	$3,335	1.26%
Non-metallic mineral products	$105,586	$1,736	1.64%
Primary metals	$194,274	$830	0.43%
Fabricated metal products	$185,986	$2,640	1.42%
Computer & electronic products	$923,113	$69,737	7.55%
- Computers & peripheral equipment	$306,605	$12,549	4.09%
- Communications equipment	$132,307	$14,987	11.33%
- Semi-conductor & electronic components	$192,258	$28,812	14.99%
- Navigation, measuring, electromed, control instrum'ts	$269,779	$12,150	4.50%
- Other electronic products	$22,164	$1,238	5.59%
Electrical equipment, appliances & parts	$172,771	$4,630	2.68%
Transportation equipment	$1,298,507	$38,221	2.94%
- Motor vehicles, trailers & parts	$776,056	$38,221	4.93%
- Aerospace products & parts	$457,250	$12,584	2.75%
- Other transportation equipment	$65,201	$1,375	2.11%
Furniture & related products	$40,754	$540	1.33%
Other manufacturing	$1,122,030	$12,956	1.15%
Non-Manufacturing			
Information	$924,731	$45,930	4.97%
- Software publishers	$317,084	$35,070	11.06%
- Services: telecommunications, Internet, Web search, etc.	$501,859	$9,308	1.85%
- Other information products & services	$105,788	$1,552	1.47%
Finance & insurance	$435,237	$1,310	0.30%
Real estate, rental & leasing	$34,898	$517	1.48%
Professional, scientific, technical services	$584,424	$30,639	5.24%
- Computer systems design & related services	$259,001	$11,262	4.35%
- Scientific & R&D services	$179,114	$14,682	8.20%
- Other	$156,308	$4,695	3.00%
Health care services	$30,438	$1,217	4.00%
Non-manufacturing other	$2,044,098	$16,711	0.82%
ALL INDUSTRY	**$10,942,915**	**$329,650**	**3.01%**

---

* Wolfe, endnote 17.

States, as product version number one is hitting the market, its replacement, product version two, is already in the Development stage, and product version three is waiting in the wings for a Go to Development decision.

- *Increased globalization:* We have access to new and foreign markets like never before, but at the same time, our domestic market has become someone else's international one. This globalization of markets has created significant opportunities for the product innovator: the world product, locally tailored, targeted at global markets; and the prospect of doing development work in emerging countries, plugging into new brain power at lower costs. It has also intensified competition in every domestic market. These global factors have sped up the pace of product innovation.

A quick review of all four drivers of product innovation reveals that none is likely to disappear in the next decade or two. Technology advances will continue to occur; so will changes in market needs and demands; globalization of markets and offshoring marches on; and competition will drive life cycles to become even shorter. Product innovation will be even more critical to corporate prosperity in the years ahead than it has been in the recent past.

Suggestion: If you haven't already done so, conduct a review of the strategic role—past, present, and future—of new products in your company. Key questions include:

1. Where will your sales growth come from? What proportion from new products? From new markets? From growth in existing markets? Or from increased market share?
2. What proportion of your current sales comes from new products introduced by you in the last three years? How does this compare to the Best Innovators in Figure 1.3? What is your projection or objective for the future? What will your portfolio of product offerings look like in five years?
3. What is your historical level of R&D spending as a percentage of sales? Has it been going up or down? How does it compare to your competitors' or the industry level (see Table 1.1)? Why is it higher or lower?
4. Are the answers to the three questions above consistent with each other? Are you investing enough in R&D and new products to yield the results that you want?

HIGH ODDS OF FAILURE

Innovative products are critical to your long-term success. They keep your business's product portfolio competitive and healthy, and in many firms, provide you with long-term and sustainable competitive advantage. The dilemma is that

> The odds of winning are about one in seven. But there are ways to beat these odds!

product innovation is a crapshoot: Boasting a steady stream of successful and high-impact new products is no small feat.

The hard reality is that the great majority of new products never make it to market. And those that do face a failure rate somewhere on the order of 25 to 45 percent. For example, our studies indicate that new products currently have a success rate of only 60.2 percent at launch, up only 1 percent since 1997 and up 2 percent since 1990.[21] These success rate figures do vary from study to study, however, depending on what the industry is and how one defines a "new product" and a "failure." Some sources cite the failure rate at launch to be as high as 90 percent. But these figures tend to be unsubstantiated and are likely wildly overstated. Note also that averages often don't tell the whole story: The success rate varies from a low of 37.6 percent for the Worst firms to a high of 79.5 percent for the Best!

Regardless of whether the success rate is 55 or 65 percent, the odds of a misfire are still substantial. Worse, the figures cited above don't include the majority of new-product projects that are killed along the way and long before launch, yet involved considerable expenditures of time and money.

The attrition curve of new products provides a more complete picture. A number of studies have revealed more or less the same-shaped curve, and Figure 1.5 is a composite: *For every seven new-product ideas, about 4 enter development, 1.5 are launched, and only 1 succeeds.*[22] That's a seven-to-one ratio for success when starting at the idea stage—pretty poor odds! The bad news continues: 44 percent of new-product projects fail to hit their profit targets; more than half are launched late; 32 percent of businesses rate their new-product development speed and efficiency as "very poor"; and 28 percent of businesses don't even measure their new-product performance results![23] These are astounding statistics when one considers the magnitude of human and financial resources devoted to product innovation. But all is not bad: Recall from Figure 1.3 earlier that a minority of firms—the 20-percent Best Innovators—do achieve an enviable 80-percent success rate at launch, 77 percent of their new products hit profit targets, and 79 percent are launched on schedule. These few firms show that it is possible to outperform the average, and by a considerable margin.

Suggestion: How well is your company faring at product innovation? Do you know—do you keep score? (Many companies cannot provide reliable statistics on success, fail, and kill rates; on resources spent on winners versus losers; or on numbers of projects hitting time and profit targets.)

Keep score in product innovation. The adage "You cannot manage what you do not measure" certainly applies in new products. Key statistics to track include:

Figure 1.5: The Attrition Rate of New-Product Projects

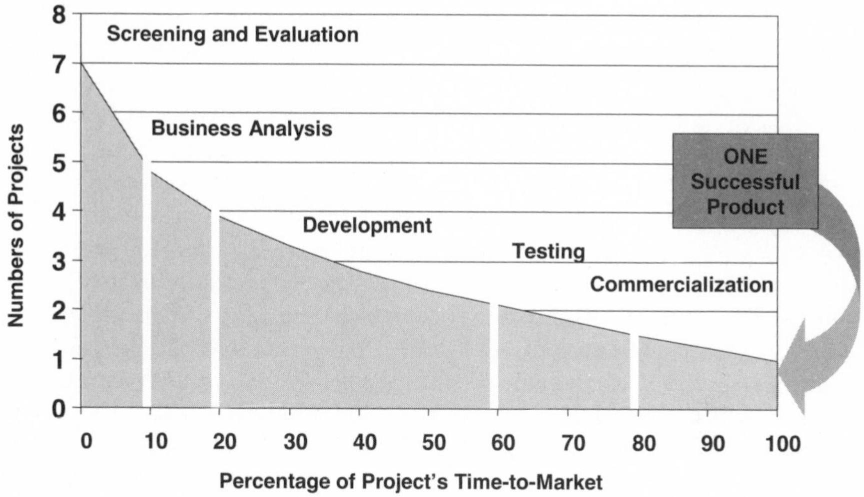

Source of data: endnote 22.

✓ Success versus failure rates at launch
✓ Attrition rates: What percent of projects continue at each stage of the process?
✓ Proportion of resources devoted to winners versus losers versus killed projects, overall and per stage
✓ Proportion of projects hitting time, profit, and sales targets

Beating the Odds

New products are much like a steeplechase horse race: Relatively few new-product projects succeed. About seven horses leave the starting gate and must clear various hurdles, hedges, or gates along the way. And only one horse in seven crosses the finish line as the winner. Racetrack gamblers try to pick the one winning horse, but more often than not, they place their bets on the wrong one.

New-product management is even more risky than a horse race. True, the odds of picking a winner at the outset are somewhere on the order of seven to one. But the size of the bets is considerably greater—often in the millions of dollars. And unlike the gambler, new-product managers cannot leave the game—they must go on placing the bets, year after year, if the company is to succeed. The new-products arena is very much addictive: Once in, it is difficult to quit!

Faced with these kinds of odds and risks, why would anyone want to play at product innovation? But there are some important differences between a horse race and new products. First, the payoff from one winning new product, like Apple's iPod or Green Mountain's single-cup K-cup system, can be enormous—enough to more than cover all your losses. Second, and perhaps more subtle, the way the bets are placed is different. At a racetrack, all bets must be placed *before the race begins.* But in new products, bets are placed *as the race proceeds.* Imagine a steeplechase horse race where bets could be placed after the horses clear each hedge or gate! Suddenly the odds are changed dramatically in favor of the shrewd gambler.

Product innovation, then, is much more like a game of five-card stud poker than a horse race. In five-card stud poker, after each card is dealt, the players place their bets. Toward the end of each hand, the outcome—who will be the winner—becomes clearer; at the same time, the betting and the amounts at stake rise exponentially. Many an amateur poker player has sat down with a professional, assuming that he had equal odds of winning. True, each player has the same odds of being dealt a winning hand: The cards are dealt randomly. But over the long term, the professionals will always win—not because they get better hands, but because of how they bet, knowing when to bet high, when to bet low, and when to fold and walk away. The trick is in the betting! The professional player counts cards and has tangible criteria for betting.

Unfortunately, too many companies play at product innovation like the amateur poker player. They start with an equal chance of winning. But because they don't count cards (that is, they don't do their homework but operate on hunch and speculation instead) and lack solid betting criteria (that is, they have poor or nonexistent decision rules for making Go/Kill decisions), they lose to the professional. And so the odds of losing—especially for the amateur player—are exceptionally high.

The point of these analogies is to show that the new-products field is much more complex than a mere horse race: Product innovation features high risks, low odds of picking a winner, large amounts at stake, and an incremental betting process, with additional and increasing bets placed as the race proceeds. The second point is that effective betting is one key to winning. We all have the same odds of being dealt a good hand, but it's how we bet—the information we gather and the betting rules or criteria we use—that makes the difference between winning and losing. Finally, there is one important difference between product innovation, on the one hand, and poker or a horse race, on the other: We can affect the outcome. That is, through the actions that product developers take, they can change the outcome of the race or the poker hand. And thus much of what is to follow in this book is about gaining insights into the practices and methods that Best Innovators use to change the outcome and to shift the odds in their favor.

DEFINING NEWNESS AND A "NEW PRODUCT"

Serious players keep score in product innovation. But in order to keep score, one must have a definition of what counts as *a new product.* One of the problems with some of the scores cited above is that they include *different types* of new products: For example, the attrition rates for truly innovative new products are much higher than for extensions and modifications of existing company products.

Product: First, a "product" is anything referred to as an *external marketplace* for sale, use, or consumption. This includes *physical products* as well as *services*, and *combinations of services and products*. But it excludes "freebies" such as might be provided by a tech service-and-support group (for example, free training or free maintenance). Products are usually associated with businesses or corporations, and the majority of my illustrations and examples are from companies. But "products" can also be from nonprofit organizations (nongovernmental organizations [NGOs], industry as-sociations, health-care and other societal organizations, or governments), al-though the term "program" might also be used. For example, the British and Canadian governments have implemented stage-and-gate systems, essentially a new-product process, to deliver new government programs to their citizens.

> Keep score in product innovation— how well are you doing? To keep score, you must have a rigorous definition of what counts as "a new product."

New product: Next, how does one define a "new product," innovativeness, or "newness"? Here are some definitions to help you when crafting performance metrics:

- One major U.S. manufacturing conglomerate defines a new product as "anything—service or physical product—that provides new functionality, features or benefits that are clearly visible to the customer or user, and which involved at least 50 person-days in development time." The notion here is that the product should be perceived as "new" by the marketplace (and not just by the firm's engineering department), and that the firm should have made some minimum investment (there is something at stake).
- Some consumer-goods firms define a new product as a new stock-keeping unit (SKU) or new bar code. Such a loose definition, although very pragmatic, allows far too many initiatives to count as new products and thus inflates the numbers. To compensate for this overstatement, some of the same firms only count *incremental sales* from these same items—that is, the *increase in sales*. So if a new version of a product is launched (a new SKU or new bar code), but it creates no new sales (that is, sales are low, or the product simply cannibalizes an existing company product), it may be a "new product" but its sales would not be counted in the tally.

Another useful scheme recognizes that there are many different types of *new products*. "Newness" can be defined in two ways:

- New to the company, in the sense that the firm has never made or sold this type of product before, but other firms might have.
- New to the market or "innovative": the product is the first of its kind on the market.

Viewed on a two-dimensional map as shown in Figure 1.6, six different types or categories of new products are identified:[24]

1. *New-to-the-world products:* These new products are the first of their kind and create an entirely new market. This type represents only 10 percent of all new products, and is shrinking.
2. *New-product lines:* These products, although not new to the marketplace, nonetheless are quite new to the particular firm. They allow a company to enter an established product category or market for the first time. About 20 percent of all new products are this type.
3. *Additions to existing product lines:* These are new items to the firm, but they fit within an existing product line the firm makes. They may also represent a fairly new product to the marketplace. Such new items are one of the largest types of new products—about 26 percent of all new-product launches.
4. *Improvements and revisions to existing products:* These "not-so-new" products are essentially replacements of existing products in a firm's product line. They offer improved performance or greater perceived value over the "old" product. These "new and improved" products also make up 26 percent of new-product launches.
5. *Repositionings:* These are essentially new applications for existing products and often involve retargeting an old product to a new market segment or for a different application. Repositionings account for about 7 percent of all new products.
6. *Cost reductions:* These are the least "new" of all new-product types. They are new products designed to replace existing company products, but they yield similar benefits and performance at lower cost. From a marketing standpoint, they are not new products; but from a design and production viewpoint, they could represent significant change. They represent 11 percent of all new-product launches.

Most firms count the first four types above—those in the upper left and right of Figure 1.6—as "new products."

Suggestion:
1. Develop a robust definition of what a "new product" is in your business. Ensure that the definition is both rigorous and operational, that is, one that is feasible (easy to use and measure, and gives reliable metrics), yet tough (does not include every minor development project or overstate the numbers).

Figure 1.6: Types of New Products on Two Dimensions—New to the Company and New to the Market

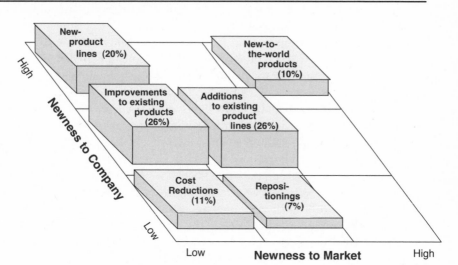

Source: Booz Allen Hamilton, endnote 24; PDMA, endnote 4.

Use this definition when determining your product innovation results to compare with industry results in Figure 1.3.

2. Next, review the new products that your business has introduced in the last three years. Then categorize them according to the six types in Figure 1.6. What is the split of projects by type (use a pie chart)? Does the split differ much from the all-industry averages shown in Figure 1.6? Why?

3. What is the breakdown by project type in terms of total resources spent— that is, to which types of projects has your money and effort been devoted? What is the breakdown by sales and profits—that is, which types of products or projects are generating the revenues and profits? What is the success rate by type? Finally, what's the ratio of sales (or profits) to spending per project type (that is, the productivity of each type)?

4. Is your current breakdown or split the desirable one? What should be the split of new products by type in Figure 1.6?

THE PATH FORWARD

In this chapter, you have seen that winning at new products plays a critical role in determining company fortunes. You have also seen some of the perfomance results, and the huge differences between sucessful innovators and the typical company, which provokes the question: Why? Four vectors that drive bold and successful innovation were laid out in the Innovation Diamond.

You have also read about some of the risks in product innovation: the huge expenditures that companies make on R&D, and the comparison of product innovation to a horse race with high odds of failure and significant rates of attrition. The key is in how you place your bets! But you can also affect the outcome. Finally, keeping score is an important facet of product innovation, so I provided definitions of "new products" and also laid out a scheme to help define and categorize new products in order for the scores to be more comparable.

In the next chapter, we take a close look at the hard evidence. Our research into new-product practices and reasons for innovation success (and failure!) over the last thirty years has been noted by the Product Development and Management Association as the most widely published research in the field and has yielded perhaps the most thorough database on new-product winners and losers—over 2,000 launches in over 500 companies in both Europe and North America.[25] And from observing these many successes and failures, we learn the keys to winning at new products. Additionally, our benchmarking studies—in which we looked at the best-performing businesses versus the rest—yield many insights into best practices and key success drivers. These investigations, both at the project level and also at the business level, provide the basis for the book.

We begin our voyage in Chapter 2, with a look at the reasons new products fail, and what goes wrong. This is perhaps a negative way to start, but it's the right place, too: Here, the hope is that we can learn from our past mistakes. We then look to new-product successes and pinpoint what separates winning new products from the losers, and also take a look at successful businesses in Chapter 3. Here, we see that there are clear patterns to success, and indeed, that new-product success is both predictable and controllable. These "success drivers" are integrated into fourteen key lessons for new-product success—the *critical success factors* that we then build into our *playbook for winning*.

Following that, Chapters 4 through 9 deal with crafting a playbook for winning. Here the focus is on the development and implementation of a *Stage-Gate®* *new-product system* for driving new products to market successfully and efficiently.* The majority of firms doing product development today already use a form of *Stage-Gate*,[26] but in Chapter 4, we introduce the newest version of our popular *Stage-Gate* methodology—a best-in-class idea-to-launch product innovation system. Here, the critical success factors and best practices identified in Chapters 2 and 3 are integrated and translated into an operational blueprint for action, with a particular emphasis on bold innovation projects.

Chapter 5 continues with *Stage-Gate* and a look into some of the additional and more innovative practices that companies have introduced into their idea-to-launch system, making it more flexible, adaptive, and open. Chapter 6 deals

---

* *Stage-Gate®* is a trademark of the Product Development Institute Inc. in the United States and Australia, and of RG Cooper & Associates in Canada. In the European Union, the trademark is held jointly by Cooper and Jens Arleth.

with Discovery—coming up with breakthrough new-product ideas—and high-lights more than twenty-five methods for generating great ideas, along with the latest results on which ones work best. Chapter 7 lowers the microscope on the "fuzzy front end"—the front-end stages of the process where success or failure is largely decided—and outlines best practices here, especially for bolder, higher-risk innovation projects. Chapter 8 deals with portfolio management and picking the winners: It focuses on ways to improve your "betting practices," improving your odds of picking the right new-product projects, and also achieving the right balance and mix of development projects. Making the right investment decisions is so vital that I devote the whole of Chapter 9 to the same topic, but with emphasis on new approaches to make gates more effective, including the concept of "gates with teeth."

Chapter 10 concludes the mapping of the *Stage-Gate* system as we move through Development and toward Launch: development, testing, and market rollout. Chapter 11 looks at implementation issues, offering insights into how to handle the difficult job of the design and implementation of *Stage-Gate* within your business (or the reinvention or overhaul of your existing idea-to-launch process).

So read on! First, witness the critical success factors in the next two chapters, and then how they can and should be built into your *innovation playbook* in your business so that you, too, can be a *big winner* at new products.

2

WHY NEW PRODUCTS WIN

I am the master of my fate: I am the captain of my soul.
— W. E. Henley, "Invictus"

THE INVISIBLE SUCCESS FACTORS

What are the secrets to new-product success? And why are some new-product projects and products so successful? Do you know? Most people don't or choose to ignore them—witness the high failure rates and the large number of businesses and new products with very poor performance here (recall the performance results in Chapter 1, and also Figures 1.3 and 1.4). That's why I refer to these success drivers as "secrets to success" or the "invisible success factors."

There is help, however! Numerous studies have probed the question of why new products win (or fail), looking at large samples of successful versus unsuccessful new products and what separates the two; some studies also lowered the microscope on businesses and their innovation performance and sought reasons for their results (see box in Chapter 1 for a quick description of the studies).[1] An understanding of these "success drivers" is vital to designing systems and approaches for conceiving, developing, and launching new products. It's much like a coach and the football team watching video replays of football games: Patterns emerge and insights are gained into what to avoid in future games and what new plays or actions should be built into the new playbook. That is, when we identify a major and consistent reason for product failure, we build into our playbook or system steps to avert such failures in the future; and when we pinpoint success drivers—factors that distinguish winning new products—again we build in steps and actions to replicate those in our idea-to-launch system. This chapter looks at the "tactical" success and failure drivers, specifically, factors that apply at the project and product level and that are immediately actionable; the next chapter focuses more on strategic and broader success drivers, which apply at the business level.

WHY NEW PRODUCTS FAIL TO YIELD THE PROFITS THEY SHOULD

Perhaps the best place to begin the quest to improve innovation results is to understand *why new products fail*. Often, an understanding of past failures, problems, and pitfalls leads to insights that ultimately result in corrective action. This is one premise of the process of continuous improvement and the learning organization.

Why do so many new products fail to live up to their financial and sales expectations? In the last chapter, we saw that almost half of development projects fail to meet their profit objectives and that as many as one-third of new products fail at launch! The following list of reasons and root causes for failure is compiled from an integration of research results from countless studies into new-product outcomes[2] and from many problem-detection sessions held in companies:

1. Me-Too, Ho-Hum, or Tired, Trivial New Products[3]

The first reason is that the product *fails to excite the customer*: It does not satisfy an unmet need or solve a major problem—in short, it looks a lot like the competitor's product. What's missing is the quest for competitive advantage and true innovations: The new-product idea is proposed, but the bar is never set high enough, and so the project team develops yet one more me-too, ho-hum, tired and vanilla product, much the same as competitors'. There is *no compelling value proposition* for users or customers; and given no reason to switch, they don't! And sales fail to materialize.

One root cause is that management does not demand that project teams rise above competitors' offerings. By contrast, in one major consumer-goods firm, the expectation is that the new product will be "differentiated, unique, and deliver superior-to-competition performance"; otherwise, the project is simply rejected! A second root cause is that businesses are missing key elements in their idea-to-launch systems: There is no emphasis on differentiated products and compelling value propositions. Indeed, if one were to slavishly execute according to the typical firm's new-product idea-to-launch guidebook, the result probably would be yet another vanilla product. Some firms' processes seem to be *designed to deliver mediocrity*.

Finally, for a variety of reasons ranging from pressure from the sales force to a pervasive risk averseness, the portfolio and development budget is consumed by an overabundance of extensions, modifications, and tweaks, so there's no room and no resources left for bold, innovative products.

2. Weak Front-End Homework

Some businesses simply fail to do the needed up-front or front-end work on projects. The necessary due diligence on new-product projects—the market study, the technical assessment, the financial analysis—is superficially done or not done at all. Figure 2.1 reveals the facts: Here, see the percentage of firms that are rated as doing a poor job on key front-end tasks (note that averages are shown, as well as results for the 20-percent worst performers). Among worst-performing businesses:

- 96 percent do a poor job on assessing the value of the product to the customer,
- 93 percent do the market research poorly or not at all,
- 77 percent carry out the technical assessment deficiently,
- and 77 percent don't do the business and financial analysis on the project well.

But these are the 20-percent worst firms, so what about the typical firm? The data are almost as damning. Typically:

- 84 percent of businesses fail to properly assess the value of the product to the customer,
- 82 percent do the market research poorly,
- 78 percent carry out the operations or source-of-supply assessment deficiently,
- and 74 percent are weak on the business and financial analysis.

These are frightening results, and they reveal a *quality crisis in the innovation process*—no, not product quality, but a crisis in "quality of execution." Simply stated, key tasks are not done, or not done well, which leads to too many underperforming new products.

When it comes to doing the front-end or due diligence work on new-product projects—market research, product value assessment, technical assessment, and building the Business Case—80 to 90 percent of typical firms are deficient, according to an APQC study (see Figure 2.1).

The result of poor front-end homework is that when it comes time to make key decisions—product design or Go/Kill investment decisions—there are many assumptions, but few hard facts. Frequently this lack of front-end work is due to no time and no money to do the work, and very often because people are too busy on other tasks. Both are lame excuses. Another cause is the desire to reduce time to market. Cutting out the homework stage in order to save a few months sounds like a compelling argument, if it weren't for the huge body of evidence that proves otherwise—that poor or no homework actually lengthens, not shortens, cycle time, as well as damaging new-product success rates.

3. A Lack of Customer or User Input and Insights

Another reason so many new products fail to reach their sales and profit targets is the lack of understanding of the marketplace and customer or user. Too often,

**Figure 2.1: Serious Deficiencies Exist in the Early Stages of Projects—
Especially for Poor-Performing Businesses**

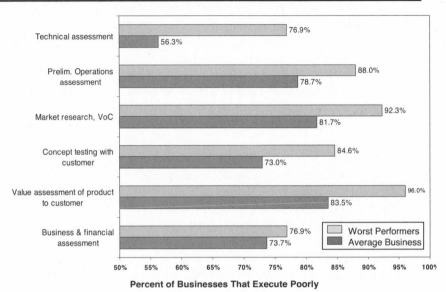

Source: endnote 1.

the project team (or an executive) develops the concept of what the product should be and do, often with very little real input from the marketplace. For example, there is no voice-of-customer work done, and no visits to users by the project team to uncover insights into real needs and customer problems. Figure 2.1 again reveals the facts: The overwhelming majority of firms simply do a poor job on the market research, concept testing with the customer, and determining the value of the product to the customer. Note that the "voice of the salesperson" or "voice of the product manager" are not substitutes for the voice of the customer! Also, if customer input is sought, it is often limited to one or only a few customers, and to immediate customers only—there is no attempt to broaden the customer base, or to move down the value chain to listen to the voices of the customers' clients, too. Further, as the product itself takes shape, and as various iterations of the product are crafted, there is little effort to validate the product with the customer until too late in the process. In short, *the customer or user is not an integral part of the development process.* And so, when the product goes to field trials, to customer tests or even to launch, it is not enthusiastically welcomed by the marketplace.

4. Unstable Product Specs and Project Scope Creep
Unstable product and project definitions, which keep changing as the project moves along, are *the number one cause of delays later in the project*, according to

some studies. In this scenario, the project team drives the ball down the field, but someone keeps moving the goalposts . . . and scoring a goal becomes next to impossible. For example, the project's scope changes: The project may begin as a simple one-customer request, and then becomes a multi-customer project. But halfway through Development, it's redefined again, this time as a new-product line serving an entire market. Or a single-country project suddenly becomes a global initiative. Another common scenario is that the product definition and specifications keep changing—the product's requirements, performance characteristics, and specifications are quite fluid, as different people who influence the project keep adding features or functionality, even as the project nears the end of the Development stage.

Sometimes unstable specs and scope creep are due to factors beyond the control of the project team, for example, a new competitive product entry or a new technology. But most often these definitional changes occur because of the arrival of *new information:* A salesperson indicates that the product needs an additional feature, or an executive sees a competitor at a trade show and wants that function added, and so on. This "new information" is not really new at all. It could have, and should have, been available to the project team near the beginning of the project. The root cause is often traced back to point #2 above, a lack of front-end homework.

5. Dysfunctional Project Teams, Too Many Functional Silos

The lack of true cross-functional project teams is *a major fail point* in many new-product projects. Indeed there is strong indication that *an effective cross-functional team is the number one key to driving cycle time down.* But many companies get it wrong. In some companies, the project resembles a relay race: the Marketing Department "owns" the project for the first lap, and then hands it off to R&D for development; after R&D completes its phase or lap, it gets handed off to Manufacturing, which throws it over the wall to the sales force for launch. In other businesses that have attempted to field cross-functional teams, often the experience is marred: The team lacks members from all the key functions (for example, often the Manufacturing or Operations person does not join the team until well into Development—too late!); the team leader is the wrong person and not really much of a leader at all; the team lacks cohesiveness and does not share a common vision of the project; some team members lack a strong stake in and commitment to the project; and team accountability is missing. What we witness are "dysfunctional teams" rather than cross-functional teams!

6. Far Too Many Projects in the Pipeline—No Focus

One of the greatest sins in product development is a senior management issue, namely, *overloading the development pipeline.* Far too many projects are approved at the early Go/Kill gates for the resources available. And there's no real attempt to deal with the resource issue later on: Projects keep getting added to the active list. The result is that projects are underresourced and people are spread far too thin. And with so much multitasking (people working on far too many projects), many inefficiencies creep into the system, as much time is wasted switching from project to project. One result is that projects take far longer than they should, as the development pipeline begins to resemble a logjam in a river. Another is that project quality starts to decline: For example, corners are cut, a needed market study gets skipped, the field trials are abbreviated, and so on, often with disastrous results.

7. A Lack of Competencies, Skills, and Knowledge

In some businesses and projects, not only are people spread too thin, there aren't even the people available with the right skills, competencies, and knowledge to undertake the project. Or the business is missing a key success driver, such as access to a marketplace or to a needed technology or technical skill. Sometimes the cause is that management approves the project yet fails to understand that key resources and competencies are indeed missing: The project, as defined, *never should have been approved in the first place*. Other times, this skills lack comes about because certain businesses have downsized so much that they've lost key technical and marketing talent: The people who are good at doing major and longer-term projects (but are not needed for day-to-day marketing and technical work) are gone. Finally, the necessary partnerships and alliances are not in place: Management does not insist that outside business partners be found to bring the missing and needed skills to the table; or the wrong partners are enlisted.

If you are typical, you've probably witnessed some or all of these seven reasons that new products fail to achieve their financial goals. No doubt, it is comforting to hear that other businesses suffer from the same maladies that you do. It's also motivating to hear that many companies have identified these and similar causes, and are taking steps to overcome them. For example, a quick review of these seven causes above reveals potential solutions—a stronger customer focus, better front-end work, fewer but better projects in the pipeline—that are built into prescriptions for improving results. So read on to see what the success drivers are and what actions can be taken.

SEVEN CRITICAL SUCCESS DRIVERS

The challenge is to design a playbook, blueprint, or process for successful product innovation—a process by which new-product projects can move from the idea stage through to a successful launch and beyond, quickly and effectively. Before charging into the design of this playbook, let's first understand the secrets to success—what separates successful innovation projects from the failures, the critical success factors that make the difference between winning and losing. Some are fairly obvious, but before you dismiss them as "too obvious," recognize

TABLE 2.1: WHY NEW PRODUCTS WIN— SEVEN CRITICAL SUCCESS DRIVERS

1. A unique superior product—a differentiated product that delivers unique benefits and a compelling value proposition to the customer or user—is the number one driver of new-product profitability.
2. Building in the voice of the customer—a market-driven and customer-focused new-product process—is critical to success.
3. Doing the homework and front-end loading the project is key to success. Due diligence done before product development gets under way pays off!
4. Getting sharp and early product and project definition—and avoiding scope creep and unstable specs—means higher success rates and faster to market.
5. Spiral development—build, test, get feedback, and revise— putting something in front of the customer early and often gets the product right.
6. A well-conceived, properly executed launch is central to new-product success. And a solid marketing plan is at the heart of the launch.
7. Speed counts! There are many good ways to accelerate development projects, but not at the expense of quality of execution.

that most firms still neglect them. We begin this insightful journey next, and as we probe each success driver, reflect on how you can benefit from each, and how you can translate each into an operational facet of your new-product system or playbook (see Table 2.1 for summary).[4]

1. A unique superior product—a differentiated product that delivers unique benefits and a compelling value proposition to the customer or user—is the number one driver of new-product profitability.

Delivering products with unique benefits and real value to users—bolder innovations—separates winners from losers more often than any other single factor. Such superior products have five times the success rate, over four times the market share, and four times the profitability of products lacking this ingredient, according to our research.[5] Product advantage, superiority, or differentiation as the key determinant of success is a recurring theme in many new-product studies.

That differentiated, superior products are key to success should come as no surprise to product innovators. Apparently, it isn't obvious to everyone: Study after study shows that "reactive products" and "me-too" offerings are the rule rather than the exception in many businesses' new-product efforts, and the majority fail to produce large profits![6] A second very popular scenario, which also yields poor results, is *the "techie" building a monument to himself*—the technical solution in search of a market.

> Superior and differentiated products—ones that deliver unique benefits and superior value to the customer—are the number one drivers of success and new-product profitability.

What do these superior products with unique customer or user benefits have in common? These winning products:

- ✓ are superior to competing products in terms of meeting users' needs, offer unique features not available in competitive products, or solve a problem the customer has with a competitive product,
- ✓ feature good value for money for the customer, reduce the customer's total costs (high value-in-use), and boast excellent price/performance characteristics,
- ✓ provide excellent product quality relative to competitors' products, and in terms of how the user measures quality, and
- ✓ offer product benefits or attributes easily perceived as useful by the customer, and benefits that are highly visible.

The "Best Innovator" businesses were introduced in Chapter 1—firms that model the way.[7] A closer look at these exceptional businesses shows that the Best Innovators emphasize certain factors in their new-product efforts—see Figure 2.2. Best Innovators are much stronger in terms of offering important product benefits, a superior value proposition, and better value for the customer in their new products, all features of bold innovations we saw in Chapter 1:

a) Best Innovators create products whose *main benefits are really important* to the customer or user, by a 4:1 ratio versus poor performers.
b) Their products offer the customer *new and unique benefits* not available in competitive products, by a huge 8:1 ratio versus poor performers.
c) They deliver new products that offer *better value-for-money* to the customer or user, compared to competitors (three times more so than poor performers).
d) Their new products are superior to competing products in terms of *meeting customers' and users' needs* (by a 4:1 ratio versus poor performers).
e) And they launch *better-quality products*—regardless of how the customer or user measures quality—than poor performers, by a 2:1 ratio.

There is a message here. These are the types of new products that really separate winning businesses in product innovation—the Best Innovators. By contrast,

Figure 2.2: A Unique Superior Product Is the Number One Driver of Performance Results

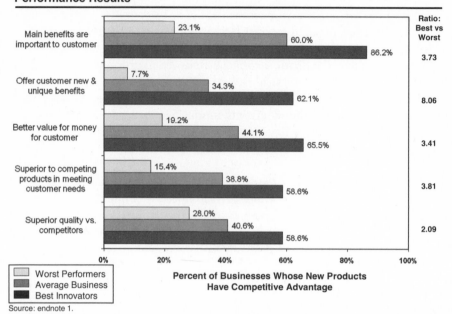

	Ratio: Best vs Worst
Main benefits are important to customer — 23.1%, 60.0%, 86.2%	3.73
Offer customer new & unique benefits — 7.7%, 34.3%, 62.1%	8.06
Better value for money for customer — 19.2%, 44.1%, 65.5%	3.41
Superior to competing products in meeting customer needs — 15.4%, 38.8%, 58.6%	3.81
Superior quality vs. competitors — 28.0%, 40.6%, 58.6%	2.09

0%   20%   40%   60%   80%   100%

Worst Performers
Average Business
Best Innovators

Percent of Businesses Whose New Products Have Competitive Advantage

Source: endnote 1.

the poor performers simply "don't get it." They consistently miss the mark on these five vital ingredients of winning new products.

A point of distinction in Figure 2.2: *Benefits* are what customers or users value and pay money for; by contrast, product attributes, features, functionality, and performance are the things that engineers, scientists, and designers build into products. Often benefits and features are connected, but sometimes the designers get it wrong, so that added product features and performance do not yield additional benefits for customers or users.

Very few firms can point to specific facets of their new-product methodology that emphasize this vital "product superiority" success ingredient. Often, product superiority is absent as a project selection criterion, and rarely are steps deliberately built into the idea-to-launch process that encourage the design of such superior products. Indeed, quite the reverse is true: The preoccupation with cycle-time reduction, the way gates are conducted, and the tendency to favor simple, inexpensive projects actually penalizes bolder projects that lead to product superiority.

The management implications are clear:

- First, these ingredients of a superior product (Figure 2.2) provide a useful checklist of questions in assessing the odds of success of a proposed new-product project: They logically become *top priority questions* in a project screening checklist or scorecard.

- Second, these ingredients become *challenges to the project team* to build into their new-product design. In short, the list of these five ingredients of product advantage above become personal objectives of the project leader and team, and must be molded into the playbook. As one team leader told me, "I stamp these on my forehead and look in the mirror every morning— these [the items in Figure 2.2] become our team's goals!"

But how does one invent or build in product superiority? Note that superiority is derived from design, features, attributes, specifications, and even positioning. The important point here is that "superiority" is defined from the customer's or user's standpoint, not in the eyes of the R&D, technical, or design departments. Sometimes product superiority is the result of new technology or a technological breakthrough. But more than technology and unique features are required to make a product superior. Remember: Features are those things that cost you, the developer, money. By contrast, benefits are what customers pay money for! Often the two—features and benefits—are not the same. So, in defining "unique benefits," think of the product as a "bundle of benefits for the user"; and think of benefits as something that customers view as having value to them:

An example: The idea for the new product started with a group of women at Mead Johnson Nutritionals (U.S.) who knew they all shared the struggle to do it all in life while still being able to appreciate it all. This Women's Health Team conducted extensive market research that concluded that women are in need of more stamina to make it through the day—and that their situation is quite serious. A nationwide survey in the United States conducted by the company (942 respondents) revealed that 60 percent of women felt that the condition of their declining vitality levels was very serious or extremely serious, with 80 percent of women feeling the negative impact of tiredness on their relationships with family and friends. A follow-up summit meeting, with dozens of the most prominent women's health experts in the country, helped to further define the problem and then brainstormed provocative solutions.

One area of focus was nutrition, with experts noting that key nutrients not sufficiently met include calcium, antioxidants, B vitamins, zinc, folic acid, and iron. A second conclusion was that women should indulge themselves more, taking care of their personal needs. Another conclusion was that snacking should be taken "out of the closet"—health experts said that women should eat less food, but more frequently, especially snack foods that are nutritious and rich in these vital but lacking nutrients. Yet another conclusion was that women found nutritional information to be confusing and contradictory—they wanted clarity and simplification.

Thus was born Viactiv™, a new-product line of women's nutritional products. The product combines the need for a healthy and indulgent snack food with vital but lacking nutrients in female diets: Viactiv Soft Calcium Chews. This is a chocolate snack product, with a tailored combination of nutrients specific to women's needs, including calcium and 100 percent of the recommended daily values for B vitamins, folic acid, and antioxidants. This simple solution to a confusing problem has been a hit with the target audience: Sales have been stunning and have exceeded management's expectations (Viactiv continues to be a big success and is now part of McNeil Nutritionals, a division of Johnson & Johnson).

The point is that "unique," "differentiated," and "superior value" must be in the eyes of the customer or user. It was through hard work by the Viactiv team that the key benefits and unmet needs of users were discovered, leading to a product with real competitive advantage.

Suggestion: The definition of "what is unique and superior" and "what is a benefit" is from the customer's perspective—so it *must be based on an in-depth understanding of customer needs, wants, problems, likes, and dislikes.*

1. *Determine customer needs at the outset—build in voice-of-customer (VoC) research early in your projects.* The goal here is to identify customer needs, not just their wants. *Wants* are usually fairly obvious, and easy for the customer to talk about. But spotting *needs*, particularly *unmet and unarticulated needs*, is more of a challenge, but often yields a breakthrough new product. So start with a user needs-and-wants study—market research and seeking customer insights—to probe customer needs, wants, problems, preferences, likes, and dislikes. Determine the customer's "hot buttons"— the order-winning criteria, the customer's problems, and what the customer is *really seeking* in a much-improved or superior product. Let the customer help design the product for you.
2. *Do a competitive product analysis.* There is no such thing as a perfect competitive product. If you can spot the competitors' product weaknesses, then you're halfway to beating them. Remember: The goal is product superiority, and that means superiority over the current or future competitive offering. Take the competitor's product apart in your lab or design department; and when you do the VoC research, be sure to ask your customers for their opinions about the strengths and weaknesses of the competitor's product. One more point: Anticipate what the competitor's product might or will be in the foreseeable future. Never assume the competitor's current product will be the competitive benchmark by the time you hit the market!
   Once these two investigations are complete, the project team can translate the information into a product definition, paying special attention to the benefits and the *value proposition* that the product will offer to the customer.
3. *Build in multiple test iterations to test and verify your assumptions about your winning-product design.* Once the product concept and specs are defined

(based on user inputs above), test the concept with users—and make sure they indicate a favorable response. That is, even before serious development work begins, start testing the product—even though you don't yet have a product!—via concept, virtual prototype, or "protocept" (between a concept and a prototype) tests.

This disciplined approach to discovering product superiority is decidedly customer focused, which leads to success factor number two, the need for a strong customer input.

2. Building in the voice of the customer—a market-driven and customer-focused new-product process—is critical to success.

A thorough understanding of customers' or users' needs and wants, the competitive situation, and the nature of the market is an essential component of new-product success. This finding is supported in virtually every study of product success factors. Recurring themes include:

- ✓ need recognition
- ✓ understanding user needs
- ✓ market need satisfaction
- ✓ constant customer contact
- ✓ strong market knowledge and market research
- ✓ quality of execution of marketing activities, and
- ✓ more spending on the front-end market-related activities.

Conversely, a failure to adopt a strong market focus in product innovation, an unwillingness to undertake the needed market assessments and to build in the voice of the customer, and leaving the customer out of product development spells disaster. Poor market research; inadequate market analysis; weak market studies, test markets, and market launch; and inadequate resources devoted to marketing activities are common weaknesses found in virtually every study of why new products fail.

Sadly, *a strong market focus is missing in the majority of firms' new-product projects*. Detailed market studies are frequently omitted (in more than 75 percent of projects, according to one investigation). Further, marketing activities are the weakest-rated activities of the entire new-product process, rated much lower than corresponding technological actions. Moreover, relatively few resources and little money are spent on the marketing actions (except for the launch), accounting for less than 20 percent of the total project cost.

The Best Innovators are leaders when it comes to a strong market focus—see Figure 2.3. Best Innovating businesses:

- work closely with customers and users to identify needs, problems, and customer "points of pain"—4.5 times more so than do poor performers,

Figure 2.3: Voice-of-Customer and Market Insight Impacts Strongly on Innovation Performance Results

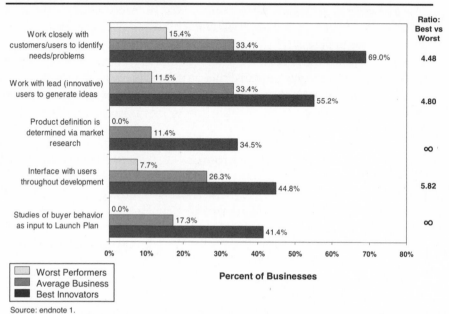

Source: endnote 1.

- work with lead or innovative users—users that are "ahead of the wave"—to generate new-product ideas (by a 5:1 ratio versus poor performers),
- determine their product definitions via market research—that is, VoC insights are a major input to the product definition (remarkably, *none* of the poor-performing businesses do this, and such input is a practice of only 11 percent of average businesses),
- interface with customers throughout the entire development process, not just at the beginning and end—by a 6:1 ratio versus poor performers, and
- seek market input to help design the launch plan.

An example: Drägerwerk is an international leader in the field of medical and safety technology, and its Dräger Safety subsidiary provides products, services, and solutions for risk management for personal and facility protection.[8] One of the company's product lines, breathalyzer testing devices, is used by police forces to test alcohol levels in suspected drunk drivers. The goal was to develop a new European breathalyzer product line, but the project needed direction and lacked blockbuster ideas.

Two VoC study teams were formed, and after some training on how to do ethnographic research, they began their camping-out exercises in the United Kingdom, the Netherlands, and Germany. In all countries, the teams spent time at police stations, conducting traditional interviews with police officers and their supervisors. But the real learning and insights came from their nighttime vigils—the camping-out exercise—in which the VoC teams worked beside the police officers as they ran their nighttime roadside spot checks on drivers. These insights provided the key to a new product with significant competitive advantage.

> Building in the voice of the customer is one of the strongest drivers of new-product profitability, and also of time efficiency. But the great majority of companies miss the mark here—with insufficient VoC and no fact-based customer insights.

For example, during the observation period, the British VoC team soon realized how difficult a job the police officers have trying to maintain order and control. One officer had pulled over a car full of exuberant young drinkers fresh from the nearby pub and issued the standard command to those suspected of being drunk: "Remain in the car!" The officer, wearing latex gloves for fear of HIV, then passed the breathalyzer device through the driver's window, instructing the driver to blow into the mouthpiece. It takes two minutes to get a full reading.

Meanwhile, the other officer had pulled over another car, so now the officers had to manage two cars full of drunk people. Quite clearly, the police officers were somewhat intimidated by the task of crowd control, as they were outnumbered and the lads in the cars were twice the size and half the age of the officers (who, incidentally, do not carry guns). Note that the officers never admitted to intimidation during the formal daytime interviews!

To overcome the problem of crowd control and intimidation, the VoC team came up with one solution: Speed up the process. The aim was to substantially reduce the two-minute waiting time that was creating the queue. This was achieved by developing a ten-second test device. A second observation was that because of the dials on the British version of the instrument, it could only be used on right-hand-side drivers. Thus, when a left-hand-side driver from France or Germany was pulled over in the United Kingdom, the police could not conduct the test quite as quickly. And because of time pressures, they really had no option but to simply wave the car through. This behavior was never revealed, neither to their supervisors nor in the formal interviews. The solution here was to design an ambidextrous testing instrument—an arm with the mouthpiece that could be swung over the top of the test device, depending on whether a right-hand-drive or left-hand-drive vehicle was pulled over.

These are just two of the ten novel feature-ideas that made the new Dräger product line a huge success. Each feature was not, in itself, a breakthrough; but when the ten new features and benefits were added together, the new product was indeed a blockbuster and absolutely delighted police forces.

Figure 2.4: A Strong Customer Focus Means Key Actions from Beginning to End in the Innovation Process

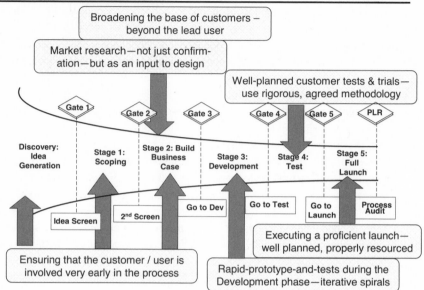

Suggestion: Huge differences in practices exist between Best Innovators and poor performers, according to the results in Figure 2.3; and these actions in Figure 2.3 are clearly "best practices." Thus, a strong market focus must prevail throughout the entire new-product project, as shown in Figure 2.4, starting with idea generation.

Idea generation: The best ideas come from customers! Devote more resources to market-oriented idea-generation activities, such as focus groups and VoC research with customers to determine customers' generic needs and their problems. Use the sales force to actively solicit ideas from customers and develop relationships with innovative or lead users. There is more to come on effective ideation in Chapter 6.

The design of the product: User and customer inputs have a vital role in the *design of the product*—when the product's requirements and specs are being defined. Often, market research, when done at all, is done too late—after the product design has already been decided and simply as an after-the-fact check. Note that market research must be used as an input to the design decisions and serves as a guide to the project team before it charges into the design of the new product. Determine customer and user needs at the outset, starting with a user needs-and-wants study (VoC research) in tandem with a competitive product analysis (competitive benchmarking).

So, build in the voice of the customer early in the project via:

- ✓ in-depth one-on-one personal interviews,
- ✓ customer site visits (done by the entire project team),
- ✓ fly-on-the wall or "day-in-the-life-of" research,
- ✓ "camping out" with the customer (extended site visits or ethnography, similar to anthropological research),
- ✓ customer panels, and
- ✓ large-sample quantitative market research.

Even in the case of *technology-push* new products (in which the product emanates from the lab or technical group, perhaps the result of a technological breakthrough or a technical possibility), there still should be considerable market input as the technology is shaped into a final product design. That is, following the technical discovery, but before full-fledged development gets under way, there is ample opportunity to research and interact with the customer to determine needs and wants, to shape the final product the way the customer wants it, and to gauge likely product acceptance.

Before pushing ahead into Development: Be sure to test the product concept with the customer by presenting a representation of the product—via models, mockups, protocepts, CAD drawings, and even virtual products—and gauging the customer's interest, liking, and purchase intent. It's much cheaper to test and learn before Development begins than to develop the product first, and then begin customer testing!

Throughout the entire project: Customer inputs shouldn't cease at the completion of the pre-development market studies. Seeking customer inputs and testing concepts or designs with the user is very much an iterative process—"spiral development" as outlined in success driver #5 below. Keep bringing the customer into the process to view facets of the product via a series of concept tests, rapid-prototype-and-tests, customer trials, and test markets, verifying all assumptions about the winning design. Don't wait until the very end of the Development stage—the field trials—to unveil the product to the customer. There could be some very unpleasant surprises!

3. Doing the homework and front-end loading the project is key to success. Due diligence done before product Development gets under way pays off!

We all learned in eighth grade how distasteful homework was. Many of us haven't forgotten: We hate homework! But then, as now, homework or due diligence is critical to winning. Countless studies reveal that the steps that precede the actual design and development of the product make the difference between winning and losing. *The Best Innovators are much more proficient when it comes to these*

Figure 2.5: Quality of Execution in the Fuzzy Front End Impacts Strongly on Innovation Success

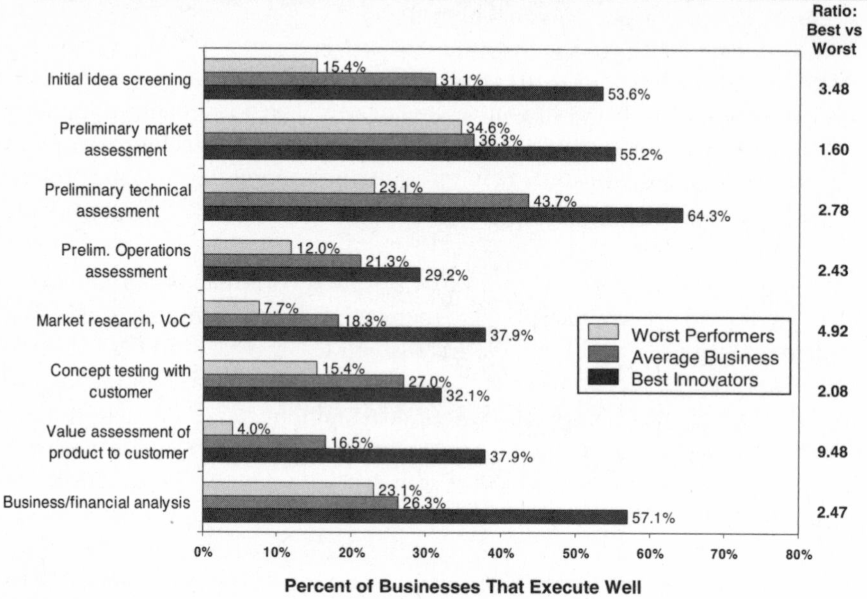

	Ratio: Best vs Worst
Initial idea screening — 15.4% / 31.1% / 53.6%	3.48
Preliminary market assessment — 34.6% / 36.3% / 55.2%	1.60
Preliminary technical assessment — 23.1% / 43.7% / 64.3%	2.78
Prelim. Operations assessment — 12.0% / 21.3% / 29.2%	2.43
Market research, VoC — 7.7% / 18.3% / 37.9%	4.92
Concept testing with customer — 15.4% / 27.0% / 32.1%	2.08
Value assessment of product to customer — 4.0% / 16.5% / 37.9%	9.48
Business/financial analysis — 23.1% / 26.3% / 57.1%	2.47

Legend: Worst Performers / Average Business / Best Innovators

Percent of Businesses That Execute Well (axis: 0% 10% 20% 30% 40% 50% 60% 70% 80%)

Source: endnote 1.

activities in the *"fuzzy front end" of projects—they do their homework* (see Figure 2.5):

- ✓ Initial screening: the first decision to get into the project (the idea screen),
- ✓ Preliminary market assessment—the first and quick market study to assess market size and likely product acceptance and sales,
- ✓ Preliminary technical assessment—a technical appraisal of the project, looking at technology risks and the likely technical route,
- ✓ Preliminary operations assessment—looking at source-of-supply, manufacturing, and operations issues,
- ✓ The detailed market study, market research, and VoC research (described above),
- ✓ Concept testing—testing the product concept with the customer or user to ensure customer liking and purchase intent (also described above),
- ✓ Value assessment—determining the value or economic worth of the product to the customer,
- ✓ The business and financial analysis just before the decision to "Go to Development" (building the business case).

Where are the biggest differences, and where do the Best Innovators excel? Compared to poor performers, the stand-out practices for the Best Innovators are: determining the economic value of the product to the customer; undertaking voice-of-customer research as input to the product's design; and the business and financial analysis as part of building the business case. But these are not easy tasks, and even the best firms struggle here.

Another issue is the *balance* within the homework stage. Best Innovators strike an appropriate balance between market/business-oriented tasks and technology activities, whereas poor performers tend to push ahead on the technical side and pay lip service to marketing and business issues in the early stages of the project. Figure 2.5 shows how much better the Best Innovators execute the homework activities, but especially the early stage marketing/business tasks. Surprisingly, most firms confess to serious weaknesses in the front-end or pre-development steps of their new-product process. Pitifully small amounts of time and money are devoted to these critical steps: only about 7 percent of the dollars and 16 percent of the effort.

More homework prior to the initiation of product design and development has been consistently found to be a key factor in success. The quality of execution of the pre-development steps—initial screening, preliminary market and technical studies, market research, and business analysis—is closely tied to the product's financial performance. And successful projects have over 1.75 times as much work (person-days) devoted to pre-development actions as do failures. One of Toyota's seven principles of innovation stipulates that projects be "front-end loaded"— that a higher proportion of work be shifted to the earlier stages of the development project.[9] Indeed, the emphasis that the Japanese devote to the planning stage of the new-product process is described by Havelock and Elder:

> Japanese developers make a clear distinction between the "planning" and the "implementation" phases of a new technology initiative ... The objective of planning is complete understanding of the problem and the related technology before a "go" decision is made. It is reported to be an unrushed process which might look agonizingly drawn out to Western eyes.[10]

The pre-development activities are important because they qualify and define the project. They answer key questions, such as:

- Is the project economically attractive? Will the product sell at sufficient volumes and margins to justify investment in development and commercialization?
- Who exactly is the target customer? And how should the product be positioned?
- What exactly should the product be to make it a winner? What features, attributes, and performance characteristics should be built into it to yield a unique superior product?
- Can the product be developed and at the right cost? What is the likely technical solution?

- What about source of supply? By us or by others? And at what cost and investment?

"More homework means longer development times" is a frequently voiced complaint. This is a valid concern, but experience has shown that homework pays for itself in reduced development times as well as improved success rates:

✓ First, all the evidence points to a much higher likelihood of product failure if the homework is omitted. So the choice is between more work early on, or much increased odds of failure: no pain, no gain!
✓ Second, better project definition, the result of solid homework, actually speeds up the development process. One of the major causes of time slippages is poorly defined projects as they enter the Development stage, that is, vague targets and moving goalposts.
✓ Third, given the inevitable product design evolution that occurs during the life of a project, the time to make the majority of these design changes is not as the product is moving out of Development and into Production. More homework up front anticipates these changes and encourages them to occur earlier in the process rather than later, when they are more costly.

Suggestion: The message is evident. Don't skimp on the homework! If you find yourself making the case that "we don't have time for the homework," you're wrong on two counts: First, cutting out the homework drives your success rate way down; and second, cutting out homework to save time today will cost you in wasted time tomorrow. It's a "penny-wise, pound foolish" way to save time. Make it a rule: No significant project should move into the Development stage without the actions described above completed, and done in a quality way. And devote the necessary resources to get the work done; that is, front-end load the project! Figure 2.5 provides a useful checklist of early stage activities that should be built into your new-product process or idea-to-launch system.

4. Getting sharp and early product and project definition—and avoiding scope creep and unstable specs—means higher success rates and faster to market.

How well the project and product are defined prior to entering the Development stage is a major success factor, impacting positively on both profitability and reduced time-to-market. Look at the facts in Figure 2.6, and notice how much better the Best Innovators get the product defined before embarking on the Development stage:

- Best Innovators clearly *define the benefits* to be delivered to the customer (by a 4:1 ratio versus poor performers).

Figure 2.6: Having Sharp, Stable, and Fact-Based Product Definition Drives Innovation Success

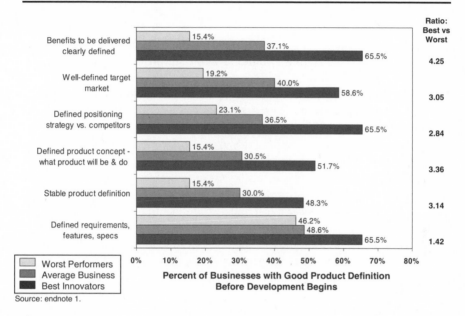

- The *target market*—who will buy the product—is clear, and so is the positioning strategy, that is, how the product will be positioned in the customer's mind and versus competitors.
- The product concept is also well defined—what the product will be and do.
- The product definition is *stable* (although this ideal is difficult to achieve).
- And the product *features, attributes, and specifications* are defined.

Note the major differences on each of these five items when Best Innovators are compared to the poor performers. These elements of product definition are vital to success and distinguish the Best Innovators.

By contrast, a failure to *define the product and project scope* before Development begins is a major cause of both new-product failure and serious delays in time-to-market. In spite of the fact that *early and stable product definition is*

> Securing sharp, early, stable, and fact-based product definition before Development begins is one of the strongest drivers of cycle-time reduction and new-product success.

consistently cited as a key to success, businesses continue to perform poorly here, as shown in Figure 2.6. Terms such as "unstable products specs" and "project scope creep" describe far too many new-product projects in our studies.

Suggestion: Build in an *integrated product and project definition step* or checkpoint before the door is opened to a full development program. This definition has six components:

a) the project scope: what the bounds of the development effort are—domestic versus international; new-product item versus platform development, and so on
b) target market definition—precisely who the product is aimed at
c) the product concept—what the product will be and do (written in the language of the customer)
d) the benefits to be delivered, including the *value proposition* for the customer or user
e) the positioning strategy (including the target price)
f) product features, attributes, performance requirements, and high-level specs (prioritized: "must have" and "would like to have")

This *integrated definition* must be fact based: It is developed with inputs and agreement from the functional areas involved: Marketing, R&D, Engineering, Operations, and so on. The entire project team must sign off on it; and senior management should also commit to the definition—the essential "buy in" or sign-off.

Unless the these six items are clearly defined, written down, and agreed to by all parties prior to entering the Development stage, then your project faces tough times downstream: Your odds of failure have just skyrocketed by a factor of three! Here's why:

1. Building an integrated product definition step into the new-product system forces more attention to the front-end or pre-development activities. If the homework hasn't been done, then arriving at a sharp definition that all parties will buy into is next to impossible.
2. The definition serves as a communication tool and guide. All-party agreement or "buy in" means that each functional area involved in the project has a clear and consistent definition of what the product and project are and is committed to it. How often have you left a meeting thinking that agreement was achieved, only to find out later that there are many different versions of what was agreed to, depending on whom you speak to? This integrated product definition is the agreement in black and white.
3. This definition also provides a clear set of objectives for the Development stage of the project, and for the technical team members. With clear product objectives, development typically proceeds more efficiently and quickly: no moving goalposts and no fuzzy targets!

Achieving a stable product definition is a challenge—even the Best Innovators struggle, as shown in Figure 2.6. Recognize that many markets are quite fluid and dynamic, and that "things change." So the notion of a traditional "100-percent design freeze" before Development is obsolete in some markets, such as IT and software. But this is no reason to throw one's hands in the air and declare that "product definition is impossible—we'll decide it as we go along." With solid front-end homework and due diligence (success driver #3 above), many elements can be nailed down before Development begins, even in fluid markets, while some elements of the product's design will remain "variable" and "to be decided" as the project proceeds.

Suggestion: The recommendation is this: For those of you who face *fluid and dynamic markets*, where product definitions are difficult to pin down before Development commences:

- ✓ Build in the necessary front-end homework, as in success driver #3. Facing fast-paced markets is no excuse for taking lazy shortcuts. So take your choice: fast failures or thoughtful successes!
- ✓ Pin down the integrated product definition as best you can *before Development begins*—use the list of six items in this definition that I outlined above.
- ✓ Specify in advance which part of the product requirements and specs are "known and fixed" versus which are "fluid, uncertain, and variable" before Development begins (one hopes that more than 50 percent is fixed on entering Development). Use two columns in your product definition: "fixed" and "variable."
- ✓ Build steps into your development process to gather data so that the "variable parts" of your product definition can be pinned down as development proceeds, which brings us to success driver #5.

5. Spiral development—build, test, get feedback, and revise—putting something in front of the customer early and often gets the product right.

Spiral development is the way that fast-paced teams handle the dynamic information process with fluid, changing information. Spiral development helps the project team get the product and product definition right, in spite of the fact that some information is fluid and some may be even unreliable when the team moves into the Development stage.

Many businesses use *too rigid and linear a process* for product development. This is wrong! The project team diligently visits customers in the pre-development or front-end stages and determines customer needs and requirements as well as possible. Front-end work or homework is properly done; and the product specs are determined and the product definition is fixed. So far, so good.

The Development stage gets under way, but proceeds in *a linear and rigid fashion*. The project team hunkers down and moves the project forward following a

Figure 2.7: Spiral Development—a Series of "Build-Test-Feedback-Revise" Iterations—Gets the Product Right with No Time Wasted

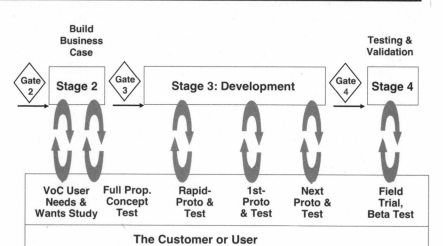

"heads down," rather than a "heads up," approach. Some ten or fifteen months pass, and at the end of this linear Development stage, the product is ready for field trials or customer tests. Then everything goes wrong. When presented with the prototype or beta product for testing, the original customers now indicate that "this is not quite what we had in mind" or that "things have changed." Or perhaps a new competitive product has been launched that alters the competitive landscape.

The point is that by proceeding in a linear and rigid process, the project team and business set themselves up for failure. Maybe the initial product requirements were not quite right: Key points were missed when the initial VoC work was done. Or perhaps things really did change in the ten to fifteen months that ensued. And now the project team must backtrack to the Development stage for another attempt at the product . . . back to the drawing board! And we witness another victim of a rigid linear process that does not adapt to changing circumstances.

Smart project teams and businesses practice spiral development (based on "agile development" as used in the IT industry). For example, Best Innovator businesses are six times more likely to interface with customers and users throughout the entire Development stage (as indicated in Figure 2.3). They build in a series of *iterative steps,* or *"loops,"* whereby successive versions of the product are shown to the customer to seek feedback and verification, as shown in Figure 2.7. These loops are a series of "build-test-feedback-and-revise" iterations (their iterative nature leads to the term "spiral development"):

- Build something, even if it's only a model or representation of the product.
- Test it—get it in front of the customer or user, and gauge interest, liking, preference, and purchase intent, likes and dislikes.
- Get feedback—find out the customer's reactions firsthand, and most important, what must be fixed or changed.
- Revise—update the product definition based on this feedback and get set for the next iteration of "build-test-feedback-and-revise," but this time with a product version one step closer to the final product.

Suggestion: *Use spirals—a series of "build-test-feedback-and-revise" iterations.* This spiral approach is based on the fact that customers don't really know what they are looking for until they see it or experience it—so get something in front of the customer, anything, even if it's still a long way from the final product; and start early. Then seek fast and confirmatory feedback, making the necessary changes to the product, getting an even more complete version in front of the customer for the next iteration. But some words of warning: Don't fully develop the product and start presenting real prototypes early in the process; the notion here is to get something in front of the customer initially that you can put together quickly and inexpensively.

> People don't know what they're looking for until they see it or experience it. So get something in front of the customer or user fast—and keep repeating these tests all the way through to formal product testing.

How does spiral development work in practice? A sample set of spirals is shown in Figure 2.7. Note that these loops or spirals are built in from the front-end stages through the Development stage and into the Testing stage, beginning with a VoC study and culminating in product tests and market launch.

6. A well-conceived, properly executed launch is central to new-product success. And a solid marketing plan is at the heart of the launch.

Emerson once said, "Build a better mousetrap and the world will beat a path to your door." The problem is that Emerson was a poet, not a businessman. This old adage may never have been true, and it certainly hasn't been true for years. Not only must the product be superior, but its benefits must be communicated and marketed aggressively. A quality launch is strongly linked to new-product profitability. Look at how the Best Innovators fare in Figure 2.8:

- They do the necessary market research—understanding buyer or customer behavior—in order to better craft the launch plan (interestingly, less than half the Best Innovators undertake such a study; but then not one poor performer does so—thus I include this action as a key difference between Best and Worst firms).

Figure 2.8: The Market Launch and Related Actions Impact Innovation Results Strongly

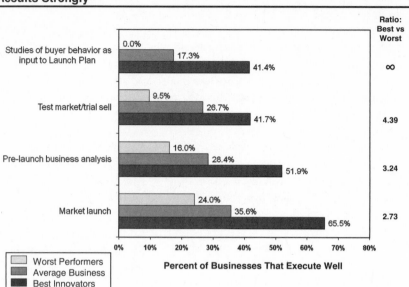

Source: endnote 1.

- Best Innovators conduct a test market or a trial sell to validate the marketability of the new product and also to test elements of the market launch plan.
- They undertake a solid pre-launch business analysis.
- But most important, Best Innovators execute the launch more proficiently— by a 3:1 ratio when compared to poor innovators.

The message is this: Don't assume that good products sell themselves, and don't treat the launch as an afterthought. Just because the launch is the last step in the process, never underestimate its importance. A well-integrated and properly targeted launch does not occur by accident, however; it is the result of a *fine-tuned marketing plan,* properly backed and resourced, and proficiently executed.

Marketing planning—moving from marketing objectives to strategy and marketing programs—is a complex process. Entire books have been devoted to the subject. But this complex marketing planning process must be woven into your new-product system. For example, defining the target market and the development of a positioning strategy, one of the core steps in developing a marketing plan, is part of the product-definition step just before Development begins (success factor #5 above). And answers to many key questions—How do customers buy? Via what channels of distribution? What are their sources of information? What servicing do they require?—are central to developing the nuts and bolts of the marketing programs. Answers to these questions must come from market re-search investigations that are built into the new-product process or playbook. More on how to craft a market launch plan in Chapter 10.

Suggestion: I make four important points regarding new-product launch and the marketing plan:

a) The development of the market launch plan is an *integral part of the new-product process:* It is as central to the new-product process as the develop-ment of the physical product.
b) The development of the market launch plan *must begin early* in the new-product project. It should not be left as an afterthought to be undertaken as the product nears commercialization.
c) A market launch plan is only as good as the *market intelligence* upon which it is based. Market studies designed to yield information crucial to market-ing planning must be built into the new-product project.
d) These who will execute the launch—the sales force, technical support people, other front-line personnel—must be engaged in the development of the market launch plan, and some should therefore be members of the project team. This ensures valuable input and insight into the design of the launch effort, availability of resources when needed, and buy-in by those who must execute the product and its launch—elements so critical to a suc-cessful launch.

7. Speed counts! There are many good ways to accelerate development projects, but not at the expense of quality of execution.

Speed to market is an admirable goal, and there are many apparently valid reasons that cycle-time reduction should be a priority:[11]

- *Speed yields competitive advantage: First in will win!* There is conflicting ev-idence on this, however; often the number-two-product entrant learns from the mistakes of the pioneer and ends up making more money. Nonetheless, on average, the first entrant usually does better, as shown in Figure 2.9, which reveals the impact of order-of-entry. Note that "first-in products" have a success rate of 70 percent at launch versus 58 percent for third-in products; and first-in have a higher profitability rating (profits achieved ver-sus targeted profits).
- *Speed yields higher profitability.* Again there is mixed evidence, with our stud-ies showing only a modest positive connection between profitability and timeliness (on-time performance and time efficiency), whereas other studies show no conclusive link between time-to-market and profits. Nonetheless, first-in products certainly have the advantage of realizing revenues sooner

Figure 2.9: First Entrant Products Tend to Do Better—Higher Success Rates and Profitability

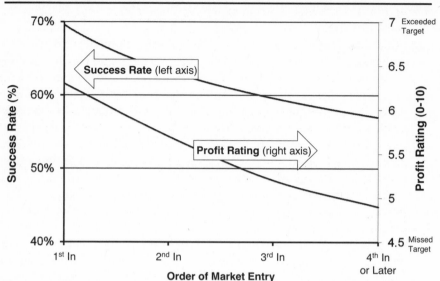

(money does have a time value!) and may also see more revenues and profits over the product's life.

• *Speed means fewer surprises.* There is much less likelihood that the market has changed if one gets to market quickly.

Another, perhaps less valid reason for speed, is the senior executive's desire to get the new product's revenue results on this year's bottom line (often a result of how the executive is measured)!

The point is: Speed is important, but not as vital as one might have assumed; and for some projects, speed must not be the overriding goal. Note that *speed is only an interim objective*—a means to an end. The ultimate goal, of course, is profitability. But many of the practices naively employed in order to reduce time-to-market ultimately cost the company money. They achieve the interim objective—bringing the product quickly to market—but fail at the ultimate objective: profitability. Too often the methods used to reduce development time yield precisely the opposite effect and in many cases are very costly: They are at odds with sound management practice.

Thus, there is a "dark side" to accelerated product development:

• Shortcuts are taken with the best intentions but far too frequently result in disaster: serious errors of omission and commission, which not only add delays to the project but often lead to higher incurred costs and even product failure. For example:

✓ moving in haste through the early stages of a new-product project—the front-end-homework and the market studies—only to discover later that the product design does not meet customer needs, and the project itself is an ill-conceived one;

✓ moving a product to market quickly by shortening the customer-test stage, only to incur product reliability problems after launch, resulting in lost customer confidence and substantial warranty and servicing costs.

- Reducing cycle time often results in focusing on easy and quick hits—the "low-hanging fruit" projects such as line extensions and minor modifications—but that means paying the price later via a lack of significant new products and loss of longer-term competitive advantage. Recall the dramatic shift from the 1990s portfolios to smaller, lower-risk, and even trivial new products in today's portfolios (Figure 1.1 in Chapter 1).
- Setting unrealistic timelines to achieve launch deadlines creates frustration, tension, and morale problems among project team members when milestones are invariably missed. Ultimately, attempting to operate via an unrealistic timeline destroys the effectiveness of cross-functional teams, as team members start blaming each other for the failure to hit deadlines.

Suggestion: Be careful in the overzealous pursuit of speed and cycle-time reduction. There are ways to reduce cycle time, however, that are totally consistent with sound management practice and are also derived from the critical success drivers outlined above. Figure 2.10 shows how some of the success drivers not only impact positively on new-product profitability, but also on time reduction or efficiency. Here are five sensible ways to *increase the odds of winning* but also to *reduce time-to-market!*

1. *Prioritize and focus:* The best way to slow projects down is to dissipate your limited resources and people across too many projects. By concentrating resources on the truly deserving projects, not only will the work be done better, it will be done faster. But focus means tough choices: It means killing other and perhaps worthwhile projects. And that requires good decision-making and the right criteria for making Go/Kill decisions. More on effective project selection and gates with teeth in Chapters 8 and 9.
2. *Do it right the first time:* Build in quality of execution at every stage of the project. The best way to save time is by *avoiding having to recycle back and do it a second time.* Quality of execution pays off not only in terms of better results but also by reducing delays.
3. *Front-end homework and definition:* Doing the upfront homework and getting clear product and project definition, based on facts rather than hearsay and speculation, saves time downstream: That means less recycling back to get the facts or redefine the product requirements, and sharper technical targets to work toward.

Figure 2.10: What Drives New-Products Profitability and Time-to-Market

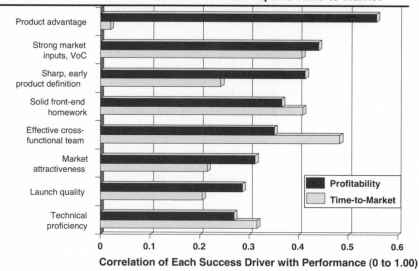

New-product profitability is measured on multiple metrics: profits relative to target (%), return-on-investment (%), and payback period (years). Time-to-market is measured two ways: time relative to scheduled time-to-market; and time efficiency – that is, time relative to fastest possible time.

4. *Organize around a true cross-functional team with empowerment:* Multifunctional teams are essential for timely development and are a topic in the next chapter. "Rip apart a badly developed project and you will unfailingly find 75 percent of slippage attributable to: (1) 'siloing,' or sending memos up and down vertical organizational 'silos' or 'stovepipes' for decisions; and (2) sequential problem solving," according to Tom Peters.[12] Sadly, the typical project resembles a relay race, with each function or department carrying the baton for its portion of the race, then handing off to the next runner or department.

5. *Parallel processing:* The relay-race, sequential, or series approach to product development is antiquated and inappropriate for today's fast-paced projects. Given the time pressures of projects, coupled with the need for a complete and quality process, a more appropriate model is a rugby game or *parallel processing*. With parallel processing, activities are undertaken concurrently (rather than sequentially); thus, more activities are undertaken in an elapsed period of time. The new-product process must be multidisciplinary with each part of the team—Marketing, R&D, Operations, Engineering, Sales—working together and undertaking its parallel or concurrent activity. Note that the play is a lot more complex using a parallel rugby scheme (versus a series approach), hence the need for a disciplined playbook.

BUILDING THE SUCCESS DRIVERS INTO YOUR PLAYBOOK

Many businesses have "operating procedures" or guides on how to do things right. Imagine you are crafting a new-product guidebook or set of operating procedures for how to do a new-product project right—for example, an "idea-to-launch playbook" or a stage-and-gate system to drive new products to market. What would be the first seven principles that might underpin your system? The seven success drivers outlined above in this chapter, of course. Here's how:

1. Make sure your idea-to-launch system includes actions as well as decision criteria that yield bold, differentiated products with a compelling value proposition for the customer. Most systems do not, and so they miss the number one profit driver!
2. Build a hefty dose of VoC and market information work into your system—make VoC a mandatory action. This tends to be a weak area generally, so it needs bolstering.
3. Ensure that projects are front-end loaded; thus, build a robust "homework stage" or two (perhaps a "light homework" stage followed by a "heavy homework" stage) before Development gets under way. Again, due diligence is missing in many development projects, so the key front-end actions must be emphasized in your system.
4. Build in a step to secure fact-based integrated product and project definitions—to plant the goalposts in the field. And get sign-off by all members of the project team and senior management.
5. Incorporate spirals into your system—a series of build-test-feedback-and-revise iterations to get the product definition right in the face of fluid information and changing requirements.
6. Execution of the market launch is vital; thus, make the development of a launch plan a key ingredient in your system (with the input and agreement of the functional areas that will execute the plan).
7. Speed (or time-to-market) is an issue and accelerated development has many potential benefits, but many downsides, too. Five sensible ways to accelerate developments were highlighted above—build these into your idea-to-launch system.

The next chapter continues with the theme of success drivers, but those that are broader and more related to the business rather than to the project. So read on and see how some businesses distinguish themselves in product innovation.

3

DRIVERS OF SUCCESS— WHY THE BEST INNOVATORS EXCEL

The secret of success is constancy to purpose.
—Benjamin Disraeli, British prime minister (1804–1881)

SEVEN CRITICAL SUCCESS DRIVERS FOR THE BUSINESS

Why are some businesses so much more successful at product innovation than others? We saw in Chapter 1 the huge differences in performance between Best Innovators and the rest. What are their secrets to success? The last chapter revealed some of these "secrets," notably, those most closely connected to how some new-product projects become big winners. Seeking unique, superior products; building in solid front-end homework and VoC input; planning and executing an effective launch; and accelerating the process (with some provisos) were but some of the drivers of success revealed in Chapter 2. In this current chapter, we continue with the theme "drivers of success," but *this time focused on the business* and not so much on the project as the unit of analysis: In short, *what distinguishes the most successful businesses* when it comes to innovation performance?

Consider now the more evident lessons—the critical success drivers that make the difference between winning and losing businesses; and reflect on how you can benefit from each, and how you can translate each into action in your business (see Table 3.1 for a summary of the seven critical success drivers at the business level).[1]

1. Successful businesses focus: They do fewer development projects, better projects, and the right mix of projects. They achieve this by adopting a systematic portfolio management method and by

building tough Go/Kill decision points into their new-product idea-to-launch system.

Most companies suffer from too many projects and not enough resources to mount an effective or timely effort on each. And there are too few of the right kinds of projects—the bolder innovations. This stems from a lack of adequate project evaluation and prioritization—poor portfolio management—with negative results:

- First, scarce and valuable resources are wasted on mediocre or low-value projects.
- Second, the truly deserving projects don't receive the resources they should. The result is the good projects are starved for resources and move at a crawl, or simply aren't done.

The desire to weed out bad projects, coupled with the need to focus limited resources on the best projects, means that tough Go/Kill and prioritization decisions must be made. That is, *effective portfolio management—making the right development investment decisions*—must be an integral part of your idea-to-launch system. This results in sharper focus, higher success rates, and shorter times-to-market.

TABLE 3.1: WHY BUSINESSES EXCEL— SEVEN CRITICAL SUCCESS DRIVERS

1. Successful businesses focus: They do fewer development projects, better projects, and the right mix of projects. They achieve this by adopting a systematic portfolio management method and by building tough Go/Kill decision points into their new-product idea-to-launch system.
2. Leveraging core competencies is vital to success—"step-out" development projects tend to fail.
3. Target attractive markets. Projects aimed at attractive markets do better, and thus certain key elements of market attractiveness are important project-selection criteria.
4. The right organizational structure, design, and teams are major drivers of product innovation success.
5. Top management support doesn't guarantee success, but it sure helps. But many executives get it wrong. There are seven habits of successful executives in leading product innovation.
6. The resources must be in place—there is no free lunch in product innovation.
7. Companies that follow a multi-stage, disciplined new-product process—a *Stage-Gate*® system—fare much better.

Figure 3.1: To Achieve Optimum Portfolios—the Best Projects and the Right Mix—an Effective Portfolio Management System Is Essential

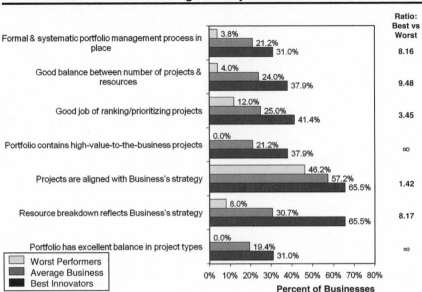

Source: endnote 1.

Project evaluations, however, are consistently cited as weakly handled or non-existent: Decisions involve the wrong people from the wrong functions (no functional alignment); no consistent criteria are used to screen or rank projects; or there is simply no will to kill projects at all—projects are allowed to get a life of their own. For example, only 31.1 percent of businesses were judged to properly screen new-product ideas, and only 26.3 percent of firms undertake a proficient business and financial analysis as part of the business case (Figure 2.5). Consider the benchmarking study results that zero in on portfolio management practices in Figure 3.1:[2]

- Only 21 percent of firms have *a formal and systematic portfolio management system* in place to help decide which product development investments to make.
- Only 24 percent have the right number of projects for the available resource—76 percent have *too many projects* for their limited resources.
- Only one-fourth of businesses do a *good job of prioritizing* and ranking projects.
- Only 21.2 percent of firms' portfolios contain *high-value projects* that benefit the corporation.
- And only 19 percent boast a *good balance* of projects—most firms have far too many small, insignificant developments.

By comparison, the Best Innovators do a much better job on project selection and portfolio management, but they, too, are far from perfect.

> Introduce tough gates with teeth and learn to "drown some puppies." The result is better focus—fewer but better development initiatives.

A critical problem is having too many projects for the limited resources available, as seen in Figure 3.1. This in turn stems from the reluctance to kill projects; there are no project priorities. As one frustrated executive put it, "We never kill projects, we just wound them." He was referring to the fact that resources are removed from projects a little at a time (rather than making a tough kill decision) and end up being spread so thinly that all projects are set up for failure. In many cases, managers confessed that projects simply aren't killed once they're into development: "Projects get a life of their own!"

What senior management must learn to do is to *drown some puppies*. No one likes to drown puppies—they're so cuddly and cute. But for the good of the litter—to control the population—the weak must be put down. And so it is with new-product projects in your portfolio. You aren't doing anyone any favors by saying "yes" to all the projects. For one thing, not all projects are equally "good"— there is a bell-shaped curve, and some projects are excellent, and some are mediocre in terms of value-to-the-business. Further, by saying "yes to all," resources get thinly spread; quality of execution suffers; cycle time and time-to-market increase; and there are too many ho-hum projects in the portfolio.

In Chapter 9, we'll see an example of a major company division that adopted a "decision-factory mentality" in product innovation.[3] The firm faced a major gridlock situation: No major projects were being launched! So it ruthlessly cut its major projects sixfold. By doing so, it reduced cycle time by almost the same ratio over a six-year period; and revenue from new products steadily increased—by more than ten times, and it continues to increase. The principle underpinning this firm's *decision factory* was: *fewer projects, better projects*. This translated into a tough prioritization exercise, real gates with teeth, and focusing resources on the very best developments. As the senior executive in charge admitted, this was not a pleasant exercise, but it was hugely successful.

Often the problem of poor project prioritization boils down to *the lack of a mechanism or system* for ranking, rating, prioritizing, or even killing projects. There are no specified decision points or gates; it's not clear who the right decision-makers are—the locus of decision-making is ill-defined; and finally, there are no formal or agreed criteria against which to judge or evaluate projects.

The many studies into success and failure provide valuable insights into what prioritization criteria to use. Indeed, new-product success is *fairly predictable*: Certain project characteristics consistently separate new-product winners from losers, and in a strong way. These characteristics can and should be used as criteria for project selection and prioritization.

Suggestion: What some companies have done is to redesign their new-product process: They have created a funneling process, which successively weeds out the poor projects; and they have built in decision points in the form of *tough gates*. At gate reviews, senior management rigorously scrutinizes projects, then makes Go or Kill and prioritization decisions. The use of visible Go/Kill criteria at gates improves decision effectiveness; fortunately, certain project characteristics have been identified that consistently separate winners from losers, which should be used as criteria in scorecard format for project selection and prioritization:

1. *Strategic:* how well the project aligns with the business's strategy, and how strategically important it is.
2. *Competitive and product advantage:* whether the product is differentiated, offers unique customer benefits, and represents a compelling value proposition to the user.
3. *Market attractiveness:* how large and growing the market is, and whether the competitive situation is positive (not intense, few and weak competitors).
4. *Leverage:* whether the project leverages the business's core competencies, such as marketing, technology, and manufacturing/operations.
5. *Technical feasibility:* the likelihood of being able to develop and manufacture the product—is this new science and a technically complex project? Or a technology re-package?
6. *Risk and return:* the financial prospects for the project (for example, NPV [net present value], IRR [internal rate of return], Payback Period) versus the risk.

These six factors, and the list of items that comprise them, should be an integral part of businesses' screening and project prioritization decision model. A scorecard composed of these questions that capture strategic alignment, product superiority, market attractiveness, leverage, technical feasibility, and profitability can be used as a tool to make more effective Go/Kill and prioritization decisions.

Project selection and picking winning new-product initiatives is only part of the task, however. Another goal is selecting the right *mix and balance* of projects in your development portfolio, seeking strategic alignment in the portfolio, and ensuring that the business's spending on development projects mirrors its strategic priorities. Figure 3.2 shows dramatically that portfolio management and project mix really do matter: The most successful innovating companies have a decidedly different development portfolio mix than the rest.[4] Note that in poor performers, 40 percent of the portfolio consists of "incremental product improvements and changes." But with Best Innovators, 65 percent of their portfolios are more innovative products—new-to-the-world products, products new to the company, and major product revisions. Many businesses have thus moved to more formal *portfolio management systems* to help effectively allocate resources and achieve the right mix and balance of development projects. We come back

Figure 3.2: Breakdown of Projects by Project Type Shows the Different Portfolios for Best Versus Worst Performers in Product Innovation

	Worst Performers	Average Business	Best Innovators
Promotional Developments & Package Changes	12%	10%	6%
Incremental Product Improvements & Changes	40%	33%	28%
Major Product Revisions	19%	22%	25%
New-to-the-Business Products	20%	24%	24%
New-to-the-World Products	7%	10%	16%

~45%	~55%	~65%

├────── 10 Point Steps ──────┤

> Best Innovators focus more on innovative and game-changing projects

Source: endnote 4.

to this vital but challenging topic of project selection and portfolio management in Chapters 8 and 9.

2. Leveraging core competencies is vital to success—"step-out" development projects tend to fail.

"Attack from a position of strength" may be an old adage, but it certainly applies to the launch of new products. Where new-product synergy with the base business is lacking, new products fare poorly.

Synergy, or *leverage,* is a familiar term, but exactly what does it translate into in the context of new products? Synergy (or leveraging core competencies) means having a strong fit between the needs of the new-product project and the resources, competencies, and experience of the firm in terms of:

✓ R&D resources (ideally the new product should leverage internal and existing technical competencies),
✓ marketing, selling (sales force), and distribution (channel) resources,
✓ manufacturing or operations capabilities and resources,
✓ technical support and customer service resources,
✓ market research and market intelligence resources, and
✓ management capabilities.

Leverage and synergy are the common thread binding the new business to the old. When translated into product innovation, the ability to leverage existing and

> The ability to leverage core competencies—both marketing and technical— are important project-screening criteria. Attack from a position of strength!

in-house strengths, competencies, resources, and capabilities increases the odds of success of the new-product project. By contrast, "step-out" projects take the firm into territory that lies beyond the experience, competencies, and resource base of the company and increase the odds of failure.

Familiarity is a parallel concept to synergy, and many companies use the "familiarity matrix" to categorize development projects: New markets and new technologies are the axes. Some new-product projects take the company into unfamiliar territory: a product category new to the firm; new customers and unfamiliar needs served; unfamiliar technology; new sales force, channels, and servicing requirements; or an unfamiliar manufacturing process. Sadly, the firm often pays the price: Step-out projects tend to have higher failure rates, so beware the unknown!

If at all possible, always "attack from a position of strength" when it comes to new products. That is, *select projects that leverage your in-house resources and skills*, seeking synergies in your product development projects. This has been the message from a number of studies into new product success and failure. The reasons for the impact of leverage are clear:

1. *Resources are available and at marginal cost*: If the new product can be developed using existing and in-house technical skills, this is often less expensive and less risky than seeking outside technology and skills. Similarly, if the product can sold to existing customers through an already established sales force or distribution channel system, then this, too, is less expensive, less risky, and less time-consuming than seeking new distribution channels, building a new sales force, or targeting unfamiliar customers.
2. *Knowledge*: Operating within one's field of expertise—either markets or technology—provides considerable "domain knowledge," which is available to the project team. By contrast, moving into new fields for the business often yields unpleasant surprises. When faced with a recent major product failure in which domain knowledge was lacking, one executive declared: "We didn't even know what questions to ask—we didn't know what we didn't know!"
3. *Experience*: The more often one does something, the better one becomes at doing it: One develops a track record, and moves "down the experience curve." If most new-product projects that the firm undertakes are closely related to (leveraged from) the current business, then one builds considerable experience with such projects—one after another after another. The result is that it costs less to do each successive project.

Two types of leverage are important to product innovation:

- *Technological leverage:* High technology-leverage or synergistic new products are those that build on the firm's existing or in-house development technology and skills, utilize inside engineering or design skills, and use existing manufacturing or operations resources and competencies.
- *Marketing leverage:* High marketing-leverage or synergistic new products are those that are sold through the existing sales force or distribution system; make use of existing customer relationships; and leverage a brand name or build off the firm's promotional and market communications skills and assets.

Look at the compelling results showing the impacts of both dimensions of leverage in Figures 3.3 and 3.4:

- New products with *high technology-leverage achieve almost three times the success rate* as those with low technology-leverage. Such "high leverage" new products also have more than double the market share and a much higher rated profitability than do new products in which there is little or no technological leverage or synergy (Figure 3.3).
- Similarly, new products that *leverage the firm's existing marketing resources* and skills have more than double the success rate. Such high market-leverage products also achieve 1.6 times the market share and have a much higher rated profitability on average than low leverage products (Figure 3.4).

Figure 3.3: Leveraging Technology Core Competencies Almost Triples the Success Rate, Doubles Market Share, and Impacts Strongly on Profitability

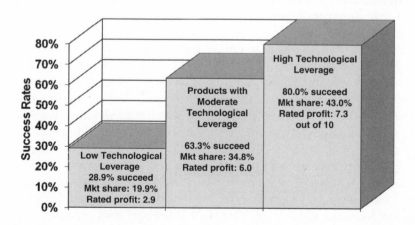

Rated profit: 10=far exceeded our expected profit; 0=fell far short; 5=just met expectations

Source: NewProd success/failure studies, endnote 1 in Chapter 2.

Figure 3.4: Leveraging Marketing Core Competencies Almost Doubles the Success Rate and Impacts Positively on Market Share and Profitability

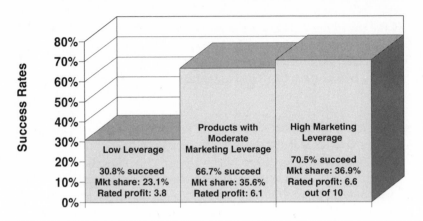

Rated profit: 10=far exceeded our expected profit; 0=fell far short; 5=just met expectations

Source: NewProd success/failure studies, endnote 1 in Chapter 2.

Suggestion: In designing new product strategies and selecting which new products to develop, never underestimate the role of leverage. Arenas and projects that lack any leverage from the base business invariably cost the firm more to exploit. Further, projects without leverage usually take the firm into new and uncharted markets and technologies, often with unexpected pitfalls and barriers. There are simply too many unpleasant surprises in arenas that are new to the firm.

These two dimensions of leverage—technological and marketing, and their ingredients—become obvious checklist items in a scoring or rating model to help prioritize new-product projects. And that's why they were included in the scorecard checklist above (success driver #1). If your *leverage score* is low, then there *must be other compelling reasons to proceed* with the development project. Leverage and synergy are not essential—there are other ways to fill the void—but they certainly improve the odds of winning.

Sometimes it is necessary to venture into new and unfamiliar markets, technologies, or manufacturing processes. Do so with caution—eyes wide open—and be aware that success rates will suffer; but note that the odds of disaster are not so high to deter making the move altogether. If leverage is low, yet the project is attractive for other reasons, then steps must be taken to bolster the internal resources and competencies. Low leverage scores signal the need for outside resources—partnering, outsourcing, or other "open innovation" approaches (more on "open innovation" in Chapters 5 and 6). But such solutions are not a panacea: There are risks and costs to both partnering and outsourcing as ways to secure the needed resources and competencies.[5]

3. Target attractive markets. Projects aimed at attractive markets do better, and thus certain key elements of market attractiveness are important project-selection criteria.

Market attractiveness is an important strategic variable. Michael Porter's "five forces" model considers various elements of market attractiveness as a determinant of industry profitability.[6] Similarly, various strategic planning models—for example, the two-dimensional GE-McKinsey map or business portfolio grid used to allocate resources among various existing business units (stars, cash cows, dogs, and wildcats)—employ market attractiveness as a key dimension of the grid.[7]

In the case of new products, market attractiveness is also important. Clearly, products targeted at more attractive markets are more successful. There are two dimensions of market attractiveness:

1. *Market potential:* positive market environments, namely, large and growing markets; and markets in which there is a strong customer need for such products, and in which the purchase is an important one for the customer. Products aimed at such markets are more successful.
2. *Competitive intensity:* negative markets characterized by intense and tough competition; competition on the basis of price; high-quality and strong competitive products; and competitors whose sales force, channel system, and support service are strongly rated. Poor competitor margins is also a negative. Products aimed at these competitive markets fare more poorly.

The significant impact of market attractiveness, measured by these two dimensions, is shown in Figure 3.5. New products aimed at attractive markets have almost double the success rate and achieve higher market shares and better profits. Consistently picking the right development projects to invest in is one way to win at innovation; and market attractiveness is an important criterion for making these correct investment decisions.

These dimensions of market potential and competitive intensity are obvious, of course, but are often overlooked or rationalized away when evaluating the odds of success for a new product, especially in the emotion of the moment:

An example: One of the speakers at a small-business conference was presenting a new product his business was launching. The product was very high-tech and used a complex mathematical algorithm on data from a digitized picture to move a robotic arm in a production setting.

The demo unit on stage had a fascinating application: packing sardines into a sardine can. We all watched the stage with anticipation as the first

Figure 3.5: Market Attractiveness Almost Doubles the Success Rate and Impacts Positively on Market Share and Profitability

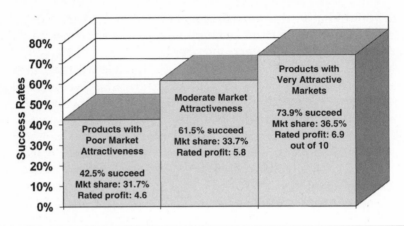

Rated profit: 10=far exceeded our expected profit; 0=fell far short; 5=just met expectations

Source: NewProd success/failure studies, endnote 1 in Chapter 2.

sardine moved up the conveyer belt; then we heard the picture being taken and watched with amazement as the small robotic arm seized the sardine and packed it just perfectly—head and tail in the right places—in the small sardine can. We all clapped.

The business owner (and his highly competent technical staff) were justifiably proud of their technical achievement and took a bow on stage. Then the tough questions started: What is the value of the product to the user? How many sardine packers on a production line will it replace? At what wage scale? How many sardine packing plants are there in high-wage countries? And so on.

It turns out that there were (at the time) three sardine plants in North America, paying decent wages to sardine packers. Most of the other plants were in low-wage countries, thus limiting the value of the automated packer. At last count, the business had sold but one machine. Lousy market, terrific technology!

The point of the story is to remind us to ask the tough questions—What is the market potential? What is the product's value to the customer? How tough is the competition? Are competitors making good margins?—*before going into Development* rather than days before launch. I see too many "clever new products" targeted at rather mediocre markets.

Suggestion: The message is this: Both elements of market attractiveness—market potential and competitive intensity—impact the new product's fortunes; and both must be criteria in your scoring or rating system for project selection and prioritization. That's why market attractiveness is part of the scorecard checklist illustrated in success driver #1 above.

> A cross-functional team, with clearly assigned and accountable team members, on the team from beginning to end, and led by a highly visible team leader, is a common denominator in Best Innovating businesses.

4. The right organizational structure, design, and teams are major drivers of product innovation success.

Product innovation is very much a team effort! Do a postmortem on any bungled new product project and invariably you'll find each functional area doing its own piece of the project, with very little communication between players and functions—a fiefdom mentality—and no real commitment of individual players to the project. Many studies concur that how the project team is organized and functions strongly influences project outcomes.[8]

Suggestion: Design your organization for product innovation. Product innovation is not a one-department show! It is very much a multidisciplinary, cross-functional effort. Organizational design—how you organize for new products—is critical. Except for the simplest of projects—simple line extensions and product updates—product innovation must cut across traditional functional boundaries and barriers. The ingredients of good organizational design should be familiar ones, but surprisingly many businesses have yet to get the message.

Our benchmarking studies find that Best Innovators organize their new-product project teams as shown in Figure 3.6. First, there is a *clearly assigned team* of players for each significant development project—people who are part of the project and *do work for it* (not just come to meetings). That is, coming out of every Go/Kill or gate decision meeting, it should be clear who is assigned to the project team (and their time commitments specified, too). What is surprising is that this practice is not evident in almost all businesses today. But it is not: Only 61.5 percent of businesses have clearly assigned project teams for innovation, with the Best Innovators outdoing the worst by a 2:1 ratio. Most important, this defined team is a *cross-functional project team*, with team members from Technical, Sales, Marketing, Operations, and so forth—a practice now embraced by the great majority of businesses. Cross-functional cooperation on the team is also critical—for example, not too much time and effort wasted on politics, conflicts, and interdepartmental prejudices. Ensuring harmony and cooperation among team members is normally the role of the project leader, but in some firms, team member training—how to be a good team player—is provided. Surprisingly, this is a moderately weak part

Figure 3.6: The Way Development Project Teams Are Organized Strongly Impacts on Innovation Performance

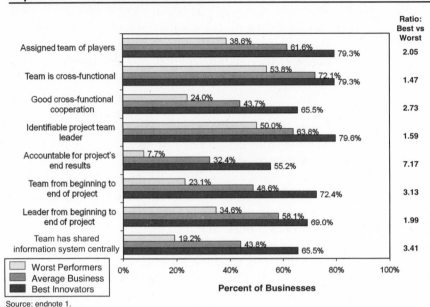

Source: endnote 1.

of most businesses' new-product efforts, with only 43.7 percent of businesses reporting good cross-functional cooperation within project teams.

There is also a clearly *identified team leader* in Best Innovators—a person who is in charge and responsible for driving the project. The team leader's role is similar to the leader of a business start-up: an entrepreneurial role, in which the leader not only leads the team—much like a team captain on a sports team—but also promotes the project, seeks resources, and handles the external interfaces of the project, especially with senior management. Some firms also appoint a *project manager*—quite a different role—especially in large projects. The project manager has an administrative and less entrepreneurial role; this person manages the day-to-day activities of the project, handles the nuts-and-bolts items, gets the team meetings organized, manages the time line and the budget—all the tasks associated with good project management.

Project team accountability is key to innovation success, as seen in Figure 3.6. That is, when a project leader and team present a business case to senior management—for example, projections of first-year sales, profit estimates, and expected launch date—and the project is approved, these projections now become commitments: They are the basis on which senior management approves the project and commits the needed resources to the project leader and team; and the quid pro quo is that the team and leader are now committed to deliver. These projections become the team's targets, and the project team is ultimately accountable for their achievement. Many firms now build in a "post-launch review" in which the team presents the *results of the project* some months or even a year or so after launch to the same group of senior executives that approved the project—a closed-loop feedback system.

Although the concept of accountability makes sense, note that only one-third of businesses actually apply the principle, but that the *Best Innovators embrace team accountability for results by a 7:1 ratio.* Team accountability is one of the greatest differences between Best Innovators and other firms.

In order to foster team accountability, it's essential that the project team remain "on the field for the entire game." In more than one firm we benchmarked, the prevailing philosophy was "launch and leave"—that is, launch the product and get onto some other assignment before the results are known. This lack of accountability and team continuity led to many negative results: wildly overestimated initial projections (in order to get the project approved), and a significant failure to follow through and work to achieve the promised results. Thus, a best practice is that *the project team remain on the project from beginning to end*—not just on the project for a short while or a single phase: Almost half of businesses practice this team approach, and it is particularly evident among Best Innovators. Similarly, although the entire team has an equal stake in and commitment to the project, one person usually stands a little higher, namely, the project leader. It's therefore essential that the *project leader remain responsible for the project from idea through to launch*—that is, the leader carries the project right through the process, and not just for one or a few stages; poor performers are weak here.

The one exception is for very long projects, such as in the pharmaceutical industry: Here the recommendation is that co-captains be appointed—a team leader and assistant captain—much like on a sports team or in the cockpit of an airplane. Either one can lead the project over a period; but both remain on the project until the end—no one gets off the plane halfway through the flight!

Another best practice is a *central shared-information system* for project team members. This usually means a centralized communications and IT system that permits sharing of project information and allows several team members to work concurrently on the same document, even across functions, locations, and countries. Using IT to support the innovation process is a particularly strong facet of Best Performers, with almost two-thirds having such an IT system. More and more, I see excellent software being employed to facilitate and even automate new-product development projects (more on this topic when we get into the topic of next-generation *Stage-Gate* in Chapter 5).

How does one design a *system that integrates* many activities and multifunctional inputs and fosters a cross-functional team approach? And how does one ensure quality of execution of these varied tasks, which are spread throughout the organization? One answer is to develop a systematic approach to product innovation—a blueprint or road map from idea to launch—that cuts across functional boundaries and forces the active participation of people from different functions. Make every stage in the process a cross-functional one. That is, the new product process builds in different tasks and provides checks and balances that require the input and involvement of these various functions:

> *An example:* At ITT Industries, a major project cannot proceed into a full-scale development effort until a detailed market assessment (including a VoC study) has been completed, and until a manufacturing or operations appraisal is complete. This requirement is an integral part of ITT's VBPD *Stage-Gate* system (VBPD is an acronym for "value-based product development"). Thus, without the active participation of both Operations and Marketing people, the project does not get released to Development—it goes nowhere! Such a requirement forces the project team leader to engage both departments, and in most cases, to put both Marketing and Operations people on the project team long before Development begins.

> *Another example:* A major Irish brewing company, with global markets, discovered that many projects were well into Development in Dublin before adequate international input had been received. Now, in their Navigate idea-to-launch system, the project leader must seek international input—interest, requirements, commitment—before the leader completes the Business Case to seek approval for Development. This simple requirement forces the inputs from global people into the project and is key to getting the product specs right and engaging international business units in the market rollout.

A second and equally important answer lies in *organizational design.* What type of organization structure will bring many players from different walks of life in the company together in an integrated effort? In short, how do you take a diverse group of players and turn them into a team?

It's clear that the traditional functional organizational structure—the way most firms are organized, into functional silos—does not suit many of the needs of product innovation. Indeed, functional and functional-matrix approaches lead to the poorest new-product performance. Companies must move to team approaches that cut across functional lines. The three approaches that appear to work best are:

- *Balanced matrix:* A project leader is assigned to oversee and lead the project; team members are assigned from functional areas. The team leader *shares the responsibility and authority* for completing the project with the functional managers: There is joint approval and direction.
- *Project matrix:* A project leader is assigned to oversee and lead the project, and again team members are assigned from the functional areas. In this model, however, the team leader has *primary responsibility and authority*

for the project. Functional managers assign personnel as needed and provide technical expertise and mentoring; the gate meetings are where resources are committed and personnel assignments are agreed on.

- *Project team:* A project leader is put in charge of a project team composed of a core group of personnel from several functional areas. Once the team members are assigned (likely at a gate meeting and by the senior functional bosses), the functional managers have *no more formal involvement or authority over their people.* The project leader is now "their boss."

Tom Peters argues strongly in favor of project teams: "the single most important reason for delays in development activities is the absence of multi-function (and outsider) representation on development projects from the start."[9] He continues: "The answer is to comingle members of all key functions, co-opt each function's traditional feudal authority, and use teams." Of the three designs above, project teams appear to be best suited for large, complex projects, whereas a project matrix approach works best for both complex and simpler projects.

Regardless of which of the three structures above you elect, strong project *leadership—a dedicated and empowered project leader*—appears essential for timely, successful projects. The leader must have formal authority (this means co-opting authority from functional heads); and the leader and team must be empowered to make project decisions and not be second-guessed, overruled, or "micromanaged" by the functional heads or senior management.*

To work well, team members should be located close to each other. "Physical proximity is one of the keys to good teamwork" is the conclusion of studies done in a number of firms. 3M reports that physical distances beyond 100 yards thwarts team interaction severely. Co-location is one solution—team members from different functions in the company are relocated in one area or department. A team office is another solution. Co-location is not possible in the case of global or outsourced projects; thus, excellent communications technology—electronic meeting rooms, with reliable and easy-to-use audio-visual links—combined with timely and periodic face-to-face meetings, are vital to success.

The final organizational ingredients essential to making this multifunctional team work are *climate and culture,* in a combination that fosters creativity, innovation, and a team approach. Climate and culture make up a huge and pervasive topic—far beyond this discussion of how to organize a project team—yet they are so critical to innovation success; the topic was highlighted in Chapter 1 and is one of the important components of the Innovation Diamond in Figure 1.2.

---

* "Micromanage" is a term used to describe the behavior of senior management, meaning day-to-day meddling in the affairs of the project team.

Figure 3.7: Executive Practices and Commitment Are Key to Driving Innovation

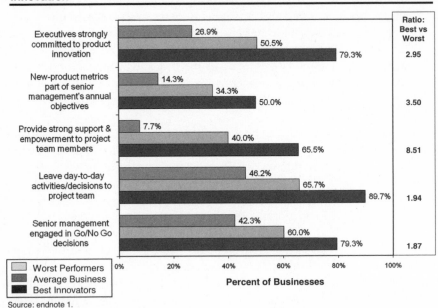

Worst Performers
Average Business
Best Innovators

Percent of Businesses

Source: endnote 1.

5. Top management support doesn't guarantee success, but it sure helps. But many executives get it wrong. There are seven habits of successful executives in leading product innovation.

Top management support is a necessary ingredient for product innovation. Look at the strengths of the impacts of senior management's role in Figure 3.7:

- In 80 percent of Best Innovating businesses, the executives are *strongly committed to product innovation*. Compare this to the 27-percent commitment in poor-performing businesses!
- New product *metrics* are part of senior management's annual objectives in half of the best firms but are noticeably absent in poor performers.
- Executives provide *strong support and empowerment* to teams and team members in two-thirds of the Best Innovators but do so in only 8 percent of poor performers.
- Across the board, executives leave the day-to-day activities and decisions to the project team—they *do not micromanage*—but this is especially true in Best Innovators.
- But senior management is very much engaged in the key Go/Kill decisions in 80 percent of the Best Innovators (versus in only 42 percent of poor performers).

Senior management support, however, must be the right kind of support. Many senior people get it wrong! Our benchmarking investigations find that top man-

SEVEN HABITS OF SUCCESSFUL LEADERS OF INNOVATION

1. They embrace and support product innovation at every opportunity—both in words and in actions:
   - They are passionate about innovation.
   - They put the resources in place.
2. They lead the creation of an Innovation Strategy for their business.
3. They are actively involved in making Go/Kill decisions at gates:
   - They practice effective gatekeeping.
   - They develop "rules of engagement" and commit to these rules.
4. They are the innovation portfolio managers:
   - They understand the business's development portfolio.
   - They play an active role at portfolio reviews.
5. They understand and embrace their business's idea-to-launch stage-and-gate system.
6. They foster the right climate and culture for innovation.
7. They keep score:
   - They hold themselves, other executives and project teams accountable for results.
   - When targets are missed, they find out why—they promote continuous improvement.

agement support is directly linked to innovation success, as shown in Figure 3.7. But one of our earlier studies of individual new-product projects found a different twist. Top managers supported failure-projects almost as frequently as successes: Those projects in which top management is committed, is involved directly in the management of the project—executive "pet projects"—and provides considerable guidance and direction for the project are only marginally more successful.

Where top management support is critical, however, is in getting the product to market. When one considers killed projects versus launched products, here top management support is important. Top management can muster the resources, cut through the red tape, and push the right buttons to get the project done.

Suggestion: The message is that top management's main role in product innovation is to *set the stage* for product innovation to occur, to be a "behind-the-scenes" facilitator, and not so much to be an actor, front-and-center. This stage-setting role is vital: Management must make the long-term commitment to internal product development as a source of growth. It must develop a vision, objectives, and strategy for product innovation that is driven by corporate objectives and strategies. It must make available the necessary resources and ensure that these resources aren't

> Innovation is a prerequisite for sustained growth. No other path to profitable growth can be sustained over time.[10]
>
> —A. G. Lafley, former CEO, Procter & Gamble

diverted to more immediate needs in times of shortage. It must commit to a disciplined process to drive products to market. And most important, senior management must empower project teams and support committed champions by acting as mentors, facilitators, "godfathers," or executive sponsors to project leaders and teams—acting as "executive champions."[11]

Senior management's role is *not to get involved* in development projects on a day-to-day basis, nor to be constantly meddling and interfering in the project, nor to "micromanage" projects. This meddling behavior is wrong for two reasons: It usurps the authority of the team (and hence defeats the "empowered team" concept); and frankly, the research evidence is that senior management doesn't do so well with "executive pet projects" or at managing such projects! The seven behaviors of effective senior management are outlined in the box.

6. The resources must be in place—there is no free lunch in product innovation.

Having a sound game plan does not guarantee success. There must be players on the field as well—not just part-time or Saturday afternoon players—but full-time dedicated resources. But too many projects and businesses simply suffer from a lack of time and money commitment to product innovation. The results are predictable: much higher failure rates, longer times-to-market, and underperforming development projects. Let's look at the hard facts.

The high failure rates and poor performance data in product innovation were highlighted in Chapter 1. Many reasons for new-product failures have been uncovered over the years, including well-known and recurring themes such as a lack of market information, a failure to listen to the voice of the customer, poor front-end or pre-development homework, unstable product definition, poor quality of execution of key tasks, and even poorly structured, ineffectual project teams.[12] We saw some of these direct causes in Chapter 2. And numerous remedies have been proposed to deal with these deficiencies.[13] In spite of the remedies, however, new products continue to underperform.[14]

A closer examination of the many reasons for failure, coupled with results from major benchmarking studies, shows that many of these problems and failure modes are themselves interlinked and are traceable to a much more fundamental or root cause, namely, *major resource deficiencies* in key areas.[15]

For example, poor quality of execution and leaving out important tasks, such as VoC work or front-end due diligence, are often not so much due to ignorance or a lack of willingness: It's more often because of a lack of time and people. As one senior project leader declared: "We don't deliberately set out to do a bad job on projects. But with seven major projects under way, on top of an already busy 'day job,' I'm being *set up for failure*—there just isn't enough time to do what needs

Figure 3.8: A Resource Crunch Exists in Product Innovation Regardless of the Functional Area—Best Innovators Are Better Resourced

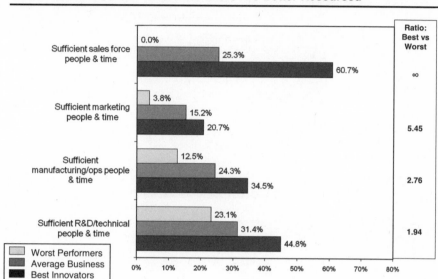

Source: endnote 1.

to be done to ensure that these projects are executed the way they should be—and so I cut corners."

This project leader is not alone in her concern. Surveys and benchmarking studies reveal that the new-product development resource deficiency is perverse and widespread. Consider the evidence:

- A lack of focus and inadequate resources are *the number one weakness* in businesses' new-product development efforts in major benchmarking studies: Project teams are working on too many projects or are not sufficiently focused on new-product development work.[16] And a lack of resources devoted to new-product development across all functions is *the number three most serious deficiency*: Only a minority of businesses indicates that sufficient resources are available to project teams to do a quality job in new-product development—see Figures 3.8 and 3.9.[17] The weakest areas are Marketing resources (85 percent of businesses judged to have inadequate resources) followed by Manufacturing/Operations resources for product development (76 percent of businesses with inadequate resources).
- Even worse, what limited resources are available to product innovation are thinly spread. Figure 3.9 reveals this lack of focus. For example, note that 91 percent of businesses are judged to suffer from people being *spread over too many development projects*; and 79 percent of businesses have their

Figure 3.9: Project Team Focus and Dedicated Resources Have a Strong Impact on Performance

		Ratio: Best vs Worst
Resources allocated based on project merit	16.0% / 38.2% / 58.6%	3.66
Adequate resources assigned to new-product projects	0.0% / 10.7% / 20.7%	∞
Team focused - not spread over too many projects	0.0% / 11.4% / 24.1%	∞
Team focused - not doing too much other work	7.7% / 21.9% / 48.3%	6.27
An innovation or NPD group exists - dedicated to new products	28.0% / 37.9% / 51.7%	1.85

Percent of Businesses

people *doing too many other tasks*—their "day jobs"—and thus are not sufficiently focused on product innovation work.

A lack of resources has many negative consequences.[18] First, *quality of execution suffers:* Corners are cut, as project teams try to meet time lines but lack the needed resources. Thus, essential market studies are truncated, front-end homework is short-circuited, the field trials are overly accelerated, and launch plans are thrown together and underresourced. And some vital activities simply don't get done at all: Lacking the time or people, key activities are simply left out as project teams scramble to meet launch dates. A second result is that cycle time or *time-to-market lengthens:* With not enough resources to handle the many projects in the pipeline, queues begin to build. The "time to get things done" is not so much execution time, it's waiting or queuing time—waiting for people to get around to doing the work (or WIP [work in process] as the process engineer would label it). And thus time-to-market suffers.

A third result is the *lack of game-changers and bold innovations:* New-product failures and being late or slow to market are the *measurable costs* of poor or untimely execution, often brought on by insufficient resources. A far greater cost is immeasurable, because it's an *opportunity cost.* How many big projects are simply not done due to a lack of resources? Given a limited resource base, human nature dictates that it be spent on lower-risk initiatives that don't cost very much—in other words, hedging one's bets. Even worse, the *active projects are dumbed down:*

That is, desirous of meeting time deadlines but lacking the people resources to get all the work done, savvy project leaders de-scope and de-feature new products, and in so doing, reduce the impact of potentially great new products.

Finally, *morale suffers*: Lacking the necessary personnel and their time commitments from functional bosses, the project team is stretched; deadlines are missed and pressure mounts; people are blamed; and team morale starts to deteriorate.

The reasons for this resource crunch? As the *competitive situation has toughened*, companies have responded by doing more with less. And so resources are limited or cut back. A related cause is a preoccupation with *short-term profitability*, driven largely by the financial community. To meet short-term financial goals, those in business unit management are caught in a dilemma: They can do what is good for the business for the longer term, or resort to short-term maneuvers— cut costs and freeze resources—in order to achieve the immediate goals set by corporate headquarters. Yet another cause is trying to do too many projects for the limited resources available, which means *a lack of focus*. Finally, many senior managements have become *speed demons*—faster, better, cheaper—thus placing far too much emphasis on cycle-time reduction and acceleration to market.

Adequate resources for projects—focused and dedicated people—are vital to innovation performance. Properly executed initiatives take time and money: "Faster, better, cheaper" is a myth! Look at the facts:

- Devoting sufficient resources to new-product development is strongly linked to new-product performance and to many of the drivers of performance.[19] Indeed, the strongest single driver of the most commonly used performance metric, namely, percentage of sales from new products, is how much the business spends on R&D (as a percentage of sales).[20] Further, note from Figure 3.8 that even though the Best Innovators are resource deficient, they suffer much less from resource gaps than do the poorer performers.
- Best Innovators are considerably more focused and boast dedicated resources for product innovation, as seen in Figure 3.9: Half of these better performers have dedicated resources to product development (project team members are not working on a lot of "other tasks"); and more than half of the Best Innovators have a ring-fenced product innovation group that does nothing but work on new products. That is, they have a focused and dedicated group—often cross-functional (R&D, Marketing, Operations, and so on)—working 100 percent on product innovation: Product innovation is their "day job"!

Suggestion: Are you suffering from a resource crunch in your new-product pipeline? The problem of too many projects and too few resources can be attacked by undertaking a current state assessment that includes a resource capacity analysis.[21] This analysis quantifies your projects' demand for resources (usually people, expressed as person-days of work) versus the availability of these people resources. You can do this analysis in one of two ways:[22]

1. *Determine if you have enough of the right resources to handle the active projects currently in your development pipeline.* Begin with your current list of active projects. Determine the resources required to complete them according to their time lines (get that data from project leaders—resources approved and realistic requirements, expressed as person-days by functional department). Then look at the availability of resources—who's available for new-product work, what percentage of their time, from what department? Develop one spreadsheet per month—projects listed and people (or departments) and person-days—and do the math! You'll usually find major gaps, especially in some departments, and hence potential bottlenecks. Finally, identify the key resource constraints—the departments, people, or capabilities that you run out of first.

2. *Determine if you have enough resources to achieve your business's new product goals and objectives.* Begin with your new-product objectives: What percent of your business's sales will come from new products? Or what dollar sales from new products? Now, determine the resources required to achieve this goal: This means figuring out the number of major, medium, and minor development projects you'll need to launch each year to achieve this goal; how many active projects you need to realize these launches (numbers of projects at each stage of the development process, idea through to launch); and therefore how many resources per year it will take to do this set of projects. Again you'll likely find a major gap between demand based on your goals, and your capacity available. It's time to make some tough choices about the realism of your goals or whether more resources are required.

Resource-capacity analysis is a start but not a solution. But it does provide information necessary to begin work on a solution. The experience in companies is that this resource-capacity analysis often:

✓ detects far too many projects in the pipeline, resulting in an immediate prioritization and pruning effort; the result is often that many lower-value projects are killed or put on hold!
✓ causes senior management to rethink its goals (often new-product goals, such as percentage of sales by new products, are based on wishful thinking or on an unrealistic corporate dictum);
✓ identifies departments or groups that are major bottlenecks in the innovation process, leading to decisions to increase or shift personnel.

Resource-capacity analysis is a fairly tactical move, but it is relatively straightforward to undertake and provides real insights into the nature and magnitude of the resource-constraint problem. So when looking at resources and resource allocation, this is a good place to begin.

Other solutions include:

- Develop a product innovation and technology strategy for your business: Such a strategy includes setting goals and quantifiable product innovation objectives for your business, as well as deciding how you intend to achieve these goals. The issue of resources invariably surfaces, and this is the time to debate whether you have sufficient resources in place to achieve your objectives; whether resources should be increased for strategic reasons; or whether your innovation objectives for the business are simply too ambitious and unrealistic.
- Ring-fence the resources: That is, make product-innovation people dedicated resources—dedicated full-time to product development—rather than dividing them among many duties (see success drivers #4 and #6 above). These ring-fenced resources, or "innovation group," includes technical people, but also Marketing and Operations people, and their full-time job is product development!
- Portfolio solutions: Consider the strategic buckets method to set aside resources for different types of projects. More on this topic in Chapter 8 on portfolio management.
- Focus: Do fewer but better projects, learn to drown some puppies. This is the theme of success driver #1 earlier in this chapter. A solid one-time pruning exercise to kick-start the process culls out the weak projects and re-focuses the resources on the excellent projects.

7. Companies that follow a multi-stage, disciplined new-product process—a Stage-Gate® system—fare much better.

The product innovation or idea-to-launch process in many companies is broken. It is a process plagued by errors of omission and commission: Things don't happen when they should, or how they should, or as well as they should! The process lacks consistency and quality of execution, and it is very much in need of repair. These are the findings of study after study. They reveal that many businesses' idea-to-launch systems are deficient or nonexistent and point to the need for a complete and a quality process.

> Leading companies have adopted a Stage-Gate® system, a method developed by the author, to accelerate new-product projects from idea to launch.

A systematic new-product process—such as a *Stage-Gate®* system*—is the solution that many companies have turned to in order to overcome the deficiencies that plague their new-product efforts. *Stage-Gate* systems are simply road maps, "cookbooks" or "playbooks" for driving new products from idea to launch, successfully and efficiently. About 68 percent of U.S. product developers had adopted early

---

* *Stage-Gate®* is a registered trademark of Product Development Institute Inc. in the United States; see www.prod-dev.com.

versions of *Stage-Gate* processes by the year 2000, according to a best-practices study done then. More recent benchmarking studies reveal that 73 percent of businesses employ such a process, and one APQC study identified a stage-and-gate process as the strongest best practice, employed by almost every best-performing business.[23] And many companies have moved to next-generation versions of *Stage-Gate*.

Managing new products without a system in place is like putting a dozen players on a football field, with no huddles and no preplanned plays, and expecting them to score. It works once in a while, but over the long run, the better-disciplined competitor will win.

The term "new-product process" or system means a conceptual and operational model for moving new-product projects from idea through to launch and beyond. It is a blueprint or road map for managing the new-product process to improve efficiency and effectiveness. The model outlines the key plays and huddles necessary to score a goal, hence the analogy to North American football.

The goal of a robust idea-to-launch system is to build the best practices outlined in this and the previous chapter into a single process or model, so that these success drivers or practices happen by design, not by accident. Operationally, an idea-to-launch system breaks the product innovation process into a series of cross-functional stages—think of these as "plays" in a North American football game. Each stage is composed of a number of prescribed "best practice" activities or tasks, undertaken by a cross-functional team, with many tasks executed in parallel. Best practices, such as front-end homework, spirals with users, planning the launch, and VoC are built into the various stages. A set of visible and prescribed deliverables is the result of each stage.

Each stage is preceded by a gate or Go/Kill decision point—think of these as the huddles in a football game. Here the team meets with management to decide whether to move to the next play, and if so what the play (actions) will be; or to stop the game and walk away from a bad situation. This stage-and-gate format leads to terms such as "gating," "gateways," "stage-gate," "phase-gate," or "tollgate" systems. The term *Stage-Gate*, now widely in use, was originally coined by me in early articles on the topic.[24] A typical *Stage-Gate* system is shown in Figure 4.10 in the next chapter for major new-product projects (note that there are abbreviated versions for smaller, lower-risk developments).[25]

The evidence in support of a systematic idea-to-launch or stage-and-gate system is strong. Booz Allen Hamilton found that companies that had implemented new-product processes are more successful; and that those firms with the longest experience here were even more successful.[26] As one vice president put it, "The multi-step new product process is an essential ingredient in successful new product development."

P&G's idea-to-launch its SIMPL stage-and-gate system is considered vital to the company's product innovation performance: "*Stage-Gate*® is not optional . . .

[it is] essential to succeed in today's environment."[27] And the payoffs of such processes have been frequently reported: improved teamwork, less recycling and re-work, improved success rates, earlier detection of failures, a better launch, and even shorter cycle times (by about 30%).[28] P&G notes that its SIMPL *Stage-Gate* system "improves functional interfaces (when and how to work together; defines responsibilities)" and "delivers individual initiatives [new products] to market effectively and efficiently. *Stage-Gate* works!"[29]

Note the measured impacts of a formal stage-and-gate process in Figure 3.10: much higher success rates and about double the proportion of projects hitting sales and profit targets.[30] A recent study by A.C. Nielsen in the consumer pack-aged goods industry reveals that best results come from an idea-to-launch system that features rigorous stages, with gates, scorecards used at gates, and an engaged governing body (often called gatekeepers)—see Figure 3.11.[31]

Suggestion: If your firm does not have an effective new-product process in place—or if it is more than three years old, or it seems a little cumbersome and creaky—the design and implementation of an up-to-date, rapid, and professional idea-to-launch system should become a top-priority task. The next chapter outlines a typical or generic process—a step-by-step procedure for turning a new-product idea into a winning new product in the marketplace.

TOWARD A *STAGE-GATE* NEW-PRODUCT SYSTEM

This chapter has highlighted seven critical success drivers of innovation that pertain to the business: better focus (doing fewer and better projects); leveraging the

Figure 3.10: A High-Quality *Stage-Gate*® New-Product System Yields Positive Results – Higher Success Rates, More Projects Hitting Sales, Profit Targets

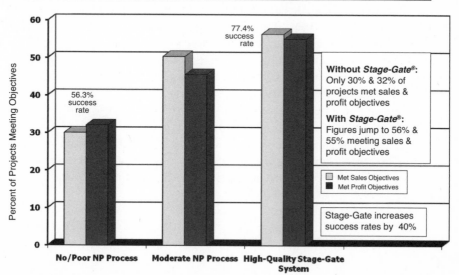

Figure 3.11: The Use of a Disciplined Idea-to-Launch Process with Gates, Scorecards, and a Governance Body Works Best for Innovation

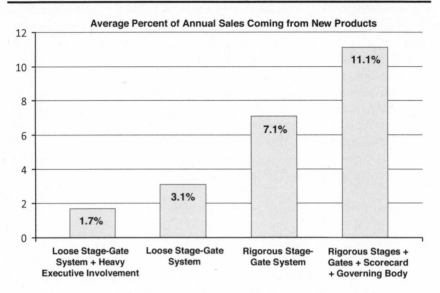

Source: adapted from: A.C. Nielsen Study (Agan, 2010); endnote 31.

business's core competencies and targeting attractive markets; fostering effective cross-functional teams and the right role for senior management; dealing with the resource crunch; and finally emphasizing the need for a well-crafted idea-to-launch system. The previous chapter delivered seven other critical success drivers, much more tactical and project-specific in nature. These success drivers from the two chapters are based not on hearsay and wishful thinking, but on facts—on the many published research studies* that have probed new-product performance, both successes and failures, at the project level as well as at the business level.

Now the challenge begins: to translate these success drivers into operational reality. That's the role of a new-product stage-and-gate system. In the next chapter, we'll fashion these success drivers into a road map, a blueprint, or a playbook that is designed to drive new-product projects from idea through to launch—successfully and in a time-efficient manner: *Stage-Gate*.

---

* By published, I mean "published in a legitimate refereed journal," not just self-published, as so many research or consulting firms do. Thus, the research and results presented here have stood the test of a rigorous and independent peer review by experts in the field. The results are therefore credible.

4

THE *STAGE-GATE*®
IDEA-TO-LAUNCH
SYSTEM*

A process is a methodology that is developed to replace the old ways and to guide corporate activity year after year. It is not a special guest. It is not temporary. It is not to be tolerated for a while and then abandoned.
—Thomas H. Berry, *Managing the Total Quality Transformation*[1]

WHAT IS *STAGE-GATE?*

Stage-Gate® is a *conceptual and operational map* for moving new-product projects from idea to launch and beyond—a blueprint for managing the new-product development process to improve effectiveness and efficiency. *Stage-Gate* is a system or process not unlike a playbook for a North American football team: It maps out what needs to be done, play by play, huddle by huddle—as well as how to do it—in order to win the game.

Stage-Gate is based on the premise that some projects and project teams really understand how to win—they get it![2] Indeed, *Stage-Gate* was originally developed *from research that modeled what the winning teams that undertake bold innovation projects do.*[3] But too many projects and teams miss the mark—they simply fail to perform. A closer inspection often reveals that these failed projects are plagued by missing steps and activities, poor organizational design and leadership, inadequate quality of execution, unreliable data, and missed time lines. So these teams and projects need help—help in the form of a *playbook* based on what winning teams do. *Stage-Gate* is simply that playbook.

---

* *Stage-Gate*® is a legally registered trademark of the Product Development Institute Inc. in the United States and Australia; of R.G. Cooper in Canada; and of J. Arleth and R. Cooper in the European Union.

Stage-Gate *Now Used in Most Leading Firms*

A world-class process for product innovation, such as *Stage-Gate*, is one solution to what ails so many firms' new-product efforts.[4] Facing increased pressure to reduce the cycle time yet improve their new-product success rates, companies look to new-product processes, or *Stage-Gate* systems, to manage, direct, and accelerate their product innovation efforts. That is, they have developed a systematic process—a blueprint or playbook—for moving a new-product project through the various stages and steps from idea to launch. But most important, they have built into their playbook the many *critical success drivers* and *best practices* in order to heighten the effectiveness of their programs. Consider these examples:

P&G's SIMPL new-product process is a *Stage-Gate* system implemented in the early 1990s—see Figure 4.1. Now in its third generation, SIMPL and related methods have been key to P&G's enormous successes in innovation in the last decade. The four-stage model was designed initially to handle internally-derived projects but has been extended to include "open innovation" projects as well.[5]

3M has traditionally had an enviable new-product track record. An innovative corporate culture and climate are often cited as 3M's secret to success. But for years 3M has also had in place various stage-and-gate systems in its businesses for managing the innovation process. Thus, creativity and discipline are blended to yield a successful new-product effort.

Corning Glass has always been a world-leading innovator, beginning generations ago with Pyrex glass and Corningware, and in more recent years, with fiber optics and glass for flat-panel displays. Corning's successes continue. What drives new products to market at Corning is the company's version of a *Stage-Gate* process, designed and installed in the early 1990s. The process has been refined and streamlined over the years, and also broadened in scope, so that today, virtually every resource-intensive project—from new or improved products through new manufacturing processes—is stage-gated.

Emerson Electric's NPD 2.0 is that firm's latest version of its stage-and-gate system, originally developed in the 1990s. "Since its introduction, Emerson New Product Development (NPD) teams have learned—quickly—that the Phase Gate process works.[6] The Phase Gate process is adapted from R.G. Cooper's *Stage-Gate*® approach which is based on large scale studies of product development practices of hundreds of international companies. The process provides a structured pathway of 'gates' to creation and product launch and beyond. 'The Phase Gate process plays to Emerson's traditional strengths of excellent execution and process,' says Randall Ledford, senior

Figure 4.1: P&G's SIMPL *Stage-Gate* Process Features Five Stages and Four Gates and Is Key to Driving the Firm's New Products to Market

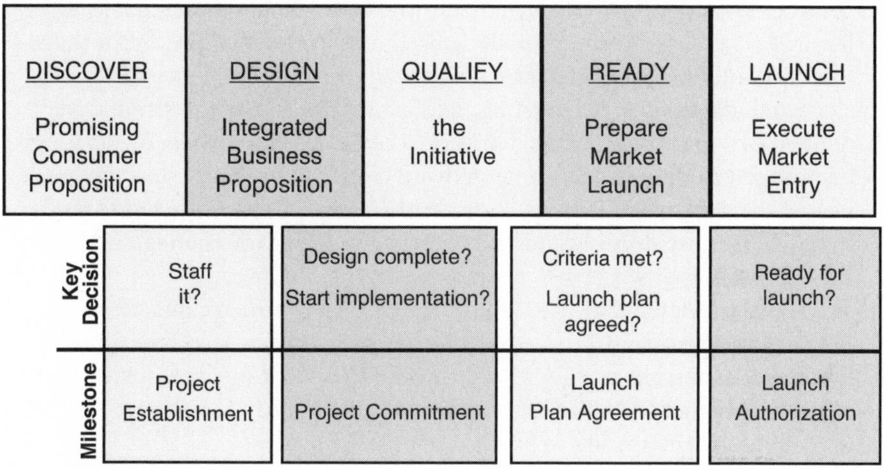

DISCOVER	DESIGN	QUALIFY	READY	LAUNCH
Promising Consumer Proposition	Integrated Business Proposition	the Initiative	Prepare Market Launch	Execute Market Entry

Key Decision	Staff it?	Design complete? Start implementation?	Criteria met? Launch plan agreed?	Ready for launch?
Milestone	Project Establishment	Project Commitment	Launch Plan Agreement	Launch Authorization

Source: endnote 5.

vice president and chief technology officer. 'So it's no surprise that we have learned so much from it so quickly.'"

Exxon Chemical began piloting a *Stage-Gate* process in its Polymers business unit in the late 1980s. So successful was the process that Exxon Chemical has rolled the method out throughout its entire chemical business, and around the world. According to the father of Exxon's Product Innovation Process, "The implementation of the PIP has probably had more impact on the way we do business than any other initiative at Exxon Chemical undertaken in the last decade." In recent years, the system has been modified and adapted to yield the company's new-generation *Stage-Gate* system.

Lego, the successful Danish toy manufacturer, replaces about one-third of its product line every year with new items—new castles, new towns, and so on. In order to accomplish this rapid introduction of new products consistently, successfully, and year after year, a process was needed. Today, Lego relies on a *Stage-Gate* new-product process to ensure that everything comes together for these many and rapid launches each year.

Stage-Gate methods work! We saw in the previous chapter the many testimonials in favor of adopting stage-and-gate idea-to-launch systems, as well as the quantitative results achieved. And the APQC best-practices study of product innovation found that having such a process was just a given. Here is an excerpt from that study:[7]

> A new-product process—a "game plan" or playbook to guide NPD [new-product development] projects from idea to launch—is another much-heralded key to NPD success. By "new-product process," we mean more than just a flow-chart; the term includes all process elements—the stages, stage activities, gates, deliverables, and gate criteria that constitute a well-defined new-product process. For more than a decade, managements have been urged to design and implement such an NPD process, and they appeared to have heeded the experts. Indeed, having a well-defined new-product process is the *strongest practice* observed in the sample of businesses [in the APQC study]:
>
> 1. A clearly defined idea-to-launch new-product process: Businesses rate very high here, with 73.7 percent of businesses having such an NPD process, and only 7.6 percent lacking a process. This result is consistent with, albeit somewhat higher than, the PDMA's best-practice study, which reported 68 percent of firms claiming to have such an NPD process.

The report goes on: "Merely having a NPD process in place, however, does not separate the Best from the Worst Performers. Nonetheless, Best Performers *overwhelmingly do have a systematic new-product process*: Having such a process seems to be just a 'given' and thus a NPD process must be considered a best practice."

SEVEN GOALS OF A NEW-PRODUCT IDEA-TO-LAUNCH SYSTEM

The challenge in this chapter is this: Given the seven critical success drivers from Chapter 2 specific to how to manage new-product projects; and given the next seven drivers from Chapter 3, pertaining to practices at the business level—drivers all gleaned from new-product success-and-failure experiences and the various benchmarking studies—how can we translate these into an operational and effective new-product playbook? For example, how does one build in quality of execution, or a strong market focus, or better pre-development homework? Let's begin with a quick look at what this new-product system must achieve.

Goal #1: Quality of Execution

The argument that the proponents of total quality management make goes something like this: "The definition of quality is precise: It means meeting all the requirements all the time. It is based on the principle that all work is a process. It focuses on improving business processes to eliminate errors." The concept is perfectly logical and essentially simple. Most smart things are. And the same logic can be applied to new-product development.

Product innovation is a process: It begins with an idea—in a best-practice system, even earlier—and culminates in a successful product launch. But processes aren't new to the business environment. There are many examples of well-run processes in business: for example, manufacturing processes, information processes, and so on.

A quality-of-execution crisis exists in the product innovation process, however. Simply stated, things don't happen as they should, when they should, and as well as they should. We saw in the last two chapters clear evidence that many key actions, from VoC work and front-end homework through to planning and executing the launch, were deficient in too many firms and projects. Serious gaps, such as omissions of steps and poor quality of execution, are the rule rather than the exception. And they are strongly tied to product failures. We also saw that these activities—their quality of execution and whether these activities are carried out at all—have a dramatic impact on success or failure, with Best Innovators typically executing these tasks far more proficiently than the rest.

This quality-of-execution crisis in product innovation provides strong evidence in support of the need for a more *systematic and quality approach* to the way firms conceive, develop, and launch new products. The way to deal with the quality problem is to visualize product innovation as a process, and to apply *process management* and *quality management techniques* to this process. Note that any process in business can be managed with a view to quality. Get the details of your process right, and the result will be a high-quality output.

Quality of execution is the goal of the new-product process. More specifically, the ideal playbook should:

1. *Focus on completeness:* ensure that key activities that are central to the success of a new-product project are indeed carried out—no gaps, no omissions, a complete process.
2. *Focus on quality:* ensure that the execution of these activities is first class; that is, treat innovation as a process, emphasize DIRTFT (Do it right the first time), and build in quality controls and checks.
3. *Focus on the important:* devote attention and resources to the pivotal and to particularly weak steps in the new-product process, notably the front-end and market-related activities.

The new-product system is simply a *process management tool.* We build into this process quality of execution, in much the same way that quality programs have been successfully implemented on the factory floor.

Goal #2: Sharper Focus, Better Prioritization

Most companies' new-product efforts suffer from a lack of focus: too many projects, and not enough resources. Earlier, adequate resources were identified as a principal driver of companies' new-product performance; but a lack of resources plagues too many firms' development efforts. And quality of execution (Goal #1 above) certainly won't be achieved until the resource problem is solved.

Sometimes this lack of resources is simply that: Management hasn't devoted the needed people and money to the business's new-product effort. But often, this resource problem stems from a lack of focus, the result of inadequate project evaluations: the failure to set priorities and make tough Go/Kill decisions. In short, the gates are weak—they lack teeth! Indeed, most of the critical evaluation points—from initial screening through to pre-launch business analysis—are characterized by serious weaknesses: decisions not made, little or no real prioritization, poor information inputs, no criteria for decisions, and inconsistent or haphazard decision-making.

The need is for a *new-product funnel*, rather than a *tunnel*. A "new-product funnel" builds in tough Go/Kill decision points throughout the process; poor projects are weeded out; scarce resources are redirected toward the truly deserving projects (the high-value ones); and more focus is the result. One funneling method is to build the new-product process around a set of gates or Go/Kill decision points. These gates are the "get-out" points where we ask, "Are we still in the game?"

Gates are analogous to the *quality-control checkpoints* on a manufacturing assembly line. They pose two fundamental questions:

- Are you doing the project right?
- Are you doing the right project?

Gates are preset at different points throughout the new-product system. Each gate has its own set of *metrics and criteria* for passing, much like a quality-control check in production. These criteria and questions deal with various facets of the project, including:

- Readiness check criteria: Is the project ready for the gate meeting? Are the deliverables in place?
- Criteria that gauge the business rationale for investing in the project— Go/Kill and prioritization criteria.
- Criteria that focus on the forward plan, resource availability, and the decision to commit resources to the project.

These gates serve to map and guide the new-product system. They signal a "Kill" decision in the event of a project whose economics and business rationale become negative, when barriers to completion become insurmountable, or when the project is far over budget or behind schedule. Gates prevent projects from moving too far ahead into the next stage until the critical activities have been completed, and in a quality fashion. And gates chart the path forward: They determine what tasks and milestones lie ahead, and the resources, budgets, and time frames for these tasks.

Goal #3: Fast-Paced Parallel Processing with Spirals

New-product project leaders face a dilemma. On the one hand, they are urged by senior management to compress the cycle time—to shorten the elapsed time from idea to launch. On the other hand, they are to improve the effectiveness of product development: cut down the failure rate—do it right! This desire to "do it right" suggests a more thorough, longer process.

Parallel processing is one solution to the need for a complete and quality process, yet one that meets the time pressures of today's fast-paced business world. Traditionally, new-product projects have been managed via a *series approach*— one task strung out after another, in series. The analogy is that of a relay race, with each department running with the project for its 100 yards. Phrases such as "hand off," "passing the project on," "dropping the ball," and "throwing it over the wall" are common in this relay-race approach to new products.

In marked contrast to the relay-race or sequential approach, with parallel processing many activities are undertaken *concurrently* rather than in series. The appropriate analogy is that of a rugby football match rather than a relay race. In rugby, the entire team runs down the field in parallel, vigorously interacting with each other all the way; and a lot happens fast!

With parallel processing, the effort is far more intense than a relay race and more work gets done in an elapsed time period: Three or four activities are done simultaneously and by different members on the project team. Second, there is less chance of an activity or task being dropped because of lack of time: The activity is done in parallel and hence does not extend the total elapsed project time. And finally, the entire new-product process becomes cross-functional and multidisciplinary: The whole team—Marketing, R&D, Engineering, Operations—is on the field together, participates actively in each play, and takes part in each gate review or scrum.

A second key is building spirals into this rugby approach—a series of "build-test-feedback-and-revise" loops, introduced in Chapter 2. Spirals confirm product design early and minimize wasted time; they prevent moving too far down the field with incorrect requirements assumptions. Spiral development is based on the premise that customers don't know what they want until they see it, so get something in front of them fast. It's the approach that some people call "fail early, fail often," except here I'm not advocating deliberate failures but rather a series of quick-and-easy tests—relying on cheap and early versions of the product (a model, virtual prototype, or protocept) to seek fast feedback and confirm the design before sinking more money into the project. Spiral development fits well into parallel processing, and both approaches lead to accelerated development, but not at the expense of quality of execution.

Goal #4: A True Cross-Functional Team Approach

The new-product process is multifunctional: It requires the inputs and active participation of players from many different functions in the organization. The multifunctional nature of innovation coupled with the desire for parallel processing means that a *true cross-functional team approach is* mandatory in order to win at new products.

I emphasize the word "true" in describing a cross-functional team, as opposed to the many "fake" or "pretend" teams one sees in business. You can tell a *fake team* when:

- So-called team members show up at meetings, but they aren't really committed to the team—they're there as *functional representatives* at a meeting.
- They aren't given release time from their "day job"—this team activity is just piled on top of an already hectic schedule.
- They promise to get things done by the next team meeting, but invariably their "real job" gets in the way and their functional boss gives them some other assignment.
- They are given lots of responsibility for the project and very little authority—the functional bosses still make the decisions about the project, often micromanaging from on high.
- Team members receive no merit points or variable pay based on the results achieved by the team.

Sound familiar? Time to have a hard look at the way you're organized for new products.

The ideal new-product system demands that every significant new-product project have a true cross-functional project team. Essential characteristics of this team are (from Chapter 3 and Figure 3.6):

- The project team is cross-functional, with committed team players from the various functions and departments—Marketing, Engineering, R&D, and Operations. Release time from their normal jobs to spend on the project is provided to team members (typically people and time commitments are decided at gate meetings).
- The project team has a clearly defined team captain or leader. This leader is dedicated to the project (not spread across numerous other duties or projects) and is accountable from beginning to end of the project—not just for one stage.
- The leader has formal authority: This means co-opting authority from the functional heads. When those in senior management approve the team's action plan at gate meetings, they also commit the resources—money, people, and release time—to the project leader and team. At the same time, senior management *transfers decision-making power* to the team. Expecta-

tions and the scope of this authority are made very clear to the team at each gate.

- Some of these resources are "ring fenced": That is, people working on the project are 100 percent dedicated to new-product efforts—to this one project and perhaps one other. New-product development *is* their full-time job!
- The team structure is fluid, with new members joining the team (or old ones leaving it) as work requirements demand. But *a small core group of responsible, committed, and accountable team players should be present from beginning to end of project.*
- Senior management holds the entire team accountable for results—all team members, not just the team leader. And rewards—such as merit increases, bonuses, or variable salary—are tied to the team's performance and results.

Goal #5: A Strong Market Focus with Voice-of-the-Customer (VoC) Built In

A market focus is the missing ingredient in too many new-product projects. A lack of market inputs and inadequate market assessment are consistently cited as reasons for new-product failure. Moreover, the market-related activities tend to be the weakest in the new-product process, yet are strongly linked to success. Although many managers profess a market focus, the evidence—where the time and money are spent—proves otherwise.

If higher new-product success rates are the goal, then a market focus—executing the key marketing activities in a quality fashion—must be built into the new-product system as a matter of routine rather than by exception. Market inputs must play a decisive role from beginning to end of the project. The following nine marketing actions are *integral and mandatory actions* in the new-product playbook (but they rarely are):

1. *Customer-based idea generation:* working with lead users and key customers to identify problems, gaps, and emerging opportunities for new solutions.
2. *Preliminary market assessment:* an early, relatively inexpensive step designed to assess market attractiveness and to test market acceptance for the proposed new product.
3. *Market research and VoC work to determine user needs and wants:* in-depth, face-to-face and on-site interviews with customers or camping out with customers (ethnography) to determine customer needs, wants, preferences, likes, dislikes, buying criteria, and so forth, as an input to the design of the new product.
4. *Competitive analysis:* an assessment of competitors—their products and product deficiencies, prices, costs, technologies, production capacities, and marketing strategies.
5. *Concept testing:* a test of the proposed product—perhaps as a virtual product or protocept—to determine likely market acceptance. Note that the product

is not yet developed, but a model or representation of the product is displayed to prospective users to gauge reaction and purchase intent.

6. *Customer reaction during Development:* continuing concept and product testing throughout the Development stage—spirals—using rapid prototypes, models, and partially completed products to gauge customer reaction and seek feedback.

7. *User tests:* field trials, preference tests, or beta tests using the finished product (or commercial prototype) with users to verify the performance of the product under customer conditions, and to confirm intent to purchase and market acceptance.

8. *Test market or trial sell:* a mini-launch of the product in a limited geographic area or single sales territory (or a simulated test market). This is a test of all elements of the marketing mix, including the product itself.

9. *Market launch:* a proficient launch, based on a solid market launch plan, and backed by sufficient resources.

Goal #6: Better Front-End Homework

New-product success or failure is largely decided in the first few plays of the game—in those crucial steps and tasks that precede the actual development of the product. Solid front-end homework and sharp early product definition are key ingredients in a successful new-product process, according to our benchmarking studies, and result in higher success rates and profitability in studies of project performance. The front-end homework helps to define the product and to build the Business Case for development. Ironically, most of the money and time spent on projects is devoted to the middle and back-end stages of the process, while the front-end actions suffer from errors of omission, poor quality of execution, and underresourcing.

The ideal new-product system ensures that these early stages are carried out before the project is allowed to proceed—before the project is allowed to become a full-fledged development. Activities essential to building the Business Case become mandatory plays before the project is given formal approval for Development.

What are these essential front-end activities in a well-designed system? They include:

- *Initial screening:* the initial decision to spend time and money on the project.
- *Preliminary technical assessment:* an initial attempt to assess technical feasibility, outline manufacturing/operations implications, and identify technical risks and issues.
- *Preliminary marketing assessment:* highlighted above, this is the first-pass market study.
- *Detailed technical assessment:* detailed technical work (not development) to prove technical feasibility and address technical risks.

- *Operations (source-of-supply) assessment:* technical work to determine manufacturing, operations or source-of-supply implications and options, capital expenditures, and probable manufacturing or delivered costs.
- *Detailed market studies:* includes the VoC user needs-and-wants study, competitive analysis, and concept tests outlined above.
- *Financial and business analysis:* probes the expected financial consequences and risks of the project.
- *Integrate product definition and business case:* integrates the results of the technical, operations, marketing, and financial analyses into a product definition, project justification, and project plan.
- *Decision on the Business Case:* a thorough project evaluation and decision to go to full Development.

Goal #7: Products with Competitive Advantage—Bold Innovations

Don't forget to build in product superiority at every opportunity—differentiated products, unique benefits, and a compelling value proposition for the customer. This is perhaps the most important driver of new-product profitability, yet all too often, when redesigning their new-product processes, firms fall into the trap of repeating current, often faulty, practices: There's no attempt to seek truly superior products. And so the results are predictable—more ho-hum, tired products. Here's how to drive the quest for product advantage and bolder innovations:

- Ensure that at least some of the criteria at every gate focus on product superiority. Questions such as "Is there a 'wow' factor in the product—will it excite the customer or user?" "Does it solve a major customer problem?" "Does the product have at least one element of competitive advantage?" and "Does it offer the user new or different benefits?" become vital to rate and rank would-be projects.
- Require that certain key actions designed to deliver product superiority be included in each stage of the process. Some of these have been highlighted above (Goals #5 and #6) and include: customer-focused ideation; VoC studies; competitive product analysis; concept and protocept tests, preference tests, and trial sells; and spirals and constant iterations with customers during the Development stage via rapid-prototype-and-tests.
- Demand that project teams deliver evidence of product superiority to project Go/Kill reviews: Make product superiority an important deliverable and discussion issue at such meetings (rather than just dwelling on the financial projections).
- Ensure that the integrated product definition, so critical to new-product success, not only includes performance requirements and specs but is also very clear about the *compelling value proposition* for the customer.

Suggestion: Take a close look at the idea-to-launch process within your firm. Does it ensure quality of execution? Is it built around a set of gates or decision points to dump bad projects and focus resources on the truly deserving ones? Does it emphasize parallel processing—a rugby match—or does it resemble a relay race; and does it incorporate spirals to confirm the design early? Does it build in an empowered, cross-functional team headed by a leader with authority? Or are you still largely functionally based? Does it promote a market focus, and what proportion of project expenditures goes to market-related actions? Do you devote enough resources to the front-end or homework stages? And do you build in activities and criteria designed to yield unique, bold, superior products with real competitive advantage (or does your system favor small, simple, me-too efforts)?

If some of the answers are no, then the time is ripe to rethink your new-product playbook. Maybe it's time to overhaul your idea-to-launch system—it's a bit dated, or too cumbersome, or misses many of the vital success drivers and goals outlined above. Perhaps the time is now to reinvent your innovation system with the objective of building in the best practices from Chapters 2 and 3, and the seven goals outlined above, to create your *Stage-Gate* system for the next decade.

HOW TO MANAGE RISK

The management of new products is the management of risk, so your playbook must also be designed to manage risk. Indeed, if you look closely, you'll see that most of the critical success drivers outlined in the previous two chapters investigate ways of dealing with risk. Total risk avoidance in new-product development is impossible, unless a company decides to avoid all innovation—and face a slow death.

Most of us know what is meant by the phrase "a risky situation." In product innovation, a high-risk situation is one in which much is at stake (for example, the project involves a lot of money or is strategically critical to the business) and the outcome is uncertain (for example, it is not certain that the product will be technically feasible or will do well in the marketplace). The components of risk are: amounts at stake and uncertainties (see Figure 4.2).

Russian Roulette: A Life-or-Death Gamble

Imagine for a moment that you are facing the gamble of your life. You've been invited to a millionaire's ranch for a weekend. Last night, you played poker and lost more money than you can afford—around $100,000. All of the other players are enormously wealthy cattle and oil barons. Tonight, they've given you the opportunity to get even. Each of the other ten players antes into the pot $1 million. That's $10 million—more money than you are ever likely to see again.

Here is the gamble. One of the players takes out a six-shooter pistol, removes all the bullets, and in full view of everyone, places one live bullet in the gun. He then spins the chamber. For $10 million, you are asked to point the gun at your head and pull the trigger. Will you take the gamble?

Figure 4.2: Development Project Risk Has Two Components—Amounts at Stake and Level of Uncertainty—and *Stage-Gate* **Manages Both**

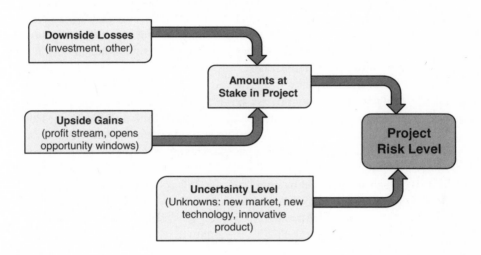

Most people would say no! But the situation exhibits the key elements of risk: a great deal at stake (the $10 million or your life) and a high degree of uncertainty—the bullet could be in any location.

Reducing the Stakes

This hypothetical gamble represents an unacceptable risk level. Yet this is precisely the way some managers play at new products: huge amounts at stake, coupled with high levels of uncertainty. Others are simply fearful of any risk, and walk away, which may also be the wrong decision. How can the risk be reduced to an acceptable level? One route is to *lessen the amounts at stake.* For example, use blank bullets along with ear protectors to deaden the noise, and point the gun, not at your head, but at your foot. The potential downside loss, if the gun were to fire, is that now you would merely be laughed at by a group of poker players.

But upside gains are inevitably tied to downside losses. So, instead of anteing up $1 million, every player now puts in $1. Will you still take the gamble? Most would reply, "Who cares?" There is no longer enough at stake to make the gamble worthwhile or even interesting. The risk is now so low that the decision becomes trivial. Lots of so-called new products are almost as trivial.

Some Gambling Rules

Rule number one in risk management is: If the uncertainties are high, keep the amounts at stake low. Rule number two is: as the uncertainties decrease, the amounts at stake can be increased. These two rules keep risk under control.

There is another way in which risk can be managed in our hypothetical example. The pot remains at $10 million, a live bullet is used, and the gun must be aimed at your head. But this time, your opponent, in plain view, marks the exact location of the bullet on the chamber. He spins the chamber and asks you to reach into your pocket and give him $20,000 in return for a look at the gun to see where the live bullet has ended up. Then you decide whether or not you still wish to proceed with the gamble. In short, he offers you the opportunity to buy an option— to "have a look"—for a much lower cost.

Most of us would consider this a "good gamble" (assuming we had the $20,000)—one with an acceptable risk level. A relatively small amount of cash buys an option or a look at the gun and the location of the bullet. Having paid for the look and determined the bullet's location, you then make your second decision: are you still in the game? It's much like buying options on a property you might wish to purchase.

The risk has been reduced by converting an "all-or-nothing" decision into a two-stage decision: two steps and two decision points. Your ability to purchase information was also instrumental in minimizing risk: Information has reduced the uncertainty of the situation. Finally, the ability to withdraw from the game— to get out—also reduced risk.

Three more gambling rules designed to manage risk evolve from this second gambling situation. Rule number three is: Incrementalize the decision process— break the all-or-nothing decision into a series of stages and decisions—in effect, buying options and doing due diligence. Rule number four is: Be prepared to pay for relevant information to reduce risk. And rule number five: Provide for getout points—decision points that provide the opportunity to fold your hand, walk away, or get out of the game.

Risks in New-Product Management

These five rules of risk management apply directly to new products. Near the beginning of a project, the amounts at stake are usually low, and the uncertainty of the outcome is very high. As the project progresses, the amounts at stake begin to increase (see Figure 4.3). If risk is to be managed successfully, the uncertainties of outcomes must be deliberately driven down as the stakes increase. Further, the stakes must not be allowed to increase unless the uncertainties do come down. Uncertainties and amounts at stake must be kept in balance.

Unfortunately, in many new-product projects, the amounts at stake increase as the project progresses while the uncertainties remain fairly high (see Figure 4.4). Additional spending fails to reduce the uncertainties! The project moves ahead with decisions based on assumptions and hearsay—a lack of facts. By the end of the project, as launch nears, management is no more sure about the commercial outcome of the venture than at day one of the project. The amounts at stake have increased, uncertainty remains high, and the risk level is unacceptably high.

For every thousand-dollar increase in the amounts at stake, the uncertainty curve in Figure 4.3 must be reduced by an equivalent amount. To do otherwise

97

Figure 4.3: As Amounts at Stake (Investment) Increase Over the Life of
the Project, Uncertainties Are Driven Down and Risk Is Managed

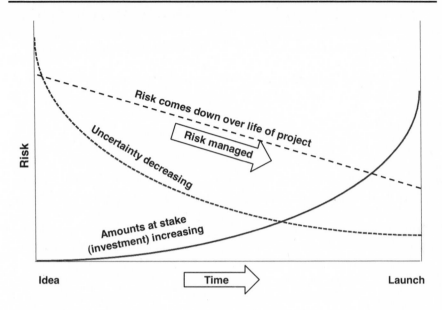

Figure 4.4: Amounts at Stake (Investment) Increase But Uncertainties
Don't Come Down Much and Risk Is Out of Control

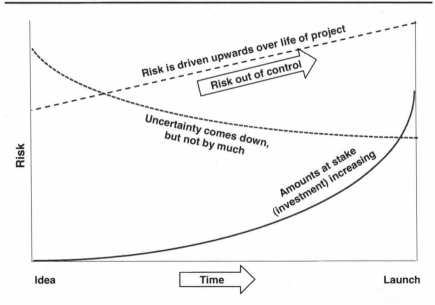

is to let risk get out of hand. In short, every expenditure in the new-product process—every notch up on the amounts-at-stake curve in Figure 4.3—must bring a corresponding reduction in the uncertainty curve. The entire new-product process, from idea to launch, can be viewed as an uncertainty reduction process involving the purchase of options. Remember the five gambling rules:

1. When the uncertainties of the new-product project are high (that is, when the prospects of success are uncertain), keep the amounts at stake low. When you don't know where you're going, take small steps—buy a series of options rather than investing the entire amount.
2. As the uncertainties decrease, let the amounts at stake increase. As you learn more about where you're going, take bigger and bigger steps.
3. Incrementalize the new-product process into a series of steps or stages. Treat it as a series of *options purchases*. Each step should be more costly than the one before.
4. View each stage as a means of reducing uncertainty. Remember that information is the key to uncertainty reduction. Each step in the process that involves an expenditure must reduce uncertainty by an equivalent amount.
5. Provide for timely evaluation, decision, and get-out points. These decision points pull together all the new information from the previous stage and pose the questions, "Are you still in the game? Should you proceed to the next stage, or kill the project now?"

Suggestion: The five decision rules outlined above apply to almost any high-risk situation. Does your company follow them in its day-to-day management practices? Review your firm's new-product practices, perhaps using an actual case, and assess whether your management group is handling risk appropriately.

A BEST-PRACTICE NEW-PRODUCT SYSTEM
The Structure of the Stage-Gate System

The seven key goals and the five gambling rules, together with the success drivers from the last two chapters, have been fashioned into a best-practice *Stage-Gate* system—a *conceptual and operational model* for moving a new-product project from idea to launch.[8] This *Stage-Gate* system is a playbook or blueprint for managing product innovation to improve effectiveness and efficiency.

Stage-Gate is elegantly simple, and makes a lot of sense: a series of information-gathering stages followed by decision-making gates. *Stage-Gate* treats product innovation as a process, and any process can be modeled and made better and more efficient. Instead of viewing product development as a black box—ideas go in and commercial-ready products come out (or a black hole—ideas go in and nothing comes out)—*Stage-Gate* breaks the innovation process into a predetermined set

Figure 4.5: The *Stage-Gate* System Breaks the Product Development Into a Series of Manageable Stages with Increasing Resource Commitments

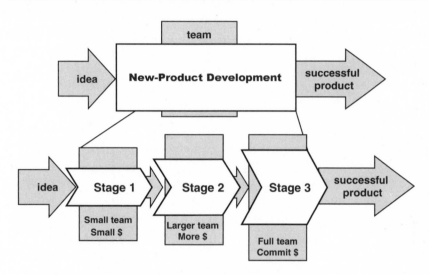

of manageable, discrete stages (see Figure 4.5). Each stage consists of a set of pre-scribed, cross-functional, and parallel activities:

- Teams of people undertaking some vital activities to gather some data
- Followed by data analysis and interpretation
- To create the key deliverables (information)
- On the basis of which senior management—the resource owners—make the Go or Kill decision

And the process repeats (see Figure 4.6). The entrance to (or exit from) each stage is a gate: The gates control the process and serve as the quality control and Go/Kill checkpoints. This stage-and-gate format leads to the name "*Stage-Gate* system."

The Stages

Each stage is designed to gather information needed to move the project to the next gate or decision point. Different types of information—market, technical, operations—is important, and so the work within each stage is cross-functional: There is no "R&D stage" or "Marketing stage." And each stage is defined by the activities within it—a set of parallel and cross-functional tasks that incorporate

- ✓ best practices, for example, the nine vital market-related actions listed above (see p. 91),

Figure 4.6: *Stage-Gate* Consists of a Set of Information-Gathering Stages Followed by Go/Kill Decision Gates

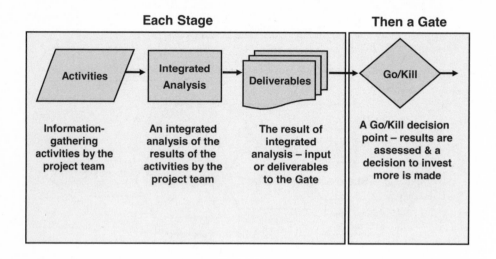

Source: Stage-Gate International Inc.

✓ some of the success drivers, for example, quality of execution and sharp, early product definition,

✓ and the seven goals, for example, the quest for a superior, differentiated product, that we saw earlier in this and the last two chapters.

Some of these activities are mandatory; others are merely prescribed and highly recommended—*Stage-Gate* is a guide, not a rule book. These stage-activities are designed to gather information and drive uncertainties down. And each stage typically costs more than the preceding one: The process is an incremental commitment one.

The general flow of the typical *Stage-Gate* system is shown pictorially in Figure 4.7. The stages are:

Discovery: pre-work designed to discover and uncover opportunities and generate ideas

Scoping: a quick, preliminary investigation and scoping of the project—largely desk research

Build the Business Case: a much more detailed investigation involving primary research—both market and technical—leading to a Business Case, including product and project definition, project justification, and a project plan

Figure 4.7: The Five Stages in the Typical Idea-to-Launch *Stage-Gate* System—from Discovery (Ideation) Through to Launch

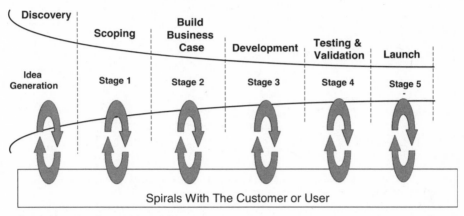

Source: Adapted from Cooper, endnotes 2 & 4.

Development: the actual detailed design and development of the new product, and the design of the operations or production process

Testing and Validation: tests or trials in the marketplace, lab, and plant to verify and validate the proposed new product, and its marketing and production/operations

Launch: commercialization—beginning of full operations or production, marketing, and selling

The Gates

Preceding each stage is a gate or a Go/Kill decision point—see Figure 4.8.* The gates are the scrums or huddles on the rugby or football field. They are the points where the team converges and where all new information is reviewed. Gates serve as quality-control checkpoints, as Go/Kill and prioritization decision points, and as points where the path forward for the next play or stage of the process is agreed to.

The structure of each gate is similar (Figure 4.9). Gates consist of:

1. A set of required *deliverables*: what the project leader and team bring to the decision point (for example, the results of a set of completed activities).

---

* Strictly speaking, the gates follow the stages—gather information, then make a Go/Kill decision. But it's more practical to treat them as entrance gates—opening the door to the next stage.

Figure 4.8: Each Stage Is Preceded by a Gate—the Decision Points or Go / Kill Points in the System

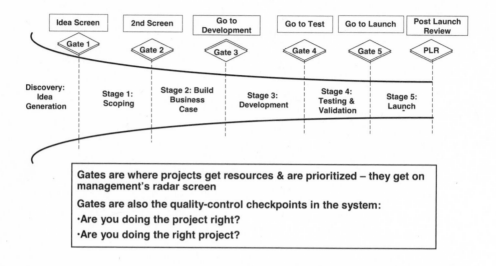

These deliverables are visible, are based on a standard menu for each gate, and are decided at the output of the previous gate. Management's expectations for project teams are thus made very clear.

2. *Criteria* against which the project is judged: These include readiness-check questions, must-meet or knock-out questions (a checklist designed to weed out misfit projects quickly), as well as should-meet criteria or desirable factors, which are scored and added (a point count) and used to prioritize projects.

3. Defined *outputs*: for example, a decision *(Go/Kill/Hold/Recycle),* an approved action plan for the next stage (complete with people required, money and person-days committed, and an agreed time line), and a list of deliverables and a date for the next gate.

Gates are usually staffed by senior managers from different functions, who own the resources required by the project leader and team for the next stage: They are the gatekeepers.

AN OVERVIEW OF THE *STAGE-GATE* SYSTEM

Now for a bird's-eye look at the *Stage-Gate* system—an overview of what's involved at each stage and gate. In later chapters, we'll lower the microscope on the Discovery stage, or how to generate breakthrough ideas (Chapter 6). We then

Figure 4.9: Gates Have a Common Format—Inputs, Criteria, and Outputs

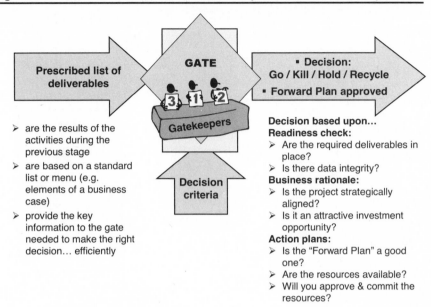

> are the results of the activities during the previous stage
> are based on a standard list or menu (e.g. elements of a business case)
> provide the key information to the gate needed to make the right decision... efficiently

focus on the front-end or pre-development stages in Chapter 7. Chapters 8 and 9 take a close look at how to design and operate gates or decision points. And Chapter 10 focuses on the middle and back-end stages of the process. But for now, let's just have a quick walk-through of the model designed for larger new-product projects, which you can follow stage by stage in Figure 4.10.

Discovery or Ideation

Ideas are the feedstock or trigger to the process, and they make or break the system. Don't expect a superb new-product process to overcome a deficiency in good new-product ideas. The need for great ideas coupled with the high attrition rate of ideas means that the idea-generation stage is pivotal: You need great ideas and lots of them.

Many companies consider ideation so important that they handle this as a formal stage in the process, the one we call Discovery—that is, they build in a *defined, proactive idea-generation and capture system*. Many activities can be part of the Discovery stage in order to stimulate the creation of great new-product ideas. Such activities include: undertaking fundamental but directed technical research, seeking new technological possibilities; working with lead or innovative users; utilizing VoC research to capture unarticulated needs and customer problems; competitive analysis and inverse brainstorming of competitive products; installing an idea-suggestion scheme to stimulate ideas from your own employees;

Figure 4.10: This Five-Stage Idea-to-Launch *Stage-Gate®* System Is for Major and More Complex Product-Development Projects

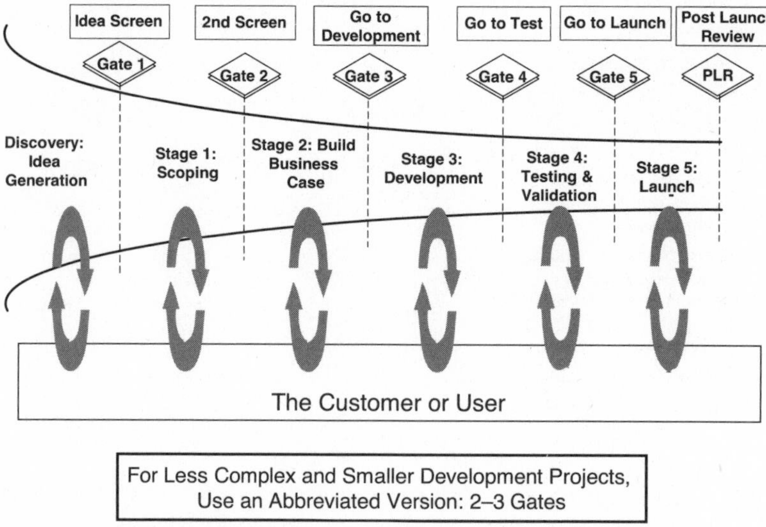

Source: Adapted from Cooper, endnotes 2 & 4.

scanning the outside world and employing "open innovation" to seek external ideas; and using your strategic planning exercise to uncover disruptions, gaps, and opportunities in the marketplace.

Gate 1: Idea Screen

The Idea Screen is the first decision to commit resources to the project: The project is born at this point. If the decision is Go, the project moves into the Scoping or preliminary investigation stage. Thus, Gate 1 signals a preliminary but tentative commitment to the project: a flickering green light.

Gate 1 is a "gentle screen" and amounts to subjecting the project to a handful of key must-meet and should-meet criteria. These criteria deal with strategic alignment, project feasibility, magnitude of opportunity and market attractiveness, product advantage, ability to leverage the firm's resources, and fit with company policies. Financial criteria are typically not part of this first screen, because so little is known, and besides, the resources to be committed are quite small at this phase. A checklist for the must-meet criteria and a scorecard (point-count rating scales) for the should-meet criteria can be used to help focus the discussion and rank projects in this early screen.

An example: Exxon Chemical has implemented its PIP (Product Innovation Process), whose initial gate has a handful of key Yes/No criteria:

Strategic fit:	Does the proposal fit within a market or technology area defined by the business as an area of strategic focus?
Market attractiveness:	Are the market size, growth, and opportunity attractive?
Technical feasibility:	Is there a reasonable likelihood that the product can be developed and produced?
Killer variables:	Do any known killer variables exist (e.g., obsolescence, environmental issues, legislative actions)?

At this "Start Gate" meeting, project ideas are reviewed against these four criteria, using a paper-and-pencil approach: This list of must-meet criteria is scored (Yes/No), and the answers to all questions must be Yes; a single No kills the project. The gatekeepers include both technical and business (marketing) people.

Stage 1: Scoping

This first and inexpensive homework stage has the objective of determining the project's technical and marketplace merits. Stage 1 is a quick scoping of the project, involving desk research or detective work—little or no primary research is done here. This stage is usually done in less than one calendar month's elapsed time, and ten to twenty person-days' work effort.

A *preliminary market assessment is* one facet of Stage 1 and involves a variety of relatively inexpensive activities: an Internet search, a library search, contacts with key users, focus groups, and even a quick concept test with a handful of potential users. The purpose is to determine market size, market potential, and likely market acceptance, and also to begin to shape the product concept.

Concurrently, a *preliminary technical assessment is* carried out, involving a quick and preliminary in-house appraisal of the proposed product. The purpose is to assess development and operations (or source-of-supply) routes, technical and operations feasibility, possible times and costs to execute, and technical, legal, and regulatory risks and roadblocks.

Stage 1 thus provides for the gathering of both market and technical information—at low cost and in a short time—to enable a cursory and first-pass financial and business analysis as input to Gate 2. A preliminary Business Case is constructed here, but based on fairly uncertain or "guesstimates" data. Because of the limited effort, and depending on the size of the project, very often Stage 1 can be handled by a team of just several people—from Marketing and Technical. Consider this example of a preliminary technical and market assessment:

An example: OMNOVA Solutions of Akron, Ohio, had the good fortune to uncover a new technology via fundamental research that has become the platform for a number of new-product projects. The new technology enables traditional polymers to have an extremely slippery surface, yet unlike other slippery materials, the resulting polymer retains its usual positive physical properties (e.g., abrasion resistance and toughness).

The first product to be launched was vinyl wall-covering with a difference—it's a relatively low-cost, dry-erase whiteboard. Before embarking on extensive development work for this project, a preliminary assessment or scoping was undertaken. The company was already in the industrial wall-covering business, so ample in-house data on markets, sizes, and trends were available. Additionally, the project leader sought and found published data—trade publications, reports, and so on—on the existing whiteboard market. Informal chats with some distributors revealed the pricing structure. Technical work was relatively limited at Stage 1, as fundamental research had already uncovered the technical possibility. Nonetheless a core group of scientists got together with Manufacturing people to discuss technical and manufacturing feasibility—note how early Manufacturing was involved in the project. Finally, a first-cut financial analysis was developed—based largely on guesstimates—but this sanity check revealed a huge opportunity.

Gate 2: Second Screen

The new-product project is now subjected to a second and somewhat more rigorous screen at Gate 2. This gate is similar to Gate 1, but here the project is reevaluated in the light of the new information obtained in Stage 1. If the decision is Go at this point, the project moves into a heavier spending stage.

At Gate 2, the project is subjected to a list of readiness-check questions, and also a set of must-meet and should-meet criteria similar to those used at Gate 1. Here, additional should-meet criteria may be considered, dealing with sales force and customer reaction to the proposed product, and potential legal, technical, and regulatory "killer variables," the result of new data gathered during Stage 1. Again, a checklist and scorecard facilitate this gate decision. The financial return is assessed at Gate 2, but only by a quick and simple financial calculation (for example, the Payback Period).

An example: ITT Industries uses a well-crafted five-stage, five-gate product *Stage-Gate* system called VBPD.[9] The second gate, called the "Value Screen" follows the preliminary investigation, namely, the "Scoping Stage," and opens the door to a more detailed investigation, "Build the Business Case." The essence of this "Value Screen" gate is a reevaluation of the proposed project in light of the additional information gained from the Scoping Stage. The gate features a combination of must-meet and should-meet criteria. The must-meet items must yield Yes answers; the should-meet items are rated on scales—a point-count system on six questions:

1. Strategic (importance and fit)
2. Product and competitive advantage
3. Market attractiveness
4. Synergies (leverages our core competencies)
5. Technical feasibility
6. Financial reward

Stage 2: Build the Business Case

The Business Case opens the door to product development, and Stage 2 is where the Business Case is constructed. This stage is a detailed investigation stage, which clearly defines the product and verifies the attractiveness of the project prior to heavy spending. It is also the *critical homework* stage—the one found to be so often weakly handled.

The definition of *the winning new product* is a major facet of Stage 2. The elements of this definition include target-market definition; delineation of the product concept; specification of a product-positioning strategy, the product benefits to be delivered, and the value proposition; and spelling out essential and desired product features, attributes, requirements, and specifications.

Stage 2 sees *market studies* undertaken to determine the customer's needs, wants, and preferences—that is, to help define the "winning" new product.

An example:[10] PumpSmart was an ill-fated project within the Goulds Industrial Pumps Division (U.S.) that was spawned by a single customer request. The customer had asked a Goulds' salesman: "Why don't you build an intelligent pump—one that can sense its own operating environment, and adjust its mode of operation to minimize wear and tear, minimize pump downtime, and maximize pump life?" A great idea, and it sailed through the Idea Gate and on into Development with little or no further customer research as the PumpSmart project. The final product consisted of an intelligent pump with multiple sensors located both upstream and downstream that measured pressure, flow, vibration, and temperature; these sensors were connected to a microprocessor (computer) that controlled a variable-speed motor. The pump could adjust its speed in response to different operating conditions and thereby reduce wear and maintenance.

PumpSmart was launched with great fanfare and proved to be a huge dud. The smart technology was brilliant, but the value proposition and product were weak. All was not lost, however. Sensing that the technology was indeed solid, Goulds' management had another try. By this time, however, Goulds' technical and marketing people had been through *extensive training on VoC*, and employed the technique on the new PumpSmart project. Teams of three people—from Technical, Sales, and Marketing—undertook indepth interviews with key users, and also undertook walk-throughs at customer facilities where pumps were used.

Their conclusions: Although pump maintenance was an issue, it was not an overriding one. The customers' major point of pain was sky-rocketing electrical power costs. These pumps, often high horsepower, run flat out and consume lots of power. What the visit teams also observed was that beside each pump is a flow valve—often in the half-closed position. "That's how we control the volume or flow," explained users.

To the Goulds team, this was absurd: "It's like driving a car with your foot to the floor on the accelerator and using the handbrake to control the speed . . . very inefficient." The new PumpSmart was obvious: a much simpler version of the original PumpSmart, with a sensor downstream and upstream to measure flow demand and supply, a simple microprocessor, and a variable speed drive. When demand is low, the pump slows down, and significant electrical power is saved. In a new installation, there's not even a need for a valve—the pump is the flow controller. In a retrofit installation, PumpSmart pays for itself in less than a year in power savings.

The product has been a huge success, but it was only through VoC work, and in particular the observation and walkabout facet of the visits, that the insight leading to the breakthrough was discovered. Same technology as the ill-fated first PumpSmart project, but a very different product definition based on in-depth customer visits.

Competitive analysis is also a part of this stage. Another market activity is concept testing: A representation of the proposed new product is presented to potential customers, their reactions are gauged, and the likely customer acceptance of the new product is determined.

A detailed *technical appraisal* focuses on the "doability" of the project at Stage 2. That is, customer needs and "wish lists" are translated into a technically and economically feasible conceptual solution. This translation might even involve some preliminary design or laboratory work, but it should not be construed as a full-fledged development project. A manufacturing (or operations) appraisal is often a part of building the Business Case, where issues of manufacturability, source-of-supply, costs to manufacture, and investment required are investigated. If appropriate, detailed legal, patent, and regulatory assessment work is undertaken in order to remove risks and to map out the required actions.

Finally, a detailed *business and financial analysis is* conducted as part of the justification facet of the Business Case. The financial analysis typically involves a discounted cash flow approach, complete with sensitivity analysis to look at possible downside risks.

The result of Stage 2 is a *Business Case* for the project: The *integrated product definition*—a key to success—is agreed to; and a thorough *project justification* and *detailed project action plan* are developed.

Stage 2 involves considerably more effort than Stage 1 and requires inputs from a variety of sources. Stage 2 is best handled by a team consisting of cross-functional members—the core group of the eventual project team.

Gate 3: Go to Development

This is the final gate prior to the Development stage, the last point at which the project can be killed before entering heavy spending. Some firms call it the "money gate": Once past Gate 3, financial commitments are substantial. In effect, Gate 3 means "go to a heavy spend." And it's here that the shape of the funnel changes, as shown in Figure 4.10, taking on a gentler slope—that is, most of the Kill decisions are made in the early gates, at Gates 1, 2, and 3; relatively few projects are killed after Gate 3. Senior management at EXFO Engineering appropriately call this the "funnel leading to a tunnel."[11] Gate 3 also yields a sign-off of the product and project definition.

This Gate 3 evaluation involves a review of each of the activities in Stage 2, checking that the activities were undertaken, that their quality of execution is sound—the readiness-check questions. Next, Gate 3 subjects the project once again to the set of must-meet and should-meet criteria similar to those used at Gate 2. Finally, because a heavy spending commitment is the result of a Go decision at Gate 3, the results of the financial analysis and hurdles are an important part of this screen.

If the decision is Go, Gate 3 sees commitment to the product definition and agreement on the project plan that charts the path forward: the Development Plan and the Preliminary Operations and Marketing Plans are reviewed and approved at this gate. The full project team—an empowered, cross-functional team headed by a project leader with authority—is assigned; and resources—person-days and funds—are formally committed.

Stage 3: Development

Stage 3 begins the implementation of the Development Plan and the physical development of the product (or mapping out the details of the service and the IT work underlying the service). Lab tests, in-house tests, or alpha tests ensure that the product meets requirements under controlled conditions. For lengthy projects, numerous milestones and periodic project reviews are built into the Development Plan. These are not gates per se: Go/Kill decisions are not made here; rather, these milestone checkpoints provide for project control and management. However, missing a milestone or two usually signals that the project is off course and that calls for an immediate and emergency gate review. The deliverable at the end of Stage 3 is a partially tested prototype of the product.

The emphasis in Stage 3 is on technical work. But marketing and operations activities also proceed in parallel. For example, market analysis and customer feedback work continue concurrently with the technical development, with constant customer opinion sought on the product as it takes shape during Development. These are the "build-test-feedback-revise spirals" in Figure 4.10—the back-and-forth or iterative loops, with each development result, for example, rapid prototype, working model, first prototype, and so on, taken to the customer for assessment and feedback. Meanwhile, detailed test plans, market launch plans, and production or operations plans, including production facilities requirements, are developed. An updated financial analysis is prepared, while regulatory, legal, and patent issues are resolved.

Gate 4: Go to Testing

This post-development review is a check on the progress and the continued attractiveness of the product and project. Development work is reviewed and checked, ensuring that the work has been completed in a quality fashion and that the developed product is indeed consistent with the original definition specified at Gate 3.

This gate also revisits the economic questions via a revised financial analysis based on new and more accurate data. The Testing or Validation Plan for the next stage is approved for immediate implementation, and the detailed Marketing and Operations Plans are reviewed for probable future execution.

Stage 4: Testing and Validation

This stage tests and validates the entire viability of the project: the product itself, the production or operations process, customer acceptance, and the economics of the project. A number of activities are undertaken at Stage 4:

- *In-house product tests:* extended lab tests or alpha tests to check on product quality and product performance under controlled operating or lab conditions.
- *User, preference, or field trials of the product:* to verify that the product functions under actual use conditions and also to gauge potential customers' reactions to the product—to establish purchase intent.
- *Trial, limited, or pilot production/operations:* to test, debug, and prove the production or operations process and to determine more precise production costs and throughputs.
- *Simulated test market, test market, or trial sell:* to gauge customer reaction, measure the effectiveness of the launch plan, and determine expected market share and revenues.
- *Revised business and financial analysis:* to check on the continued business and economic viability of the project, based on new and more accurate revenue and cost data.

Sometimes Stage 4 yields negative results, and it's back to Stage 3:

An example: All was proceeding well for the OMNOVA dry-erase wall covering. A successful trial production run in Stage 4 yielded sufficient semi-commercial product to permit customer trials in several test office buildings. The product had been extensively tested in the lab on all known performance metrics—temperature, humidity, scuff resistance, and so on. But one small factor was overlooked—as so often happens. Some customers used a certain brand of dry-erase markers with a unique solvent. The result:

When left on the whiteboard for several days, writing from this one brand of marker proved difficult to completely erase. And so "ghosts" appeared. This *ghosting problem* was never identified until real customers started using the product. But OMNOVA was alert and acted on the field-trial results. The problem was rectified, and now the commercial product meets all customer requirements.

Gate 5: Go to Launch

This final gate opens the door to full commercialization—market launch and full production or operations start up. It is the final point at which the project can still be killed. This gate focuses on the quality of the activities in the Testing and Validation stage and their results. Criteria for passing the gate focus largely on whether the Stage 4 test results are positive; the expected financial return; whether the launch and operations startup plans remain solid; and the readiness check—that all is commercial-ready for the launch. The Operations and Marketing Plans are reviewed and approved for implementation in Stage 5, and in some firms, so is the Product Life Cycle Plan (the plan that takes the product well beyond the launch phase, into maturity and even to product exit).

Stage 5: Launch

This final stage involves implementation of both the Market Launch Plan and the Operations Plan. Production equipment is acquired, installed, and commissioned (although sometimes this is done earlier in Stage 4, as part of the Stage 4 production trials); the logistics pipeline is filled; and selling begins. And barring any unforeseen events, it should be clear sailing for the new product . . . another new-product winner!

Post-Launch Review

At some point following commercialization (often six to eighteen months later), the new-product project is terminated. The team is disbanded, and the product becomes a "regular product" in the firm's product line. This is also the point where the project and the product's performance are reviewed. The latest data on revenues, costs, expenditures, profits, and timing are compared to projections to gauge performance. Finally, a post-audit—a critical assessment of the project's strengths and weaknesses, what you can learn from this project, and how you can do the next one better—is carried out. This review marks the end of the project. Note that the project team and leader remain responsible for the success of the project through this post-launch period, right up to the point of the Post-Launch Review.

An example:[12] Emerson Electric's NPD 2.0 stage-and-gate system builds in a rigorous post-launch follow-up as a way to ensure team accountability for achieving the project's sales and profit objectives. "Post-Launch Review also sets up a systematic way to provide continuous learning and improvement of the NPD process through closed-loop feedback." These reviews occur one to two months after launch, and again twelve to twenty-four months after launch. "The initial follow-up would allow corrective action and a complete review of team performance. The latter review would provide accountability for results, and determine the next steps for the project or change the new NPD [new-product development] process."

Like Emerson Electric, many firms undertake two Post-Launch Reviews: one shortly after launch to make immediate course corrections and to undertake a retrospective analysis of the project while memories are still fresh; and the final review some twelve to eighteen months after launch to review actual versus promised results and terminate the project.

So there you have it—very simple in concept, yet remarkably robust as a way to drive new products to market. Before getting into the details of how the process works, and some of the added sophistication, flexibility, and new techniques that some companies have built in (outlined in the next few chapters), let's first make sure we're all on the same page regarding what *Stage-Gate* is and is not!

DEBUNKING THE MYTHS ABOUT *STAGE-GATE*—WHAT *STAGE-GATE* IS NOT!

The concept sounds simple, but it is surprising how some people get it so wrong. They read the book and claim to have implemented a stage-and-gate process "just like in the book"; but something gets very lost in the translation. Here are some of the frequent ways people misread, misapply, and abuse an otherwise excellent system. What *Stage-Gate* should not be:

Not a Functional, Phased Review Process[13]

Don't confuse *Stage-Gate* of the twenty-first century with the traditional "phased review" process of the 1960s–1980s. Surprisingly, some companies still use this ponderous phased-review system. The phased-review process, endorsed by NASA and others, broke the innovation process into stages, each stage reporting to a function or a department. Implemented with the best of intentions, the process managed to almost double the length of developments. Why? The process was designed like a relay race—activities in sequence rather than in parallel; there were handoffs throughout the process, as one function passed the project on to the next department (and with handoffs, there arise the inevitable dropped balls or worse yet, just throwing it over the wall!); and there was no commitment to the project from beginning to end by any one group—accountability was missing. Moreover, the process was a technical one, not a business process; and gates were more like milestone review points or *technology readiness checks* (projects were rarely killed).

By contrast, today's *Stage-Gate* system is built for speed. The stages are cross-functional, and not dominated by a single functional area: This is a *business process*, not an R&D, Engineering, or Marketing process. The play is rapid, with activities occurring in parallel rather than in series. The governance process is clear, with defined gates and criteria for efficient, timely Go/Kill decision-making. And the project is executed by a dedicated and empowered team of players, led by an entrepreneurial team leader or team captain.

Not a Rigid, Lockstep Process

Some companies' idea-to-launch systems resemble rule books—a lockstep process full of rules, regulations, mandatory procedures, and "thou shalts" that every project should follow, regardless of the circumstances. If this describes your process, no wonder people try to avoid it or circumvent it!

Stage-Gate is a map to get from Point A (idea) to Point B (successful new product). As in any map, when the situation merits, detours can be taken. For example, many companies tailor the model to their own circumstances and build lots of flexibility into their process:

- Not all projects pass through every stage or every gate of the model.
- In any project, activities and deliverables can be omitted or bypassed.
- Similarly, activities can be moved from one stage to another—for example, moving an activity ahead one stage in the event of long lead times.

More on these facets of flexibility in the next chapter.

Not a Linear System

Because of the visual graphics associated with *Stage-Gate*, some people see it as a linear model, with both the stages and the activities within each stage being linear. They miss the point that although the stages are laid out one after the other, within each stage, activities and tasks are anything but linear. Indeed, inside the stages there is much looping, iterating, and back-and-forth play as the project proceeds; some activities are undertaken sequentially, others in parallel, and others overlapping. And then there are the ever-present spirals outside the company and system to customers and users. Even the stages are allowed to overlap (beginning one stage before the previous one is completed), and often the project must iterate back to a previous stage. So the process is anything but linear, even though the traditional graphics depict a neat, linear, and logical process.

Not a Project Control Mechanism

I visited an internationally renowned company near Frankfurt, Germany, and was introduced to its *Stage-Gate* process via a PowerPoint presentation. The title slide said it all: "Project Controlling System," and the presentation went downhill from there. *Stage-Gate* is not, and never was, intended to be a *control mechanism* so that executives, auditors, and financial people could control, or worse yet, micromanage projects from their lofty offices. Rather, *Stage-Gate* is a playbook designed to enable project teams and team leaders to get resources for their projects and then speed them to market using the best possible methods to ensure success.

Not a Dated, Stagnant System

Although *Stage-Gate* has endured many years, today's versions are almost unrecognizable from the original model. It has evolved a lot over time. The world has been the laboratory for *Stage-Gate*, and ingenious people from every continent have made many improvements and adaptations to the system. Many novel improvements have been built into the standard model outlined in this chapter; you'll see more in the next chapter.

To put things in perspective, the *marketing concept* was first published in 1960, and its principles—putting the customer first—are still valid today;[14] but the way we practice marketing today is very different from the way it was in 1960. It's the same with *Stage-Gate*—the principles still hold. But today's modern *Stage-Gate* system bears little resemblance to the original model. It has evolved considerably to include new principles of lean and rapid product development; it has built in a number of new best practices that were not envisioned back in the early days; and now there are many different and tailored versions of *Stage-Gate*.

The point is that *Stage-Gate* is not a static tool; rather, it's a comprehensive, integrated, evolving, and evergreen system that builds in many best practices and methods. And it's always changing. Many pundits promote one favorite tool or a particular method as the "answer" or replacement to *Stage-Gate*. Although some of these new tools are no doubt useful and indeed many *Stage-Gate* users incorporate them into their *Stage-Gate* process, be careful—these tools are typically not a replacement for or alternative to *Stage-Gate*. For example, *lean product development* offers some very good techniques, principles, and methods for removing waste in the innovation process, which companies simply build into *Stage-Gate*. Six Sigma is another valuable tool, and a number of firms such as Ethicon (division of J&J) have integrated DFSS (Design for Six Sigma) right into their *Stage-Gate* process.[15]

Not a Bureaucratic System

Sadly, some managers see *any system* as an opportunity to impose more paperwork, lots of forms, unending meetings and committees, and needless red tape. Remember: The objective here is a systematic, streamlined process, not a bogged-down bureaucratic one. Take a hard look at your idea-to-launch process. If any procedure, meetings, committee, mandatory activity, or form does not add value, then get rid of it!

> *An example:* A major Swiss firm engaged in the power-transmission and belting industry faced a time-to-market challenge. On first arriving at the firm (and coming from a company that used *Stage-Gate* effectively), the new CTO was alarmed at how slowly the company's gating process moved. "It was heavy with bureaucracy," he declared. Thus, at the CTO's insistence, a task force was set up; the process was reinvented and streamlined, and all unnecessary activities and procedures removed, so project leaders could get on with their job of driving their product to market. The process works now!

Not a Data-Entry Scheme

A notable producer of automotive tires in the United States installed its version of a *Stage-Gate* process, which I was asked to review. What surprised me was that the entire system design was led by the IT department (which knew little about product development), and that software constituted the dominant part of the process. When I logged on to the new system, the first screen asked me for information such as "customer requirements for the new tire" and "intended vehicles and their volumes."

What the system appeared to be was an order entry, but it was not; it was their take on what a *Stage-Gate* process should be. There were no gates in the process; and the stages were just nominal ones, each stage asking for additional information. But nowhere were best practices, such as doing some voice-of-customer work, undertaking a competitive analysis, or doing a technology assessment, ever mentioned. Indeed, as one astute employee pointed out: "If I were prepared to 'fake the numbers,' I could get through the entire idea-to-launch system without even leaving my keyboard." And this tire company is not alone. I have since seen similar IT-driven models in other well-known companies whose managements should know better.

Stage-Gate is *not* a data entry system or an IT model. Although software, with its required data entry, can be a valuable facilitator to the process, don't let the tail wag the dog here. *Stage-Gate* comprises a set of information-gathering activities; the data that these activities yield can be conveniently handled by IT to facilitate document management and communication among project team members. But the software and data entry are a tool, not the process!

Not Just a "Back-End" or Product-Delivery Process

One executive in a large engineering and manufacturing firm boasted to me, "Once the product is defined and the business case accepted, then our stage-and-gate process kicks in and it's usually clear sailing from there. It's all that front-end stuff—before we get into our stage-and-gate process—that causes the problems." Shocked at his lack of understanding of *Stage-Gate*, I politely explained that "all that front-end stuff" is very much part of *Stage-Gate*. Look at the flow chart in Figure 4.10: Three of the stages (or half the model) happen before Development begins. The fuzzy front end—ideation, scoping the project, defining the product, and building the business case—is perhaps the *most critical part* of *Stage-Gate*! Indeed, the game is won or lost in the first few plays, and so the front end of *Stage-Gate* is vital, and the part of the model that contributes the most to much higher success rates.

Not the Same as Project Management

Stage-Gate is a *macro* process—an overarching process. By contrast, *project management* is a *micro* process. *Stage-Gate* is not a substitute for sound project management methods. Rather, *Stage-Gate* and project management are used together. Specifically, project management methods are applied *within the stages* of the

Stage-Gate process. For example, during the larger, more complex stages (Stages 3, 4, and 5, Development, Testing, and Launch in Figure 4.10), project management methods must be applied, such as:

✓ A team initiation task to define the project—its mission and goals
✓ Team-building exercises
✓ Computer-generated time lines and critical path plans
✓ Parallel processing (undertaking activities concurrently rather than sequentially)
✓ Milestone review points (built into the action plans approved at each gate)
✓ Regular project reviews

BUILT-IN SUCCESS DRIVERS

The logic of a well-designed playbook, such as the *Stage-Gate* system in Figure 4.10, is appealing because it incorporates many of the factors and lessons vital to success and speed that were highlighted in the previous chapters. For example:

1. The system is front-end loaded: It places much more emphasis on the homework or pre-development activities. Stages 1 and 2—the Scoping and Build Business Case stages—are essential steps before the door to Development is opened at Gate 3.
2. The system is multidisciplinary and cross-functional. It is built around an empowered, cross-functional team. Each stage consists of technical, marketing, operations/production, and even financial activities, necessitating the active involvement of people from all of these areas. The gates are cross-functional, too: Gates are staffed by gatekeepers from different functions or departments in the firm—the managers who own the resources needed for the next stage—in order to achieve alignment across functional areas.
3. Parallel processing speeds up the system. Activities in each stage are undertaken concurrently, rather than sequentially, with much interaction between players and actions within each stage—a rugby approach.
4. A strong market focus is a feature of the system. Marketing inputs begin at the Discovery stage and remain an important facet of every stage from beginning to end of the process. Projects cannot pass the gates until the market-related actions have been completed in a quality way.
5. Spirals are a vital part of the process, a method borrowed from the fast-paced IT industry. Using "build-test-feedback-and-revise" iterative loops, teams move quickly to confirm the product design and resist moving too far downfield with a project based solely on assumptions.
6. There is more focus. The system builds in tough Go/Kill decision points in the form of gates. These gates weed out poor projects early in the process

and help focus scarce resources on the truly deserving projects. They are the quality-control checkpoints: Are you doing the project right? And are you doing the right project?

7. An integrated product definition step is built into the system in Stage 2, Build the Business Case. It is here that the project and product are both defined and justified. This product definition is a key deliverable to Gate 3; without it, the project cannot proceed to Development.

8. There is a strong emphasis on quality of execution throughout. The stages and recommended activities within each stage lay out a playbook for the project leader and team: There is less chance of critical errors of omission. Templates and deliverable requirements establish clear expectations for teams. And the gates provide the critical quality-control checks in the process: Unless the project meets certain quality standards, it fails to pass the gate.

Suggestion: As soon as you finish this chapter, take a hard look at your own new-product idea-to-launch system. First, do you have such a process? If yes, lay it out in front of you. Go through the eight characteristics listed just above and ask yourself: "Does my new-product process build in each of these items? Where? Can I point to them? Are they clearly visible?"

If yes, then answer the next question: "Is my system really operational, or is it just a 'paper process' or high-level conceptual model?" The APQC benchmarking study cited earlier in the chapter (endnote 7) uncovered the key features of *Stage-Gate* that translate the model from a handful of PowerPoint slides to a fully operational system—see Table 4.1. Review the list in Table 4.1, asking whether your system passes. If the answers are no to these questions, then please read on, for it's time to reinvent your firm's idea-to-launch system and to get it operational and practiced.

TABLE 4.1: A GOOD CHECKLIST—
CHARACTERISTICS OF AN OPERATIONAL STAGE-GATE SYSTEM*

(Based on the APQC best practices in innovation study)

Clearly defined stages: An overwhelming majority of businesses use a series of defined stages—for example: Ideation, Scoping, Build Business Case, Development, Test, and Launch (72.4 percent of businesses [in the APQC study] have well-defined stages).

Activities defined for each stage: Some NPD processes lack specifics, for example, no clearly defined activities or expectations in each stage. Not so for our sample of firms: Activities and tasks are defined for each stage of their NPD (new-product development) process for 73.8 percent of businesses.

Defined Go/Kill gates: An important part of a well-constructed NPD process is gates or Go/No Go decision points. At gates, management meets with project teams to review the project, evaluate its merits, and make Go/No Go and resourcing decisions. Gates are a strong facet of most businesses' NPD processes, with 73.8 percent of businesses claiming proficiency here; only 13.3 percent of businesses lack gates.

Defined Go/No Go criteria at gates: Go/Kill criteria are considered important in order to better evaluate the merits of NPD projects and to assist management in making the Go/No Go decision. In spite of the logic of having such gate criteria, the lack of these criteria is fairly widespread (21.9 percent of businesses lack these criteria; only 46.7 percent claim to have well-defined gate criteria), and indeed this is a somewhat weaker facet of businesses' NPD processes.

Deliverables defined for each gate: A menu of what the project team is expected to deliver to each gate in the NPD—their "deliverables"—is a positive feature of best-in-class new-product processes and is also common among the sample of businesses. Overall, having well-defined deliverables is rated moderately strong, with 71.0 percent of businesses having such an explicit menu of deliverables to guide project teams.

Gatekeepers designated for each gate: Often it is unclear just who should undertake project reviews and whose signatures are needed for an NPD project to proceed. The locus of decision-making—the people who make the Go/No Go decisions at gates—is also an important feature of many firms' NPD processes. So it is with the sample of businesses: Most have the gatekeepers very well defined (71.9 percent of businesses), whereas 15.2 percent do not at all.

---

* Taken from APQC study, endnote 7.

A visible, documented process: Some firms claim to have an NPD process; but on closer inspection, it's more a high-level and conceptual process—a few flow diagrams with boxes and diamonds and little more. To be operational, an effective new-product process should be well mapped-out, visible, and well-documented. Again, the sample of businesses does fairly well: 66.7 percent of businesses indicate that they have a well-documented and visible NPD process; only 14.3 percent do not.

Whether the NPD is really used: The true test of an NPD process is whether or not it is really used; or is it merely window-dressing in the business—a paper process? There is clear evidence that some businesses really are using their NPD process to drive new products to market, with the majority of projects operating within the process: More than half of businesses (52.4 percent) really make use of their NPD process. Somewhat disturbing is that although the great majority claim to have some type of NPD process in place (only 7.6 percent claimed not to have a process), 19 percent claim that their process is not really used.

An enabling process for project team: Another test of one's NPD process is whether or not it is a facilitating process, helping project teams get their products to market (rather than a bureaucratic process that stands in the way). This is one of the weakest elements of the NPD process, with 56.7 percent of businesses claiming that they have built too much bureaucracy into the process.

An adaptable and scalable process: Is the NPD process a flexible one, adapted to the needs, size, and risk of the project? Or is it a rigid one-size-fits-all process, failing to recognize the difference between major and minor projects? Two-thirds of the businesses in this study (65.2 percent) view their NPD process as flexible, adaptable, and scalable.

A process manager in place: A number of firms have designated a process manager—full- or part-time—to shepherd their NPD process, ensuring that it works. Duties often include: coaching project teams, facilitating gate meetings, ensuring project deliverables are ready and distributed to gatekeepers, training, keeping metrics, and so on. The lack of a process manager is fairly evident for a great many firms: 31.4 percent do not have this person in place; but 41 percent of businesses do.

5

NEXT-GENERATION *STAGE-GATE®*— HOW COMPANIES HAVE EVOLVED AND ACCELERATED THE SYSTEM

Learning and innovation go hand in hand. The arrogance of success is to think that what you did yesterday will be sufficient for tomorrow.
—William Pollard, English clergyman (1828–1893)

GLOBAL INPUTS TO REINVENT *STAGE-GATE*

The world has become a living laboratory for *Stage-Gate*. Countless corporations globally have task forces working on designing and installing next-generation versions of *Stage-Gate* systems. I am fortunate because I often see the results of their labors, especially the successes. Here now are some of the ways that progressive companies have modified, adjusted, and adapted *Stage-Gate* and have implemented the next-generation idea-to-launch process: seven of the more important improvements to *Stage-Gate*, designed to make an already solid system even better—faster and more productive:[1]

1. Firms have made their *Stage-Gate* systems *scalable*—scaled to suit different risk levels, sizes, and types of development projects.
2. They have made the system *adaptable* in order to accelerate the process— spiral or agile development, concurrent activities, overlapping stages, and conditional Go decisions.
3. Some companies have introduced *lean manufacturing principles* in order to remove waste and bureaucracy from their idea-to-launch systems—lean product development.

4. *Continuous improvement,* also a facet of lean development, has been made operational through better metrics, the use of success criteria, and rigorous post-launch reviews.
5. *Stage-Gate* systems have been adapted in order to accommodate *"open innovation"*—seeking ideas, technology solutions, and even finished products from outside the firm, and selling underutilized intellectual property externally.
6. Life cycle management systems have been integrated with the development process, so that *Stage-Gate* is now part of the total *life cycle management model*—from product creation to product exit many years later.
7. *Stage-Gate* is *automated* in some companies, which have installed excellent software to support their idea-to-launch systems. Many software products are now *Stage-Gate* certified.

There are other major improvements that firms have made as their *Stage-Gate* systems have evolved. For example, the vital issue of product innovation governance is a topic that many firms have focused on and improved; but it's so large a topic that I deal with it separately in Chapters 8 and 9, on project selection and gates with teeth, respectively. Another huge improvement to *Stage-Gate* is the inclusion of ideation—Discovery—as a stage in the process (previously it had been assumed that ideas just appeared magically). So important is this Discovery stage that I devote an entire chapter to it, Chapter 6, coming up next.

Suggestion: If your idea-to-launch process is more than five years old, or if it's bogged down with bureaucratic baggage that's been added over the years, it's time for a good overhaul and modernization. Read on, and take a look at the seven key best practices that users have implemented to accelerate their *Stage-Gate* system or to improve productivity; then audit your process versus these practices. Maybe it's time to set up a "renew and reinvent" task force to modernize your innovation system.

1. SCALED TO SUIT DIFFERENT RISK LEVELS AND TYPES OF PROJECTS

One size does not fit all. Different versions of *Stage-Gate—Full, XPress,* and *Lite*—are needed for projects of different sizes and risk levels, as in Figure 5.1.

Perhaps the greatest change in *Stage-Gate* over the last decade is that it has become a *scalable process,* scaled to suit very different types and risk levels of projects—from very risky and complex platform developments through to lower-risk extensions and modifications, and even to handle rather simple sales force requests.[2]

When first implemented, there was only one version of *Stage-Gate* in a company, typically a five-stage, five-gate model.[3] And the rule was that "one size fits all." But users quickly realized that some projects were too small to push through the full five-stage model, and so they circumvented it. The problem was that these smaller projects—line extensions, modifications, sales force requests, and so on—did not use many resources individually, but collectively they consumed the bulk of resources. Thus, a contradictory situation existed, whereby projects that represented the majority of development resources went "outside the system."

Management recognized that each of these projects—big and small—has some element of risk, consumes resources, and thus must be managed; but not all need to go through the full five-stage process. The process has thus *morphed into multiple versions* to fit business needs and to accelerate projects. We saw in Chapter 4 that risk is some combination of how much is at stake in a project (development cost and potential payoffs) and the uncertainties of the project, for example, how new the product, technology, or market is. The general rule is: The higher the risk, the more one adheres to the full *Stage-Gate* model shown in the last chapter—stay on the highway! But for lower-risk projects, detours and shortcuts are possible and indeed recommended. Figure 5.1 shows some examples:

- *Stage-Gate® Full* (across top of Figure 5.1) is the usual five-stage, five-gate process, designed for genuine new-product projects—typically larger, more uncertain, and somewhat higher risk. We saw this model in the last chapter. Although this is the standard model, in practice most development projects are smaller and lower risk, hence do not go through this "full model"—it's reserved for the *true innovation projects*!
- *Stage-Gate® XPress* (middle of Figure 5.1) is for projects with moderate risk, such as improvements, modifications, and extensions. These projects often represent the majority of projects in the development pipeline—they are the *sustaining innovation* or "renovation" projects, designed to keep the product line fresh, up-to-date, and in good repair; as a result, they are usually lower cost and more predictable to do. Note that the *Stage-Gate* system is reduced to three stages and three gates for these lower-risk developments. The activities list per stage is similarly truncated, and the deliverables package and templates shortened. Gatekeepers are typically not the senior leadership team, but mid-management.
- *Stage-Gate® Lite* (across bottom of Figure 5.1) is for very small projects, such as simple customer requests or salespeople's submissions. Usually these projects represent minor modifications to existing products, and though small, collectively they often consume a substantial percentage of company R&D resources. Thus, these small projects should also be "in the system"; they, too, need to be managed and scrutinized, and not every request is undertaken (otherwise R&D become "busy fools"). Note that the model has been reduced to two stages; the activities and deliverables are also reduced, and the gatekeepers are often mid-management from technical groups and the sales force.

Figure 5.1: Next-Generation *Stage-Gate* Is Scalable to Suit Different Projects

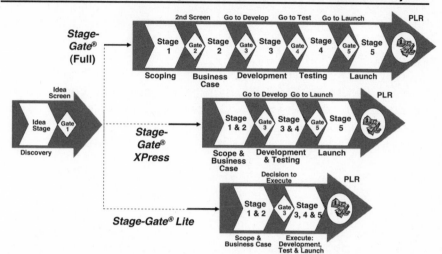

Major new-product projects – true innovations – use the Full Five-Stage process (top)
Moderate risk projects – extensions, modifications & improvements – go through the *XPress* version (middle)
Sales force & Marketing requests – minor changes – use the *Lite* process (bottom)

In Figure 5.1, all ideas or proposed development projects enter Gate 1 on the left for an initial screen, so that Gate 1 is in effect a "clearinghouse." The idea-screening decision is made here, as is the routing decision—what type of project this is, and therefore what version of *Stage-Gate* it should be in. The principle for electing which version of *Stage-Gate* to use is simple: The higher the risk, the more one adheres to the full five-stage process across the top of Figure 5.1.

A word of caution: Visible rules must be in place to ensure that higher-risk projects are not incorrectly routed through *Stage-Gate Lite* or *XPress*, perhaps by an aggressive project leader wishing to circumvent the correct process. Thus, guidelines in terms of market and technical newness and dollar costs of the project must be developed in order to ensure correct project routing in Figure 5.1.

Request-for-Proposal Projects

When the firm does much large-scale custom-development work for single customers—such as in response to a request for quotation—*Stage-Gate* systems have been similarly modified for such projects. Examples include *Stage-Gate* developed for the defense industry or government contract work. The first few stages of such systems deal with whether or not to submit a bid (often the cost of proposal preparation is quite high), but once the bid is won, the project is Go from that

STAGE-GATE TD FOR TECHNOLOGY DEVELOPMENT PROJECTS

A typical *Stage-Gate* system for technology developments and technology platforms (TD) is shown in Figure 5.2; it consists of three stages and four gates across the top of the chart.[4]

Discovery or idea generation (Stage 1) is the trigger for the process. Idea generation is often done by scientists or technology people, but it can also be the result of other activities, such as a strategic-planning exercise, technology forecasting, or a technology road-mapping exercise.

Idea Screen: The first gate is the idea screen, the initial decision to commit a limited amount of time and money to the TD project. This gate is a *gentle screen* that poses the question: Does the idea merit expending any effort at all? Criteria for Go are largely qualitative—strategic, potential impact, leverage, and technical feasibility. The Gate 1 gatekeeper group is typically composed of senior R&D people: the corporate head of Technology, other senior R&D people, along with representatives from Corporate Marketing and Business Development to ensure commercial input.

Scoping: The first stage is Project Scoping, whose purpose is to build the foundation for the technology development project, define the scope of the project, and map out the forward plan. The effort is limited, typically taking not much more than several weeks. Stage 1 activities are conceptual and preparation work, and include a technical literature search, patent and IP search, competitive alternatives assessment, resource gaps identification, and a preliminary technical assessment.

Second Screen: Gate 2 is where the decision is made to begin limited experimental or technical work in Stage 2. Like Gate 1, this gate is also a relatively gentle screen and poses the question: Does the idea merit undertaking limited technical and physical work? Gate 2 is again largely qualitative and does not require financial analysis (because the resulting product, process, or impact of the technology are still largely unknown). The gatekeepers are the same as at Gate 1.

Technical Assessment: The purpose of Stage 2 is to demonstrate technical feasibility under ideal conditions. This stage entails preliminary experimental or technical work, but should not take more than one to two person-months' effort and should last no longer than three to four months. Activities here typically include undertaking a thorough conceptual technological analysis; executing feasibility experiments or definitive technical work; developing a partnership network; identifying resource needs and solutions to resource gaps; and assessing the potential impact of the technology on the company.

Gate 3: This is the decision to deploy resources beyond one to two person-months and opens the door to a more extensive and expensive investigation, Stage 3. This gate thus involves a more rigorous evaluation than at Gate 2 and is based on new information from Stage 2. Gate criteria resemble those for Gate 2, but with more and tougher sub-questions, answered with benefit of better data. The Gate 3 gatekeepers usually include the corporate head of technology, other senior technology or R&D people, Corporate Marketing or Business Development, and the heads of the involved businesses who will commercialize the technology.

Detailed Investigation: The purpose of Stage 3 is to implement the full experimental or technology-development plan, to prove technological feasibility, and to define the scope of the technology and its value to the company. This stage could entail significant expenditures, potentially person-years of work. Besides the extensive technical work, other activities focus on defining commercial product or process possibilities, undertaking market, manufacturing, and impact assessments on these possibilities, and preparing an implementation business case. Sound project management methods are employed during this lengthy stage, including periodic milestone checks and project reviews.

Applications Path Gate: This is the final gate in the TD process, the "door opener" to one or more new-product or process-development projects (see Figure 5.2). Here, the results of technical work are reviewed to determine the applicability, scope, and value of the technology to the company; and next steps are decided. Note that this Gate 4 is often combined with an early gate in the usual product-development process (for example, with Gate 1, 2, or 3, as shown across the bottom of Figure 5.2). Gatekeepers are typically the senior Corporate R&D people, Corporate Marketing, or Business Development, plus the leadership team from the relevant business that will assume ownership of the resulting commercial development projects.

point onward (that is, subsequent gates are not Go/Kill, but Go/Recycle). These custom-work *Stage-Gate* systems are similar to the "full model" in Figure 5.1, but with some important differences to deal with request-and-quote situations.

Versions to Handle Platform and Technology Development Projects

There is no longer just *Stage-Gate* for new-product projects. Other types of projects—platform developments, process developments, or exploratory research projects—compete for the same resources, need to be managed, and thus also merit their own version of a stage-and-gate process. For example, Exxon-Mobil Chemical has designed a three-stage, three-gate version of their *Stage-Gate* process to handle upstream research projects;[5] numerous other organizations (Timex, Lennox, Sandia Labs, Donaldson) have adopted a three-stage, four-gate system to handle fundamental research, technology development, or platform projects.[6]

Platform or technology platform projects are increasingly important in product innovation. The PDMA Handbook defines platform projects narrowly as: "the *design and components* that are shared by a set of products in a product family"[7]— for example, an engine-transmission assembly by an automaker, from which multiple different automobiles are designed and built. The notion of platforms has been broadened to include a *capability* that might spawn multiple products. The analogy is that of an oil-well drilling platform—it is constructed at huge cost, but once built, permits multiple holes to be drilled at lower cost per hole. Thus, a technology platform project is one in which the "deliverable" is not a new product per se, but rather a *capability or technology* upon which multiple new products can be created. A process for such projects is outlined in the *Stage-Gate TD* box.

Note that because such TD projects involve many technological uncertainties— for example, new science and invention may be required—the TD process (across the top of Figure 5.2) is very flexible: It is iterative and features loops within stages, and potentially to previous stages. And gates rely less on financial criteria and more on strategic criteria.

Other Stage-Gate Models and Applications

Stage-Gate is employed well beyond the bounds of new-product and technology development. For example, Exxon Chemical expanded the use of *Stage-Gate* to include capital projects (for example, production plant expansions or modernizations) as well as internal IT projects. Kennametal, a U.S. tool manufacturer, has developed a version of *Stage-Gate* for mergers and acquisitions. And numerous firms, where much of R&D is focused on *process* rather than *product* development, have tailored *Stage-Gate* for process development—a similar model to that across the top of Figure 5.1, but focused internally with the firm's production facility as "the customer." These applications are beyond the scope of this book, however; nonetheless, the point is made that *Stage-Gate* sees many applications well beyond those originally envisioned, and though the process is heavily tailored to the specific application, the principles of *Stage-Gate* still apply.

Figure 5.2: The Technology Development Process (top) Handles Technology Developments and Technology Platform Projects, Which Spawn Multiple New-Product Projects (bottom)

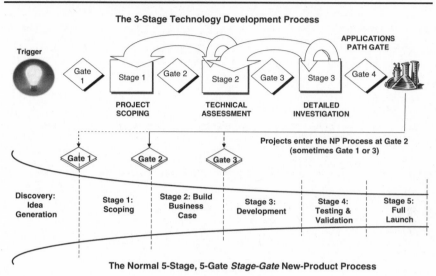

The 3-Stage Technology Development Process

The Normal 5-Stage, 5-Gate *Stage-Gate* New-Product Process

Suggestion: One version of *Stage-Gate* likely won't handle your many development needs. Consider setting up three different versions to handle light, medium, and heavy projects, much like in Figure 5.1. Most projects will likely go through the medium and light models, reserving the "full" process for bolder, higher-risk new-product projects. And if you undertake technology platform or technology projects, consider installing a methodology for these, too, much like in Figure 5.2.

2. AN ADAPTABLE, FLEXIBLE, AND AGILE PROCESS
Spiral or Agile Development

Stage-Gate has also become a much more *adaptable* innovation process, one that adjusts to changing conditions and fluid, unstable information. The concept of *spiral* or *agile development,* introduced in Chapter 2, is built in, allowing project teams to move rapidly to a finalized product design through a series of "build-test-feedback-and-revise" iterations.[8] Spiral development bridges the gap between the need for sharp, early, and fact-based product definition before development begins versus the need to be flexible and to adjust the product's design to new information and fluid market conditions as development proceeds. Spiral development allows developers to continue to incorporate valuable customer feedback into the design even after the product definition is locked in before going into Stage 3. Spiral development also deals with the need to get

Figure 5.3: Sample Spirals Throughout the *Stage-Gate* System Are Built in by Design—These Are Deliberately Built into the System

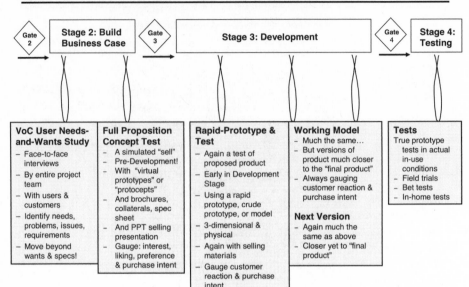

mock-ups in front of customers earlier in the process (in Stage 2 rather than waiting until Stage 3 or 4).

How does spiral development work in practice? A sample set of spirals is shown in Figure 5.3. Note that these loops or spirals are deliberately built in from the front-end stages through the Development stage and into the Testing stage— they are deliberately designed into the system and don't simply occur accidentally! The first loop or spiral is the *VoC study* undertaken early in Stage 2, during which project team members visit customers to better understand their unmet needs, problems, and benefits sought in the new product. At this point, the project team probably has very little to show the customer; and that's the way it should be: The purpose of this visit is to listen and watch, not to "show and tell."

During the second spiral, the full proposition concept test in Figure 5.3, the project team presents *a representation of the proposed product*. Depending on the type of product and industry, this representation can be a computer-generated virtual prototype, a handmade model or mock-up, a very crude protocept, or even a few computer screens for new software. The product obviously does not work at this early stage and, in some presentations, is only two-dimensional. But it is enough to give the customer a feel for what the product will be and do. The product presentation should be accompanied by simulated collaterals or selling materials: a dummy brochure, a simulated spec sheet, a sales presentation on

PowerPoint, or even a storyboard with sound track to simulate a television ad. Interest, liking, preference, and purchase intent are thus established even before the project is a formal development project.

Feedback is sought on dislikes and changes required, and the project team moves to finalize its product definition as part of the Stage 2 Business Case. Note that the product definition should specify *that which is fixed* (and not likely to change) *versus that which is fluid* (and may change as new information becomes available). The notion of the perfectly locked-in product definition at Gate 3 does not work in fluid market situations.

> *Stage-Gate* must be agile, adaptable, and flexible. Spirals, along with moving activities forward—overlapping stages and activities (concurrent activities)— are the way to do this.

Moving into the Development stage in Figure 5.3, within weeks the team members produce the next and more complete version of the product, perhaps a crude model or a rapid prototype. They test this with customers, and again seek feedback, which they use to rapidly revise and build the first working prototype—and so on, with each successive version of the product getting closer to the final product, and at the same time, closer to the customer's ideal.

A Flexible Process

The notion of a rigid, lockstep process is dead.[9] Today's fast-paced *Stage-Gate* is flexible, as opposed to a rigid "book of rules and procedures" to be religiously followed. *No activity or deliverable is mandatory. Stage-Gate* is a guide that suggests best practices, recommended activities, and likely deliverables. But the project team has much discretion over which activities it wants to execute and which it decides against. Every project is unique and merits its own action plan. The project team presents its proposed "go-forward plan"—its best attempt at defining what needs to be done to make the project a success—at each gate. At these gates, the gatekeepers commit the necessary resources, and in so doing, approve the go-forward plan. But note that it is the *project team's plan*, not simply a mechanistic implementation of a standardized process!

Another facet of flexibility is *simultaneous execution*.[10] Here, key activities and even entire stages overlap, not waiting for perfect information before moving forward, as shown in Figure 5.4:

- Project teams can move activities forward by executing them in parallel rather than in series. The rule is: Move forward when the information is reliable and stable. In this way the project can be accelerated—a rugby approach with multiple parallel activities, rather than a relay race, with activities strung out in series in a painfully slow fashion.
- In some cases, it is even acceptable to move activities from one stage to an earlier one, and in effect, *to overlap stages*, also shown in Figure 5.4.

Figure 5.4: Overlapping Activities Within Stages, and Even Between Stages, Saves Time – But Increases Risk

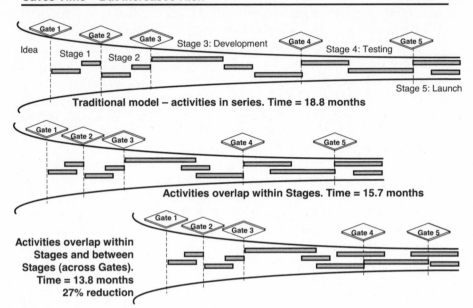

Note the time savings in Figure 5.4. The upper diagram is the traditional model (18.8 months to market), but by overlapping activities within stages (middle diagram), the time is cut by three months, or 16.5 percent. But by overlapping stages—Stages 4 and 3, and Stages 5 and 4—time is reduced by five months, or 27.6 percent.

An example: At Toyota, the rule is to synchronize processes for simultaneous execution.[11] Truly effective concurrent engineering requires that each subsequent function maximize the utility of the stable information available from the previous function as it becomes available. That is, development teams must do the most they can with that portion of the design data that is not likely to change. Each function's processes are designed to move forward simultaneously, building around stable data as they become available.

Concurrent engineering has been around for some time; less well-practiced, however, is concurrency across multiple cross-functional activities in order to accelerate the process. The chart in Figure 5.5 provides some guidelines for when it is acceptable to move activities forward. The information the project team has should be judged in terms of:

- Reliability—is the information fact-based or is it hearsay, speculation, and opinion?
- Stability—is the information likely to change, or is it relatively stable over time?

Figure 5.5: Use This Chart to Determine Which Information Is Stable and Reliable and When to Move Forward

	Information Stability	
	Fixed	**Fluid**
Fact-Based	Stable & reliable information: Base your key decisions on information here, e.g., Design, Go/Kill	Unstable information. Do not use for key decisions. Build in steps to get constantly updated & current data
Opinion	Can base early decisions (Go/Kill; prelim. Product Definition) on this information. Undertake studies to get facts	Poor & unstable information. Do not base decisions on this

(Vertical axis label: Information Reliability)

A project team's review of the "quality of information" it possesses often identifies some information that is both reliable and stable (upper left quadrant of Figure 5.5) and thus points to some activities that can be moved forward.

A word of caution: As noted in Toyota's principles of lean development, only use that portion of the data that is not likely to change.[12] Working with early and fluid data will result in much waste—you think you are saving time, but it will actually take longer than the traditional linear process. So, review the available data (example: design requirements), noting that which is fact-based and solid versus that which is speculative and fluid. And use the four-quadrant chart in Figure 5.5 to help classify the information.

Simultaneous execution usually adds risk to a project. For example, the decision to purchase production equipment before field trials are completed, thereby avoiding a long order lead-time, may be a good application of simultaneous execution. But there is risk, too—the risk is that the project may be canceled or change direction after dedicated production equipment is purchased. Thus, the decision to overlap activities and stages is *a calculated risk*, but the risk must be calculated! That is, the cost of delay must be weighed against the cost and probability of being wrong—see Table 5.1.

Conditional Go Decisions
Gates can be accelerated by allowing a fifth possible decision outside the four normal Go/Kill/Hold/Recycle decisions: Conditional Go. From time to time, all

TABLE 5.1: CALCULATE THE RISK OF MOVING FORWARD

First, determine the Cost of Delay (the actual cost in dollars per day of delay):

1. The cost of the deferred income stream:
   - Money has a time value!
   - Look at your projected cash profit stream after launch.
     - ✓ Determine its present value (PV in $000).
     - ✓ Multiply the PV by your cost of capital per day (%).
     - ✓ That's the daily cost of deferring or postponing your income because of delay.
2. The lost window of opportunity:
   - If your product has a limited window of sales opportunity,
   - Determine the cost of these lost sales (on a per-day basis).
3. The extra development and testing costs:
   - Any project that lasts longer invariably ends up costing more than it should.
   - Estimate the marginal cost per day of the project for "hanging around" longer than it should (this marginal cost is less than the full cost per day of development, but more than zero).
4. Loss of competitive advantage:
   - In fast-moving and competitive markets, where being first-in really matters.
   - This is an estimate—the impact of lost market share.
5. Other costs—examples are:
   - The costs of delivering late to a key customer (sometimes there are contractual penalties).
   - The cost of delaying a partner's launch of their product.

Add up items 1–5 above. Use this cost-per-day of delay ($000) in your calculations when you determine whether or not it makes sense to move forward.

Moving forward in an accelerated fashion is a calculated risk—so do calculate the risk!

Cost of delay (number of days x cost-per-day of delay)

Versus

Cost of being wrong x Probability of being wrong

The cost of being wrong can usually be determined—for example, having to cancel an order on production equipment or write off development of some marketing and launch materials. If the cost of delay far exceeds the cost and probabilities of being wrong, move forward! Move the long lead-time items ahead!

deliverable requirements for a Go decision are met except one, which is identified as a gap at the gate meeting. The issue: Should one hold up the project awaiting the completion of the outstanding task, or move ahead? Some companies allow a "Conditional Go" decision—move ahead—but steps are taken to ensure the completion of the final task to the satisfaction of one nominated gatekeeper.

An example: a company was developing a proximity warning system for container-handling cranes in a shipyard area, and the project team had just entered Gate 3, "Go to Development." All was in order. All the deliverables were in place, and the project looked good except for one thing: an astute gatekeeper noted that an issue of legal liability—what if the warning system failed and someone was injured?—had not been dealt with. Should they hold the project up, awaiting legal counsel, which might take weeks? The project team had momentum and was poised to move forward into Development.

The decision was made to go ahead into Development—get under way—but the team was instructed to seek legal opinion immediately and was given four weeks to get an answer; within four weeks, the team was to submit the legal opinion to the head gatekeeper. If he was satisfied, then the "conditional go" would become simply a "go." Otherwise, the project would be put on hold at that future date until the legal issue was resolved.

The key here is discipline—ensuring that the outstanding task does indeed get done, and satisfactorily—by providing some type of feedback or closed loop, in this case, back to the head gatekeeper. Otherwise, the option of Conditional Go simply becomes an "easy out" for tasks not completed on time.

Suggestion: Take steps to make your idea-to-launch system agile, flexible, and adaptive. Build in the spirals with users—build-test-feedback-and-revise iterations—to quickly confirm that the product is right and to ensure purchase intent early. Build in concurrency, allowing activities within stages to overlap, not waiting for perfect information before moving ahead. And consider overlapping stages—moving one activity forward into the previous stage in order to save time. But note the risks, and balance the cost of delay versus the cost of being wrong.

> Use lean manufacturing techniques—value stream analysis—to remove all waste and non-value-added work from your idea-to-launch system.

3. EFFICIENT, LEAN, AND NO WASTE
Too Much Bureaucracy

Having a well-defined and efficient system that speeds new products to market is the goal. Instead, what some companies have done is to design a cumbersome, bureaucratic process with a lot of make-work and non-value-added activities. Here are two of the common pitfalls I see:

A. Deliverables Overkill

Most companies' new-product processes suffer from far too much information delivered to the gatekeepers at each gate. The project team screams "too much bureaucracy and too much work to prepare for gates" while the gatekeepers complain that they must plow through pages of materials, much of it not relevant to the decision. Several factors create this deliverables overkill:

- Because the project team is not certain what information is required, they overdeliver—they prepare an overly comprehensive report, and in so doing, *bulletproof* themselves. What is needed is a better understanding between project teams and gatekeepers regarding just what information is needed at each gate: Expectations must be made clear on both sides.
- The fault can also be the design of the company's *Stage-Gate* system itself. The system often includes very elaborate templates that must be filled out for each gate, regardless. Some experts argue that templates are mind numbing and encourage unneeded work; others argue that in any process, templates are a useful guide and help to structure the data. Either way, overly detailed templates, replete with pages of fields to be filled in, can lead to deliverables overkill.

Although some of the information that gating systems demand may be interesting, often much of it is not essential to the gate decision. Detailed explanations of how the market research was done, or sketches of what the new molecule looks like, add no value to the decision. Restrict the deliverables and their templates to the essential information needed to make the gate decisions:

> *An example:*[13] Johnson & Johnson's Ethicon Division has an effective *Stage-Gate* process that begins with Stage 1 "Understanding the Opportunity" and ends with "Launch." A positive feature of the process is "lean gates." Previously, the gate deliverables package was a thirty- to ninety-page presentation, obviously a lot of work for any project team to prepare. Today, it's down to the bare essentials: one page with three backup slides. The expectation is that gatekeepers arrive at the gate meeting *knowing the project* (the gate meeting is not an educational session to describe the project in detail to a poorly prepared gatekeeping group). Senior management is simply informed at the gate review about the *risks and the commitments required*. Finally, there is a standardized presentation format. The end result is that weeks of preparation work have been saved.

B. Demanding Much Non-Value-Added Work

Some companies' processes build every possible activity into each stage, and long lists of required tasks and activities per stage are the result. Moreover, many *Stage-Gate* processes over time become far too bulky as more and more make-work gets added to the system.

An example:[14] ITT Industries boasts a very effective *Stage-Gate* process, part of its *value-based product development (VBPD)* initiative (which incidentally helped to drive sales from new products from 15 percent in 2002 to 33 percent by 2010). One of the bureaucratic forces that ITT management constantly had to guard against was the tendency for each function to require far too much from the project team. For example, when the Corporate Environment, Health and Safety group got hold of the process, it added a huge amount of work in Stage 2 for the project team—a long list of twenty tasks that resulted in a seven-page deliverable template, longer than the full business case! It seemed as though each department was trying to outdo the next one in terms of how comprehensive it could make its section of the documentation. Instead, the departments created a bureaucratic nightmare that no project team could have fought its way through. Had it not been for a very tough-minded executive who oversaw the entire VBPD *Stage-Gate* process, this added work would have killed their system. Today the process is slim, trim, and effective—and it delivers results!

No Pain, No Gain

The implementation of any system requires some effort, and indeed *Stage-Gate* makes certain new demands on project teams, leaders, and gatekeepers. For example, project teams are expected to meet a certain standard in terms of front-end homework and get the facts on their project—something that may be new to people who are used to pulling numbers out of the air. Similarly, gates do take a bit of effort and represent new demands both for gatekeepers and project teams, especially in a company used to casual or intuitive decision-making or one-person executive-edict gate meetings.

All of these new demands may seem like extra work to those new to *Stage-Gate*. The argument voiced is that "all this extra work is bureaucratic—we can skip over these tasks and save ourselves lots of time and money." This argument would be convincing, if it weren't for the evidence: The extra work is well worth the effort and pays for itself many times in terms of increased success rates, greater project profits, and often shorter times to market in the long run.

The point is that one must be very careful not to confuse *avoiding bureaucracy* (defined as doing work that adds no value) with *intellectual laziness* or *sloppy execution* (skipping key tasks that do add much value, but do take a little more time and effort to do them right). Many project teams and companies are guilty of the latter.

Using "Lean Techniques" to Remove Waste

Smart companies have made their next generation *Stage-Gate* process *lean*, removing waste and inefficiency at every opportunity. They have borrowed the concept of *value stream analysis* from lean manufacturing and have applied it to their new-product process.

Figure 5.6: Construct the "Value Stream Map" of Your New-Product Process

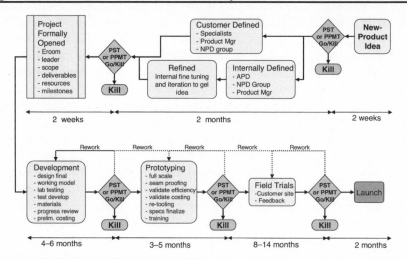

Source: Manufacturer of process equipment. Disguised & abbreviated. The actual process chart was drawn on a 10-meter length of paper, but reduced for this book. Times to complete each task are noted, along with recycles/rework (deficiencies in the process are also noted on the original chart – not shown here).

A *value stream* is simply the connection of all the process steps with the goal of maximizing customer value.[15] In product development, a value stream represents the linkage of all value-added and non-value-added activities associated with the creation of a new product or service. The tool known as the *value stream map* is used to identify and document value streams in product innovation and is critical to identifying both value-added and non-value-added activities, hence is an essential tool to improving your idea-to-launch process.[16]

In employing value stream analysis, a task force creates a map of the value stream—your current idea-to-launch process—for typical development projects in your business (an example is shown in Figure 5.6). All the stages, decision points, and key activities in a typical project are mapped out, with typical times for each activity and decisions indicated. In undertaking this mapping, it becomes clear that there is often a difference between the way the process is supposed to work, and the way it works in reality.

Once the value stream is mapped out, the task force lowers the microscope on the process and dissects it, critically assessing each step and activity in the process and posing four key questions:

- What work gets done at this step, stage, or activity?
- How well do we execute this activity? How long does it typically take?
- Is this step or activity really needed?
- If so, how can it be made better? How can it be made faster?

All procedures, required deliverables, documents and templates, committees and decision processes are examined, looking for time wasters. Once problems, time wasters, and non-value-added activities are spotted, the task force then works to remove them.

Such a disciplined approach invariably spots non-value-added work in the system, and steps can then be taken to modify the system to remove it:

An example: Acme Company develops important components for paper machines in the pulp-and-paper industry. (Paper machines are huge $100+ million machines that make paper continuously, occupying a space the size of an aircraft hangar.) The value stream map in Figure 5.6 is an abbreviated map from this firm.

One particularly troublesome aspect of the process in Figure 5.6 centers on field trials: It takes eight to fourteen months to undertake field trials on a real paper machine; and often the trials don't work, so they must be repeated. Field trials can thus add months, even years, to projects!

The task force undertook a *root cause analysis*, which revealed the following: field trials are done at customers' plants—a paper mill—so Acme must wait until a scheduled customer plant shut-down. The field trial is fairly expensive for customers, so they are somewhat reluctant to do these all the time. Besides, there's no real incentive for customers to undertake field trials for Acme. More insights: The frequent recycles, which really slow the project and add cost to the customer, are largely due to a lack of understanding of users' needs and applications, or serious technical problems with the solution.

Additional analysis revealed that the main competitor does not have the same problem, as it does initial field trials on an in-house *pilot plant paper machine* owned by the company. The pilot machine replicates a full paper machine very well and thus reduces risk to the customer. The trial product is largely proven and so recycles are largely eliminated: The competitor got the product almost right before conducting a full customer field trial.

Then the task force worked hard to find solutions to the defined problems. Here are the solutions as a result of this value-stream and root-cause analysis that the task force proposed and implemented:

Get access to a pilot plant paper machine: The task force investigated this option and found several pilot machines available; for example, several universities had such machines and they were available for rent.

Better up-front homework and VoC work: A VoC Task Force was set up, sponsored by the Chief Marketing Officer, to probe how to do this. VoC methods were investigated and some recommended; and VoC became a mandatory step in their idea-to-launch process: time and actions devoted to determine needs, application requirements, operating conditions, customer benefits sought, and so on.

More incentive for the customer: Project teams were directed to seek a better understanding of the value-in-use for customer (the result of better VoC and front-end homework). Further, incentives for the customer were built in (for example, some degree of exclusivity regarding product use).

More selectivity on new-product projects: Management put some tougher gates and policies in place: "Don't do every customer request—only those projects with a demonstrable, visible benefit to the customer and with a strong incentive to cooperate."

Technical issues: Technical skills were rated number one in the world. But a better understanding of the customer problem, benefits sought, and operating conditions would help focus the R&D work.

These five action items were implemented. They dramatically reduced the field trial problem and greatly accelerated the innovation process—another value stream analysis success!

Suggestion: Get rid of the waste, bureaucracy, and excess baggage! If it does not add value, cut it out. Use methods borrowed from the field of lean manufacturing, including value stream analysis to identify non-value-added activities; and use root cause analysis to rectify problematic steps and tasks in your process.

4. METRICS, TEAM ACCOUNTABILITY, AND CONTINUOUS IMPROVEMENT

Next-generation *Stage-Gate* systems build in a tough Post-Launch Review in order to instill accountability for results and, at the same time, foster a culture of continuous improvement. Continuous improvement is one of the main tenets of lean manufacturing and lends itself readily to application in the field of product innovation.

Continuous improvement in new-product development has three major elements:[17]

a. *Having performance metrics in place.* These metrics measure how well a specific new-product project performed. For example, were the product's profits on target? Was it launched on time?

b. *Establishing team accountability for results.* All members of the project team are fully responsible for performance results when measured against these metrics.

c. *Building in learning and improvement.* When the project team misses the target, or when deficiencies occur, focus on fixing the cause—stop this from happening again—rather than putting a Band-Aid on the symptom, or worse yet, punishing the team.

An example: At Emerson Electric, traditionally, post-launch reviews were absent in most divisions' new-product efforts. But in the new release of Emerson's idea-to-launch process (NPD 2.0), a post-launch review is very evident. Here, project teams are held accountable for key financial and time metrics that were established and agreed to much earlier in the project. When gaps or deficiencies between forecasts and reality are identified, root causes for these variances are sought and continuous improvement takes place.[18]

Emerson benefits in three ways. First, estimates of sales, profits, and time-to-market are much *more realistic* now that project teams are held accountable for their attainment. Second, with clear objectives, the project team can focus and work diligently to achieve them: Expectations are clear. Finally, if the team misses the target, causes are sought and improvements to the process are made so as to prevent a recurrence of the cause—using closed-loop feedback and learning.

> Team accountability is achieved by putting metrics in place and holding a full Post-Launch Review. Build in continuous improvement—no punishment!

It works much the same way at Procter & Gamble:[19] "Winning in the marketplace is the goal. In many firms, too much emphasis is on getting through the process; that is, getting one's project approved or preparing deliverables for the next gate. In the past, P&G was no different. (By contrast, the great majority of businesses still do not conduct post-launch reviews on projects; and even fewer hold their project teams accountable for achieving agreed-to project results)." Instead, this P&G principle emphasizes winning in the marketplace as the goal, not merely going through the process. The text continues: "Specific success criteria for each gate relevant to that stage are defined for each project. Examples include: expected profitability, launch date, expected sales, and even interim metrics, such as test results expected in a subsequent stage. These criteria, and targets to be achieved on them, are agreed to by the project team and management at each gate." And the project team is held accountable post-launch for achieving results when measured against these success criteria.

The Post-Launch Review is the final *point of accountability* for the project team. Actual results achieved are determined, then compared to the projections—to the original success criteria. Accountability issues are high on the agenda of this vital review: Did the team achieve what was promised when measured against the success criteria?

Continuous Learning

Continuous learning and improvement must be in place, too: If results are measured and deficiencies are identified but no action is taken, the same mistakes keep getting repeated. Thus, at the Post-Launch Review, when a project team

Figure 5.7: Undertake a Thorough Post-Launch Review

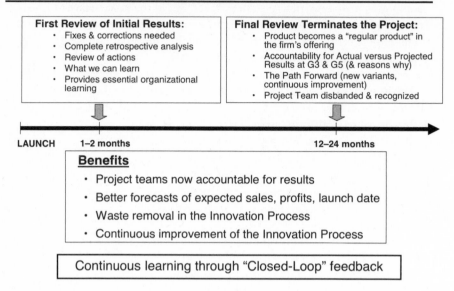

misses the target, a *root cause analysis* ensues to determine the cause of the deficiency and to prevent its recurrence. The focus is on continuous improvement—a learning organization—rather than on blaming the team and creating a culture of fear and retribution.

> *An example:* EXFO Engineering (winner of the PDMA's outstanding corporate innovator award) boasts a solid *Stage-Gate* system, coupled with an outstanding portfolio-management process. EXFO has added an additional gate in its process—Gate 5—whose purpose is to ensure the proper closing of the project (Launch is Gate 4.1 in this company's numbering scheme). At this final post-launch gate meeting, management reviews the project to be sure that all the outstanding issues (manufacturing, quality, sales ramp-up, and project) have been addressed and closed. Feedback is presented based on a survey of initial customers; the project postmortem is reviewed, which highlights the project's good and bad points, as are the recommendations for improvement from the team. Typically, Gate 5 occurs about three months after initial product delivery to customers. Additionally, sales performance and profitability (return on investment, or ROI) of the project are monitored for the first two years of the life of the product.[20]

The Post-Launch Review

Many companies adopt a double Post-Launch Review, as shown in Figure 5.7. The first review takes place shortly after launch, while team members are still available. An initial results assessment is undertaken, and corrections and fixes needed are identified. Most important, the team conducts a *retrospective analysis of the project*—a blow-by-blow review of their project from beginning to end. This assessment is much like the value stream analysis outlined above, except that it is for a real project recently completed. Once the map of the project is created, then the four key questions are asked:

- What work was done at this step, stage, or activity?
- How well did we execute this activity? How long did it take?
- In hindsight, was this step or activity really needed?
- If so, how could we have done it better? How could we have done it faster?

The goal is to gain insights into how to do the next project better and faster: every project better than the one before! This retrospective analysis, or Kaizen exercise, is a key facet of continuous improvement in innovation management.

An example: Kennametal, a major U.S. tool manufacturer (yet another winner of the PDMA's outstanding corporate innovator award), regularly conducts Post-Launch Reviews shortly after launch. The goal is to find ways to improve and accelerate the process. Such reviews have led to the identification of a number of activities that could be done in parallel rather than sequentially, and also tasks and decisions that could be moved forward. For example, the capital request usually is made after the Go to Launch gate, but by moving it forward into the Testing stage, much time could be saved in the case of acquisition of long lead-time production equipment.

The final Post-Launch Review occurs typically twelve to twenty-four months after launch and is the point of final accountability for the project team. It is here that the project team presents the results achieved versus the commitments made at both Gates 3 and 5 (two key commitment gates in the system). Often, these results are versus success criteria, as at P&G, such as:

- First year sales—actual versus promised
- Profitability (for example, revised NPV based on one year's operating results) versus forecasted
- Launch date (on time or late?)
- Customer satisfaction achieved

This final Post-Launch Review occurs in front of the senior gatekeepers—the same group that approved the project at the two money gates, Gates 3 and 5. Note that the project team remains accountable for the results of the project, although its members have probably moved on to other tasks before this review occurs. The project is formally terminated as a "new-product project" and becomes a "regular product" in the firm's product portfolio.

Suggestion: Build in a tough Post-Launch Review—perhaps two reviews as in Figure 5.7—and ensure that project teams remain accountable for promised results until this review takes place. Most firms don't! When gaps are spotted, shift into a mode of continuous improvement, taking steps to prevent the problem from recurring. But avoid punishment—there is a fine line between accountability and punishment; innovation and creativity cannot flourish in a culture of fear!

5. *STAGE-GATE* FOR "OPEN INNOVATION"

Major corporations face a major threat—the fact that their own internal R&D has not been the engine of innovation in their industries and that they have missed opportunity after opportunity. Indeed, many of the breakthrough ideas, products, and technologies over the last decades have come from outside major corporations.[21] For example, lots of ideas, inventions, and innovations come from smaller, entrepreneurial start-ups funded by venture capitalists.[22] Many of these create breakthrough technologies and ideas and new business models to disrupt established categories and markets. Thus, competitive advantage now often comes from leveraging the discoveries of others. And the implication of that trend is unavoidable.

> "Open innovation" is here to stay. Create an *Open Innovation Stage-Gate* system to handle these projects and put in place the infrastructure, new metrics, and the culture change to make open innovation work.

Does your organization suffer too much from NIH—the "not invented here" syndrome? Leading companies have recognized the need for *open innovation*—for a healthy balance between internally and externally generated ideas and new products. And they have put in place the processes, IT support, teams, and culture to *leverage external partners and alliances* in the quest for new ideas, inventions, and innovations from outside the firm.

Stage-Gate has thus been modified to accommodate *open innovation*. Companies, such as Kimberly Clark, Air Products & Chemicals, GE, BASF, and P&G, have moved to *open innovation*. In doing so, they have modified their *Stage-Gate* process—built in the necessary flexibility, capability, and systems—in order to enable this network of partners, alliances, and outsourced vendors from idea generation right through to launch. For example, P&G's SIMPL 3.0 version of its *Open Stage-Gate* system is designed to handle externally derived ideas, IP, technologies, and even fully developed products; and some GE companies have also reinvented *Stage-Gate* (its Toll-Gate system) to handle open innovation, both outbound and inbound.[23]

In the traditional or *closed innovation model*, inputs come from internal and some external sources—customer inputs, marketing ideas, marketplace information, or strategic planning inputs. Then, the R&D organization proceeds with the task of inventing and developing new products or technologies for commer-

Figure 5.8: *Open Innovation Stage-Gate* Features External Interfaces (In-Bound and Out-Bound) at Multiple Points in the Process

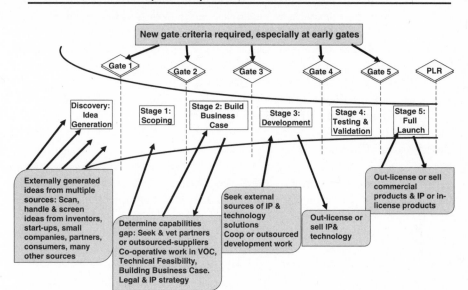

cialization, immediately or at a later date.[24] By contrast, in open innovation, *companies look inside-out and outside-in, across all three aspects of the innovation process*, including ideation, development, and commercialization. In doing so, much more value is created and realized throughout the process—see Figure 5.8. For example:[25]

Ideation or Discovery Stage

Here, not only do companies look externally for customer problems to be solved or unmet needs to be satisfied, but now also to inventors, start-ups, small entrepreneurial firms, partners, the general public, and other sources of available ideas and technologies that can be used as a basis for internal or joint development. Thus, an *external idea scanning, scouting, handling, and screening system* must be built into *Open Stage-Gate.*

New "open innovation" activities that are incorporated into this early Discovery stage include:[26]

✓ Identification of existing and embryonic technologies, leading players and strategic analysis—a focus on state-of-the-art.
✓ Mapping of pertinent local and global technical expertise.
✓ Use of technical watch tools for discovering potential partnerships, collaboration opportunities, and new ideas (for example, Goldfire, Innography).

- ✓ Establishing a scouting group to seek out entrepreneurs, small businesses, and innovators (for example, at conferences, trade shows, online).
- ✓ Accessing trend experts and agencies that map or hunt trends (for example, www.trendhunter.com).
- ✓ External benchmarking (industry forecasts, road maps, and innovation strategies).
- ✓ Holding and promoting value-added research consortia.
- ✓ Actively soliciting external ideas via Web pages and contests (more on these approaches in the next chapter).

Building the Business Case

New tasks are now incorporated in this critical pre-development stage, including actions that involve potential partners or outsourced suppliers that will provide technological or marketing capabilities to develop and commercialize the product. Such "open innovation" actions include:

- ✓ Identifying the need for partners or outsourced suppliers early in your project (identifying missing internal capabilities).
- ✓ External calls for "expressions of interest" for partners and collaborators.
- ✓ Seeking potential partners or suppliers and vetting candidates (including mechanisms and criteria for guiding the choice of partners).
- ✓ Developing partnering strategies.
- ✓ Handling the IP and legal issues with external firms—developing an IP strategy for the project.
- ✓ Cooperatively undertaking VoC work and technical feasibility work—the two partner project teams working together.
- ✓ Building the Business Case with your partner.
- ✓ Executing the various legal documents, including, for example, a memorandum of understanding (probably in Stage 1), a letter of intent (probably in Stage 2), and a legal contract (exiting Gate 3).

An example: To facilitate the legal aspects of open innovation, Hydro Québec has developed an internal Web page that contains all the legal document templates for project teams to use and guidelines for their use. This has proven to be a great help to project team members, who were often mystified by the legal facets of partnering projects.

Development Stage

In the *Open Stage-Gate* system, companies seek help in solving technology and development problems from suppliers, partners, or independent technical people external to the corporation and thus build in "partners" in this stage. Additionally, operational project management tools that include external players in internal innovation processes are used here. Further, the option to acquire external innovations that have already become productized or even commercialized by others must also be built in.

In another form of "open innovation," in the Development stage, companies can *out-license* or sell technologies and intellectual property that are internally developed but are determined to be outside the core business. Thus, seeking of potential buyers and out-licensing or IP-selling actions might be built into this stage.

Launch or Commercialization Stage

The *Open Stage-Gate* system allows the business to sell or out-license already commercialized products when more value can be realized elsewhere; or to in-license—acquiring an already commercialized product that provides immediate sources of new growth for the company.

Running the Gates

External partners are often invited to gate meetings throughout the *Stage-Gate* system, and the decision to move forward is made jointly. Clearly having both executive groups attending changes the flavor of the gate meeting, and thus it's imperative that agreed gate procedures be used. For example, what happens in the event of a "split vote"? More on gating procedures and details in Chapter 9.

Go/Kill or *investment criteria* must also be modified in the *Open Stage-Gate* system. In the traditional gating model, criteria such as "leverages our core competencies" and "strategic fit with our business" are no longer directly applicable (or must be adjusted). For example:

- In the open innovation gating system, not having all the capabilities to develop or execute a project—whether marketing or technological—is not a "Kill," but leads to seeking a partner or outsourced supplier to handle the missing elements. And so new criteria must be introduced, dealing with partner or supplier vetting and selection and their capabilities.
- Similarly, not having a strategic fit with your business, traditionally a "Kill" outcome, could lead instead in the *Open Stage-Gate* model to selling the technology or out-licensing the product.

Thus, different sets of gate criteria must be developed for the *Open Stage-Gate* system.

Performance Metrics

Traditional performance metrics, such as percentage of sales by new products or on-time performance must be augmented with new metrics that capture how well the open facet of your "open innovation" is working. Examples of such metrics include:

- Value-created indicator: tracks the value of partner and collaborator contributions.
- Openness indicator: Ratio of the number of partnerships or collaborative efforts at Stages 1 and 2 to the total number of projects at Stages 1 and 2.[27]

Organization and Infrastructure

Open innovation is not free: The necessary people and infrastructure must be put in place to make it work. Companies have installed the necessary organization to seek and handle external ideas and IP: For example, BASF and Hydro Québec have created Scouting Groups; and Swarovski (the Austrian crystal company) has set up its I-Lab. Other firms have dedicated groups not only to seek ideas but to manage the entire open innovation process, working closely with outside sources of innovation and technology: for example; P&G's Connect & Develop team; Nokia's Venturing Group; and Air Products Corporate Technology Partnerships Group.

Suggestion: If "open innovation" is in your plans, then put in place the necessary systems, IT support, and organization—a *scouting, connect, and development* team—to handle open innovation. This also includes a highly modified *Stage-Gate* system for open innovation projects, as in Figure 5.8.

One word of caution, however: Many different types of development projects fall under the general heading "open innovation." There is both *outbound* innovation (in which you license or sell the technology or developed product to others) as well as *inbound* (in which you seek ideas, solutions, IP, development, and marketing help from external others). These two types of projects are quite different, and thus both types require *different open innovation Stage-Gate models*.

In a similar vein, *where* the external interface occurs—in the idea stage, during Development, or at Launch—also creates different types of projects: Seeking external ideas is quite different than development with a partner or supplier, which is a different type of project than in-licensing a finished product.

So don't expect a "one-size-fits-all" solution. Determine which open innovation model is the logical one for you (inbound, outbound, ideation, co-development, licensing-in, licensing-out, or co-marketing) and develop the appropriate *Open Stage-Gate* system(s) for that open innovation model. It will resemble your normal *Stage-Gate* approach, but will have some important differences, too.

6. LIFE CYCLE MANAGEMENT AND *STAGE-GATE*

Progressive companies integrate the idea-to-launch process with "life after launch," namely, Product Life Cycle Management. The goal is to ensure that the product development team simply does not dwell solely on the immediate development of its project and fail to consider the future. Saab Aerospace (Sweden) has integrated its well-crafted stage-and-gate process into a life cycle management model; it begins with idea generation and goes right through to product phase-out and end of technical support . . . many years into the future.

Goals of Life Cycle Management

The main goals of life cycle management are to ensure that there is a vision for where the development project is heading, long after the initial launch period, and that investments in the project also consider the long term. A second goal is to identify some of the "must do" initiatives that will be required as part of the new product's evolutionary plan, so that these subsidiary projects can get under way in time for when they are needed.

> Your *life cycle model*—from idea to launch and through to product exit and termination—includes *Stage-Gate,* but a number of other gates and stages as well.

Another goal—and this is important to firms that must spend millions supporting their current products—is to map out the new product's exit strategy, including when support will no longer be needed for the new product years ahead (or alternately, what other company products must be pruned in order to make room for the new product, and their exit strategies). The motivation here is that if new products keep getting added to the product line, and no plans are made for removing existing products, the business's product offering gets heavier and heavier, and thus more difficult to support.

Finally, for some firms, the product life cycle plan deals with product disposal—for example, how to dispose of, recycle, or reuse the components in ten-year-old automobiles ready for that junk pile.

The Life Cycle Stage-Gate Model

A typical life cycle model is shown in Figure 5.9, with nine gates or decision points from idea to phase-out.[28] The right side of the diagram contains the traditional product development gates, namely, Gates 1–5 in *Stage-Gate*, plus some broader decisions: when to include the project in the product road map and when in the development portfolio. The first gates are:

G-1: Idea screen, analysis of the opportunity
G-2: Opportunity approved or rejected as a road map candidate, mini-business case approved
G-3: Development approved, opportunity included in the development portfolio
G-4: Start of investment in commercialization and marketing; field trials approved; visibility in product catalog; approval of PLC Plan
G-5: Commercial launch, start of Sales.

After the commercialization gate, Gate 5, there are four more gates that continue through to phase-out and termination:

Figure 5.9: Build *Stage-Gate* (right side) into Your Product Life Cycle Management Model

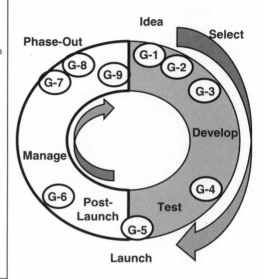

G-1: Idea screen, analysis of the opportunity
G-2: Project approved as roadmap candidate, mini-business case approved
G-3: Development approved, project included in the development portfolio
G-4: Start of investment in commercialization & marketing, field trials, production trials approved, approval of PLC Plan
G-5: Commercial launch, start of Sales & Production
G-6: Post-Launch Review; product approved for all markets, declared successful, project team disbanded. Product Evolution Plan implemented

Then follows a long period of product management & evolvement (G-6 to G-7):

G-7: Start of Phase-Out, considering commercial impacts & plan to transition users
G-8: Successful end of Phase-Out Plan & decide/announce end-of-support date; migrate remaining users
G-9: End of Life – product terminated

G-6:   Product is available for all markets, acceptance of the quality and business model.

Then some years may pass.

G-7:   Start of Phase-Out, considering commercial impacts and last-time-buy date
G-8:   Confirmation of Phase-Out Plan and end-of-support date
G-9:   End of Life—product terminated.

The life cycle plan thus takes the project beyond the first few months of launch, and indeed many years into the future. The life cycle plan deals with many product and marketing elements such as:

- *Expected sales and revenues*, beyond the launch period, so that these can also be factored into the initial investment decisions. For example, a new product may be projected to achieve an admirable two-year payback period (recover its development and launch costs in two years), and a respectable NPV. So not much thought is given to sales and profits beyond the time horizon of the payback or NPV calculation. But if the vision is for the product to continue on for many years, and to evolve into a full and robust product family, then this financial vision must be factored into the original investment decisions—for example, the decision may be to spend even more in the early days to build a stronger foundation and team—perhaps even a platform for growth, and in effect invest for the longer-term future.

- *Product strategy and the product evolution plan*, noting which new versions, updates, and extensions of the new product will be required after the initial launch, and their timing.
- *Pricing over the life cycle*—for example, that initial pricing might be premium in order to skim the high-value users, and then shift lower as volumes and competition both increase, moving more to a penetration pricing strategy over time.
- *Positioning, promotion, and marketing communications*—the plan may be to shift the marketing, communication, and positioning emphasis over the life cycle, as the product ages and meets heavier competition.
- *Used products (or pre-owned products)*—decisions are required on the strategy for used products after initial purchasers begin to sell them (or refurbishing products and extending their life); or a decision not to be involved in these secondary markets.
- *Product disposal*—how to deal with the worn-out product at the end of its life, but in a responsible way. For example, can components be reused or recycled? And can the original product design build in reusability and recyclability, making disposal easier or greener?
- *Product phase-out*—how and when to stop selling and producing the "new" product once it is old, and a plan to deal with the current population of owners. (Alternately, the new product's life cycle plan can also deal with the phase-out of other company products that will no longer be needed as a result of this new product—in order to make room for the new product—and how their exit strategies will be handled. A "pruning" or culling exercise is sometimes part of the life cycle plan. Such strategic considerations regarding existing products overlap traditional *product-line portfolio management*.)

An example: Product managers in banks face huge legacy problems every time they withdraw an aging financial service. Although the new product may be many times better than the old product, many bank customers will prefer to stay with the old product—inconvenient to switch, happy with the old product, know how to use it, nothing new I must learn, and so on. Thus, the product manager faces the difficult challenge of when to phase out the old product (stop selling it), when to terminate support for the old product, and how to migrate the old customers to the replacement product. Unless this strategy is in place, the bank's existing product portfolio gets larger and larger, with mounting costs to support these old legacy products, most of which are IT-based.

Integrating *Stage-Gate* into a more comprehensive life cycle plan makes sense for many organizations, and indeed the proposed life cycle plan is often a required deliverable to Gates 4 and 5 in *Stage-Gate*. Note, however, that the right side of Figure 5.9 is essentially the same *Stage-Gate* system we saw in Chapter 4, typically taking place over a one- to two-year period, and with some additions noted above. But once past Gate 5 and into the left side of Figure 5.9, the time horizon increases dramatically, uncertainties mount as forecasts that far out are difficult, and the time between gates is years rather than months. In spite of the challenges, however, integrating *Stage-Gate* into the life cycle model is considered a best practice.

Suggestion: Life cycle management is practiced in an increasing number of firms; and many others should begin looking into the concept—managing products from idea through to launch, and then well beyond launch, even to product exit and death. Issues such as product evolution (extension, updates, modifications) as well as product termination, transitioning of customers, and product disposal or recycle, are vital issues and should be part of this life cycle plan.

If your current product portfolio is getting heavier and heavier, and new products keep getting added, with no plans to withdraw old products; or if product evolution is problematic; or if product disposal or recycle is a concern, then it's time to extend your idea-to-launch system and transform it into a life cycle model. The chart in Figure 5.9 provides a guide.

7. AUTOMATED *STAGE-GATE* SYSTEMS

Progressive companies recognize that automation greatly enhances the effectiveness of their new-product process.[29] Although many companies have attempted to implement a solid idea-to-launch process, often a business struggles with adoption. That is because, too often, the processes they've put in place are administratively burdensome and difficult to use.

Software Reduces the Workload

One increasingly popular way of enabling process adoption and adherence is the use of *automation software*. The benefits of automation are twofold: Less time is required to complete process activities and deliverables; and the administrative task load associated with process execution is dramatically reduced. For example, project team members can more easily create gate deliverables, search for documents, and perform other routine

> Excellent certified software exists to automate *Stage-Gate*. The payoffs are significant in time and work savings.

tasks because they have ready access to embedded templates and best-practice content. Some automating systems pre-populate templates for key deliverables (such as status reports, presentations, and resource charts) with project information that has been recorded elsewhere in the system. As a result, documents and other materials that previously took hours or days to prepare can be completed in minutes. The templates further serve as how-to references that project team members follow as they complete tasks, helping to ensure that key process steps are followed. Automation can also help project leaders by providing them with pre-formatted models for the creation of new projects, including definitions for each stage and gate and listings of corresponding deliverables. Such pre-formatted models also help to ensure consistency in process execution.

Streamlines Communications

Another benefit associated with *Stage-Gate* automation is the streamlining of communications and knowledge sharing among project team members and with gatekeepers or executives. Everyone from project team member to senior executive has access to the right view of relevant information—the information that they need to move their project forward, to cooperate with other team members globally on vital tasks, to stay on top of projects, or to help make the Go/Kill decision. By allowing critical project information to be stored in one central location, automating software makes it possible for the *Stage-Gate* process manager or project leader to assign and track tasks online across multiple product development projects. As team members complete tasks, they can share deliverables, work on them collaboratively, and communicate status reports immediately. This greatly simplifies the project reporting process for the project leader.

Automation also gives executives the ability to view all the active projects in their business's product portfolio at a glance and to drill down into the details of individual projects. For example, most of the automation systems have extensive built-in portfolio management tools, complete with the portfolio displays such as those outlined in Chapter 8. These displays are generated automatically from the software database. Having access to this information allows executives to spot at-risk projects, to rank projects (for example, according to criteria such as NPV, the productivity index, or the project score, or any other stored parameter or characteristic of projects), or to determine the impact of shifts in resource allocations and project priorities on the product portfolio.

Certified Software for Stage-Gate

In order to realize these benefits of information access, decision-support system, and time savings, automation software tools are increasingly being adopted by leading businesses and must be considered part of the next-generation *Stage-Gate* system. Many of these tools integrate strategy, portfolio management, *Stage-Gate*, resource management, and idea management—a business-decision support system for making new-product investment decisions more effectively and efficiently. A number of software products designed to support *Stage-Gate* systems have been reviewed and are certified "*Stage-Gate* ready"—see www.stage-gate.com.

Additionally, standard off-the-shelf versions of *Stage-Gate*—a "*Stage-Gate* in a box"—as well as Web-based versions, also exist. These *Stage-Gate* tools, although not automation per se, also facilitate the implementation and use of an idea-to-launch process. They can also be quickly adapted and implemented in your business (see, for example, SG-Navigator™).[30]

Suggestion: Many larger firms have invested in software in support of their *Stage-Gate* process. In the last decade, such software solutions have made enormous gains, so that today the various software products improve just about every facet of product development from idea capture and handling through to resource management. And the many legitimate case studies from these solutions suppliers show positive results, including significantly increased productivity. However, be sure to check out the validity of the various software offerings and only use *Stage-Gate Certified* software.

COMMON ERRORS IN DESIGNING A NEXT-GENERATION *STAGE-GATE* SYSTEM
Misapplying Cost-Cutting Models to Innovation Projects

A number of companies have implemented methods such as Six Sigma and Lean Manufacturing and then tried inappropriately to apply this same methodology to the innovation process. Wrong! Six Sigma was originally designed to reduce product defects and improve product quality, hence the term "Six Sigma," or six standard deviations in terms of defect rates. Later, when popularized at GE, the method evolved to encompass cost-reduction and problem-solving activities. But it was never intended, nor should it be used, as an idea-to-launch new-product process. Why? Simply because the method *assumes a problem* and then converges on a solution; but it fails to allow for divergent, creative, and right-brain behavior that typifies the fuzzy front end of most firms' innovation processes. A noted Six Sigma expert acknowledges that the "define, measure, analyze, improve, control" (DMAIC) mindset doesn't entirely gel with the fuzzy front-end of invention. "When an idea starts germinating, you don't want to overanalyze it, which can happen in a traditional DMAIC framework."[31]

Consider the predicament that 3M found itself in when a number of 3M businesses replaced their successful innovation processes with Six Sigma. As noted in a *Business Week* article:[32]

> The very factors that make Six Sigma effective in one context can make it ineffective in another. While process excellence demands precision, consistency, and repetition, innovation calls for variation, failure, and serendip-

ity. The impact of the Six Sigma regime at 3M was that more predictable, incremental work took precedence over blue-sky research. "You're supposed to be having something that was going to be producing a profit, if not next quarter, it better be the quarter after that," a former 3M researcher says. Defenders of Six Sigma at 3M claim that a more systematic new-product introduction process allows innovations to get to market faster. But Fry, the Post-it note inventor, disagrees. In fact, he places the blame for 3M's recent lack of innovative sizzle squarely on Six Sigma's application in 3M's research labs.[33]

Similarly Lean Manufacturing methods work well in the factory to reduce waste and non-value-added activities. But be careful in the overzealous application of lean methods to the innovation process—manufacturing is a very different process than innovation.

Trying to Do Portfolio Management Without a Stage-and-Gate Process

Some executives mistakenly believe that they can get by with only portfolio management and no stage-and-gate process in place. The argument is that their gates lack the real teeth necessary to make Go/Kill decisions and prioritize projects, and so portfolio management is the answer. Earlier, the point was made that Go/Kill and prioritization decisions occur at the gates; but the gates must have teeth!

An effective *Stage-Gate* system is essential to sound portfolio management for several reasons. First, by having tough gates in place, the poorer projects are eliminated early in the process—through the funneling effect—and thus the overall result is a better portfolio. Perhaps more important is that a solid stage-and-gate process leads to *data integrity:* Best practices and key tasks built into the stages insure that better data are acquired, while the gates define what information is required from the project team—the deliverables.

Data integrity (or its lack) is one of the top issues identified in a recent APQC portfolio management study.[34] Without a good *Stage-Gate* process in place, project teams are left on their own about what data to gather and how to obtain it. The end result is that inconsistent data are gathered on projects, and in different ways. Thus, it becomes difficult to compare and rank projects against each other, and so effective portfolio management is next to impossible.

Too Much Reliance on Software as a Solution

Some product developers see IT tools solving everything. Not so: The mistaken belief is that the purchase of a software tool will be a substitute for a robust idea-to-launch process or can be the fix for an ineffective innovative system. Software is *a great facilitator* of a stage-and-gate process, yielding many benefits. For example, software tools available for *Stage-Gate* enable project team members to communicate more effectively and to work on shared documents; they provide an electronic *Stage-Gate* manual, complete with all deliverables templates, lists of tasks within stages, and accompanying worksheets; and they track projects and provide tailored views of all the projects in the pipeline. Thus, IT can greatly facilitate the implementation and use of *Stage-Gate*. But an IT tool per se is not a substitute for a robust idea-to-launch process: You need a solid innovation process first, and then software becomes the enabler.

Other IT issues are that the software is too cumbersome and may even overwhelm project teams. Additionally, some software requires a lot of unexpected work to configure. Finally, a few software vendors oversell their products, and make unsupported claims, such as that their software is *Stage-Gate* ready when it is not. When seeking IT in support of your innovation process, take a very close look, ask many questions, and use certified software.[35]

Expecting the Impossible from a Process

Stage-Gate is not a panacea, and it's only one piece of the puzzle. As the creator of P&G's SIMPL *Stage-Gate* process notes: "*Stage-Gate* is not stand-alone. Not recognizing this slowed us down—it took us five years to learn this, and five years to implement it [get a solution]."[36]

Many companies face myriad problems in product innovation. The installation of a visible idea-to-launch process is too often assumed to be the magic bullet, the hope being that all these other problems will disappear. Actually, quite the reverse is true. By making the innovation process much more visible and transparent, the other weaknesses in the firm's approach and methods become even more apparent.

> *An example:* Many companies suffer from too many projects and not enough resources to do them well. In short, there is gridlock in the development pipeline, and not much gets through. Although *Stage-Gate* may bring some relief—the gates will kill some weaker projects and thus free resources—the full solution is likely to lie elsewhere, perhaps via a resource capacity analysis or the implementation of an effective resource-tracking and portfolio-management system. For example, P&G's Initiatives Diamond shows its SIMPL stage-and-gate system as one and only one of the four pillars of success.[37] Two others are portfolio management and resource allocation. All three must work together.

MAKING IT WORK

An effective *Stage-Gate* system yields positive results in terms of getting new products and services to market quickly, efficiently, and profitably. The fact that many well-managed companies have made it work to their advantage is the proof. At the same time, as with any management approach, some struggle with the concept. Chapter 4 outlined the background, theory, and some of the details of *Stage-Gate*. And some new approaches that firms have built into their next-generation *Stage-Gate* systems have been outlined in this chapter—making the system more flexible, adaptive, and scalable; streamlining the system and removing waste and bureaucracy; incorporating accountability and continuous improvement; adapting the system to include "open innovation" and life cycle management; and finally, automating the system via IT.

6

DISCOVERY—THE QUEST FOR BREAKTHROUGH IDEAS

Lack of money is no obstacle. Lack of an idea is an obstacle.
—Ken Hakuta, American inventor, author, and TV personality

A SHORTAGE OF BLOCKBUSTER NEW-PRODUCT IDEAS

Most companies don't lack for ideas—*they lack for big ideas!* In spite of the desire for breakthrough new products, recent data suggest that quite the opposite is occurring. We saw in Chapter 1 that the nature of new-product development portfolios has shifted dramatically—away from bolder, larger, and more innovative projects to smaller, lower-risk projects (see Figure 1.1). Clearly, companies cannot achieve their aggressive product-innovation goals if they continue to focus on small, incremental development products and projects.

The quest for competitive advantage and achieving significant increases in sales and profits though product innovation means that the portfolio of projects must change. Making that happen will require new, bold, and innovative product ideas—*some real game-changers and blockbuster ideas*. Of many management practices studied in a major investigation of innovation, five top best practices were identified, including having an idea-to-launch process, resource management, an innovation strategy, and market insights—see Figure 6.1. But of these five important drivers, *idea management has the strongest impact*.[1] Having effective idea management results in a dramatic extra 7.2 percent of sales from new products!

Feeding the Innovation Funnel

The trigger for your *Stage-Gate*® system is a new-product idea: in other words, when technological possibilities are matched with market needs and expected market demand. A good new-product idea can make or break

> Of the five most important drivers of businesses' new-product performance, idea management has the strongest impact.

Figure 6.1: The Five Most Important Drivers of New-Product Performance

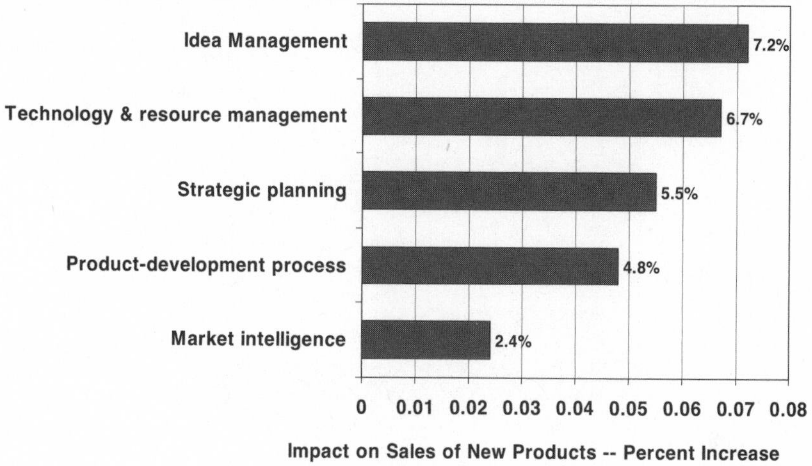

Idea Management — 7.2%

Technology & resource management — 6.7%

Strategic planning — 5.5%

Product-development process — 4.8%

Market intelligence — 2.4%

0   0.01   0.02   0.03   0.04   0.05   0.06   0.07   0.08

Impact on Sales of New Products -- Percent Increase

Source: A.D. Little Innovation Excellence Study, endnote 1.

the project: Ideas are the *feedstock for the innovation process.* But don't expect a well-oiled new-product process to make up for a shortage of quality ideas: If the idea was mundane to start with, don't count on your *Stage-Gate* process to turn it into a star!

Our major benchmarking study reveals that only 19 percent of businesses have a proficient ideation front-end to feed their development funnel; and only 31 percent of firms have an effective method for selecting which ideas to invest in—see Figure 6.2.[2] To a certain extent, the Best Innovating businesses model the way in this benchmarking study: More than three times as many Best Innovators boast well-executed ideation when compared to the poorer-performing firms. But even among Best Innovators, there is much room for improvement. Similarly, 54 percent of Best Innovators have an effective idea-screening system in place, almost four times as many as for poor-performing firms.

So important is idea generation that I now treat this as a separate stage in the *Stage-Gate* system, namely, the "Discovery stage." In earlier editions of this book, the idea stage was treated as a given and portrayed as a light bulb in the model: It was always assumed that there are lots of ideas sitting around waiting to be worked on. This may be true for some firms, but even here, the *quality of these ideas is lacking*—lots of little ideas. So a vital facet of a successful new-product effort is designing and installing an effective idea-generating system.

Suggestion: Review your new-product pipeline. Is there a shortage of really great projects—products that promise major revenues or will have a high impact on

Figure 6.2: Best Innovators Have Superior Idea Generation & Handling Practices Versus the Rest of Firms

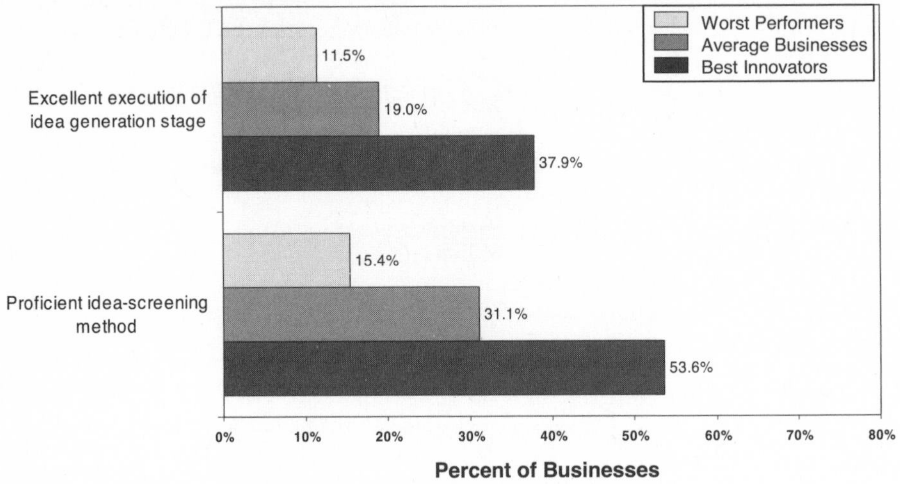

Source: Benchmarking study, endnote 2.

your business? If so, maybe it's because you're neglecting the Discovery stage of the process. Ask yourself some questions: Where do new-product ideas come from? Where should they be coming from? Are the ideas good ones? How does your company actively solicit new-product ideas? Do you have a new-product idea-generating system? If the answers to these questions make you uneasy, don't worry: This chapter suggests some concrete actions that can be taken to improve idea generation.

WHERE TO START? A PRODUCT INNOVATION AND TECHNOLOGY STRATEGY

A prerequisite to effective idea generation is having a *product innovation strategy for your business*. This strategy, among other things, defines the *arenas of strategic focus* or "strategic arenas"—in short, where you want to focus your R&D efforts and thus where you want to hunt for ideas. The development of a product innovation and technology strategy for your business is a huge topic and hence beyond the scope of this book.[3]

These *strategic arenas* must be both attractive (large, growing markets; weak competition; good opportunities to develop new products) and where you can leverage your core competencies in technology, marketing, and production to advantage. The hope is that you select arenas that will be *your next engines of growth*—"oasis arenas," lush with rich fruit and full of many bold new-product ideas!

These arenas become your idea "search fields." Delineating *search fields* or *strategic arenas* is important for idea and opportunity identification, because it specifies what's in bounds, and perhaps more important, what's out of bounds. This specification makes the quest for great new-product ideas much more directed and focused, hence more effective— you avoid the scattergun approach often found in traditional idea search. Your innovation strategy also helps to provide validation to new ideas: The first question at every gate meeting is: "Does this idea (or project) align with our innovation strategy?" Without a well-defined innovation strategy, it's hard to make the right choices in project selection.

> A product innovation and technology strategy is a prerequisite to effective ideation. It defines the "search fields" and helps to validate new ideas.

SET UP AN IDEA CAPTURE AND HANDLING SYSTEM

Ideas are like grapes on a vine! Unless they are picked, they wither and die. How many times have I heard, "There's no shortage of ideas in our company," but when I ask, "Where are they?" I get blank looks. They're in people's heads, on their computers, in a file—but not moving ahead. Thus, no matter the source of the idea, there must be a mechanism in place to capture the ideas, evaluate them, and then move the promising ones forward. Figure 6.3 shows a typical idea-handling model. So, the place to begin is to install such an idea-management system like the one in Figure 6.3—it's a high-impact best practice, as we saw in Figure 6.1!

Reach out to many sources of ideas, both inside and outside the company, establishing communications or "idea flow lines" to stimulate the flow of ideas. These "flow lines" can be connecting with universities, undertaking formal market research, or having an internal idea contest for employees. More on the best sources and methods later.

Next, consider installing *an incubation center*, as shown in Figure 6.3, where ideas get a chance to breathe and "grow legs." One problem with submitting ideas directly to a business review or gate meeting is that many good ideas are too raw and will be instantly killed: *The best ideas are often the most fragile ones!* The I-Group denoted in Figure 6.3 works on the ideas, massages them, and puts some meat on them prior to a gate review. So when they reach the idea screen, these raw ideas are a little more robust.

Next is the decision gate or idea screen: Gate 1. Here, the best ideas are selected for work and to move forward into Stage 1, and the rest go into the idea vault—they are the dead ideas or on-hold ideas. Some firms have purchased idea-management software that allows others in the company to see the ideas in the vault and make suggestions—an open system much like an online blog.

An example: The Austrian crystal company, Swarovski, seeks about 350 solid new ideas annually and has created a professional front-end or idea-management system in its *Stage-Gate* process, shown in Figure 6.4. Ideas are gathered from many sources, and concurrently, scouting research into

Figure 6.3: Install an Idea-Management System – A Systematic Idea Capture and Handling Process

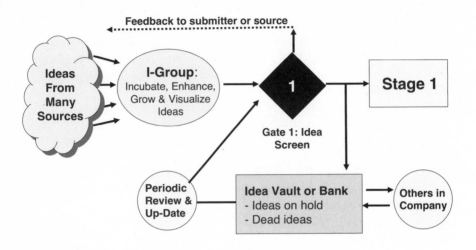

trends, fashion, and technology produces many ideas. These ideas are "sucked" into the system (upper left), where they are subjected to a strategic pre-screen—a "pre-gate"—that poses only strategic, impact, and leverage questions (no financial ones!). Next, members of the i-Lab enhance the idea in the creative and enrichment phase. Then the idea is subjected to an informal evaluation—sent to knowledgeable people in the firm via their internal IT-system, i-Flash—for a quick assessment and feedback. If positive, the idea is "visualized" and developed further, and finally submitted to a business unit's Gate 1, idea screen, in Swarovski's *Stage-Gate* system.[4]

If the idea is Go, usually an interim project leader is assigned, along with a few other people in order to undertake Stage 1, Scoping. Note that Scoping is a preliminary investigation only, so the commitment at Gate 1 is pretty small—the decision does not have to be a perfect one! In fact, the data are so limited and the commitment so small that I recommend a qualitative (nonfinancial) scoring scheme—a scorecard—for this early idea screen.

THE SOURCES OF THE BEST IDEAS

Now the task is to *identify potential sources of ideas to reach out to*: Where do the good ideas come from? And more important, where should they be coming from, and which valuable sources are you missing? We do have some new data on eighteen different sources of new-product ideas that show the *most popular* versus

Figure 6.4: Swarovski's Idea-Management System, Called the i-Lab Process, Feeds Hundreds of Solid and Pre-Screened Ideas to Gate 1

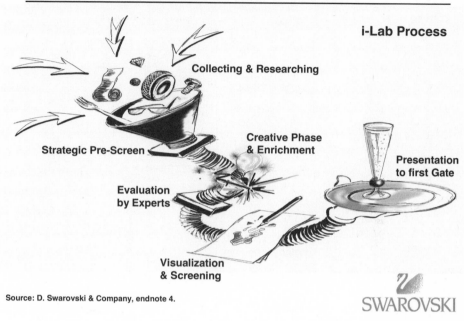

i-Lab Process

Collecting & Researching

Strategic Pre-Screen

Creative Phase & Enrichment

Presentation to first Gate

Evaluation by Experts

Visualization & Screening

SWAROVSKI

Source: D. Swarovski & Company, endnote 4.

the *most effective sources*—see the ideation diagram in Figure 6.5.[5] (Popularity is measured by percentage of firms that extensively use each method, shown on the horizontal axis. Rated effectiveness of each method is shown as a 0–10 scale on the vertical axis in Figure 6.5, but only for users of that method.)

VOICE-OF-CUSTOMER METHODS

Eight voice-of-customer (VoC) methods are highlighted in the ideation diagram of Figure 6.5, including ethnography, focus groups, and lead user analysis.[6] Some VoC methods are very extensively used, notably, customer visit teams, focus groups to identify customer problems, and the lead user method, as noted by the diamonds inside the upper circle in Figure 6.5. Other newer methods, such as ethnography, forming a community of enthusiasts, or letting the customer help design the product, are less popular.

Regardless of popularity, however, VoC methods *are rated highly* by users in terms of effectiveness in generating breakthrough new-product ideas and constitute *the top five best-rated methods*. Indeed, most of the VoC methods fare very well, receiving solid effectiveness scores from users—all in the top half

> Voice-of-customer ideation methods are among the most popular and are rated the most effective sources of new ideas.

Figure 6.5: The *ideation Four-Quadrant* Diagram Shows Effectiveness Versus Popularity For Each of 18 Ideation Methods

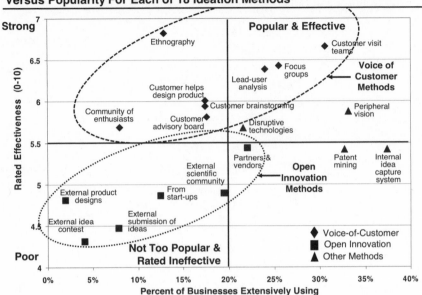

Source: Cooper-Edgett ideation study, endnote 5.

of the ideation quadrant diagram in Figure 6.5. In rank order of effectiveness—best to average—let's look at each VoC method:

1. Ethnographic Research, or "Camping Out"

If you want to study gorillas, a few focus groups is probably not the answer; nor is asking your salespeople about gorillas, or sending out an online survey. What is required is *real field research*—buy a tent and a backpack and move into their village, much like the anthropologist Jane Goodall did.

Ethnography, the term used in marketing for cultural anthropology, involves camping out with customers or observation of customers for extended periods, watching and probing as they use or misuse products. Although ethnography has become a popular topic in product innovation literature, the method is not so popular among practitioners, as seen by its unique location in the upper left quadrant in Figure 6.5. The method sees limited use for ideation, ranking number thirteen in popularity with only 12.9 percent of firms extensively using ethnography. But in spite of its lack of popularity, this method gets *top marks for effectiveness,* with the highest effectiveness rating:

An example: ICI Paints (U.S.) discovered a simple phenomenon through ethnography that led to a major and winning new product. Folks from ICI literally camped out with professional painters who worked in housing developments. Every morning and afternoon, the coffee wagon showed up, and all the workers dropped what they were doing to enjoy a coffee break and perhaps a cigarette outdoors.

The observers watched the painter who was halfway through painting a ceiling white when the coffee break occurred. Upon returning to his task, the paint had dried, so the painter couldn't see which half he had already painted and which was unpainted, especially in the case of the second or third coat. His solution: He simply painted the entire ceiling again—not a problem for the painter, but costly for the contractor: wasted paint and time.

The solution that ICI created: pink paint. The paint goes on pink at first, and stays pink until fully dry, whereupon it turns white. So the painter returning from his break can see in an instant which half of the ceiling is unpainted. A simple solution, indeed almost humorous, if it weren't for the huge payoffs to ICI.

Ethnography is a relatively new method for identifying unmet needs, although this general type of research—cultural anthropology—has been around for many decades. The main advantage is the depth of knowledge that one gains. Thus, of all methods, ethnography provides perhaps the greatest insight into the user's unmet and unarticulated needs, applications, and problems, according to users, and hence is a very powerful source of breakthrough ideas.

The main disadvantage is exactly that: Because it is so deep, it takes much time and is expensive to undertake. On the other hand, look at the payoffs and the fact it is rated number one in terms of effectiveness! The time can be reduced by shortening the length of visit per customer site; for example, Fluke, a manufacturer of handheld instruments, spends about one day per customer site in its "day-in-the-life-of" research. Proxy methods can also be used: For example, Johnsonville Sausage, a major U.S. food producer, installs video cameras in household kitchens to observe consumers as they cook meals, looking for new opportunities for sausages.

Another word of warning is that this observational method relies very much on the skill of the observer. If your people lack observation and listening skills, or are poor at drawing inferences and integrating information, then the method loses effectiveness. Some talent and training is needed.

Additionally, the method does not suit all product types and markets. For example, employing ethnography at a construction site, or in a factory or hospital is quite feasible; but camping out in someone's kitchen or bathroom is a bit more of a challenge. In spite of low usage and some of these limitations, the method is proven to work and is *definitely recommended*!

2. Customer Visit Teams

Here, teams visit customers or users; and they employ in-depth interviews based on a carefully crafted interview guide to uncover user problems, needs, and wants for new products. The method is ranked number four in popularity, with 30.7 percent of firms extensively using this method. Note, however, that the method *is ranked number two by users for effectiveness.* In terms of a combination of popularity and effectiveness, this method is number one—in the far upper right corner in Figure 6.5.

In practice, customer sites are identified and agreement with the customer for such a visit is obtained. If a business-to-business (B2B) customer, the interviewers try to arrange for a small group of customer people to be available, namely, the *key purchase influencers.* The typical interview team is about three people, and is cross-functional—from Marketing, Sales, and Technical. Technical people must be involved so that they can acquire face-to-face learning, too (rather than receiving the information secondhand and filtered).

When conducting the interviews, a structured and well-crafted conversation guide is essential. This guide lays out the questions and topics, ensures completeness and consistency across interviews, and provides a place to record answers. Needs, functions, and benefits sought by users are explored, not just features, and thus the best questions are *indirect and inferential:*

> Example: "When you lie in bed at night and think about this product, what keeps you awake?"

Direct questions, though more obvious, tend to yield obvious answers and hence are not too useful:

> Example: "What do you want in your new product?"

The indirect questions yield much greater insights into users' likes, dislikes, problems, points of pain, and unmet and unspoken needs.

Once the interview is complete, the interview team should do a walkabout, spending time with the customer where the product is actually used. Often, by watching people use, misuse, and abuse the product, further insights into unmet needs are gained.

> *An example:* VoC using visit teams uncovered multiple ideas that led to a new product in the specialized field of hard-surface drills and saws. The company, Dr. Fritsch GmbH, is a small German firm (about 100 people) with annual sales of about 12 million euros. It manufactures production machinery that it sells to customers who produce diamond-hardened tools—grinding wheels, saw blades, drill bits, and the like.
>
> The task was to seek input for a new product in the firm's core market. One of the goals of the VoC study was to find out more about customers' products, their processes, and their customers' requirements, and thus their requirements for new production machinery.
>
> First, the team defined hypotheses about the expected results. This was vital, especially because sales people had often said: "We already knew all of what came out of the VoC research." One of the hypotheses was that a

new product and technique of setting the diamonds introduced by a Taiwanese customer (called Arix*) would not succeed commercially.

Thirty customer visits were undertaken by cross-functional teams of two to three people globally. A "manual" or protocol for the customer visits was created, and everyone on the visit teams was trained before going out to see customers. Questions asked focused on needs, problems, issues, and challenges faced by customers and users. One revelation was that the setting of the diamonds within the cutting segments is critical for customers, and that the new Arix machine was indeed making believers out of skeptics in the marketplace.

The VoC results were then condensed in a workshop involving eighteen people, and an ensuing creativity (brainstorming) session took the VoC input and generated about eighty ideas; these were subsequently pared down to seven "hot topics" and rough concepts. Preliminary work was done on the concepts, and a second evaluation reduced the set to three best bets. The firm finally elected the "ideal product" (now called DiaSet), a technology to set diamonds automatically to yield the desired diamond arrays for the new product. With the product defined conceptually, the technical challenge for Dr. Fritsch was to develop a production technique that could be integrated into the company's sintering machines to help their customers produce pre-set diamond-cutting segments efficiently. But by first understanding the customer needs and requirements, the technical work proceeded more effectively toward a clear target and solution! As this book is being written, the new product is completing one year of sales, and is ahead of target—a success.

There are several points to note in this example: First, this is a relatively small company, thus VoC using field visit teams is not just for larger firms. Second, this is a very technical product category; effective market research can and should be done for such products, and not just restricted to simple consumer products. The study was done globally—it did not focus just on a few nearby and convenient customers. Next, a broad-based workshop was held to interpret the results and insights of the VoC study (too often, when the researchers alone interpret results, they get it wrong). Finally, note that the team had an open mind, so that when VoC results came back that contradicted the original hypothesis, they did the needed 180-degree turn (too often, when VoC results are inconsistent with the views of the product managers or sales force, the research is attacked as "bad research"). One final point is that the small German firm did reach out and get professional help in designing and conducting the study and workshop.[7]

In-depth customer interviews have a number of strengths as a VoC technique. Because customer visits are a *field research technique*, they are valuable for gaining real insights into the customer's world. The major advantage users claim is the ability to identify and focus on customer problems and unspoken needs during these interview sessions, a vital source of product ideas. Additionally, closer

relationships can be developed with customers. And because the interview structure is flexible and the questions are open-ended, they allow the opportunity for
surprises, which might not be gained by other tools such as quantitative research.
Finally, using cross-functional interview teams promotes a shared vision and understanding of what customers need and expect.

The main challenges are getting customers to cooperate (to agree to the session, and to provide honest answers), finding the time to do this valuable study
(in-depth interviews at multiple customer sites do take more effort than most of
the methods), training the interviewers, and designing a robust interview guide
with the right questions. In spite of the challenges, however, this VoC visit team
method is *definitely recommended*!

3. Customer Focus Groups Doing Problem Detection

In this VoC method, focus groups are run with customers or users to identify
needs, wants, and problems, points of pain, and suggestions for new products.
(Note that in product development, focus groups are most often *used to test concepts*, not to generate ideas; this is the exception.) The focus group moderator
skillfully focuses the discussion on problems or wants, and helps users walk
through their problems.

> *An illustration:* A U.S. manufacturer of lawn-and-garden tractors invites a
> group of small tractor owners to a Saturday morning event at a local ex-
> urban hotel. Demonstration tractors are in the parking lot for the invitees
> to ride on and make comments about. Company people mingle with the
> crowd, listening and taking notes.
>
> Having sample products on display as customers gather for the event
> helps to promote discussion and problem detection. Customers are encour-
> aged to interact with the products, make comments, and get in the right
> mood. Company people can also mix with the customers to listen, probe,
> and gain insights, and even video record users as they interact with products
> at the event.
>
> Then the focus group moderator moves the twelve-person customer
> group into a meeting room and begins the focus group discussion with a
> broad nonthreatening question: "Introduce yourself and tell us about your
> lawn tractor." The idea behind focus groups is to start very broadly and then
> to narrow down and focus on specific issues that arise.
>
> The next question is: "Think of the last time you used your tractor and
> something bad happened to you—please tell us about it." As the discussion
> questions become more narrow and focused, issues begin to arise and are
> discussed at great length. Whenever a major issue or serious problem arises,
> the moderator drills down into the issue—she directs the discussion there.
> But solutions are not sought; problems are merely identified and defined.

Meanwhile, in another room, watching the proceedings on closed-circuit television, is a group of company people: design engineers and some marketing people. Once problems are identified by the customer focus group, the company room shifts into brainstorming mode. Solutions are proposed and sketched on flip charts.

Next, the proposed solutions, one flip-chart sheet at a time, are taken into the customer focus group room for discussion and evaluation. Here, the tractor owners rip the conceptual solutions apart, and in so doing, devastate the design engineers still watching all this on TV. And more problems and issues are raised. Armed with this new information and feedback, the design engineers continue brainstorming and come up with even better solutions.

And round and round the process goes—from the brainstorming group to the focus group and then back again. It's a series of iterations, until an ideal solution is proposed—one that the designers think is feasible, and that the customers agree that they like.

Groups are a cost-effective and time-efficient way to tap into the voice of the customer, and thus they get much use, especially in gaining insights in consumer goods markets. The method shares the same strengths as the visit team approach above, namely, the ability to identify problems and to drill down into these problems.

Group discussions involving eight to twelve people are often much more animated, insightful, creative, and provocative than an interview involving just two or three people, simply because one group member feeds off another group member's comments, and the conversation and energy level build. Groups also have the advantage that even though the sample size is small, with care, a reasonably representative group of customers can be assembled fairly easily. Additionally, much of the legwork can be outsourced to a market research firm.

There are several words of caution about groups, however. Challenges include getting the right customers to agree to participate (a particular problem with B2B customers); finding the right moderator with focus group skills and product knowledge; and cost. The sample size of group attendees may be quite limited and may not be totally representative of the market. The small size also makes drawing quantitative conclusions all but impossible. In B2B situations, it is often more difficult to assemble a group of customers from different geographic areas, although a trade show venue can be used. One must also be careful not to invite competitors to the same session. Another drawback is potential biases in the group discussion, for example, that one dominant person sways the entire group to a certain conclusion. Finally, group effectiveness is dependent to a large extent on the skill and neutrality of the group moderator; a biased or ineffective moderator will direct the group to an invalid conclusion or produce few profound conclusions at all. In spite of the challenges, however, this method is *definitely recommended*!

4. Lead-User (Innovative User) Analysis

This VoC method has been around since the 1980s but has only caught on in the last decade. The theory is this: First, your customer has ideas for your next new product. Second, if you work with the average customer, you'll get average ideas. But, if you identify a select group of *innovative* or *lead users* and work closely with them, then expect much more innovative new products.[8] Research by Eric Von Hippel reveals that many commercially important products are initially thought of and even prototyped by users rather than manufacturers. He also found that such products tend to be developed by "lead users"—innovative companies, organizations, or individuals that are well ahead of market trends and even have needs that go far beyond the average user. The trick is to track down lead users, who are by definition rare—on the far right tail of the bell-shaped curve.

The lead-user method has four main steps:[9]

1. Identify the target market and company goals for innovation in this market.
2. Determine the trends: Talk to people in the field who have a broad view of emerging technologies and leading-edge applications.
3. Identify lead users, either via a networking process or a survey. In networking, begin by briefly explaining the quest to people with apparent expertise on the subject: for example, research professionals or people who have written about the topic. Then ask for a referral to someone who has even more relevant knowledge. It's usually not long before one reaches the users at the leading edge of the target market. In a survey approach, customers and users are identified and then contacted, for example, by phone. A cleverly crafted questionnaire asks questions to try to identify more innovative users—for example, for a tool company, one might use questions such as "Have you ever modified this tool?" or "Have you ever tried to build a better tool or jig for this application?"
4. Develop the breakthroughs: Host a workshop with the identified lead users and key in-house technical and marketing people. Participants work in small groups at first, then as a whole, to define final product concepts. Normal group techniques such as brainstorming and inverse brainstorming are used, but the difference is that you are working with abnormal people—folks who are very innovative and creative.

The method is positioned very close to customer focus groups in Figure 6.5 and proves to be quite popular, with 24.0 percent of firms extensively using the approach. And the method is quite effective, ranked number four on average by users.

An example: At Hilti, a leading European manufacturer of demolition, fastening, and concrete drilling equipment, lead-user analysis is extensively used. First, lead users are identified—leading edge, innovative customers in the construction or demolition field. Hilti's direct sales force provides guidance here. Hilti's Innovation Management Department then invites a group of these lead users for a weekend retreat—they watch and they listen, attempting to understand lead users' problems. Suggestions and possible solutions from lead users are fashioned into tentative new-product concepts. Hilti management claims that this lead-user technique has been used with great success across a wide variety of product groups within the company.

The advantage of the method is that innovative customers, who are ahead of the wave, are quite likely to have the industry's next new product, and this method is one way to uncover what it is. And the method works: For example, some businesses at 3M in the United States swear by the approach; others are more neutral in their assessment.

The major challenges are identifying who the innovative users are, getting them to participate in an off-site workshop, and then structuring and running the workshop session properly. Using referrals is one approach to identifying possible participants, but this can be tedious and problematic. 3M surveys customers and asks questions about whether or not the customer has modified the product. This lead-user method is *definitely recommended*.

5. The Customer or User Designs

This novel method has received much attention in recent years and has been made possible in part because of new IT and Internet tools. Here, customers or users are invited to help the product developer design the next new product, and in so doing, provide many ideas for significant product improvement. The "customer designs" method has not caught on widely. But in spite of its limited popularity, however, it *ranks number five in terms of effectiveness* in Figure 6.5.

An example: Witness Lego's Web-based "DesignByMe," which permits you and your child to log on and develop customized Lego kits. Your child downloads a simple CAD software package from the DesignByMe Web page—Lego Digital Designer—so that he can design his own Lego toy.

It's a win-win for everyone. Young designers can create their own designs, even if they don't have all the physical parts at home. They can share their ideas with other "enthusiasts" in the Lego Gallery; and they can order all the parts online for their custom design (including their own custom-designed box). The kit is all delivered to their home at a known price (good news for the parents). The best is: The Lego Product Design Team gets to know what their target customers *really* want!

The big advantage of this method is that informed users are in the best position to design the next breakthrough new product simply because they know their needs and what they want. But the method can only be applied to certain categories of products. For example, allowing users to design products where the science is beyond the knowledge of the user—pharmaceuticals, aerospace equipment, telecommunications equipment—won't work. But it does work for some categories. Additionally, there is the challenge of employing effective tools (for example, the right Web-based tool kits) to allow users to create product designs. Nonetheless, in spite of only modest popularity, "the customer designs" method is *definitely recommended* for certain industries and product types.

6. Customer Brainstorming and Inverse Brainstorming

This VoC method is often employed at a customer event in the case of B2B markets, or instead of a focus group session for consumer products. It entails gathering a group of users, then employing formal brainstorming sessions with customers or users to come up with new-product ideas. Often *inverse brainstorming* is used to begin the session in order to uncover product deficiencies and shortcomings. Then brainstorming follows to propose solutions to the identified deficiencies:

> *An example*: C&K, an ITT Industries business unit based in the United States, manufactures a complete range of industrial switches—for example, the on-off switch found on your printer, laptop, or desktop computer. The head of the business hosts a "customer day" on innovation. Salespeople work diligently to ensure that knowledgeable and key customers attend: from the automotive industry, the computers and servers sector, industrial equipment manufacturers; and the lab and scientific equipment industry. Guest speakers are invited to provide enlightening talks on the innovation topic, so that customers receive good value for the day. As part of the day, two group sessions are held:
>
> Session I: Attendees are split into groups by industry and assigned the challenging question: "What's wrong with switches in your sector or in your equipment?" Also included on each team are company people—Technical and Marketing—from C&K. This inverse brainstorming session identifies many problems with switches: The fact that switches occupy too much space on servers, with servers becoming smaller each year; or that seat belt switches in autos—the switch that turns that beeping off when you buckle up—are problematic because they take so much abuse. Each of the four teams reports back with a long list of very creative ways in which the current products are deficient.
>
> Session II: Later in the day, the same teams are asked to select the three greatest problems identified in the inverse brainstorming session and then to brainstorm for about thirty minutes on each major problem. Here the rules of brainstorming are applied—no criticism allowed! At the end, the teams quickly identify the best ideas and report back with a short list.
>
> One idea in response to the problematic seat belt switch is the idea of a switch with no moving parts—one that relies on a magnetic field. Cur-

rently, C&K and a major automaker are working together to replace the electro-mechanical seat belt switch with a magnetic one—a huge potential for C&K.

The inverse brainstorming approach followed by traditional brainstorming is a tried-and-proven methodology for ideation, and many users claim that great ideas are the result of such sessions. But there are costs and difficulties: Organizing the event can be time-consuming; getting business customers to participate is always a challenge; and there are difficulties in setting up a group session when members from the same industry (potential competitors) are involved. This approach is *recommended* in spite of its limited popularity.

7. Customer Advisory Board or Panel

This VoC approach has been around for decades and entails using a customer advisory board or ongoing user group to advise on problems and what new products are needed. In spite of its durability, the method is only moderately popular, with only 17.6 percent of firms extensively using it for ideation. Users rate the effectiveness of advisory boards for ideation above average, number eight in ranking in Figure 6.5.

Few users had much good to say about advisory boards as a solid source of quality ideas, but part of the problem is the way the meetings are organized—more as a discussion session than a structured attempt to identify hot new-product opportunities. Thus, customer advisory boards are fine to use for maintaining good customer relations but are *not at the top of the list for idea generation.*

8. Community of Enthusiasts

Netnography is a new twist on ethnography, except it's done on the Internet . . . "listening" to people as they blog, post items on bulletin boards, or tweet. By undertaking content analysis, one can identify themes, problems, and potentially new ideas for products:

> *An example:* Del Monte (U.S.) Foods (pet foods division) found a winner via Netnography.[10] Step 1 was the "I love my dog" initiative. The firm gathered and analyzed data from online blogs, forums, and message boards, identifying themes and trends in the pet-food marketplace. Most important, they identified one key segment: "Dogs are people, too"—the dog owners who treat their dogs just like real people.
>
> Next, Del Monte built an online community, "I Love My Dog," designed for continuous consumer interaction. This community was by invitation (500 consumers in this "dogs are people" segment) and password protected. The community enabled Del Monte to undertake deeper consumer listening and understanding: Consumers discussed issues, blogged, chatted, shared photos, found resources, and participated in surveys.

Dog owners in this segment, it was discovered, treat their dogs like real people, dressing them up, strolling them in baby carriages, and even purchasing dog furniture. They also give their dogs real people-food; so if steak is on the adult menu, the dog gets some steak, too! But content analysis of the online community discussions revealed that breakfast was a problem—bacon, sausage, and eggs for the dog? The result was a new product: Snausage Breakfast Bites, which filled the need.

This community of enthusiasts method is not popular at all as a source of ideas, with only 8.0 percent of firms extensively using it. Similarly, the method is rated the least effective of the eight VoC methods (ranked number nine in effectiveness), but that's still above average.

The major advantage is that once set up, this community can be maintained fairly inexpensively. By analyzing the comments and messages, as Del Monte did, one gains insights into what is really going on in the user community, learning about users' problems and desires. The challenge is that this method requires considerable skill, insight, and time to undertake content analysis. A second challenge is that the method likely only applies to a handful of product classes, for example, sports equipment, computer software, pets—high-involvement product categories in which customers are likely to band together into enthusiast groups or clubs. In spite of very low usage, the method *should be considered for applicable product categories.*

> A variety of strategic or "top-down" methods of ideation exist. Several prove very effective.

STRATEGIC METHODS FOR GENERATING IDEAS

Let's now turn to *strategic methods* or "top-down" methods for generating new-product ideas. These approaches are much more strategic in nature and rely on methods used to help fashion a business's innovation strategy; but they are also useful in identifying new-product ideas and opportunities.

1. Look for Big Problems and Disruptions in Your Market

Big ideas solve big problems! And big problems often come from major shifts or disruptions in an industry. Strategic ideation approaches can be used to identify shifts, dislocations, or disruptions in the industry or marketplace, which often signal an emerging market or a major new-product opportunity.

Begin by assessing your customers' industry—your marketplace. Unmet or unarticulated needs are often the result of changes and shifts in a user industry. Questions include:

- What changes are occurring in your customers' needs? In your value chain? How will they affect your industry and its key players?

- What new opportunities could emerge from these changes—from new value chains and workflows to help make your customers more successful?
- Are there opportunities to better meet customer needs or capitalize on a changing market environment?

These are good questions but getting the answers involves legwork—it's not just a desk exercise! Start by developing a map of the *value chain*, identifying the various types of players all the way down to the end-user. Next, *assess their futures*: their changing roles, who will gain, and who might be dis-intermediated (cut out). And always be on the lookout for "aha's" and "wows"—are there opportunities for you?

Next, *identify customers' industry drivers* and potential shifts in these drivers. That is, try to assess what factors make them (or their competitors) profitable and successful. Is it cost of materials or low-cost production? Or response time to customer requests? And how are these changing—especially in a way that might open up opportunities for you? And finally, can *you* provide solutions here to help your customers be more profitable?

Then *analyze historical trends and estimate future trends;* spell out a scenario (or alternate scenarios) of where your customer's industry—your marketplace—is heading. Next, *follow the money!* Market Maps is a good tool to see where the profits can be made: This is simply a chart that shows which types of players have what piece of the revenue in the industry—see Figure 6.6. A similar and useful tool is Profit Pool Maps, which identifies the activities in an industry, percentage of revenue by each, and profit margins in each.[11]

The result of this assessment of your customer's industry should be the identification of the most attractive arenas (segments or parts of the marketplace where you should focus your search for ideas). Assessing your customer's industry, when coupled with face-to-face VoC research (above) and working with lead users (above), is a powerful technique: It leads to the identification of emerging or unmet customer needs, and new opportunities for new products and solutions.

2. Employ a Core Competencies Assessment

In parallel, conduct an internal assessment on your own business—a strengths, weaknesses, and *core competencies assessment*. Core competencies are skills and knowledge that differentiate you from your competition in a way that gives you a significant edge or advantage.[12] This competencies assessment gives those in senior management a place to start when deciding which areas or arenas they wish to focus on for innovative new products and solutions—adjacencies (related markets or product categories) where you might leverage your strengths to advantage. And often a core competency assessment directly identifies new-product ideas that build on your strengths.

Figure 6.6: Use Market Maps to "Follow the Money" (Example: Financial Institutions—Transactions, Custody, Trust, and Settlements)

Reveals the distribution of an industry's profits along 2 dimensions – activities and type of firm

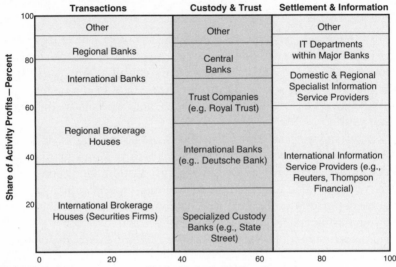

Source: Disguised data from a
major bank, based on endnote 11.

An illustration: You are in the competitive world of airline reservations systems. You currently sell a reservation system aimed at travel agents. An industry analysis, as described above, reveals provocative results. Increasingly, travelers are using the Internet to book their flights, especially with major carriers with easy-to-use Web pages. A Profit Pool Map reveals that for airline travel, the travel agents' margins have been squeezed by the major carriers. The travel agent, your principal customer, is in danger of becoming dis-intermediated and is quickly becoming the least profitable link in the value chain. This disruption threatens your business but also opens up new possibilities. A core competency assessment reveals that you have the best reservation system or "engine" in the world to serve your traditional customers, travel agents.

End-user market research reveals that not all travelers are satisfied with booking flights on airlines' Web pages: They must search through the Web pages of multiple airlines to get the best price deal; and often they end up with a higher price than an experienced travel agent could obtain. This VoC research reveals new opportunities for an IT product, but this one aimed directly at the end-user: a single booking system that includes all airlines and hunts for the best deal. And so you conceive, develop, and launch your new product: an online travel booking service that promises best prices and best schedules across multiple carriers (essentially your existing "engine" with a new front-end or user-interface bolted on). Thus, Travelocity® was launched!

Figure 6.7: Disruptive Technologies Create New Products That Underperform Current Products— but Note the New Performance Dimension

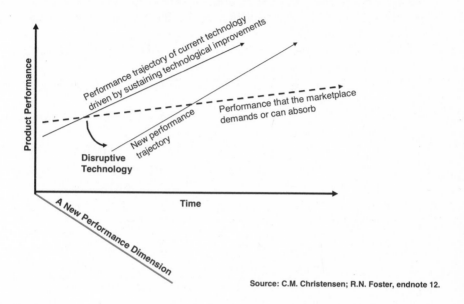

Source: C.M. Christensen; R.N. Foster, endnote 12.

Suggestion: Undertake a thorough industry and market assessment. Analyze the value chain; identify the industry drivers; and review historical trends and develop scenarios of the future. Look for gaps, emerging needs, and disruptions in your market or your customer's industry. These gaps and problems may signal your next major new-product opportunity. Take a close look at your own core competencies to determine where you have strategic leverage, which might lead to new-product opportunities.

3. Exploit Disruptive Technologies in the Search for Ideas

Periodically, radical or step-change innovations occur that dramatically alter the landscape of an industry.[13] These *disruptive technologies* often yield products with inferior performance initially, and so the new products based on the disruptive technologies are not usually adopted quickly by the mainstream market. But they do pose a potential threat or opportunity for the future: Witness the impact that the digital cameras, Internet, cell phones, and hybrid cars have had on their industries.

Figure 6.7 shows the situation. The current technology in most industries usually advances over time, driven by a number of small improvements—sustaining innovation—as noted by the solid inclining line (left) in Figure 6.7. Such was the case for 35 mm cameras, the dominant technology prior to digital cameras. Performance of the existing products (vertical axis) can be measured in a number of ways—for example, picture resolution or ease of use. In fact, what usually happens is that the dominant technology improves so much over time that it exceeds the needs of many users (the dotted line in Figure 6.7).

Along comes a new disruptive technology, denoted by the solid inclining line (right), whose initial products are inferior to the dominant technology when measured on the traditional performance metrics—picture resolution, ease of use (remember the first digital pictures—not exactly award winners). So at first glance, it appears that the new technology is doomed!

What is missing in this two-dimensional diagram is the third dimension—the new performance dimension—shown as the Z axis in Figure 6.7. This new dimension here is "a digitized picture." For most camera users, this was not a relevant dimension; but for a handful of very specialized users—for example, commercial property salespeople, or property insurance adjusters—who needed to get pictures (not award winners) to their client or to their head office, the new performance dimension was critical; and they were prepared to endure the pain of inferior performance in other dimensions (picture quality) to get the new performance benefit: a digitized picture.

The conventional competitors making 35 mm cameras and film unfortunately were living in a two-dimensional world—"flatworld"—and either did not see the third dimension or underestimated its impact. But the new digital camera producers had the advantage of living in a three-dimensional world. The rest is history.

The point is that disruptive technologies create *huge threats to the dominant firms* in an industry and *great opportunities* for others. In the last century:

- Digital watches almost destroyed the Swiss watch industry.
- Handheld calculators devastated mechanical calculating devices.
- Ballpoint pens, the Xerox machine, and the jet engine created great dislocations.

When disruptions occur, the dominant firms beforehand are most often no longer the dominant firms afterward. The phenomenon is called the *tyranny of success.*[14] What made firms successful in the first place then sows the seeds of defeat: confidence leading to arrogance; constancy of purpose, leading ultimately to the inability to change; and huge investments in the technology (now the "old technology") that become golden handcuffs. Even more dangerous, these disruptions are also *stealthy.* They often occur almost unnoticed: Because their first products have inferior performance, the industry experts, forecasters, and market researchers dismiss the new products and the new technology.

So much for the theory! But how does one predict whether or not an emerging technology will be disruptive? And how does one seek ideas from the new technology?

1. First, continually monitor the outside technology landscape in your own industry. And identify technologies that might address your current customers' needs better than your own technology does.

2. Next, monitor the technologies in those industries working on related problems. Again look for new technologies there.
3. When an emerging technology is spotted, assess its likelihood of success. Understand the dynamics of innovation and substitution—there are reasons that new technologies emerge:
   - An unmet customer need that the current technology cannot meet; or
   - A new customer need, the result of shifts in the external environment.
   Determine whether the new technology is likely to satisfy that need better. In order to anticipate disruptive technologies, *don't start with the technology but with customer needs* and an understanding of what the customer sees as having value.
4. Look beyond what customers ask for, and look further than the mainstream market and users. Try to identify the handful of *potential customers who stand to benefit the most from the new solution*—the insurance adjustor or property salesperson in the digital camera example.
5. Finally, be sure to do lots of fieldwork: face-to-face discussions with early adopters and potential users, so that your people can learn firsthand about applications and users' potential for adoption.

Once a potential disruptive or radical and step-change technology is identified, then shift to assessing its impact on your industry, market, and products; and if needed, begin to identify what new products you will need and when (see the IOTA [Impact of Opportunities and Threats Analysis] later in this chapter).

In spite of all the hype, exploiting disruptive technologies is ranked only number ten out of eighteen in terms of effectiveness in generating breakthrough ideas and is about equal to the least effective of the VoC approaches—see Figure 6.5. Predicting the impact of a new technology remains difficult: Why were cell phones so successful, when an equally excellent, perhaps better technology, satellite phones, met with limited success? Some argue that analyzing disruptive technologies is a *better tool to explain the past* than to predict the future! Further, disruptions do not occur on a regular basis in most industries, so one might wait decades to see such product ideas come about. The method is *definitely recommended* but with the caveats noted above—disruptions are difficult to predict, and they occur infrequently.

4. Peripheral Vision as an Idea Source

The biggest dangers are *the ones you don't see coming!* Understanding these threats and anticipating the opportunities requires strong peripheral vision.[15] For example, Mattel's failure to recognize preteen girls maturing at an younger age led to a surprising and big drop-off in sales of Barbie Dolls—it caught them unaware. Simply stated, little girls began to outgrow Barbie Dolls at a much earlier age and shifted to older, more mature, more sophisticated dolls such as Bratz. Interestingly, also in the toy industry, Lego faced a similar problem—little boys growing up more quickly and shifting to computers and electronic games. But unlike Mattel,

Lego acted, introducing high-tech products that feature robotics, electronic bricks, sensors, and controller motors: Mindstorms, Power Functions, Technic, and even Lego computer games.

Another sad story of the failure of peripheral vision—they didn't see it coming—is DuPont's inability to recognize and deal with the threat of low-cost polymers. DuPont invented many of the polymers that we take for granted: Nylon, Orlon, Dacron, Lycra, and Teflon, to name some. In spite of DuPont's technology prowess, patents had run out and other chemical companies built Asian and Middle Eastern plants with access to lower-cost feedstock and lower-cost labor. DuPont did little: Instead of taking bold action—for example, building Asian or Middle Eastern polymer plants with the advantage of DuPont's superior technology—DuPont slowly retreated from its polymer markets, which led in turn to under-utilizing of its production capacity, higher costs, and thus even greater vulnerability. DuPont's polymer business today is a shadow of its former self.

Most companies are blindsided by unexpected events: In a strategic survey, two-thirds of companies were surprised by up to three high-impact competitive events in last five years.[16] And 97 percent lack an early warning system! Because most firms are blindsided by major external events, they miss opportunities for new products.

Peripheral vision is simply a strategic method for generating new-product ideas: It is a deliberate and formal strategic exercise whereby you assess the external world, identifying trends and threats, and in the process, define potential new products. Key questions that are helpful in a peripheral visioning exercise include:

1. Who in your industry picks up on advance warnings and acts on them?
2. What have been your blind spots in the past?
3. Is there a relevant analogy from another industry?
4. What are peripheral customers (adjacent markets, former customers) and non-direct competitors saying?
5. What new futures could really hurt (or help) you?
6. Is there an unthinkable scenario of the future?[17]

Peripheral visioning proves to be a very popular approach to generating new-product ideas (perhaps also under a different name), and is ranked number two out of eighteen, with 33.1 percent of firms extensively using this strategic approach, as shown in Figure 6.5. Effectiveness is also positively rated: a number seven ranking from users. *Definitely recommended!*

5. The Value of Future Scenarios

One of the most significant strategic decisions ever made was when AT&T turned down a free offer to take control of the Internet.[18] In the late 1980s, the National Science Foundation (U.S. government) wanted to withdraw from its role of administering the Internet and offered AT&T a free monopoly position. But AT&T

had a mental map of the future—namely, a scenario or picture of the future in which their centrally switched technology would remain dominant. The notion of a packet-switched, decentralized switching technology (what the Internet uses) would never be the future. The technical experts at AT&T concluded that the Internet was insignificant for telephony and had no commercial significance in any other context.

What AT&T should have done—and indeed what your company should do—is to develop *alternate scenarios of the future*. Yes, develop the scenario of the "official" or expected future . . . in AT&T's case, with centrally switched architecture remaining dominant. But develop an alternate scenario, too—in this case, an alternative in which new markets for Internet services and new kinds of telephony challenge the dominant AT&T architecture. Such a scenario at minimum would have given decision-makers a sense of the Internet's potential and might have led them to consider alternate courses of action. But developing alternate scenarios also helps decision-makers become much more *sensitive to signals of change*. As Peter Schwartz, who advocates the use of scenarios in planning, declares: "What has not been foreseen is unlikely to be seen in time." For example, AT&T executives, by defining the alternative scenario, might have been more alert when increasing numbers of users began to go online, when Web pages began to mushroom, and when PC sales to home users grew by leaps and bounds in the early 1990s.

Developing alternate scenarios of the future usually involves senior people taking part in extensive discussions and work sessions. Because your purpose is to arrive at new-product opportunities, restrict the discussion to scenarios that are relevant to your business and deal with the external (or extended market) environment. For a bank, this might be: "Describe the future of financial and related markets, and the financial industry as a whole."

Questions to work on include:

1. What is the best future scenario? Try to describe in as much detail as possible what your (company's) world will look like in the future (five to ten years), given the best-case external environment assumptions.
2. What is the worst possible scenario of the future for your company's external environment?
3. What are some relevant dimensions that characterize these scenarios (for example, in AT&T's case, a relevant dimension was "centralized versus decentralized switching": The best scenario was at one end—namely, centralized switching; the worst case was at the other—decentralized or packet-switching dominant).

Then identify the *primary decisions* that you face. In order to identify new-product opportunities from scenarios analysis, the questions are:

- Should you launch new businesses or business models?
- Should you invest in new technologies or technology platforms?

- What types of new products should you be seriously looking at?

Scenarios are utilized by imagining that one or another "future scenario" will be true and then assessing the consequences of making each decision, assuming each alternate future.

Finally, markers or signals of each scenario occurring should be identified, so that managers can spot telltale signs over the next months or years as to which way the world is moving. For example, one banking scenario is that there will be no retail bank branches in the future—that bricks and mortar will be history. Telltale signals over the next decade might be: the number of new e-banks launched; the proportion of users in various age groups moving to e-banking; and the development of new communication devices that make the Internet more portable and functional. If such trends or devices gain rapid momentum, then look for total branchless banking around the corner.

Suggestion: Develop scenarios of the future; but do more than just developing the most likely scenario or your "official future." Develop *alternate scenarios*— best case and worse case. Imagine what would happen if each alternate scenario came true—how would it alter your new-product decisions? And what would be the financial consequences of making decisions assuming the official scenario, if indeed one of the alternate scenarios were to come true (as AT&T's did). Assign just a small probability to these alternate scenarios occurring, and reconsider your new-product investment decisions! And use brainstorming and creativity techniques to uncover imaginative ideas, given that each scenario—official and alternate—occurs.

6. Competitive Analysis
A final strategic approach to ideation is to take a hard look at your competitors. The goal here is to understand their strengths and weaknesses, why they are winning or losing, and what you can learn. Inverse brainstorming competitors' products—ripping them apart and identifying their weaknesses—is a useful tool. And be sure to build questions on competitor products—what customers like or dislike about them—into your market research.

An example:[19] Rust-Oleum, a major U.S. supplier of paint, coatings, and related renovation products, undertakes a "brand deconstruction exercise" in order to generate new product ideas. Marketers in the company pick a competitive brand in their category, one that is doing something right, and get into this competitor's shoes. They do a SWOT (strengths, weaknesses, opportunities, threats) analysis: Questions include: What is the competitor thinking? What keeps those folks up at night? They also shop competitors' products and ask customers about them. They take their competitor's product apart in the lab and also pose questions in consumer and customer research

Figure 6.8: Summarize Your Strategic Exercises with an IOTA Chart— Impact of Opportunities and Threats Analysis

Area of focus for Peripheral Vision Scanning	List: Threats, major changes & trends, disruptions, danger signals, key issues and events	How likely?	How imminent (timing)?	Impact— so what?	What opportunities: new products, new services, new businesses, new business models?
Market changes and shifts—your customers					
Changes in your competitors and their strategies					
Changes in members of your value chain (e.g., retailers, distributors)					
Technology trends, changes & disruptions					
Legislative & political changes, events, dangers					
Social & demographic trends, changes					
Economic changes, threats, dangers					

about the competitive brand. Management then takes the findings and acts on them, often coming up with new strategies or new-product ideas.

Putting Your Strategic Exercises to Work

To wrap up your strategic exercises—strategic analysis, forecasting market and technology disruptions, peripheral visioning, creating alternate scenarios, and competitive analysis—hold an *integration session or workshop*. Here you review all the trends, events, threats, opportunities, and forecasts that you have identified (the left column of Figure 6.8, the IOTA chart). Next, indicate the timing and likelihood of these events or trends: Are they here and now, with 100-percent likelihood of occurring? Or perhaps they're sometime in the distant future and should be ranked as a "maybe." Next, discuss the impact—for example, the impact of little boys and girls growing up quickly would be disastrous to both Lego and Mattel. Now for the final column in Figure 6.8—so what? What can you do about it? Here you identify the new products or new businesses that this IOTA exercise points to.

OPEN INNOVATION AS A MAJOR SOURCE OF IDEAS

Chapter 5 introduced the concept of *open innovation*, noting that many companies now look to externally generated ideas, technology, IP, and even finished products to supplement their internal development effort.[20] In spite of all the talk about open innovation, when it comes to idea generation, it is surprising that these open methods prove not to be very popular, nor are they perceived to be particularly effective as sources of new-product ideas. Indeed, as a group, most are in the lower left quadrant in the ideation quadrant diagram of Figure 6.5 (the solid boxes inside the lower circle).

"Open innovation" is a relatively new source of innovation ideas. In spite of limited popularity and rated effectiveness, it's recommended for certain product categories.

Six different open innovation approaches to getting new-product ideas were investigated. There are others. Note that the most popular approach—ideas from partners and vendors—has been around for a long time, and though it is an open innovation method per se, it certainly is not a new method. The three *most effective open innovation methods* (as judged by users, see Figure 6.5) are ideas from partners and vendors, ideas from the external scientific community, and ideas from start-up businesses. None of these open innovation approaches is as effective as an idea source as the eight VoC methods are, however, perhaps because of their newness, or perhaps because of their limited applicability.

Open innovation has the advantage of tapping into inventors, scientists, designers, vendors, consumers, and small businesses for ideas, IP, technology, and even finished products—a huge number of sources well beyond the limited capabilities of your own engineering or R&D departments. The major disadvantage is that as a source of new-product ideas, many of the open methods only apply to certain product categories (for example, P&G endorses the method strongly, as evidenced by their effective "Connect & Develop" Web page; whereas GE argues that seeking ideas for locomotives or jet engines from the outside world is a little impractical). A second challenge is the amount of time and work it takes to scan, solicit, handle, and process the ideas or IP.

The reasons for the lack of popularity and perceived effectiveness may be that some of the open innovation approaches are relatively new, and thus many companies have yet to experiment with them. And being so new, it's too early to evaluate their effectiveness. Others dispute this and argue that open innovation is *not so new*—that "firms have always been open to some degree and that the benefits differ depending on their line of business."[21] Those in industries with simpler technologies and B2C (business-to-consumer) products (such as Procter & Gamble) are good candidates for open innovation, with millions of consumers and would-be inventors the target; but companies in advanced technology and complex products may find inviting ideas from the outside world less fruitful.

Yet another critique comes from capital-intensive industries, where products take a long time to develop and remain on sale for years. GE's CEO Jeff Immelt observes that his firm is a leader in a number of fields, such as making jet engines and locomotives, which requires "doing things that almost nobody else in the world can do" and where intellectual-property rights and a degree of secrecy still matter.[22]

Mark Little, head of GE research, is even more skeptical and notes that outside ideas "don't really stick well here." He professes great satisfaction with the output of GE's own research laboratories: "We're pretty happy with the hand we've got."

From most effective to least, here are the open innovation methods for idea generation:

1. Partners and Vendors

This open innovation method entails seeking new-product ideas from outside partners and vendors. It is not a new approach, and it is quite popular, with 22.1 percent of firms extensively using it to generate ideas. In terms of effectiveness, the use of vendors and partners as a source of ideas is down the list at number eleven out of eighteen.

The advantages are that vendors and partners bring to the table technical capabilities that may be beyond your scope of expertise. Buried within these capabilities are the seeds of your next great new product. The trouble is that vendors or partners may be equally as uncreative at ideation as you are, so don't expect a plethora of great ideas from this source. Nonetheless, because it is a tried-and-proven approach, is quite popular, and yields decent effectiveness ratings, the approach is recommended; it is also the only open innovation method even close to the desirable upper right quadrant in Figure 6.5.

2. Accessing the External Technical Community

This open innovation approach solicits ideas and technology solutions from the external scientific and technical community. A number of online tools, such as NineSigma, Yet2.com and Innocentive, make this access much easier today. The method is fairly popular, with 19.5 percent of firms extensively using it. Note, however, that the method tends to be used more for *seeking technology solutions* during the Development stage than for seeking new-product ideas.

3. Scanning Small Businesses and Business Start-Ups

This open innovation approach accesses small and start-up businesses and gets ideas from these entrepreneurial firms. The argument here is that you can bet that somewhere today there is a scientist or designer with the great next new product in your industry. The trouble is, that person probably doesn't work for you but is employed in a small business or start-up firm. Indeed, the track record of large and dominant firms in commercializing breakthrough innovations in most industries has been dismal, with the true innovations coming from newer or smaller firms. One challenge is that there are hundreds, perhaps thousands, of smaller enterprises that could be sources here, and accessing and vetting all the potential sources is no small task. A second challenge is the protectiveness often exhibited by the start-up entrepreneur—an unwillingness to give up "his baby" or even 50 percent of it in exchange for much higher profits.

4. External Product Designs

This open innovation method involves using the Internet to invite the general public—customers, users, and many others from the external world—to submit *finished product designs* (not just ideas). The method is sometimes called "crowd-sourcing." Examples are Threadless, a T-shirt company in Chicago that runs on-line contests for T-shirt designs; Muji, a Japanese furniture company that asks its catalogue members to submit furniture designs;[23] and Lego's Web-based Design-ByMe, aimed at kids, mentioned above.

Letting outsiders design products is a very novel and step-out method, and I included the customer-focused aspect of this method in the VoC section above. As an open innovation method, it goes beyond customers and lets the *whole world* participate, and as a result, it seems that both popularity and effectiveness drop off, as noted in Figure 6.5.

The advantage of the method is that the world becomes your product design house—you can capitalize on people's desire to design and develop products, often for little or no financial gain. The example of open-source software is often cited by proponents. Once again, however, this method has limited applicability—and is restricted largely to consumer products and relatively simple and creative goods (note that the examples given above are all creative design products about which outsiders are likely to have creative insights).

5. External Submission of Ideas

In this open innovation approach, your customers, users, and others in the external world are invited to submit their new-product ideas, often via the Internet and your Web page. P&G's Connect & Develop system is an example.[24] But few companies have tried this: The popularity of this method ranks number sixteen out of eighteen, with only 7.9 percent of firms extensively using it. Surprisingly, and in spite of the positive note in articles written about P&G's system, the effectiveness of external submission of ideas ranks almost dead last.

On the positive side, users of this method indicate that the entire world becomes your source of ideas, greatly magnifying the possibilities beyond your own employees' creative abilities. The major weaknesses are that the technique probably only applies to the world of consumer and technically simple products. Further, it takes "an army of internal people," as one executive commented, to review the ideas, assess, and evaluate them, and get back to the submitter with a proposal. For example, one major European consumer-goods company tried the approach for a while but then gave it up as far too time-consuming—"a lot of work for the very few good ideas we obtained."

6. External Idea Contest

This is another open innovation method, namely, hosting an ideation contest and inviting the external world to submit ideas:

An example: Swarovski Enlightened™ invited professional designers and creative people generally from all over the world to engage in a watch-design community.[25] The community was an online (Internet) design contest, which was open to designers (for example, design students) and also to people who are generally interested in watches and gemstones. Users were invited to submit designs and to vote on the designs created by other users.

The contest was conducted in two ways: Using a watch configuration tool kit, participants were able to create or configure their own watch designs by selecting from twenty-four components (case and bezel, wristband, background, clock face) in various colors and through the selection and placement of 108 different gemstones. In the second method, freely created watch designs could be submitted by contestants. Monetary prizes were offered for the three best freely created designs, with non-cash prizes for the best configured designs.

The lively community spread like a virus across cultural boundaries, from Austria to the United States, and even created a buzz in China, India, Russia, Turkey, and Iran. Within eight weeks, the website had more than 7.5 million hits. Websites, design communities, and even magazines and blogs referred to the contest without any Swarovski advertising or promotional spending.

More than 1,650 participants joined the community to showcase their talent and submit their designs. In total, they created over 2,000 watch designs in different segments ranging from classic to sporty and from abstract to realistic. The best designs were presented at Baselworld, the largest global watch fair, and are now available.

This method is an extension of open method number five above—external submission of ideas—and shares the same positives, except there is the added incentive (and a little excitement) of a contest with prizes for the submitter. But like number five, the method is limited to simple consumer goods. Additionally, there is the added cost and time of setting up a professionally managed contest—all the rules, administration, and awarding of prizes. In summary, external idea contests are not popular at all, but they do get good reviews from some heavy users. This method is worth a look but clearly is not the ideation method of choice for most firms.

Suggestion: You cannot ignore the world of *open innovation* to generate new-product ideas (and perhaps even secure technology and finished products ready to license). There are numerous ways to access ideas through open innovation:

- Scouting teams that investigate small businesses, inventors, and start-ups by visiting conferences, trade shows, and also tracking developments online and in publications—globally.

- Web pages inviting the public to submit ideas, technology, and finished products, as does P&G.
- Interfaces with university technology transfer centers (go with a shopping list!).
- Regular sessions with suppliers and their technical people, and involving your R&D and Marketing people.
- Web pages that allow customers to design their own products, as does Lego's DesignByMe.

Open innovation ideation takes effort, however: You must put the resources in place—a *scouting, connect, and develop team*—to work with the external submitters; and you must strive to establish the right climate and culture for open innovation, ensuring that your existing employees are not threatened by the new business model.[26]

TECHNOLOGY DEVELOPMENT AND FUNDAMENTAL RESEARCH— CHANGING THE BASIS OF COMPETITION

Do you have a central research facility? Most firms cannot afford a "corporate lab," but if your company does fundamental research or develops new technology, be sure to engage this research unit in your Discovery stage. Fundamental research and technology development will often lay the seed for a great new product, product family, or platform, and hence is a vital source of new-product ideas.

The trouble is that much fundamental research is *undirected, unfocused,* and *unproductive*—which is why so many CEOs have shut it down. If fundamental research is not yielding the breakthrough projects it should, then provide direction via your *innovation strategy*; and introduce a little *Stage-Gate* discipline. I outlined *Stage-Gate TD* in Chapter 5, specifically designed for new technology, knowledge-build, or fundamental research projects. Some scientists may scream their disapproval, but remind them that this is not a university where curiosity-based research is the rule—this is a business. Other scientists will welcome the opportunity to become more engaged in value-producing research for the corporation.

> **Be sure to leverage your technology development and basic research effort. Ensure that this research is directed by your innovation strategy.**

Suggestion: If fundamental research, science projects, or technology developments are undertaken in your business, try introducing a stage-and-gate process similar to that in Figure 5.2 in the last chapter in order to provide a little more direction and focus. Here, the Applications Path gate should be the trigger for new-product ideas. But note that the process—its stages, gates, activities, and gate criteria—will differ substantially from your new-product process. Don't try to force fit these science projects through your normal *Stage-Gate* process!

PATENT MAPPING

Patents are an outstanding but all too often overlooked source of valuable information, including ideas for new products.[27] The amount of knowledge contained in patents is enormous but somewhat overwhelming to access and interpret.

Patent mapping involves the distillation and interpretation of large amounts of often complex patent data into one or more high-value representations useful in making business decisions. The goal is to generate actionable intelligence from raw patent information, enabling timely, informed decisions. For innovators, patent mapping helps the user to conceptualize the IP space and serves as a trigger for new-product ideation and selecting development areas to focus on. For example, if considerable patent and filing activity is noted in a particular field or area, that is a signal—a signal that technologists somewhere are onto something, and more important, that management sees that this area is sufficiently interesting to spend the time and money to file a patent.* Thus, *hot areas in technology* can be spotted—emerging areas, and areas that are seen as having potential.

Patent mapping and patent mining are well known and quite popular, as seen in Figure 6.5. Although the techniques are useful for identifying areas of competitive activity and hence potential areas of focus, they do not generate new-product ideas per se. As a result, effectiveness is ranked lower, at number fourteen on average, well below the VoC methods.

GETTING GREAT IDEAS FROM YOUR OWN EMPLOYEES

Your own employees are excellent potential sources of new-product ideas. Yet all too often, internally generated ideas are either mundane or not acted upon. Here are some ways to change that.

Internal Idea Capture

Setting up an internal idea capture system is, not surprisingly, the *most popular ideation method.* This typically involves formally soliciting new-product ideas from your own employees (often via an internal Web page or using purchased software), and then screening and handling these ideas via some form of formal and structured process. Number

> Your own employees can be excellent sources of new-product ideas. Set up an internal idea capture system. But many companies get this wrong.

---

* Note that patent filing is expensive and consumes scarce IP people resources; therefore, companies are selective about what they file, thus revealing what they consider important.

one overall in terms of extensive usage, effectiveness is disappointing, ranked number twelve.

Suggestion: Implement a professional internal idea suggestion system to tap into the creative juices of your own employees . . . but with some important caveats. The problem is, like everything else worth doing, the details do matter. And many businesses get the details of internal idea generation wrong. Here are some tips:

- Put someone *in charge* of your internal idea suggestion scheme. The problem is, ideation is everyone's job and no one's responsibility, so it falls between two stools.
- Publicize the idea suggestion scheme widely—it's surprising in how many firms I visit, folks are not sure whether there is such an ideation system in place!
- Separate the "ideas for new products" system from general purpose "idea suggestion boxes." The latter tend to attract lots of minor cost- and time-saving ideas; but you don't want your innovation ideation scheme mixed in with that!
- Welcome all ideas and do not belittle people for submitting offbeat ideas. And make it easy for employees to submit ideas—virtual suggestion boxes, as at GE, work for most people (an internal Web page), but paper-based submissions may still be a route for some.
- Make the system accessible broadly—in Saint-Gobain's scheme (the French glassmaker), even suppliers and customers can participate!
- Provide guidance: On your internal Web page, outline the "search fields" where you are actively seeking ideas; and then provide some background and data to flesh out some of the search fields. When Guinness first introduced its idea scheme to employees, the first batch of ideas was awful—all over the place and little to do with their beer business. Then search fields were defined—the female beer drinker; the metro-sexual young male; packaging innovations to bring the pub experience into the home; and so forth—and the quality of ideas improved markedly.
- Provide a fast response—on average two weeks. People get tired of waiting and soon lose interest and stop submitting ideas. And provide some feedback; it's not enough to say to the submitter: "On October 18, we reviewed your idea, and the idea screening committee unanimously agreed that your idea sucked." Use a scorecard and give feedback on the relevant dimensions—where the idea scored high and low.
- Provide incentives—rewards or recognition. Recognition works best, according to some studies, and is less problematic.[28] Some rewards, instituted with the best of intentions, have the opposite effect. For example, one firm established significant prizes for good ideas, with the rule that in the event of two identical submissions, the first submission took the prize. The result:

Ideas dried up, as everyone became very protective of their ideas, did not share and discuss, and thus creativity dropped!

- Annually review the system and track the ideas—numbers of ideas, sources, and what happened to them.

Run an MRG or Off-Site Idea-Generating Event

MRG means *major revenue generator*. And an MRG event is an off-site company event designed to produce or scope out at least several major ideas at the end of a few days' tough work. It's fun and it works! The principle is that your own people, including senior people, often have the seeds of great new products within them. By harnessing the creative energy of the entire group, unexpected outcomes are often the result. An MRG event is a way to stimulate creativity but in a structured fashion. Here's how to proceed:

An annual off-site company conference of senior and middle people is the venue. We've all been to these—two or three days of assorted speakers, some from inside the company, others from outside. A nice event, but not much happens as a result of these.

> Get more "bang for the buck" from your off-sites. Run an MRG event. Done right, the result should be five to ten big ideas.

This year, make the event yield a different result. Invite fewer speakers, but instead, build in a series of MRG exercises. Let's assume a two-day meeting:

Morning of Day 1: After the usual opening speech, split the audience into breakout teams. Here's the assignment: "You have ninety minutes to identify the major trends, shifts, changing customer needs, and potential disruptions that are taking place in our marketplace." Be sure to challenge teams to answer the money question: "So what? Do these shifts suggest any major new opportunities?" After the breakout session, teams report back. Pick some teams at random to present their conclusions.

Afternoon of Day 1: Same breakout teams but a new assignment: This time, they identify the major technology shifts in their and their customers' industry that will impact the market, and might change the way you do business. Again pick teams at random to report back.

Other breakout sessions over the first 1.5 days deal with similar topics, including an assessment of internal company strengths and core competencies that might be leveraged to advantage; and also shifts in the industry and value chain structure—what new players and competition are there, and what old ones may disappear? But always the challenge to all breakout teams and sessions is: "So what—what opportunities do these changes suggest to you? Do you see any aha's?"

By noon of Day 2, shift to *opportunity mapping*. That is, task the teams with mapping out some of the opportunities that their assessments have suggested—this usually means identifying and listing some of the bolder ideas and aha's.

Then, ask each team to present its list of major opportunities or ideas—post these on flip-chart sheets on the wall. Finally, the large group votes on the ideas, using scorecards, and then "green dots" the top-scoring ideas.

Before the event ends, be sure to identify the "best bets" and have teams put together a go-forward plan on each—the next steps and a team to work on the idea—as the final exercise of the two-day event.

It's a great exercise and it works! To make it even more effective, I recommend some pre-work. Teams meet in advance to undertake a few tasks: some VoC work with customers; a technology forecast; and a market trends forecast. And during Day 1, interspersed among the exercises, teams present the results of their pre-work to stimulate discussion.

The result of such MRG events is usually five to ten major opportunities identified and partially defined, a core of enthused people willing to work on each, and the beginnings of an action plan.

Set Up an Internal Innovation Show

Leading firms stimulate creativity and move good ideas forward by hosting innovation shows, much like a trade show, but internal. Here, employees set up booths and display their capabilities, technologies, and hot ideas for the future.

> *An example:* Kellogg's (a U.S. food company) hosts "moonlighting" events, essentially innovation shows where employees and units set up booths, much like a trade show, to display their ideas and technologies.[29] The show is attended by huge numbers of employees, and also senior executives. Attendees vote on the best ideas, and there are "people's choice" winners. This has proven to be an effective way of communicating ideas within a large corporation, and also for highlighting winners and gaining visibility for them.

Suggestion: If you seek breakthrough new products, try rethinking your idea stage using the proven Discovery approaches above. Figure 6.9 shows the activities that flow and converge to generate great new-product ideas. Use strategic approaches, in which you undertake a thorough analysis of your external environment, looking for shifts and disruptions that signal new opportunities (top part of Figure 6.9). Concurrently, undertake an internal core competencies assessment. Pinpoint arenas of strategic focus where you can concentrate your idea-hunting activities—your "search fields." Develop alternate scenarios of your future, and identify the opportunities for new products (left of Figure 6.9)—but don't get caught in the "official futures trap" that AT&T did!

Next, lower the microscope on customers and users in this arena (right side of Figure 6.9). Employ VoC research, with a particular emphasis on understanding customer problems. Then seek solutions leading to great new products. There are varied examples here from all industries—from the ICI's pink paint

Figure 6.9: The "Discovery Stage" in *Stage-Gate*—Multiple Activities Converge to Generate Great New-Product Opportunities

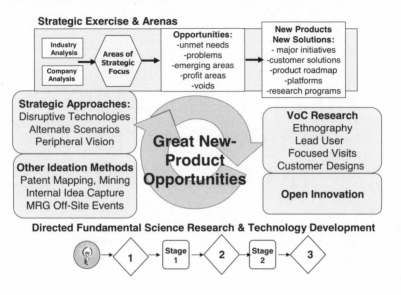

through to Del Monte Snausage and the DiaSet machine. Working with lead users, as practiced at 3M or Hilti, may be right for you—it's VoC work, but with a different twist. And fundamental technical research is a source. But harness your technical talent by engaging them in your Discovery stage: Introduce a tailored *Stage-Gate* approach—*Stage Gate TD*—to your technology development people (bottom of Figure 6.9).

Tap into the creativity of your own employees with an internal idea capture system, but in a professional way, using the tips outlined above. Hold a major revenue-generating event, described above, instead of your annual conference—that's time much better spent! Finally, host an innovation show as at Kellogg's.

An effective Discovery stage, as shown in Figure 6.9, is fundamental to coming up with great ideas to feed your product innovation system. Seeking extraordinary ideas sometimes means doing some extraordinary things!

7

THE FRONT-END WORK— FROM DISCOVERY TO DEVELOPMENT

Ideas won't keep. Something must be done about them. When the idea is new, its custodians have fervor, live for it, and if need be, die for it.

—Alfred North Whitehead,
English philosopher and mathematician

THE FIRST FEW PLAYS OF THE GAME

The game is won or lost in the first five plays! In Chapter 2, we saw that the seeds of disaster were often sown in the early stages of a new-product project—poor homework, a lack of customer focus, and poor quality of execution. Also in Chapter 2, we observed that the keys to new-product success often lie in the front-end or pre-development activities: getting the homework right, undertaking solid VoC (voice-of-customer) work, and getting sharp, early, and fact-based product definition. Just how important is the front-end work? As any venture capitalist will attest, a solid dose of due diligence before investment pays off! Figure 2.10 from Chapter 2 shows the impacts vividly: Here we see eight key drivers of time-to-market and profitability. Not surprisingly, the strongest driver of profitability is launching a unique, superior, differentiated product. But look again at Figure 2.10:

> The game is won or lost in the first five plays. Front-end load your projects and then manage the front end of the innovation process— get rid of the fuzziness!

- Solid front-end, pre-development homework is the number four driver of profitability, and the number two driver of time-to-market.

- Voice-of-customer work (a strong market focus) is the number two driver of profitability and the number 3 driver of time-to-market.
- Sharp, early product definition (before development begins) is the number three driver of profitability and the number five driver of time-to-market.

All three drivers are intimately connected, and all three are key to new-product performance: profits and time. Sadly, these early stages receive little time, effort, and attention—note from Figure 2.1 how poorly the front end is executed, with typically about three-fourths of businesses doing a poor job on each key front-end activity! The vital nature of the front-end work, coupled with poor quality of execution are the reasons I emphasize the front end of development so heavily and devote an entire chapter to these stages.

The Fuzzy Front End—Not Really So Fuzzy!

The steps that take an idea and transform it into a winning-product concept and solid product definition, all backed by a solid Business Case—a project ready for development—is the topic of this chapter, specifically for major projects or bolder innovations. Some people call this the "fuzzy front end" of product innovation. It may be fuzzy in your company, but in the Best Innovators, it's anything but fuzzy—*it's managed.* In this chapter, I show you how to *professionalize the front end*—turning some of the "fuzziness" into a science. You'll see the critical front-end actions that precede the physical development of the product, yet are so crucial to the product's ultimate success. These are the steps that take us from the project's inception—the Discovery or idea stage—through Stages 1 and 2 to a robust Business Case as the deliverable to Gate 3, the door to Development, as shown in Figure 7.1.

ON TO STAGE 1: SCOPING

Assume that you've done a solid job of idea generation to yield lots of good ideas. Now the task is to sift and sort through these ideas to see which ones are worthy of more time and money. That's the role of the Idea Screen, Gate 1. Designing these gates, screens, or decision points is no easy task, so I devote Chapters 8 and 9 to this endeavor. But for now, let's walk the idea through the first two stages of the new-product process: Let the idea pass Gate 1 and give it a green light for Stage 1, Scoping.

The spirit of Stage 1 is to "spend a little money, gather some information, so that the project can be reevaluated at Gate 2 in the light of the better information." Therefore, this first stage is a quick and inexpensive assessment of the technical merits of the project and its market prospects. Preliminary market, technical, and financial assessments make up Stage 1.

Expenditures at this preliminary stage are quite small: Note that Gate 1, the initial screen, is a fairly tentative commitment to the project—a flickering green

Figure 7.1: The Pre-Development Stages in the S*tage-Gate*® System Make or Break Major New-Product Projects

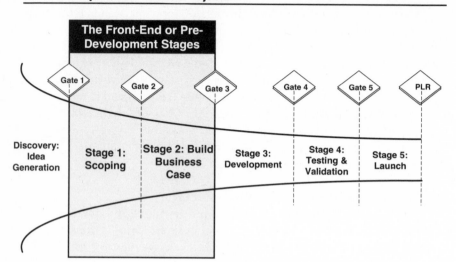

light. Indeed, some firms place a tight limit or ceiling on Stage 1 spending and time. In short, the output of a Go decision from Gate 1 can be expressed thus: "On the basis of the very limited information available, this idea or proposal has merit. Spend no more than $5–$10,000 and ten person-days, and report back in one month at Gate 2, armed with much better information for a more definitive review."

Here are some of the actions in Stage 1, Scoping—see Table 7.1 for a summary:

Preliminary Market Assessment

Preliminary market assessment involves a quick-and-dirty market study. The purpose is to determine if the proposed product has any commercial prospects:

- ✓ to assess market attractiveness and potential,
- ✓ to gauge possible product acceptance,
- ✓ to size up the competitive situation, and
- ✓ to shape the idea into a tentative product design.

> Not a full market research study, but a quick and cheap assessment of the market opportunity.

The task is to find out as much as you can about market size, growth, segments, customer needs and interest, and competition—quickly (usually in less than one month) and for minimal cost.

Given the limited cost and the short time duration of the study, this type of market assessment is clearly not professional and scientific market research. Rather, it's detective work and desk research: getting hold of available information in-house (for example, talking with the sales force, distributors, and technical service people); examining secondary sources (for example, reports and articles published by trade magazines, associations, government agencies, and research and consulting firms); contacting potential users (for example, via a phone blitz or focus groups);

TABLE 7.1: SUMMARY OF STAGE 1 ACTIONS—SCOPING

Purpose of Stage 1:	Stage 1 is a relatively quick, internal scoping of the idea for the proposed project. This is not a detailed investigation, but a *quick assessment* to determine whether the project is worth further investigation in Stage 2.
Actions in Stage 1:	
Preliminary Market Assessment	Quick scoping of the market prospects for the product: potential, acceptance, requirements. Not detailed market research, but detective and desk research only, relying on readily available & in-house sources.
Preliminary Technical Assessment	Conceptual assessment of technical feasibility, probable technical solution, technical risks, manufacturability (or source-of-supply), and intellectual-property issues. Check for partners.
Preliminary Business & Financial Assessment	A business sanity check: a rudimentary and quick check of the business rationale and financial prospects; the possible Payback Period (no spreadsheets or NPVs here!).
Recommendation and Action Plans for Stage 2	A Go/Kill recommendation; and proposed Action Plans (timeline; resources, people, and person-days; deliverables and date for next gate).

and canvassing outside sources (for example, an industry expert, magazine editor, or consultant). It's tough work, much like playing detective and following up on leads, but it's surprising how much information about a product's market prospects can be gleaned from several days of solid sleuthing.

Here are some sources of market information that can be accessed relatively inexpensively for Stage 1:

- *Undertake an Internet search:* There's a wealth of information out there, and much of it is available via the Internet. But you need someone who knows how to do an Internet-based market analysis. Hunt through trade magazines, journals, reports, and other published items looking for information on your market, the product type, and your competitors. For example, do a search on your competitors' names.
- *Your own library:* Your reference librarian may be worth his or her weight in gold in conducting a preliminary market assessment. If your company doesn't have its own library, try a major public library or a library at the local university's business school.
- *Search internal reports:* In larger firms, there are often numerous reports and surveys undertaken annually—customer surveys, satisfaction surveys, industry studies, and so on. Often, the information you need is buried somewhere in one of these many studies. So start with your own library or market research department—both locally and globally.
- *Key customers:* Stage 1 is premature for a detailed, large-sample customer survey or even multiple on-site and in-depth interviews. But insights from a limited number of leading, key, or trusted customers can prove very useful at this early stage: Have direct, face-to-face discussions with a few customers. These need not be based on a detailed questionnaire and can even be unstructured and exploratory. For B2B products, try to pick trusted yet representative or leading users. Talk to several people within each firm. If budgets are tight and time is pressing, use telephone interviews.
- *Hold focus groups* with a handful of customers. In spite of their limitations, focus groups remain a cost-effective way to gain insights into customer needs, wants, and preferences, and relatively quickly. And by including multiple concepts per focus group, the cost of research per concept is kept appropriately low.
- *Competitors' advertisements:* Get your hands on your competitors' advertisements and trade literature. Find out what they are saying about their products—features and performance characteristics, as well as how competitors are trying to position their products. Search for your competitors' brochures (and pricing) online.
- *Your own people:* Interview your own sales force and service representatives. They are your front-line troops—the eyes and ears of the company. Often, they can provide you with superb information on customer habits, likes,

and dislikes and the order-winning criteria, on product preferences, and on the competitive situation and pricing practices.

- *Consulting and research firms:* Some consulting and research firms publish multi-client or standardized reports that provide an overview of an industry. Although perhaps not specific to your new product, these reports or studies are a cost-effective way to gain information on market size, trends, competition, and so on.
- *Financial houses:* Brokerage houses spend lots of money researching industries and companies. So talk to your Finance Department to help you get this information from financial institutions. Annual reports of potential competitors are a help, as is the 10K report that publicly listed firms must submit to the Securities and Exchange Commission (SEC) in the United States.
- *Government agencies:* Governments collect a myriad of data. Finding this information is the problem. But don't give up before you begin. Often, a phone call to a state, provincial, or federal government office will identify the right department; and that department just happens to have the report or statistics that you were looking for.
- *Industry experts:* Hire an industry expert or guru for a day or two, and pick her brain. Although the per diem fee may be high, the knowledge gained may save you weeks of work.
- *Editors:* Editors of trade magazines are not the normal source of market information, but on occasion, they have proven very useful in tracking down reports, studies, and even subject-matter experts. A good editor usually has a good breadth of knowledge about what's going on in an industry.
- *Trade associations:* Some industries have excellent trade associations that provide superb market data. Contact these associations. And while doing so, be sure to talk to the association secretary or president to seek advice about where to find the other information you're looking for.

When undertaking your preliminary market assessment, do not neglect the international dimension. Gather market information for multiple international markets, not just your domestic one. And engage international business units, too: For example, Guinness, the Irish brewer, builds "an international alert" into Stage 1 of its Navigate new-product system: Here, brand managers around the world are contacted by the project team to see if they are interested in participating in the project, and what the market prospects for the product might be in their country.

Preliminary market studies need not be expensive and can generate many valuable insights relatively quickly; a study like this is much like what the venture capitalist does. These quick studies are not a substitute, however, for a full market study or real VoC research—a much more thorough investigation of users' needs in Stage 2 of the project.

Preliminary Technical Assessment

The *preliminary technical assessment,* a second facet of Stage 1, subjects the proposed product to the business's technical staff—R&D, Engineering, and Operations—for appraisal (usually there is at least one technical person on the project team at this point). The purpose is to establish preliminary rough technical and product performance objectives, undertake a very preliminary technical feasibility study, and pinpoint possible technical risks. Specific tasks might include discussions among in-house Technical and Operations people (occasionally, outside experts will be used); a preliminary literature search (for example, a titles search); a preliminary patent search; and acquisition and review of competitive literature. If outside technology resources might be needed, an internal resource gap analysis is conducted, and a preliminary search for possible suppliers is conducted.

> Just a quick technical assessment in Stage 1— it's too early for bench work, model building, or detailed design work.

The key questions concern the technical viability of the product:

- Approximately what will the product requirements or specs be? (Note that the product definition may still be fairly vague and fluid at this early stage.)
- How would these requirements be achieved technically—is there a technical solution that can be envisioned? Or is invention and new science required? What's the size of the technical gap?
- What are the odds that the product is technically feasible? How, and at what cost and time? What are the potential technical risk and barriers? How might these be handled?
- Do you have the technological capability to develop it yourselves? Or do you need a partner or outside supplier for some development work? What are some potential sources of external technology?
- Can the product be manufactured or produced? How, with what equipment, and at what cost? Or should you consider outsourcing or a partner? What partners might be available?
- What about intellectual-property and product regulatory issues? (Note that regulatory and patent issues are introduced and considered at this early stage! Run this quickly by your company patent, legal, IP, and regulatory people at this point.)

The potential for partnering merits special mention. Working with a partner can bring the necessary and missing skills and resources to the project, but there are also risks and costs. Our research into partnering projects reveals *no performance enhancement*—partnering projects were no more successful, profitable, or faster than comparable projects done alone. But many of the partnering projects *would not have been done at all,* were it not for the partner's skills and resources![1] The message is: Be realistic—don't expect partnering to be a panacea for new-product success. Partnering is like marriage: Some relationships are born in heaven, others are not; and we found the new-product partnering divorce rate to be about 50 percent! When partnering in product innovation, having three factors in place makes all the difference, according to our study:

- Make sure it is a *win-win situation for both partners*—that one partner does not walk away with all the rewards, leaving little for the other partner (we saw much evidence of partnerships that were like a chicken-and-pig partnership in the bacon-and-eggs breakfast business—decidedly one-sided partnerships; the loser soon lost interest in the project).
- Make sure both partners have *done their homework*—that they understand clearly how the value gets shared, and the resource commitments and work effort that each must make.
- Finally, executives on both sides must *trust each other*—so that when one executive says "the work will be done in two weeks," it really is!

Preliminary Business and Financial Assessment

Following preliminary technical and market assessments comes the preliminary business and financial assessment. The strategic and competitive rationale for the project is mapped out. Similarly, a core competencies assessment (Do you have what it takes to win here?) is undertaken, which may identify the need for a partnering or outsourcing relationship. And then comes a first-pass financial analysis.

At this early stage, estimates of expected sales, costs, and investment required are likely to be highly speculative and largely conjecture. Nonetheless, it makes sense to undertake a cursory financial analysis here, more as a "sanity check"—to ensure you're not spending $10 million on a $1-million opportunity. This financial analysis amounts to little more than a payback calculation based on ballpark estimates: What's the investment required in the venture; what's the probable annual income; and how many years before we get our money back?

> This is a preliminary financial analysis based on rough estimates. It's too early for definitive and detailed spreadsheets!

A preliminary risk assessment should also be conducted as part of the business analysis. The risk assessment is similar to the FEMA (Failure Modes Effects Analysis) in engineering design work. First, list all that could go wrong with the project; then note the likelihood of each occurring; next, the impact; and finally, the "so what?"—what do you do to mitigate the risk?

Table 7.1 provides a summary of Stage 1. At the end of this Scoping stage, a recommendation for the project is developed, along with the proposed Action Plan for Stage 2. The project now moves to Gate 2, where is it again subjected to scrutiny. But this time, the decision is to move to a much more *extensive and expensive* stage, namely, Build the Business Case.

ON TO STAGE 2: BUILD THE BUSINESS CASE

Building the Business Case is the last of the front-end stages before serious product development work begins. It is perhaps the most difficult and certainly the most expensive of the pre-development stages; moreover, this is the *critical homework* stage—the one that makes or breaks the major project. It's here that you take a good idea or sometimes a fragile concept and translate it into a blockbuster new-product definition supported by a robust Business Case. Coincidentally, this is the stage that we found is so often weakly handled (Stage 2 actions are summarized in Table 7.2).

> Don't shortcut this stage! It's vital to do this well—a key factor in success.

What Is a Business Case?

The *Business Case* is the *key deliverable to* Gate 3, the decision point that opens the door to a full-fledged development project. The Business Case has three main components:

- The product and project definition
- The project justification
- The Action Plan or path forward

Consider each component of the Business Case—see Figure 7.2:

1. *Product and project definition:* This answers the "what and for whom?" questions. Here the *product is defined*—that is, the all-party agreement spells out who the product will be targeted at, and exactly what the product will be: its benefits, features, and design requirements. Remember the importance of having sharp product definition prior to the development work beginning! This definition was discovered to be one of the key factors in success: It provides a target for development and forces discipline into Stage 2. Otherwise, the development team faces a vague product definition, one that is often a moving target.

Inherent in the product definition is the need to put "meat" on the product idea—to move from the fairly preliminary and "rough outline" product definition (the one we had in Stage 1) to a *sharp, clear, and complete definition* by the end of Stage 2. Also implicit in this definition is the need to build in the ingredients of *product superiority:* This is the opportunity to shape the product's requirements, features, and specs into a set that delivers unique and real benefits to customers. The Integrated Product Definition includes:

- The project scope: what the bounds of the development effort are—is it a single new product? Or a family of products or a new series of releases? Or a platform?
- The target market definition—precisely who the product is aimed at.
- The product concept—what the product will be and do (written in the language of the customer or user).

Figure 7.2: The Objective Here Is a Robust Business Case, the Key Deliverable to Gate 3

I	II	III
The Product defined: **What will we develop & deliver?** • Target market • Product concept • Positioning and benefits to be delivered • Value proposition • Attributes, features, requirements • High-level specs	**The Project justified:** **Why should we invest?** • Business analysis • Financial analysis & justification • Risk assessment	**The Action Plans developed:** **How will we get there?** **Who will do the work?** **When?** **What resources?** • Detailed Action Plan for next stage (Development) • Tentative Action Plans through to launch • Prelim. Launch Plan • Prelim. Operations Plan

- The benefits to be delivered to the user or customer, including the *value proposition* for the customer.
- The positioning strategy—how the product will be positioned versus competitive products (including the price point).
- The product features, attributes, and performance requirements.
- The high-level specifications.

In the case of very fluid markets, where it is difficult to pin down the product definition before development begins—recall the section on fluid product definitions in Chapter 2—use the same list of items in this definition outlined above. But specify in advance which part of the product requirements and specs are fixed, and which are fluid before development begins. In practice, when defining the product, use two columns: that which is "fixed and known"; and that which is "fluid and variable"—see Figure 7.3. Then build steps into the development process to gather data so that the "fluid components" can be pinned down as development proceeds. Note that allowing a partially fluid product definition is not an excuse for failing to do the front-end homework—I'm not advocating intellectual laziness here! Rather, it's simply a practical solution to the problem that some markets truly are fluid.

2. *Project justification:* This second component of the Business Case answers the "why" question. That is, why should your company invest in this project? This question boils down to a review of business, financial, profitability, and risk considerations. Because financial data are likely to be somewhat in error, note that

TABLE 7.2: SUMMARY OF STAGE 2 ACTIONS—BUILD THE BUSINESS CASE

Purpose of Stage 2:	To refine the proposed product concept into a winning-product definition, and to establish a sound basis for taking the project into Development. The result of Stage 2 is a defined product, target market and understanding of technical feasibility supported by a sound Business Case. It is where detailed market and technical investigations result in a Business Case, which includes the Integrated Product Definition, project justification, and project Action Plans. Stage 2 can be a time-consuming stage, especially for higher-risk projects. Time will vary depending upon the project.
Actions in Stage 2:	
VoC User Needs-and-Wants Study	VoC research to determine product requirements; face-to-face interviews or camping out (ethnography)—in-depth market research. Determines what is "value" and what is a "customer benefit"; seeks to define a winning-product concept from the user's or customer's perspective. Probes customer needs, wants, and preferences; their problems, choice criteria, likes, dislikes, and trade-offs regarding product requirements and design; also the customer's use system and product's value-in-use (economics). Seeks insights to build into the *compelling value proposition*.
Competitive Analysis	A detailed look at the competition—both direct and indirect. Determines who they are, product strengths and weaknesses, anticipated future products, pricing, competitors' other strengths and weaknesses, how they compete, and their performance.
Market Analysis	Pulls together all market information from the two studies above, plus secondary sources in more depth. Determines market size, trends,

segmentation and size, buyer behavior, and competitive situation. Relies on similar sources as in Stage 1, only much more in-depth.

Detailed Technical Assessment

Translates these market inputs into a technically feasible product design or concept (on paper). May involve some physical technical work (modeling, lab work). Maps out the technical solution and technical route; highlights technical risks and solutions; reviews intellectual-property issues and develops IP strategy; assesses possible technical partners and develops partnering strategy. Also looks in depth at manufacturability and source-of-supply: production route, costs, and capital (equipment) requirements.

Concept Testing with User

Market test prior to full commitment to develop the product—the first real "build-test-feedback-and-revise" spiral. Tests the proposed product concept with the customer or user (product concept, model, virtual prototype). Involves face-to-face interviews; gauges interest, liking, preference, differentiation, purchase intent, and price sensitivity.

Financial & Business Analysis

Looks at the business rationale for the project. Includes strategic assessment (fit and impact). Also a core competencies assessment and partnering (or outsourcing) strategy is mapped out, along with the role of international units. A detailed financial analysis is developed: NPV, IRR, Payback & sensitivity analysis. Also a risk assessment.

Action Plans

Develops recommendation for project (Go/Kill) and a detailed Action Plan for Stage 3 (Development Plan)—timeline, resources required, deliverables at end of Development. Also tentative plans for Stage 4, Testing, as well as Stage 5 (both preliminary Market Launch and Operations Plans). A launch date is specified.

Figure 7.3: The Integrated Product Definition -- Define the Product, Noting Fixed and Variable Elements

Components	Known & Fixed	Fluid & Variable
Project Scope		
Target Market		
Product Concept		
Benefits to Be Delivered, Value Proposition		
Positioning & Price Point		
Features, Attributes, Performance Requirements		
High-Level Specs		

And what the product will not be!

this justification should also be based on nonfinancial criteria and considerations as well: qualitative issues such as strategic rationale, competitive advantage, leverage, and market attractiveness. Solutions such as partnering and outsourcing are also part of the justification assessment. The project risk assessment is included here as well.

3. *The Action Plans:* This final component of the Business Case answers the questions "how, by whom, and when?" It lays out the plan of action from Development through to Launch, usually in the form of a time line or perhaps a critical path plan. Resources required—money, people, and equipment—are also spelled out. And a launch date is specified in the Business Case, complete with preliminary marketing launch and operations, manufacturing or source-of-supply plans. Given the uncertainties of future events, however, most often these plans through to Launch are very tentative. The recommendation is that the plan for the next stage (Stage 3, Development) be defined in some detail—activities, events, milestones, time line, and resources required; and that plans for subsequent stages be sketches or "throwaway plans."

A Map of What Happens in Stage 2
So what makes up this pivotal Stage 2? Figure 7.4 maps out the key actions. Building the Business Case involves, first of all, thorough market studies: a user "needs-and-wants" study—VoC work—to define in detail what must be built into the

Figure 7.4: Make Sure That These "Build Business Case" Actions Are in the "Build Business Case" Stage of Your Idea-to-Launch System

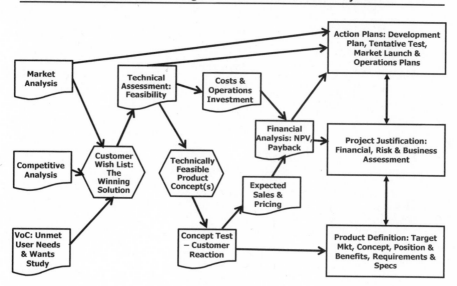

product; a competitive analysis; and a concept test of the product to gauge market acceptance. Technical work, largely conceptual, translates the market "wish list" into a technically feasible concept. A Business Case is developed for the project: the product definition is agreed to; and a thorough project justification and detailed Action Plan are developed.

Let's look at each of these Stage 2 actions in more detail.

UNDERTAKE VOC RESEARCH: A USER NEEDS-AND-WANTS STUDY

A user needs-and-wants study is the VoC market research that is so often omitted, with disastrous consequences. Its purpose is to probe the customer in order to put meat on the idea—to take a rather skimpy idea and develop a complete description of the product: benefits, value proposition, features, performance characteristics, and design requirements. The breathalyzer example, the Viactiv calcium chews project, and the PumpSmart case from earlier chapters demonstrate the nature of work that is intended here. The problem is that *most of us already have a fixed idea of what the customer is looking for,* so we conveniently skip over this critical market study. We usually get it wrong, because we have not listened well to the customer!

> This VoC work is perhaps the most important task in Stage 2 to get right—it makes all the difference between winning and losing!

Figure 7.5: The Means-End Link That Determines Product Value to the Customer or User

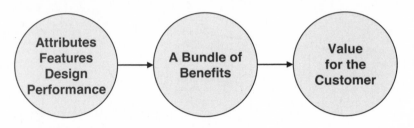

- ❑ **"Value" is in the eye of the customer or user**
- ❑ **Must study the customer to determine:**
  - ➤ What is "value"?
  - ➤ What is a benefit?
  - ➤ What is a "better product"?

A superior product—one that delivers *unique benefits to customers*—is the number one success factor. Never forget this fact! But how do you define this unique and superior product? This user needs-and-wants study provides the big opportunity: It enables you to translate your sketch of a product idea into a concrete and winning new-product concept. The goal of this study is to identify customers' needs, wants, and preferences, what they're looking for in a "winning" product, and what will absolutely delight them!

The ultimate objective is to deliver a product with real value—a compelling value proposition—to the customer (see Figure 7.5). Product value is in turn derived from the benefits built into and surrounding the product. And these in turn come from the product's design: its features, attributes, and performance characteristics, and even its positioning.

The Means-End Link in Delivering Customer Value

The point is that you must understand the means-end chain between value, benefits, and product features and performance (shown in Figure 7.5). So listen to the voice of the customer in order to get the product design right! That's why this user needs-and-wants study is so critical.

Specific research questions to address in this study include:

- What is valuable to customers? What do they really value and by how much?
- What is a benefit? That is, what specific product deliverables would the customer see as being of benefit—enough to pay more for?
- What features, attributes, and performance characteristics translate into benefits and value for the customer?

Only by understanding the interrelationships between physical characteristics (that is, product features) and customer perceptions (that is, a customer-perceived benefit) are you in a position to sit down and design the winning new product.

The VoC user needs-and-wants study identifies these relationships and answers the key research questions above about value and benefits. You can start with simple research—for example, focus groups of customers—to gain some insights into product value and desired benefits. But a focus group is only a start, and certainly not a substitute for a broader-based study. Face-to-face, in-depth, and on-site interviews, or ethnography, are usually required in order to gain the depth of understanding needed to proceed with product design.

The specific information objectives of this VoC user needs-and-wants study usually include:

- ✓ to identify customer problems with the current solution—problems that require a new solution or a new product
- ✓ to determine customers' unmet, unspoken, or unarticulated needs
- ✓ to identify their wants and preferences in a new product
- ✓ to pinpoint areas of likes and satisfaction with current (competitive) products, and also areas of dislikes and dissatisfaction with these products
- ✓ to identify the order-winning criteria, and their relative importance
- ✓ to study how customers use the products—their use system—and what problems they face in its use, and
- ✓ to understand the customer's economics of use—the total life cycle costs to the customer.

Understanding Unspoken Needs

Real customer needs are difficult to uncover. Often, customers don't know what they need, so how can they put these needs into words?[2] Customers can tell you what they want—often they describe their "product wants" in terms of a competitive product—but that's not the same as what they need. If Henry Ford had asked people what they wanted, they would have said "a faster horse." But a VoC study done at the time would have revealed many unmet needs: faster, yes, but also: more reliable, longer distance, more comfortable, easier to drive and control, for the whole family, a cleaner and an easier to maintain and keep mode of transportation—the needs that the Model T automobile ultimately met.

Needs can be understood by discovering:

- The *benefits* that the products or service features deliver to the customer or user
- The *problems* that customers would like to have solved
- What the product *lets the customer or user do*
- "Customer murmurs"—those things customers say under their breath, often in frustration

> A functional orientation (benefits). What the product should be and do for the user—not a list of the features and specs.

Undertaking the VoC Study

There are several ways to undertake a VoC user needs-and-wants study. First, you can *become customers* or users yourselves—ensure that the project team uses and endures the product during the project. Second, *live with and critically observe customers* or users—camp out with customers and undertake ethnographic research. Another approach is to *identify lead or innovative users* (those ahead of the wave) and work with them. Finally, and perhaps the most traditional approach, *listen to customers and users*—which is quite different than talking at them! Hear their voices, via:

- In-depth personal interviews
- Focus groups with customers and users
- Market surveys, including phone and Webex, e-mail surveys, and various Internet tools (such as Survey Monkey)

Note that you must define the *target market* first: VoC research is not a "shotgun" approach.

Questions to Pose in a VoC Study

Here are ten specific questions that are frequently addressed in customer (or user) interviews as part of a VoC user needs-and-wants study:

1. How are potential customers now solving their problem? What is the current solution? For example, what current product are they using, and why this particular product, make, brand, or supplier?
2. What unsolved problems are customers or users experiencing via the current solution? What are their points of pain? What really annoys them about the current products or solutions? What keeps them awake at night? Are there opportunities here for a new solution or new way of doing things? Remember: Find big problems, look for big solutions!
3. If customers had a choice, which solution, product, or brand would they buy now? Why this one? Which one or ones would they not buy? And why not?
   Questions like this are important in that they are methods of inferring what customers are looking for, and what they wish to avoid. Here, you're trying to uncover what the customers' unmet and unarticulated needs are; also, what they see as having value, what a new solution might look like, and what their "hot buttons" are!
4. What are customers' choice criteria—the criteria that they use to make a purchase decision—price, certain features and functionality, service, and so on? Why do they (or would they) buy what they buy? And what is the relative importance of each criterion in the decision?

5. How do current (competitive) products rate on each of the choice criteria? Which competitor scores highest on each criterion? Who's the lowest? And why do customers say this—what is it about their products that causes customers to rate them so high or low on each criterion?

    These fairly traditional questions on choice criteria and competitive ratings are important for several reasons. First, an understanding of how customers make their purchase choice and what criteria are used is a critical input into product design: At minimum, your new product must address and score high on the important criteria. Second, understanding how competitors' products score identifies areas of potential opportunity—for example, a competitive product weakness—that can be exploited via an improved design. A knowledge of the reasons that underlie these competitive ratings also provides valuable insights to the product designer regarding what to build into your new product and what to avoid. Finally, different patterns of responses among customers may suggest the existence of two or more market segments, and point to a market niche that was missed by competitors and can be successfully targeted by you.

6. What do customers specifically like about competitive products or current solutions? And what do they dislike? What problems do they have when using competitive products?

    Often, competitive products do have many positive design aspects, which can be borrowed and built into your new product. There's nothing wrong with copying the good facets of a competitor's product, providing you go beyond a mere copy. A knowledge of what the positive facets of competitive products are is obviously a valuable input to the designer. Similarly, identification of dislikes and problems that customers see with competitive products opens up opportunities for significant design improvement. Remember: The objective is to design a superior product, and that means superior to the leading competitive products. So an understanding of where the competitor fails—where its Achilles' heel is—is half the battle!

7. What specifically are customers looking for in a new product? What features, attributes, and performance? Which of these are "must haves" and which are only "desirable but not essential"?

8. What tradeoffs are customers prepared to make (for example, tradeoffs among various possible performance deliverables, or product features, or features versus price)?

    An understanding of customers' stated requirements—both musts and shoulds—is obviously a critical design input. But note that this customer-stated wish list is usually fairly sterile, and not enough upon which to build a winning new-product design. A knowledge of customer tradeoffs reveals the relative preference among various product features and attributes, and indicates relative value or importance of different design features to the customer.

9. How do customers use (and misuse or abuse) the product? What is the customer's "use system" in which the product must operate? And how does it fit into (or interact) with other components of the system?

10. What are the customers' economics? And how does your potential product affect their economics in use?

These last two questions are both critical and difficult. The first looks beyond the product itself: It probes the role the product plays in the total use system. The question applies to products from prepared food entrées (the kitchen and household are the system) through to telecommunications components and software. The economics or "value in use" is fundamental to understanding how you can deliver a product that yields better economic value—for example, by saving the customer money over the total life of the product or in some other facet of the customer's system.

Using VoC Research to Define Your New Product

Fine in theory, you say. But how do you put this into practice? There is no standard formula to listen to the voice of the customer in order to uncover unmet needs and translate these into potential winning solutions. But there are some patterns. I gave you the examples of blockbuster projects where VoC made the difference: the Dräger Safety breathalyzer testing device—recall how on-site visits and camping out (ethnography) with police officers revealed many problems (in Chapter 2). And Chapter 4 outlined the heavy VoC work—largely in-depth site visits by visit teams—by the PumpSmart team; and the Viactiv project team in Chapter 2 spared no effort to seek VoC input and used a variety of methods.

> This is research—not just a few casual visits. It must be carefully designed and executed, but worth every minute of effort!

Tips and Hints in Doing the VoC Study

1. Think carefully about your *information objectives*. Information only has a value to the extent that it improves a decision. So outline the key design decisions you must make and then identify the information that you need to make these decisions. And only then begin crafting the questions you wish to address to customers.

2. Use a *structured questionnaire* for interviews. You may think that you're good at interviewing—at directing the conversation and remembering answers. But if you plan on interviewing more than one or two customers, you'd better develop a questionnaire. Why?
   - ✓ *completeness:* so you cover all the questions you want answers to
   - ✓ *consistency:* so each respondent is questioned in the same way, with the same wording
   - ✓ *recording:* so you have a consistent method of recording the responses

3. This is *not selling, but listening.* Don't present product concepts or solutions (except perhaps at the end of the interview)—this is not a "show and tell" session! Instead, listen to the customers: They can tell you about product excellences, product shortcomings, problems, desired benefits, and points of pain. When users mention problems, lead them through their problems. And the word "why" is as important as the word "what"—"why did you mention that problem, why is that such a big issue for you?" And use indirect questioning rather than direct questions: They give you more insights into real needs.

4. Adopt a *functional* orientation—look for benefits sought and what the product should be and do for the user—not simply a list of the features and specifications.

5. Are you seeking the *right information?* Do a "pre-posterior" analysis—that is, before charging out to do interviews, imagine that the study is already done—that you have the answers to the questions. Given these answers, can you make the design and project decisions? If there are any doubts, now is the time to rethink and revise your questionnaire—not after the interviews are finished! And do some mock interviews first—perhaps with salespeople posing as customers—to make sure your questions sound right.

6. Make sure the interviewees are *representative*—not just a handful of people or customers selected strictly for convenience. For B2B customers, never rely on one or two interviews per client firm. Cast the net broadly! Remember: One person does not speak for his or her company! There are many influencers in the purchasing company, and focusing on one or two people in the mistaken belief that they represent the company can lead to very erroneous information.

7. *Move down the value chain.* It's not enough just to research your immediate customer. I often use the words "user" and "customer" interchangeably, but obviously they are different people in most industries. It's usually necessary to move down the value chain, beyond your immediate customer, to seek insights into market needs. There are multiple purchase influencers in any value chain, and they need to be contacted to gain full market insight. Sometimes, conflicts between different members of the value chain are identified—for example, your customer's customer wants a certain feature or performance, but your immediate customer does not. Armed with information about each value-chain member's needs, you're in a better position to make informed decisions on such trade-offs.

8. Get your *technical people involved* in the interviews, too. Seeking market information is too important to be left solely to the marketer. The interview or visit team should be two or three people, ideally three, both Marketing and Technical. This is especially true for technology-based products, and for technically sophisticated customers. The salesperson may be best for setting up the interviews, with the marketing person leading the design of

the questionnaire and handling the general questions; but the technical person has much more depth of knowledge about what is technically possible and what is not, and can engage the customer in a much more probing and profound conversation, which can lead to identification of desired product features and performance that the marketer would have missed.

9. *Do the interviews yourself*—the entire project team—so that you gain first-hand learning. Hiring a market research firm is fine, but they get the benefit of the learning, and you get a sterile report! If an outside firm is hired, go with its employees on the interviews and ensure that they teach your people how to do such interviews for future projects.

10. Study the *customer's system or use environment* and how the product fits into the whole system. And try to gain an understanding of how the system works, so that you can better appreciate the needs for and demands placed on your product. And watch people using the products—using, misusing, and abusing, again to gain insights to needs.

Suggestion: Does your company do a solid job in terms of a VoC user needs-and-wants study? Do you go to your customers, and via face-to-face meetings, try to understand their problems, needs, wants, likes, dislikes, and preferences before development begins—in short, finding out everything you'll need to know to sit down and design a truly superior product? Or are you like most firms: You arrive at a concept internally; you then use market research strictly to test product concept; but you don't really listen to the voice of the customer to help you develop and refine the concept.

In your next significant new-product project, why not build in a VoC user needs-and-wants study before Development begins. Let the *results of this study help shape your product design* or product specs, translating an otherwise mundane idea into a real winner!

DO A COMPETITIVE ANALYSIS

A second key to building a superior new product is competitive analysis. There are several purposes to such an analysis. The first is to understand the competitor's product and its strengths and weaknesses. If your objective is to deliver product superiority, then the benchmark for comparison—the competitor's product—must be totally understood. Second, a knowledge of how your competitors play the game—how they compete and where and how they are getting customers—can provide valuable insights into the keys to success and failure in this business. Finally, an appreciation of competitive strategy and

> Most project teams lack fact-based knowledge of competitive products, pricing, and strategies. They're usually based on hearsay and a few people's opinions.

how the competitor's product fits into its portfolio may give clues about expected competitive response to your product launch: For example, will it invoke a strong defense?

Key Questions in a Competitive Analysis

Here are some of the vital questions to address in a competitive analysis:

1. Who are the key players—the direct or indirect competitors—whose product yours will replace (or take business away from)?
2. What are their products' features, attributes, and performance characteristics? What are their products' strong points and deficiencies?
3. What is their product offering likely to be by the time you get to market (anticipate their new products, features, and performance)?

   It's important to understand just who the adversary is and the exact nature of the product that yours must overtake. Understanding its strong points gives clues as to what to build into your product; its weaknesses reveal areas to exploit in a superior design.
4. What other strengths and weaknesses does each competitor have—for example, sales force, customer service, technical support, branding, advertising, and promotion? For what is each competitor held in high regard? And where are its weak points?

   You must compete not only on the basis of product but also on nonproduct elements. Although product advantage is clearly desirable, sometimes the main points of competitive advantage will be found in other elements of the marketing mix.
5. How does each competitor play the game? For example, on what types of customers (or segments) does each competitor focus? And what is the basis for competition? That is, how does each competitor get business—by pricing low? Via product advantage? By having a highly skilled sales force? Or via a heavier promotional effort?
6. How well are the competitors doing? What are their market shares, and what has been the trend for each? And why is each doing so well (or poorly)—what's the secret to its success (or demise)?

   Here the focus is on what it takes to win. Take a close look at the players with their different strategies and approaches, and observe their results. From this come valuable lessons about what succeeds and what fails in this marketplace.
7. (If possible) What are the competitors' cost pictures? Their production volumes and capacities? And their profitability—both contribution and net? And how important a product is this one to their operations and to their total profitability?

   These often-confidential data give insight into the strategic importance of the competitors' products to this business, their ability to respond (for example, how far they could cut price), and their likelihood of mounting an aggressive defense against your new product.

Ways to Get Competitive Intelligence

Unlike customer-oriented market research, there are no tried-and-proven methods for competitive analysis. It's more like playing detective and tracking down a variety of leads. Some suggestions:

- Get your hands on all possible *competitive literature* and competitive *advertising.* This is all in the public domain: Your own sales force should be able to help with trade literature, and clipping (or securing) advertisements displayed in print (or electronically) is straightforward. And use the Internet to get information on their existing products, to learn about their new products, to download their brochures, instruction manuals, and installation instructions, and to get pricing information.
- Do an Internet search through various *trade publications,* looking for information on competitors: announcements, new-product introductions, plant expansions, or financial results.
- Try to acquire your *competitors' products.* If they are openly for sale and not too expensive, this is no problem. A friendly customer may also help out here as well, giving you access to a competitive product. And if the product is intangible—a new service product—utilize "mystery shopping" by posing as a customer and experiencing your competitors' service product firsthand.
- Map your *competitors' product road map*—their recent product introductions and their timing, along with features and performance. Try to project this roadmap into the future. You can use *patent mapping and mining* to anticipate their introductions in technical fields: Usually one has to file patents well ahead, giving you about a two-year advance notice of forthcoming products or technologies.
- Visit *trade shows.* Where else can you find under one roof the best and the newest that your competitors have to offer? And also observe customers' reactions at the trade show—much like a mini-concept test! It's all there, open for public viewing.
- Talk to your own *sales and service people.* They spend much time in the field and have the opportunity to see competitive products, practices, and prices. They also attend conferences and trade shows, and often have friends in other firms. In many cases, they are a storehouse of valuable competitive information.
- While doing your VoC *user needs-and-wants study,* be sure to build in questions that seek opinions from your target customers about competitors: ratings and insights on competitive products, their sales force, service, and pricing.

- Talk to *suppliers* about your competitors. From suppliers, you might be able to learn about the installed competitor capacity (what equipment and capacity it has), and current production volume (based on materials purchased).
- Use *financial sources.* For example, obtain a copy of their annual report and ask your investment house for its appraisal of the competitor. To be publicly traded, the SEC requires considerable information on the operations of a company. Ask your investment house to secure this information from the securities people—for example, the 10K report. And undertake a keyword search through the many financial papers and magazines, hunting for your competitors' names—*Fortune, Business Week,* the *Wall Street Journal, Financial Times of London,* and so on.
- Hire a *consulting firm* that is expert on competitive intelligence. Often such firms have detailed intelligence files as well as considerable experience in employing some of the methods listed above.

REVISIT THE MARKET ANALYSIS—THIS TIME IN MORE DEPTH

These two market studies outlined above—the VoC user needs-and-wants study, combined with the competitive analysis—are crucial to designing a superior product. But more information about the market is also required in Stage 2. The numerous secondary and other sources of market information highlighted in the Scoping stage (Stage 1) should be reaccessed, but this time, much more thoroughly for Stage 2 (refer back to the Preliminary Market Assessment section in Stage 1 earlier in this chapter for a complete listing of information sources).

The goal here is to develop a detailed portrait of the marketplace—a market analysis—that includes:

- ✓ market size, growth, and trends
- ✓ market segments: their size, growth, and trends
- ✓ buyer behavior: the who, what, when, where, and how of the purchase situation
- ✓ the competitive situation

When you develop a detailed market launch plan, this market analysis becomes even more essential. We see this market analysis again in Chapter 10, where we'll take a closer look at developing the launch plan.

TIME FOR A DETAILED TECHNICAL INVESTIGATION

The VoC user needs-and-wants study coupled with the competitive analysis should yield a set of guidelines—a wish list of what should be built into your new product to delight the customer and to upstage the competitor. This customer

> Spend enough time and money here so that you are reasonably confident that the product could indeed be developed . . . but *don't Develop* the product.

wish list must now be translated into something that is technically and economically feasible. This is where market needs and wants and technical possibilities must be married, in order to arrive at a proposed product design. In short, technical people must find a means of satisfying expressed customer needs and preferences. This is a creative process involving the entire project team, not just technical people. It may involve:

✓ discussions among your technical people—both people on the project team and from outside the team—to arrive at the likely technical solution on paper
✓ creative problem solving to deal with major technical issues
✓ brainstorming to arrive at creative solutions
✓ techniques such as Quality Function Deployment to translate marketing requirements into technical specs
✓ a detailed literature search and a patent search
✓ seeking help from outside experts
✓ and even some physical technical work, too:
  - definitive experiments or lab work (proof of concept)—but not full product development!
  - modeling
  - developing a crude mock-up or "protocept"
  - visioning the likely solution
  - creating a few screens, and writing some code, in the case of software products

To a large extent, this successful technical translation depends on the technological prowess and brainpower of your technical people. But *a clear definition of what is required to meet customer needs* and yield competitive advantage will certainly sharpen and focus this creative process.

Key Questions in a Detailed Technical Assessment
The questions that are addressed in this detailed technical investigation include:

1. What is the probable technical solution that will yield a product to meet marketplace requirements? Can you envision a solution?
2. What is involved in arriving at this technical solution? Is invention and new science required? Or is this simply a matter of applying fairly well-known technology?

3. What are the technical risks and potential roadblocks? And how might these be dealt with? Can alternate technical solutions be pursued in parallel?
4. Do you have the necessary skills, competencies, and track record to develop the technical solution? Can these gaps be filled by potential partners? Who?
5. If partnering in development: What is the technological competence of your partner? What role will the partner play—tasks, deliverables, commitments?
6. What are the key steps involved in arriving at a prototype product? How long will each step take and how much will each cost? What are the personnel requirements?
7. What legal or patent, regulatory, and safety issues might arise? And how would you deal with each? Do you have a patent or intellectual-property strategy in place?
8. How might the product be manufactured or produced (source-of-supply)? In your plant or operations facilities? Or would new facilities, equipment, and production personnel be required? What would the production volume be? At what capital cost? Do you need a production partner or outsourcing here?
9. What is the cost per unit of producing the product? What materials and components are required and are they available? At what cost?

The end result is a solid idea of what the product will be from a technical standpoint, what the probable technical solutions and technical route are, and a reasonably high confidence that this solution and route are technically feasible. Although some technical work—for example, lab work, experimental work, or modeling—may occur here, *limit this technical work* in Stage 2. Be careful that work more appropriate to Stage 3 does not move forward into this Business Case stage. The depth of technical work here in Stage 2 was put nicely by Rohm and Haas's Biocides business unit in their new-product process:

> If lab work is conducted in Stage 2, the purpose is not to produce a prototype or final product; rather the spirit is to spend a limited amount of time to see if one can arrive at something remotely close to the desired product, enough to provide confidence that with more effort, it could be done.

My usual rule of thumb is to spend no more than 10 percent of the Stage 3 Development costs here in Stage 2—that is, spend 10 percent to gain the knowledge and confidence to justify spending the remaining 90 percent. But don't spend the 90 percent here!

TEST THE CONCEPT WITH THE CUSTOMER—START THE SPIRALS

Will the new product be a winner? Before pushing ahead into Stage 3 with product development, you must be certain that the product will meet customer needs and wants better than competitive products and will achieve your sales targets. Remember that your product is the new entry into the market, and it has to give the customer a reason to switch.

A problem faced by many project teams is one of interpretation and translation. A thorough market study is undertaken that identifies customer needs and wants. The project team then translates these into a conceptual product design—a set of product specs. But something goes wrong in the translation. The final product isn't quite what the customer wants, or it lacks that special something that differentiates it from what the customer is already buying: It just doesn't quite delight the customer or lacks that "wow factor."

In order for this needs-identification-and-translation process to work well, two assumptions must be true:

1. Customers understand their needs (or at minimum the problems they wish solved, or the benefits they seek) and are able to verbalize these to you during the VoC user needs-and-wants study.
2. You interpret these needs correctly and do a good job of translating these needs into the technical solution and final product specs.

Both are assumptions! Even the most knowledgeable customer may not totally understand or be able to articulate his or her needs, problems, or desires, or these may not be accurately conveyed or understood during the face-to-face discussions. Even if needs are understood, there may be errors in translation: The needs and wants are misinterpreted by you, resulting in the wrong set of product specs. Or your technical solution falls just a little short of the ideal product.

The concept test is the final test prior to the Development stage that validates that the product concept (and hence, the proposed product) is indeed a winner: It checks that customer needs were correctly understood, interpreted, and translated, and makes final course adjustments in the product design before it is too late.

There is another good reason to introduce a concept test here. Recall from Chapter 2 the argument that "customers don't know what they're looking for until they see it." Thus, while all the VoC user needs-and-wants studies above may yield valuable insights into customer needs, they may also miss the mark. So *get something in front of the customer*—early and often—and gauge feedback before you charge into development. That's the role of the concept test—it's the first test in these "build-test-feedback-and-revise" iterations in the spiral development approach in Figure 5.3.

Prospecting Versus Testing

It makes sense to build in a concept test as part of Stage 2 and before proceeding to product development. There is a fundamental difference between this concept-test market study and the user needs-and-wants study outlined above. The VoC user needs-and-wants study is for *prospecting:* No product or product concept was available to show the customer, but hints, clues, and insights were obtained from the customer about what should be built into a winning-product design.

Once the technical investigation has yielded a technically feasible concept, then a full proposition concept can be shown to the customer—a model, a set of drawings, a storyboard, a spec sheet, a dummy brochure or a virtual prototype— and customer response can be gauged: "Given what you've told us, this is what we've come up with in terms of a proposed product; now, what do you think of it? Would you buy it?"

The concept test is not a prospecting study, but rather a *test or validation* that the proposed product concept is indeed a winner—intent to purchase is established. Note that at this early stage you still don't have a developed product. The purpose of this concept test is to see if you're heading in the right direction. By this time, you should have at minimum a written description of the product and its benefits, features, performance characteristics, and likely price. In addition, you may have something concrete to show the customer—drawings, artists renderings, a model, a PowerPoint slide show, a crude working model or mock-up, or even a virtual prototype on your laptop.

Designing the Concept Test

The design of a concept test is similar to that of the VoC user needs-and-wants study. At minimum, you might use focus groups of customers to gauge reactions to the proposed product. Although such focus groups give useful feedback on the product, remember that the limited sample size, the fact that group members are often not representative of the entire market (for example, a self-selected group), and the nature of the group dynamics mean that the group's vote on the product may not be a true reflection of your target market. So a broader and more representative sample of customers should be contacted via a survey: by telephone, Internet, or personal interview, or some combination of these.

Concept tests differ from user needs-and-wants studies in two major ways: First, in a concept test you *have something to show the customer* to solicit feedback; and second, you are seeking very different types of information than in a user needs-and-wants study.

Presenting the New-Product Proposition or Concept

In order to respond intelligently, the customer must fully understand the product as it will be. The better you are able to convey what the final product will be and do, the more accurate gauge of purchase intent you will get. So get as close to the "final product" as you can in your concept presentation:

- Use verbal descriptions in conjunction with visuals: artists' sketches of the product, line drawings, dummy spec sheets, dummy brochures, or perhaps even a PowerPoint show or computer animation showing the product in simulated use.

- For consumer goods, pictures or drawings showing the product and its packaging can be displayed. Better yet, use a storyboard presentation with a sound track.
- Use models (for example, crude working models or mock-ups) or inexpensive rapid prototypes to show to the customer. Often a crude prototype or sample can be put together quickly and inexpensively as part of the detailed technical investigation in Stage 2. Some food companies call these "protocepts"—partway between a concept and a prototype.
- Get creative and use the capability of your laptop and available software. Create a virtual prototype on your laptop—using CAD to draw the product, having it rotate in space before the customer's eyes. Or show the product operating via computer animation. For software concepts, developing a few screens helps to anchor the product in the user's mind, and to even enable the customer to experience it.
- If your project's risk and amounts at stake are great enough, try a full proposition presentation using a video show or perhaps an interactive presentation on your laptop.

What Information to Seek

A concept test seeks customer reaction to the product in an attempt to assess market acceptance and expected sales revenues. Information objectives typically include the following:

- ✓ a measure of the customer's interest in the proposed product and why
- ✓ a measure of the customer's liking for the product concept, and which facets are liked the most and the least
- ✓ degree of differentiation—how different from competitive products the customer sees the proposed product to be
- ✓ a comparative measure—a measure of the customer's preference for the concept relative to competitive brands or products the customer now uses, and the reasons for these preferences
- ✓ an indication of what the customer might expect to pay for the product
- ✓ an indication of the customer's purchase intent at a specified price
- ✓ information useful in finalizing the position strategy

Figure 7.6 shows a typical questionnaire. Note that there is a combination of closed-ended questions (to which the customer selects an answer, for example on a one-to-five scale), and open-ended questions (which result in a verbal answer or discussion). The closed-ended questions provide concrete, numeric data that can be aggregated and analyzed across many customers. But numbers alone tend to be sterile, hence open-ended responses are also sought to lend richness and greater understanding.

Figure 7.6: Questions in a Concept Test—Can Be Displayed on a Screen

1. First, what's your reaction to the product? (Product concept is shown & described)

Very negative	Somewhat negative	Neutral	Somewhat positive	Very positive

2. Why so positive (or negative)?
3. How interested are you in the product (concept)?

Not at all	Not too interested	Neutral	Somewhat interested	Very interested

4. Why are you so interested (or not interested)?
5. How different is is this product compared to others you are familiar with? Which one(s)?

Not at all different	Marginally different	A little different	Quite different	Very different

6. Why it is (not) different – what stands out?
7. To what extent do you like the product (concept)?

Not at all	Not too much	Somewhat	Like it quite bit	Love it

8. What three things do you like most about it? Three things liked least?
9. What would you expect to pay for this product compared to Product X: (dollar amount; or answer on scale)

Much less than	Somewhat less than	The same	Somewhat more than	Much more than

10. Why more (less) than?
11. What is the likelihood that you would buy this product, assuming it were available at a price of $XX?

Definitely would not	Probably would not	Maybe	Probably would buy	Definitely would buy

12. Why (or why not)?

Be sure to use a structured questionnaire to ensure that all relevant questions and issues are covered and that answers are recorded in a consistent way. Even when conducting personal interviews, it is good practice to follow a standardized questionnaire or interview guide, perhaps even showing the customer the written questions on your laptop screen. Seek quantitative answers where possible: Let the customer indicate responses on the various scaled measures, using a pointer and a scale, for example, to express an opinion.

It is also good practice to design a standard format for a concept test and to use that format consistently from product to product. In this way you will develop a history of data and establish benchmarks for comparison. For example, when 30 percent of those surveyed check off the "definitely would buy" box in Figure 7.6, what does this mean—is this a good result or poor one, and what market share might this score translate into?

Using the Results of a Concept Test

Use the results of a concept test with caution. They merely provide an indication of likely product acceptance—there are no guarantees. Nor should the results be used blindly. For most new products, particularly concepts in categories familiar to the customer, concept tests are likely to *overstate the market acceptance*. For example, a result of "30 percent of respondents definitely would buy" is not likely to translate into a market share of 30 percent for several reasons. First, respondents tend to have a positive response bias. There are many reasons for this: the so-called Hawthorn effect, whereby people under observation tend to respond more positively or enthusiastically than those not being studied; the desire to give socially acceptable or pleasing answers to the interviewer; and the fact that it's easy to say yes when there's no money or commitment involved. Second, although respondents might say that they'll buy your product, in the case of a frequently repurchased product, they may continue to buy the competitor's as well, that is, split purchases. If they buy both equally, the "30 percent definitely would buy" actually translates into a 15 percent market share. Third, not all potential buyers in your defined target market will be exposed sufficiently to your new product. Your advertising, promotion, distribution, and sales force may reach less than half of the total target market. The "intent to purchase" figure must be cut down by a factor that reflects your market exposure (or audience reach) on launch.

There are other problems as well that render the concept test results suspect. A common problem is obtaining feedback from the wrong respondents: This is particularly troublesome in B2B settings, where the one person interviewed may not speak for the entire company. Another problem is overselling the product concept—either promising things that the final product will not or cannot deliver, or using too much hype in the presentation of the concept (this is a test, not a sales pitch!).

For very innovative products—new or unfamiliar product categories to the customer—concept test results may *understate the product's acceptance.* Unfamiliar concepts tend to elicit a negative response initially, and it may be only after customers have had a chance to use the product for a while that they begin to appreciate the product's benefits. In short, there is a learning process here that occurs over time, one that cannot be measured in the short time frame of a snapshot concept test. For example, the initial consumer reaction to the introduction of automatic teller machines (ATMs) by banks was very negative—it was an alien, somewhat scary concept. It was only after we used these machines for several years that we saw their advantages, and our comfort level increased. A purchase-intent concept test today would yield very different results than one done in the early 1970s (which would have predicted a very low market acceptance).

> Face-to-face concept tests are best. But you can also do these online (for example, Survey Monkey, Insight Express, Market Reader PRO, National Market Measures, MRSI's ConSelect).

Tips and Hints in Doing Concept Tests

1. *Be realistic* in preparing the concept presentation. The concept presentation should reflect the real-world environment that will exist when you launch your product. Control your zeal, and only highlight benefits and performance characteristics that will be realistically included in the final product, and which you will be able to communicate to the customer at Launch.

The importance of being realistic is obvious. But countless examples exist where lack of realism was the culprit. A well-known firm in the female personal products business investigated the viability of a new woman's body lotion. A concept test was undertaken, in which the concept description showed a unique product with a number of benefits. Based on the high-scoring concept test, the company moved the product into development and finally test market. The commercials for the test market were skillfully prepared, but in a thirty-second time slot, only one of the key benefits could be stressed. The test market was a failure.

The company assumed there was something wrong with the advertising or marketing support, so it took a second shot. The elements of the marketing mix were revised and the advertising stressed a different benefit. Again the product failed. The reason was clear: There was no way to convey all the features and benefits that had been displayed in the concept test in a live launch situation—a thirty-second commercial, with lower viewer attention levels and less time to tell the story, made the task impossible. The key lesson to be learned here is this: Don't develop or test a concept presentation that can't be replicated in the real world!

2. *Don't oversell.* Remember—this is a test to gauge customer reaction to the product concept; it is not a test of your selling ability; nor is it a pre-selling exercise. Overselling what the product can do and the use of too powerful a presentation can lead to inflated and misleading results.

   In a similar vein, the use of emotionally loaded words in your concept presentation may actually backfire—it may act as a lightning rod, eliciting negative reaction and biasing the results downward:

   ✓ A new financial service may not be "sophisticated" and "elegant." The language is too powerful or simply inappropriate, causing customers to focus on this issue and fail to perceive other benefits.

   ✓ A supermarket ice cream brand could be "luscious," "rich," and "thick," but "gourmet" in a supermarket line may simply not be believable.

3. *Be clear.* Customers must fully understand the concept, if the responses and feedback they give are to be meaningful. Too often a product description is given that is vague, confusing, or superficial, and then the customer is queried about whether he or she would buy the product or not. The results are pure guesses on the part of the customer. Keep it simple, clear, and understandable, and use whatever communication tools—including visuals and models—might help explain the concept most clearly to the prospective customer.

4. *Contact the right potential customers or users.* Make sure that the customers you involve in the concept test are indeed representative of your target market. If your target user is upscale, upmarket, higher-income professionals, there is no sense taking a sample of average consumers. Similarly, for B2B, if your target market is an entire industry, then undertaking a concept test

solely on leading edge or innovative users is foolish—they're likely to give a much more positive response than the typical customer. Further, make sure that you seek opinion and feedback from a variety of people within the buying firm: There are often many purchase influencers in the decision to buy a new product.

Predicting Success and Sales

With all its weaknesses, the concept test is still the best way of gauging likely product acceptance before you have actually developed a product. For familiar products in familiar categories (which are the bulk of product-development efforts), it has proven quite predictive both in B2B and B2C situations. The top box score or top two boxes in Figure 7.6 (the percentage of people who replied "definitely would buy" or "definitely" and "probably would buy") are your best early indicator of how your product will fare, short of a test market, trial sell, or full launch.

Sadly, there are no simple formulas for translating this top box score into a predicted market share. Some market research firms have developed elaborate models, such as BASES, for estimating initial trial rates for certain types of consumer goods; and this initial trial rate, combined with repurchase intent and launch coverage, yields expected market share. But such formulas and norms tend to be very specific to certain industries and even product categories within industries. Figure 7.7 shows some of these relationships for frequently repurchased consumer goods.

Perhaps as important is the information obtained from the open-ended questions in a concept test, questions such as, "What did you like most about the product?" and "Why did you rate brand X so much better?" If the concept is failing the test, then answers to these questions provide critical insights into what needs to be done to fix the product. Even for a successful test, these answers provide clues about how to fine-tune the product design to make it even more attractive to the customer. Finally, the comments that potential customers make in response to the product provide hints about how the product might be positioned and communicated to users—what customer "hot buttons" have been hit.

Suggestion: Are you using concept tests effectively in your new product system? Do you take the time to verify that the proposed new product really is the right one before you charge off into Development? Or do you assume that you have it right, and that you'll take your chances?

Build a concept test into your next important new-product development *before Development begins.* You don't need a prototype or sample product—just a solid idea of what the product will be and a representation of it. Present the product proposition as clearly as possible to selected customers, and remember: Be realistic; don't oversell; be clear; and make sure you're speaking to the right people. Measure the customer's interest, liking, preference, and purchase intent—use scaled questions, and get quantitative answers (even in B2B interviews!). You'll

Figure 7.7: Calibration Curve Showing the Relationship of the "Top Box Score" to Trial Rate and Probability of Launch (Consumer Packaged Goods)

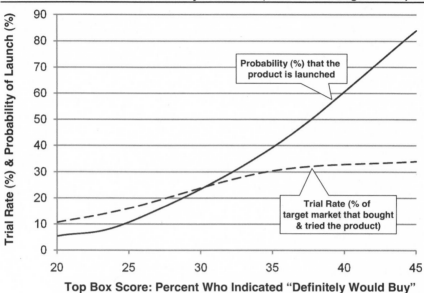

be surprised at the insights you'll gain about your proposed product's commercial prospects. But exercise care in the use of these concept-test results: Intent-to-purchase figures don't translate directly into market share!

BUILD IN THE SPIRALS

Stage 2 begins the use of the spirals in the spiral development approach—see Figure 7.8. The first spiral is the VoC user needs-and-wants study—the study that helps you understand customers' and users' unmet, unspoken, and often hidden needs, highlighted earlier—like breathalyzer and PumpSmart studies. This study is key to coming up with a differentiated, superior product with a compelling value proposition.

The second spiral is the concept test, the first test in the "build-test-feedback-and-revise" spirals. Here you show a representation of the product—a model, virtual prototype, animation, or CAD drawings—and seek feedback. This spiral is key to helping you sharpen your product design, pin down some of the "variable" components of the product definition, and ascertain purchase intent and likely sales.

> Start the spirals here in Stage 2. These are deliberate spirals—build-test-feedback-and-revise—built into the project plan by design. They are not a knee-jerk reaction to a problem. The spirals start here and continue all the way through to just prior to Launch.

Figure 7.8: "Build-Test-Feedback-and-Revise" Spirals Begin in Stage 2 and Continue Throughout the Process Right up to Launch

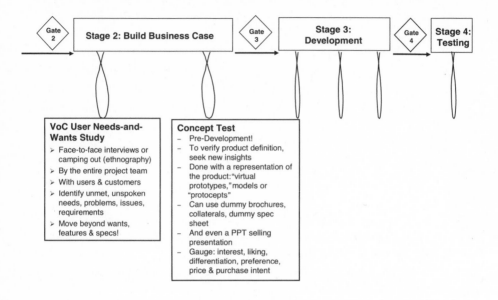

More spirals will follow in Stages 3 and 4—but it's vital in Stage 2 to begin the process of getting something in front of the customer or user—fast, early, and often!

BUSINESS AND FINANCIAL ANALYSIS

The various market studies—the VoC user needs-and-wants, the competitive analysis, the market analysis, and the concept test—help to map out the product definition. The target market is now sharply defined; the product concept and positioning strategy are confirmed; the benefits to be delivered and the value proposition are defined and validated, as are the physical attributes of the product—features, specs, and performance requirements. The technical assessment confirms technical and source-of-supply feasibility, investment, and costs. What remains is a business and financial justification of the project before moving full speed into the Development stage in Figure 7.1.

Here, the strategic rationale and competitive reasons for undertaking the project are laid out in detail. So, too, is the core competencies assessment, along with how additional resources and capabilities will be supplied by partners or via outsourcing. (If you are outsourcing or partnering, a review of their capabilities and roles has been undertaken, and a letter of intent or memorandum of understanding has been written by the end of Stage 2.) As well, the role of international units in making the product a success is included here.

The financial analysis is obviously key as you move into Gate 3. Reasonable estimates can now be made for many of the inputs for a financial analysis. Following the sequence in Figure 7.4, market size and share estimates together with pricing analysis should yield expected revenues. The product's design characteristics are now known, so the detailed technical assessment should yield cost estimates and thus reasonable projections of profit margins. The technical and operations assessment should also provide rough estimates of capital or equipment needs and costs. Marketing requirements and the expected launch costs have been investigated, and additional project costs in Stages 3 and 4 have been forecast. These estimates are the inputs to a financial analysis.

Two types of financial analysis have merit as you move into Gate 3:

- Calculating the Payback Period—how many years before you get your investment back?
- Undertaking a fairly straightforward discounted cash flow analysis (net present value [NPV] and internal rate of return [IRR])—typically five years out for a major new-product project. More on these in the next chapter, where we explore project evaluation methods.

A Risk Assessment

In addition to the expected payoffs from the project, most executives also want to see a risk assessment in the Business Case. Two types of risk assessment should be included:

- *Financial risk:* Here you build in a sensitivity analysis. There are few things that we are certain about in product development, except one fact—*your numbers are always wrong!* Those carefully constructed financial spreadsheets have an air of authenticity, except the evidence strongly suggests that many of your numbers are in error, and sometimes by orders of magnitude, especially on major and step-out projects. A sensitivity analysis simply lists the key financial assumptions and tests each assumption—best-case and worst-case estimate. More about sensitivity analysis in the next chapter.

> There are few things that we are certain about in product development, except one fact—your numbers are always wrong!

- *Project risk:* This analysis outlines all that can go wrong in the project, the likelihoods and resulting impact, and the "so what's" (this risk assessment was mentioned earlier in the chapter as part of Stage 1). Such a risk assessment should be redone here, but more thoroughly and with benefit of better insights than you had back in Stage 1—see Figure 7.9 for a guide. The important column in Figure 7.9 is the far right one—the "so what," or what action is needed to deal with the risk.

Figure 7.9: Undertake a Risk Assessment of the Project—What Could Go Wrong and What Mitigating Actions Are Required?

What Could Go Wrong?	Likelihood of Occurring?	Impact If It Occurs?	So What? What Mitigating Action?

ACTION PLANS

The final component of the Business Case is the "go forward plan" or the Action Plan. Usually, the rule is that a detailed plan of action should be put together for the next stage, with tentative plans for subsequent stages all the way through to launch. Following this rule, the Business Case plans consist of:

- ✓ A recommendation on the future of the project: Go versus Kill versus Hold.
- ✓ The detailed Development Plan—its components are described in Chapter 10.
- ✓ Plans for Stage 4, Testing and Validation. Actions frequently undertaken in Stage 4 are also shown in Chapter 10.
- ✓ A preliminary manufacturing, operations, or source-of-supply plan.
- ✓ A first-draft market launch plan (also outlined in Chapter 10).

ON TO STAGE 3: DEVELOPMENT

> The vital homework is done! The foundation is laid ... Now, on to Development!

The market has been researched. The product has been defined. The technical route has been mapped out. The financial and business justification has been prepared. And the Action Plan or path forward for the next stage (and subsequent stages) has been developed. The Business Case is now ready. These are the deliverables to the pivotal Gate 3 or Go to Development decision. This critical gate opens the door to a significant commitment of resources and to a full-fledged development program. But because the homework has been proficiently undertaken in Stages 1 and 2, described in this chapter, development should proceed more smoothly: You now have clear and defined targets to speed toward.

8

PICKING THE WINNERS— INVESTING IN THE RIGHT PROJECTS

Take calculated risks. That is quite different from being rash.
—George S. Patton, U.S. general

IT'S TOUGH TO MAKE THE RIGHT INVESTMENT DECISIONS

There are two fundamental ways to win big at product innovation:[1]

1. The first way is *doing projects right:* Ensure that an effective cross-functional team is in place and that its members do the front-end homework; build in the voice of the customer; strive for a differentiated, superior product; be time-driven, and so on. Having a first-rate idea-to-launch system to guide how projects should unfold and building in the many best practices outlined thus far in the book—the topics of Chapters 2 through 7—is the solution that many firms have adopted.
2. The second way is *doing the right projects.* As one executive put it: "Even a blind man can get rich in a gold mine, simply by swinging a pickax. You don't have to be a good miner—just be in the right mine!" Thus, *project selection* becomes paramount to new-product performance. And that's the topic of this chapter—picking the right new product and development projects to invest in.

For most businesses, development resources are too valuable and scarce to waste on the wrong projects. But many projects in firms' development pipelines are weak: Either they fail commercially (or underperform) in the marketplace, or they are canceled prior to product launch; so only *one in seven concepts* actually becomes a commercial winner. Project selection—the ability to pick the right

Figure 8.1: Project-Selection Practices Are Lacking in the Majority of Firms

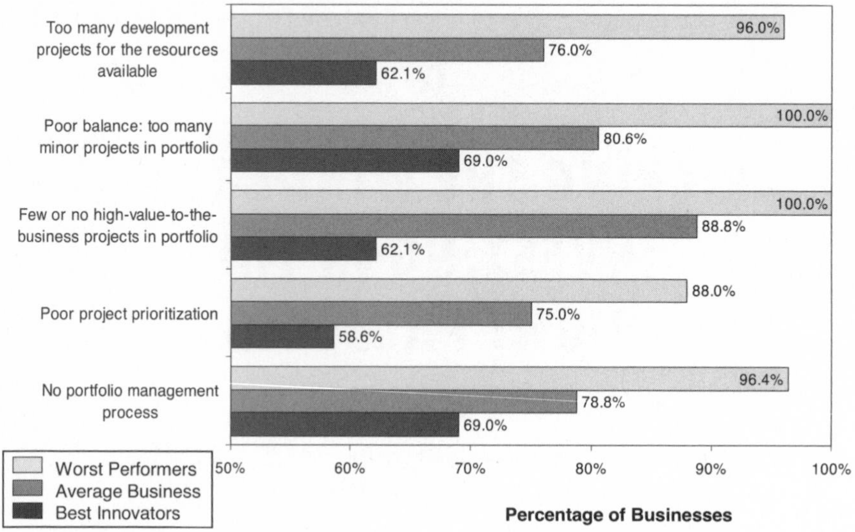

Source: Benchmarking study, endnote 9 in Chapter 1.

projects for investment—therefore becomes a critically important task for the leadership team of your business in order to *maximize productivity from your development spending.*

Many Challenges in Project Selection

Making the right investment decisions is one of the most problematic facets of product innovation. The majority of firms undertake selection in a haphazard, unprofessional way and fail to utilize many of the best-practices approaches available. Look at the benchmarking results in Figure 8.1 (Figure 8.1 is simply the data in Figure 3.1, but shown in reverse format to point out deficiencies):

- More than three-fourths of businesses do *too many projects* for the limited resources available. Overloading the development pipeline is a result of not knowing *how to say no* or a *failure to prioritize effectively*. And it has many serious side effects—projects take too long; project teams cut corners and quality of execution suffers; and projects get "dumbed down"—products are de-featured and de-specified.
- Eighty percent of firms have *very unbalanced development portfolios* or pipelines: They undertake too many small, insignificant projects—tweaks, modifications, minor updates, small sales force requests—to the detriment of higher-payoff, more innovative, and longer-term projects. Look at the breakdown in Figure 3.2 back in Chapter 3, which reveals that 43 percent of developments are very minor projects and only 10 percent are true "new

products." Recall in Chapter 1 (Figure 1.1) seeing the disturbing trend toward less-significant development projects. One result is that almost 90 percent of businesses have "few or no high-value projects" in their development portfolios (Figure 8.1).

- Almost 90 percent of firms *lack effective project prioritization*. And the great majority of businesses (79 percent) have *no professional portfolio management* or project-selection methods in place.

Even more astounding is how abysmal the *worst-performing businesses* fare on these same five criteria: 100 percent of worst performers have too many minor projects and no or few high-value projects under way; 96 percent have too many projects and no formal portfolio management system; and 89 percent have poor project prioritization. No wonder these firms perform so badly!

The end result of such poor practices is that many of the projects currently in businesses' development portfolios are weak—they are simply bad projects with limited potential. Indeed, in typical portfolio reviews undertaken within firms, we usually find that *about half the projects under way should be killed.* Many should never have been approved in the first place; and others, though fine at the outset, have deteriorated over time, yet nobody had the guts to shoot them. The bottom line is that you've got to learn to be tough—to make the difficult decisions to cull the weak project from your development portfolio.

> Project selection and portfolio management are among the weakest facets of new-product management.

A second major issue is that most firms face *a serious resource crunch* when it comes to product development. Businesses generally lack the necessary resources to undertake projects properly or on time:[2] Only 10.7 percent of firms were judged to devote sufficient resources to their new-product projects—that is, in 89 percent of firms, projects are typically underresourced![3]

The *simplistic solution* is to rank your projects from best to worst—with the high-value ones at the top of the list. Next, go down the list, and *lop off the bottom half* of projects; then reallocate those resources to the top half—the best projects— and get them done fast! The trouble with this solution is that you'll have to make some tough decisions and kill some projects—which no management group seems comfortable doing. So most senior managements elect the default option— *do them all!* Another problem with this simple solution is just how to rank projects from best to worst—it's no small feat to define and measure "best" or "value-to-the-company."

Suggestion: Before becoming too critical of the worst performers in Figure 8.1, take a look at how your business compares on these five criteria. Do you have *too many projects* for your limited resources—are your projects underresourced? And what side effects does overloading your pipeline create? Does your development portfolio suffer from *too many small projects*, while the more innovative, larger, and longer-term projects suffer? If yes, read on: It's time to install a professional project selection or portfolio-management system in your business.

PROJECT SELECTION IS BUT ONE COMPONENT OF PORTFOLIO MANAGEMENT

Project selection—making the right Go/Kill and investment decisions on development projects—is part of the broader topic of "portfolio management." Portfolio management is a term borrowed from the financial community. In product innovation, every development project is viewed as an "investment"; and these investments can be managed using decision tools and techniques fairly similar to those used in financial markets. One component of portfolio management is the gates—the decision points in your *Stage-Gate*® system where the vital Go/Kill decisions are made and where resources are committed to projects.

What Is Portfolio Management in Product Innovation?

Portfolio management is about resource allocation. That is, which new-product and development projects from the many opportunities the business faces should the business fund? And which ones should receive top priority and be accelerated to market? It is also about business strategy, for today's new-product projects decide tomorrow's product-market profile of the firm. Finally, it is about balance: about the optimal investment mix between risk versus return, maintenance versus growth, and short-term versus long-term development projects.

Portfolio management is formally defined as follows:[4]

Portfolio management is a dynamic decision process, whereby a business's list of active new-product (and development) projects is constantly updated and revised. In this process, new projects are evaluated, selected, and prioritized; existing projects may be accelerated, killed, or de-prioritized; and resources are allocated and reallocated to active projects. The portfolio decision process is characterized by uncertain and changing information, dynamic opportunities, multiple goals and strategic considerations, interdependence among projects, and multiple decision-makers and locations.

The portfolio decision process encompasses or overlaps a number of decision-making processes within the business, including periodic reviews of the total portfolio of all projects (looking at all projects holistically, and against each other), making Go/Kill decisions on individual projects on an ongoing basis, and developing a new-product strategy for the business, complete with strategic resource allocation decisions.

Two Decision Levels in Portfolio Management

Portfolio management and resource allocation can be treated as a hierarchical process, with two levels of decision-making. This hierarchical approach simplifies the decision challenge somewhat (see Figure 8.2):[5]

Figure 8.2: The Portfolio Management System Features Two Levels of Decision-Making

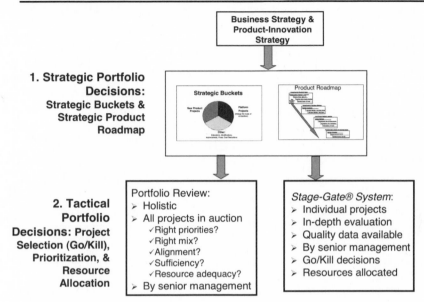

- **Level 1—Strategic portfolio management:** Strategic portfolio decisions answer these questions: Directionally, where should your business spend its development resources (people and funds)? How should you split your resources across project types, markets, technologies, or product categories? And on what major initiatives or new platforms should you concentrate your resources? Establishing Strategic Buckets and delineating Strategic Product and Technology Road Maps are effective tools here, and are outlined later in this chapter.

> Project selection is part of the broader topic of portfolio management. It's necessary to look at the broad topic— portfolio management—in order to be effective at project selection.

- **Level 2—Tactical portfolio decisions (individual project selection):** Tactical portfolio decisions focus on individual projects, but obviously follow from the strategic decisions. They address these questions: What specific new-product projects should you do? What are their relative priorities? And what resources should be allocated to each? Such tactical decisions are shown at the bottom part of Figure 8.2 and are the main topic of this chapter.

Gates and Portfolio Reviews

Two decisions processes must be in place in order to handle the tactical portfolio decisions well: *gates*, part of the *Stage-Gate* system, coupled with periodic *portfolio reviews* (the bottom part of Figure 8.2). Note that many of the tools and methods introduced in this chapter see double duty—they can be employed at gates as well as at portfolio reviews, but used slightly differently at each. Let's look at what gates and portfolio reviews are, and then delve into the best-practice methods for project selection and prioritization.

1. *Gates* (bottom right of Figure 8.2): Embedded within your idea-to-launch system are Go/Kill decision points called "gates." Gates provide an in-depth review of individual projects, and render Go/Kill, prioritization, and resource allocation decisions—hence gates must be part of your portfolio management system. Effective gates are vital to product innovation: They weed out the bad projects early, and they commit the needed resources to the deserving projects.

But gates are not quite enough! Many companies have a gating process in place, but they confuse that with a comprehensive portfolio management system. Doing the *right projects* is more than simply individual project selection at gate meetings; rather, it's about the *entire mix* of projects and new-product or technology investments that your business makes:

- Project selection *deals only with the "trees"*: Go/Kill decisions are made on individual projects, each judged on its own merits.
- Portfolio management *deals with the "forest"*: It is holistic and looks at the entire set of project investments together.

2. *Portfolio reviews:* The second decision process is the periodic *portfolio review* (bottom left of Figure 8.2). Senior management meets about four times per year to review the portfolio of all projects. Here, senior management also makes Go/Kill and prioritization decisions, where *all projects* are considered on the table together, and all or some could be *up for auction*. Key issues and questions at the typical portfolio review are:
    - Are all of your projects strategically aligned (do they support your business's innovation strategy)?
    - Do you have the right priorities among projects?
    - Are there some projects on the active list that you should kill? Or perhaps accelerate?
    - Do you have the right balance of projects? The right mix? Or are there too many small, insignificant ones?
    - Do you have enough resources to do all these projects? Or should some be cut or put on hold?
    - Do you have *sufficiency*—if you do these projects, will you achieve your stated product-innovation goals—for example, your annual sales objectives from new products?

Both decision processes—gating and portfolio reviews—are needed and must work together harmoniously. Note that the gates are project-specific and provide a thorough review of each project, in-depth and in real time. By contrast, the portfolio reviews are holistic: They look at all projects together, but in much less detail on each project. In many businesses, if the gates are working, not too many decisions or major corrective actions are even required at the portfolio review. Some leadership teams indicate that they don't even look at individual projects at the portfolio review but only consider projects in aggregate! But in other businesses, the majority of decisions are made at these quarterly or semiannual portfolio reviews.

Suggestion: Establish a hierarchical or *two-level approach to portfolio management,* as in Figure 8.2. Recognize that there are strategic decisions (directional and high-level) and tactical decisions (project selection and prioritization). For the tactical decisions, two decision processes complement each other here: your idea-to-launch *gating process,* which focuses on individual projects; and your *portfolio review* approach, which looks at the entire set of projects. Use both!

THE TOOLS TO USE FOR EFFECTIVE GATES AND PORTFOLIO REVIEWS

At gates and portfolio reviews, a number of tools can be used to help achieve your portfolio goals, namely, maximize your portfolio's value, achieve the right balance and mix of projects, and ensure portfolio sufficiency, without overloading the development pipeline.

MAXIMIZING THE VALUE OF YOUR PORTFOLIO

Maximizing the value of your development portfolio is a principal goal for most businesses. It's analogous to "buying low and selling high" on the stock market. You invest a certain amount of money or resources in development, and desire that the value of the resulting portfolio of projects be maximized. An admirable goal, but often difficult to achieve! For one thing, how do you measure the *value of your portfolio*?

The methods used to achieve this goal range from financial tools through scorecard models. Each has its strengths and weaknesses. The end result of each is a rank-ordered or prioritized list of "Go" and "Hold" projects, with the projects at the top of the list scoring highest in terms of achieving the desired objectives: The portfolio's value in terms of that objective is thus maximized. Here are the specific methods:

Rank Your Projects Using Their Economic Value or Net Present Value (NPV)

The simplest approach is merely to calculate the NPV (net present value) of each project on a spreadsheet. Most businesses already require the NPV and a financial spreadsheet as part of the project's Business Case, so the NPV number is already available. If the NPV is positive, the project is a Go at the gate; and at portfolio reviews, you can rank-order your projects—best to worst—by the NPV. Sounds easy!

The NPV is a proxy for the *economic value* of the project to the business and is generally accepted by financial people as the correct economic indicator of the shareholder value of any investment within the corporation. Additionally, popular spreadsheet programs (such as MS-Excel) come with the NPV calculation built in as a standard routine, so finding and using the technique should be no problem.

NPV is a form of discounted cash flow analysis (DCF). DCF analysis requires a year-by-year cash flow projection of the project's incomes and expenditures; further, in the DCF method, the net cash flows for each year are discounted to the present using a discount rate. This stream of future cash earnings, appropriately discounted to the present, is then added and initial outlays are subtracted to yield the Net Present Value (NPV). Explaining the details of how the NPV works—the fine points of the formula and calculation—is beyond the scope of this book, but good explanations of the theory and calculations underlying NPV are available from a number of sources.[6]

The NPV can be used in two ways:

- First, make Go/Kill decisions at gates based on NPV. Require that your project teams use the minimum acceptable financial return or *hurdle rate percent* for projects of this risk level as the discount rate when calculating their projects' NPVs. If the NPV is positive, then the project clears the acceptable hurdle rate. So NPV is a key input to Go/Kill decisions at gates. Additionally, the project's NPV can be compared to other active projects' NPVs right at gate meetings in order to gain insight into the relative position or prioritization level for the new project.
- Second, at portfolio reviews, rank all projects according to their NPV. The Go projects are at the top of the list. Continue adding projects down the list until you run out of resources. Draw a line across when you hit the resource limit: Those projects above the line are Go, and those below the line are put on hold or killed. In this way, you end up with a prioritized list of projects, which logically should maximize the NPV of your portfolio.

DCF analysis has certain advantages as a profitability indicator:

✓ It recognizes that money has a time value, and it penalizes those projects with more distant launch dates and distant future revenue streams.
✓ It is a cash flow method and avoids the usual problems of accounting and accrual techniques.
✓ It places much less emphasis on cash flow projections that are many years into the future (that is, the result is not particularly sensitive to estimates made for many years out, particularly if the discount rate is high).

In addition to determining the NPV, you can also calculate two other numbers using the same data, so they're an easy addition to your spreadsheet:

- The *internal rate of return,* or IRR, which is simply the value of the discount rate that forces the NPV to zero; it gives the project's true return-on-investment as a percent.
- The *Payback Period*, namely, how many years before you get your initial investment back. This is a useful metric, and although not a DCF method per se, it is often used by entrepreneurs, because it answers the question: "When can I start sleeping well at night?" Shorter paybacks are obviously highly desirable: The return-on-investment is high (the ROI is related to the inverse of the Payback Period); and with short paybacks, you don't have to count on earnings far into the future. So the Payback Period captures both risk and return.

THE RIGHT HURDLE RATE?

In determining the NPV, normally, the discount rate used is the firm's cost of capital adjusted for the *risk level* for that type of project.

An interesting twist to the NPV is to use a discount rate equal to the *lowest rate achieved by projects* of this type currently under way in your portfolio (use the IRR of the lowest-return project of that type). This rate will be a higher rate than the minimum acceptable hurdle rate, and thus raises the cutoff bar: Any project with a negative NPV means that its return is less than the worst project of that type in the current portfolio, and thus should be killed. By only accepting projects with rates higher than this rate, this method thus automatically improves the value of the portfolio with each added project.

More: Because the "lowest rate" is *above the minimum acceptable hurdle rate*, the method thus introduces an "opportunity cost"—the best return available from an alternate investment. If all your other projects are earning quite low rates, barely above the minimum acceptable rate, then that's the hurdle rate you use. But if all your other projects are earning high returns, use the lowest of those— that's what your new project is competing against for investment resources.

The method also eliminates the need to set *arbitrary minimum hurdle rates* for different types of projects: The existing portfolio of projects is the basis for establishing the hurdle rate.

These three numbers—the NPV in dollars, the Payback Period in years, and the IRR as a percent—denote the profitability of the project well.

To help identify project risks, *sensitivity analysis* is recommended. This procedure is quite easy to do, especially if your project data are already in a spreadsheet format. In sensitivity analysis, key assumptions are tested: For example, what if the revenue drops to only 75 percent of projected; what if the manufacturing cost is 25 percent higher than expected; or what if the launch date is a year later than projected? Spreadsheet values are changed, one at a time, and the financial calculations are repeated. Some managements require best-case and worst-case calculations, also done via sensitivity analysis.

If the returns are still positive under these different "what if" scenarios, the conclusion is that the project justification is not sensitive to the assumptions made. However, if certain "what if" scenarios yield negative returns, then these assumptions become critical: Key project risks have been identified.

Suggestion: Ask your Finance Department to develop a *standardized spreadsheet* for the NPV, IRR, and Payback Period calculations, so all project teams produce consistently calculated profit figures. Also, ask your Finance Department to develop a table of *risk-adjusted discount rates* for project teams to use to determine the NPVs for different risk-levels of projects: low risk (for example, a cost reduction) to high risk (genuine new product, first of its kind). The higher discount rates appropriately discount (or penalize) future earnings well into the future much more so for higher-risk projects; and the further into the future, the higher the discount.

Additionally, request that a *fairly standard sensitivity analysis routine* be built into the spreadsheet to yield best-case and worst-case scenarios, and also to identify the most critical assumptions.

An example: Using the NPV to rank and prioritize projects is shown in Figure 8.3, using disguised data from a large materials company. Here, six fairly comparable projects are shown with disguised names, Alpha through Foxtrot, in the first column. In column two, the PV, or present value, is the sum of the future earnings of the projects, taken out five years and discounted by the firm's discount rate for major development projects (this company uses Strategic Buckets and thus groups projects into buckets—these six projects are in the "major projects" bucket, hence the large dollar values for PV).

Also shown are the development costs and commercialization costs (this is a capital-intensive business—most major projects require capital equipment, hence again large dollar values for commercialization costs), shown in columns three and four. The NPV is shown in column five, simply the income stream (PV) less the development and commercialization costs. For project Alpha, for example, the NPV is 30 less 3 less 5 equals $22 million.

Now the decision rule: Rank the projects according to their NPV. This ranking is shown in column six, with Foxtrot being number one with an

Figure 8.3: Use Projects' NPVs to Rank and Prioritize Projects

1	2	3	4	5	6	7
Project	PV (present value of future earnings)	Develop-ment Cost	Commer-cialization Cost	NPV (net present value)	Ranking Based on NPV	Decision
Alpha	30	3	5	22	4	Hold
Beta	64	5	2	57	2	Go
Gamma	9	2	1	6	5	Hold
Delta	3	1	0.5	1.5	6	Hold
Echo	50	5	3	42	3	Hold
Foxtrot	66	10	2	58	1	Go

All figures are $ M.
Using this method, the top four projects are Foxtrot, Beta, Echo, and Alpha.
There is a resource limit of $15 M Development budget, however.
Thus, only two projects are Go: Foxtrot and Beta (these two top-rated projects consume all the $15 M). The value of the portfolio is NPV = $115 M from these two projects.

NPV of $58 million. Beta is a close second at $57 million, and so on through to Delta, which is last.

As in most firms, there is a limit to how many projects can be done. The firm has two constraints—the capital budget (equipment budget) and the R&D budget (full-time equivalent people, but expressed as a dollar figure). I'll only show the method for the R&D budget constraint, which is $15 million (but recognize that this firm redoes the numbers, the second time with the capital budget constraint, and then merges the two sets of results).

The total time to do any one of the six projects is about one year; but if we decided to do all six—the comfortable "default option" that most of us would elect—we see that the total development costs (add up column three) come to $26 million. This means we could start all six projects, but *it will take almost two years to get them done.*

Perhaps this is a wise option, because it means we don't need to make a decision on which projects not to do—*just do them all!* On the other hand, the astute financial person recognizes that this approach guarantees that all projects move at half the speed they could, and defers our income for an extra year ... a considerable cost, since money has a time value. So the more aggressive manager says, let's focus—let's pick our "best bets" and get them done!

So let's focus: Based on this NPV method of ranking projects, you do the number one project, Foxtrot—this consumes a whopping two-thirds of the

R&D budget; and next you do Beta, which consumes the rest of the budget. So the decision is: "Do two projects—Foxtrot and Beta; consume all the $15 million on these two; put the other four projects on hold; but get the two 'best bets' done and on the market in one year." These decisions are shown in the last column, column seven. Note that the total value of your portfolio is $58 + $57 = $115 million, which is quite good for your R&D spending of $15 million!

"But just a minute!" you say: "Isn't that a bit risky—putting all your eggs in one basket? Shouldn't we try to 'hedge our bets' and spread the risk by doing more projects than just two? And surely we can find some combination of 'more efficient' projects." You're right on both counts, but I come to that in the next section where the topic is the Productivity Index method.

Using NPV to make Go/Kill and prioritization decisions is fine in theory, but there are some problems: The NPV method assumes that financial projections are accurate (they usually are not, especially at the earlier gates, precisely when you're making the first Go/Kill decisions!); it assumes that only financial goals are important—for example, that strategic considerations are irrelevant; and it ignores probabilities of success and risk (except by using a risk-adjusted discount rate). A final objection is more subtle: the fact that NPV assumes an all-or-nothing investment decision, whereas in new-product projects, the decision process is an incremental one—you buy the project a piece at a time—more like buying a *series of options* on a project.[7]

This NPV method has a number of attractive features, however. First, it requires that the project team members submit a financial assessment of the project: That means they must do some research, make some fact-based projections, and think through the commercial implications and outcomes of the project. One always learns something from doing a robust financial analysis, often how unreliable the data are! Second, a discounted cash flow (DCF) method is used, which is the correct way to value investments (as opposed to the ROI, EVA [economic value added], or Payback Period). Finally, all monetary amounts are discounted to today (not just to launch date), thereby appropriately penalizing projects that are years away from launch.

The method is a good one—both for use at gate meetings and at portfolio reviews—and is recommended. But you can do better, especially for ranking projects.

Rank Your Projects Using the Productivity Index

Here's an important modification to the NPV-ranking approach in order to maximize the value of your portfolio, but recognizing that you have limited resources.[8] The problem is that some projects—for example Foxtrot and Beta in Figure 8.3— are great projects and have huge NPVs, but they consume a lot of resources, thus making it impossible to do other and lower-value but perhaps far more efficient projects. How does one decide?

> Use NPV to help make Go/Kill decisions on projects, and the Productivity Index to rank and prioritize them.

Simple: The goal is to maximize the bang for the buck. And the way to do this is to take the ratio of what one is trying to maximize (in this case, the NPV) divided by the constraining resource (the R&D dollars required)—and voilà, the best bang for the buck.* You may choose to use R&D people or work-months, or the total dollar cost remaining in the project (or even capital funds) as the constraining resource. This bang-for-the-buck ratio, or Productivity Index, is shown in column four in Figure 8.4:

$$\text{Productivity Index} = \frac{NPV \text{ of the project}}{\text{Total resources remaining to be spent on the project}}$$

Figure 8.4: Rank Projects According to the NPV-Based Productivity Index

1	2	3	4	5	
Project	NPV	Develop-ment Cost	Productivity Index=NPV/ Dev Cost	Sum of Dev Costs	
Beta	57	5	11.4	5	
Echo	42	5	8.4	10	
Alpha	22	3	7.3	13	Limit
Foxtrot	58	10	5.8	23	reached
Gamma	6	2	3.0	25	
Delta	1.5	1	1.5	26	

The Productivity Index is used to rank projects until out of resources. The horizontal line shows the limit: $15 M Development Costs is reached.

Go projects are now Beta, Echo, and Alpha. (above the line) Foxtrot drops off the list. The value of the portfolio is NPV = $121M from these three projects. Add Gamma to consume the last $2 M, and the portfolio value is now $127 M…. up from $115 M in Figure 8.3.

---

* This decision rule of rank order according to the ratio of what one is trying to maximize divided by the constraining resource is an effective one. Simulations with a number of sets of projects show that this decision rule works very well, truly giving "maximum bang for the buck"!

The example continued: Now it's time to re-sort the list of projects. But first the constraint: The R&D spending constraint is $15 million for new products in this business; development costs per project are shown in column three in Figure 8.4, and add up to $26 million. To select the "Go" projects, simply calculate the Productivity Index—NPV/Development Cost—as shown in column four. Note that Beta is the best project, with a Productivity Index of 11.4. This means that for every dollar you spend on R&D, project Beta delivers $11.40 of value! By contrast, Delta is far less productive: Every R&D dollar spent there delivers only $1.50 of value. So which project would you invest in?

Now re-rank the project list, ranking projects according to the Productivity Index (this reordering is shown in Figure 8.4, with Beta at the top of the list and Delta at the bottom). Then go down the list until you run out of resources; column five shows the cumulative resource expenditure. You run out of resources—hit the $15 million limit—after project Alpha. (There is still $2 million left, and being a wise manager, following the rule of "use it or lose it," you spend the last $2 million on project Gamma to use up the entire annual budget.)

Thus, your Go decision is now: Beta, Echo, Alpha, and Gamma. The NPVs for these four projects total $127 million, an increase of $12 million versus the ranking in Figure 8.3. Thus, the Productivity Index method gives a better set of projects.

The point to note here is that introducing the Productivity Index and constrained resources dramatically changes the ranking of projects. Compare the ranked list in Figure 8.3 with that in Figure 8.4: Note that Foxtrot, previously the number one project, drops off the list entirely when you use the Productivity Index.

This Productivity Index method yields benefits in addition to those inherent in the straight NPV-ranking approach in Figure 8.3. By introducing the Productivity Index, the method favors those projects that are almost completed (the denominator is small, hence the Productivity Index is high). And the method deals with resource constraints, yielding the best set of projects for a given budget or resource limit.

Suggestion: Use the Productivity Index for ranking projects, best to worst. It's a relatively simple extension of the NPV method, but gives a higher-value portfolio. The additional calculation is quite simple—it adds another line to your spreadsheet—and all the data are available on the spreadsheet.

Introduce Risk by Using Options Pricing Theory or Expected Commercial Value (ECV)

DCF or NPV methods have weaknesses. First, they fail to deal well with risk and probabilities of success. Second, they assume an "all-or-nothing" decision situation,

Figure 8.5: Expected Commercial Value of a Project Is Determined Via a Decision-Tree Approach

A model of a two-stage investment decision process: First, invest $D in development, which may yield a technical success (or technical failure). Then invest $C in commercialization, which may result in a commercial success (or failure). If successful, the project yields an income stream whose present value is $PV. More sophisticated versions of this model would entail more stages than the two shown here, and an array of possible outcomes from each stage.

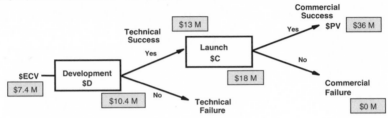

$ECV = Expected Commercial Value of the project

Probability of Technical Success = 80%

Probability of Commercial Success (given technical success) = 50%

$D = Development Costs remaining in the project = $3 M

$C = Commercialization Costs = $5 M

$PV = Net Present Value of project's future earnings (discounted to today) = $36 M

Source: *Portfolio Management for New Products*, endnote 1.

and thus are appropriate for capital expenditure decisions; but new-product projects are *purchased one piece at a time*—in increments. At each gate, management is in effect *buying options on the project*; and these options cost far less than the full cost of the project, hence are an effective way to reduce risk. The argument is that *options pricing theory* rather than NPV is the appropriate way to evaluate the worth of a new-product project at each gate.

The Expected Commercial Value (ECV) method approximates the *options pricing model* used in financial markets.[9] It introduces the notion of *risks and probabilities*—the gates are *a series of incremental purchases of options on the project*. The calculation of the ECV is based on a decision-tree analysis and considers the future stream of earnings from the project, the probabilities of both commercial success and technical success, along with both commercialization costs and development costs (see Figure 8.5 for the calculation and definition of terms).

An example: Let's revisit project Alpha from Figure 8.3. Recall that this project has an income stream of $30 million, and development and commercialization costs of $3 million and $5 million, respectively, for an NPV of $22 million.

Now the new risk information. Project Alpha has a fifty-fifty chance of commercial success (let's simplify the situation by portraying only two outcomes—success and failure; in a more realistic model, you would use an array of outcomes, from "big success" through "moderate successes" to "utter failure"). There is also a technical risk—an 80-percent chance of technical success; if a technical failure, we simply stop the project in Development.

Figure 8.5 portrays the situation for Alpha. Start at the right-hand side of the figure—the ultimate outcomes, success and failure. If the project succeeds, we receive the income stream of $30 million, but if it fails, we get nothing. These amounts are shown in the two shaded boxes at the right in Figure 8.5. Thus, the "expected value" of the project the day before launch is $15 million. To calculate the expected value, take each consequence multiplied by its probability of occurring, and add these up:

$$\text{Expected value before Launch} = 0.5 \times \$30 \text{ million} + 0.5 \times 0 = \$15 \text{ million}$$

But to get to Launch, we must spend $5 million on commercialization costs; so subtract $5 million from $15 million to get $10 million (shaded box). Thus, just before we decide to commercialize, the project is worth $10 million.

But to get to the commercialization decision point, we need a technical success . . . this has an 80-percent probability. Thus once into Development, the expected value is:

$$\text{Expected value once in Development} = 0.8 \times 10 \text{ million} + 0.2 \times 0 = \$8 \text{ million}$$

But to get through Development costs $3 million; so subtract $3 million from the $8 million. Therefore, the ECV just before Development begins is $5 million. That's the value of the project at our Gate 3: $5 million.

This ECV of $5 million is far below the original $22 million we originally valued the project at—there's a huge impact of introducing risk and probabilities. On the other hand, we mitigate risk somewhat by making a decision to kill the project partway through and not spend the last $5 million on Launch if things are going badly—the *options facet* of the model. And the ECV of $5 million reflects that as well.

The ECV is a powerful method and can be used at gate meetings as an input to the Go/Kill decision, much like the NPV—except risk and probabilities are built in. For portfolio reviews, in order to arrive at a prioritized list of projects, consider what resources are limiting, much like the NPV–Productivity Index example above in Figure 8.4. Then, take the ratio of what you are trying to maximize—namely, the ECV—divided by the constraining resource to yield another version of the Productivity Index. Projects are rank-ordered according to this new Productivity Index until the resource limit is reached. The method thus ensures the greatest "bang for the buck"; that is, the ECV is maximized for a given resources limit.

This ECV model has a number of attractive additional features when compared with the NPV approach: It includes probabilities and risk, which are inherent in any new-product project; it recognizes that the Go/Kill decision process is an incremental one (the notion of purchasing options—a stage-wise decision process); it deals with the issue of constrained resources, and maximizes the value of the portfolio in light of this constraint.

Try a Financial Simulation Model for Major Projects

Another way to introduce risk and probabilities is the use of a computer-based Monte Carlo Simulation model. Here's how these models are used: Instead of merely imputing a point estimate for each financial variable in your spreadsheet, such as Year One Sales, Year Two Sales, and so on, input three estimates for each variable: a best case, worst case and likely case. A probability curve (much like a bell-shaped curve) is drawn through each set of estimates. So each financial estimate—sales, costs, investment, and so forth—has a probability distribution.

The model begins by calculating multiple scenarios of possible financial outcomes, all based on your probability distributions. Tens of thousands of scenarios are quickly generated by the computer, each one yielding a financial outcome such as the NPV. The distribution of the NPVs generated from these thousands of scenarios becomes your profitability distribution—an expected NPV as well as a probability distribution of NPVs.

Use the expected NPV and its distribution to help make the Go/Kill decision at gates; and then take the expected NPV and divide by the costs remaining in the project and rank the projects according to this probability-adjusted NPV, much like in the Productivity Index method above.

These models are commercially available and relatively easy to use, and some of the *Stage-Gate Certified software* cited in Chapter 5 have Monte Carlo Simulation calculation packages already built in. But there are a few quirks or assumptions in these models that cause problems. For example, the model fails to deal with the *options facet* of a new-product project; further, it permits the generation of all-but-impossible scenarios that human intervention would have prevented. Nonetheless, it's a fine method, particularly appropriate for projects that involve large capital expenditures and where probability distributions of input variables can be estimated.

Use a Scorecard Approach to Rate and Rank Development Projects

What are the telltale signs of a winning new-product project? Do you know? Surely there are some key indicators, markers, or descriptors of projects that are good predictors of success. If we knew what these predictors were, then we could *develop a scorecard* and use that to *rate and rank projects* in a much more professional and predictive way.

In a scoring model system, at gate meetings, senior managers each rate the project on a number of criteria on 1–5 or 0–10 scales on a scorecard. The scores

> Scorecards work! They yield efficient, effective Go/Kill decisions and suit management's style.

from the gatekeepers at the gate review are tallied and combined, and the Project Attractiveness Score is computed: the weighted or unweighted addition of the question ratings. This attractiveness score is the basis for making the Go/Kill decision at gates and can also be used to rank-order projects at portfolio reviews.

Sounds great in theory. For decades, people have been trying to develop such "predictive models" to pick winning racehorses, winning dogs at the dog track, winning stocks on the stock market, and so on—without much luck. But the situation is quite different for new products. Indeed, there have been some impressive research investigations that have probed the *key markers* or *predictors of success* in product innovation.[10] Much of this research has been published and now is in the public domain, so we know what these markers are. And some firms have privately done internal investigations of their past projects and have come up with their own scoring models or scorecards for rating projects; some are now public.

These proven success predictors include factors such as:[11]

- *Strategic fit and alignment:* Projects that fit within your innovation strategy and are targeted at defined strategic arenas have a higher likelihood of winning. The hope is that your strategy defines arenas that are attractive (large growing markets, good margins, many opportunities) and in which you have the core competencies and strengths to win. After all, that's why you have a strategy—to point you toward more lucrative arenas.
- *Product advantage:* A unique, superior, differentiated product with a compelling value proposition is the number one driver of new-product success and a key marker or predictor. We saw this in Chapter 2, and so this factor must be front and center as a scorecard question in your project selection model.
- *Leverages core competencies:* We also saw in Chapter 3 that leveraging core competencies is another key to success and that step-out projects that do not build on the business's strengths have a much higher likelihood of failing.
- *Market attractiveness:* This is another factor outlined in Chapter 3 that impacts strongly on success. Thus, market attractiveness—the size and potential of the market as well as the competitive situation—becomes yet another question in the scorecard.

Other proven scorecard factors are risk versus reward and technical feasibility. Note that when crafting a scorecard system, it is best to keep the number of questions to ten or less. More than that, and the evaluators tend to tire of doing the

Figure 8.6: Use This Proven Scorecard for New-Product Project Selection

Factor 1: Strategic Fit & Importance
- Alignment of project with our business's strategy
- Importance of project to the strategy
- Impact on the business

Factor 2: Product & Competitive Advantage
- Product delivers unique customer or user benefits
- Product offers customer/user excellent value for money
- Differentiated product vs. competitors
- Positive customer/user feedback on product concept (concept test results)

Factor 3: Market Attractiveness
- Market size
- Market growth & future potential
- Margins earned by competitors in this market
- Competitiveness – how tough & intense competition is (negative)

Factor 4: Core Competencies Leverage
- Project leverages our core competencies & strengths in:
  - technology
  - production/operations
  - marketing/communications/branding
  - distribution/sales force

Factor 5: Technical Feasibility
- Size of technical gap
- Familiarity of technology to our business
- Newness of technology (base to embryonic)
- Technical complexity
- Technical results to date (proof of concept?)

Factor 6: Financial Reward versus Risk
- Size of financial opportunity
- Financial return (NPV, ECV)
- Productivity index
- Certainty of financial estimates
- Level of risk & ability to address risks

Projects are scored by the gatekeepers at the gate meeting, using these six factors on a scorecard (0 - 10 scales on each of the 6 factors above).

The Project Attractiveness Score is the weighted or unweighted addition of the scores, taken out of 100.

A score of 60/100 is usually required for a Go decision.

This scorecard is for Gate 3, Go to Development. Similar scorecards are used at earlier gates.

scoring. But do *make sure that these are robust questions—proven predictors of success*, and that you can prove it! A best-practice scoring model, research-based and proven, for *well-defined but major new-product projects* is shown in Figure 8.6 for Gate 3, Go to Development.

Suggestion: Use scoring models (scorecards) at gate meetings in conjunction with financial models to help select the right projects; and use the Project Attractiveness Score along with the Productivity Index to rank projects at portfolio reviews. Scoring models are generally praised in spite of their limited popularity: According to research, they produce a strategically aligned portfolio that reflects the business's spending priorities; they yield effective and efficient decisions, better than financial tools; and they result in a portfolio of high-value projects.[12]

Try Success Criteria[13]
Another selection method, employed with considerable success at firms such as P&G, is the use of *success criteria*:

An example: "The company [P&G] relies primarily on success criteria to help make better Go/Kill decisions on projects. Specific success criteria for each gate relevant to that stage are defined for each project and are agreed to by the project team and management at each gate. These success criteria are then used to evaluate the project at successive gates.[14]

Success criteria typically include metrics on profitability, first-year sales, launch date, and even expected interim metrics, such as test-market results. The method allows the project team to custom-tailor criteria to suit the nature of the project. Further, it has the added benefit of instilling project team accountability: At the Post-Launch Review, the project's results are compared to the original projections made by the team. Thus, the method *forces the team to make much more realistic and accurate sales, costs, and time projections*, which provide better data for management to make the Go/Kill decision.

Comparative Approaches: Q-Sort and Analytic Hierarchy Approaches

Comparative approaches require the gatekeepers to compare one proposal to another proposal or to some set of alternative proposals; they include such methods as Q-sort, project ranking, and paired comparisons. The decision-maker must specify which of the proposed new-product projects is preferred, and, in some methods, the strength of preferences. In certain of these methods, a set of project benefit measurements is then computed by performing mathematical operations on the stated preferences.

The *Q-sort method* is one of the simplest and most effective methods for rank-ordering a set of new-product proposals, especially at the *idea-screening gate*.[15] Each member of the gatekeeping group is given a deck of cards, with each card bearing the description of one of the projects. Following a discussion on all the projects, each member then sorts and re-sorts the deck into five categories, from a "high" group to a "low" group (or into simple "Yes" or "No" categories), evaluating each project according to a prespecified criterion. (The criterion could be, for example, expected profitability, or simply Go/Kill.) The gatekeepers' results are anonymously tallied on a chart and displayed to the entire group. The group is then given a period of time to debate the results informally. The procedure is repeated, again on an anonymous and individual basis, followed by another discussion period. By the third round, the gatekeeper group usually moves to consensus on the ranking of the projects on each criterion. The method is simple, easy to understand, and straightforward to implement; it provides for group discussion and debate; and it moves the group toward agreement in a structured way.

Comparative methods such as Q-sort do have their limitations. Perhaps their weakest aspect is that gatekeepers must give an overall opinion on a project. Individual facets of each project—for example, size of market, fit with distribution channels, likelihood of technical success—are never directly compared and measured across projects. It is left to each decision-maker to consider these individual elements and to somehow arrive at an integrated assessment. This may be asking too much of some evaluators. Moreover, the group discussion may focus on a few facets of the project and overlook other key elements. A second problem is that no cutoff criterion is provided; projects are merely rank-ordered. It is conceivable that even those projects ranked highest will be mediocre choices in a field of poor ideas. Finally, a complaint voiced at some companies is that the decision process is not very transparent to those people outside the gatekeeping group—the entire process reeks of being political, without the use of any criteria.

The *analytic hierarchy process* (AHP) overcomes some of the objections to Q-sort above, for example, the lack of decision criteria. AHP is an approach to decision-making that involves structuring multiple choice criteria into a hierarchy, assessing the relative importance of these criteria, comparing projects on each criterion, and determining an overall ranking of the projects. The evaluation is based on paired comparisons of both projects and criteria. Software, such as Expert Choice, enables a team of managers to arrive at the preferred set of projects in a portfolio.[16]

In spite of the fact that sorting techniques and AHP methods have been around for decades and have been featured in academic articles as far back as the 1980s, they don't appear to have caught on in the business community. Although somewhat obscure to the practitioner, these methods have definite merit for early gate screening where qualitative rather than financial factors dominate, and thus deserve consideration.

Evaluate New Technology Platforms Differently

Many companies seek a target proportion of breakthroughs, radical innovations, disruptive technology, and technology-platform projects within their development portfolios, perhaps 10–20 percent of the total. This is a laudable goal, as evidenced from the portfolio breakdown of top-performing businesses in Figure 3.1.

Tactically, however, these same organizations often cannot cope with such projects once they enter their idea-to-launch framework. In Chapter 5, I recommended adoption of a special version of *Stage-Gate* to handle these venturesome projects: the *technology development process* in Figure 5.2.[17]

If you undertake technology development and technology-platform projects, then be sure to recognize that such projects are less predictable and more loosely defined. Thus, *use different Go/Kill criteria* for these types of projects, criteria that are more visionary and less financial. Figure 8.7 shows a sample scorecard used for *advanced-technology and radical-innovation* projects[18]—a scorecard that

> Financial methods really don't work well for technology-platform and advanced-technology projects. Use a scorecard with much more strategic and qualitative criteria instead.

is quite different from the scorecard for normal new products shown in Figure 8.6. Note that in this best-practice model, the key factors include strategic fit and importance, strategic leverage, likelihoods of commercial and technical success, and reward. Here, the reward questions are quite broad and require only rough estimates; and out of the nineteen questions, only two require financial estimates.

Suggestion: If you undertake advanced-technology projects, technology development, or technology-platform developments, then design and implement a custom-tailored system for such projects. Don't force them through your regular

> Strategy drives your portfolio. Strategic Buckets is one tool to translate your innovation strategy into reality.

stage-and-gate process, but instead adopt *Stage-Gate TD* as outlined in Figure 5.2. As part of this model, recognize that the gate criteria will be different—much more strategic and less financial. A scorecard is best suited to operationalize these more qualitative criteria (shown in Figure 8.7) and is recommended for evaluating such technology projects.

STRATEGIC PORTFOLIO MANAGEMENT

Driving the tactical portfolio decisions is strategic portfolio management, namely, the top part of Figure 8.2. From strategy, all else flows! A business's *product innovation and technology strategy* defines its *goals and objectives* for product innovation and development; it specifies the *strategic arenas*—where innovation and development will be focused. And it maps out *attack plans*—for example, how the business intends to win in each strategic arena. The attack plans can even specify the *major initiatives* that must be undertaken in order to win, and thus comes very close to strategic road mapping.

Establish Strategic Buckets

Strategic Buckets operates from the simple principle that *implementing strategy equates to spending money on specific initiatives.** Thus, operationalizing your strategy really means "setting spending targets." When translating your business's strategy into strategic portfolio decisions (middle part of Figure 8.2), one major challenge faced is your *spending breakdown or deployment:* That is, where does senior management wish to spend its resources when it comes to product innovation—what types of projects, and in what product, market, or technology areas? And how much does it wish to spend in each area?

The method begins with the business's strategy and requires senior managers to make *forced choices* along each of several dimensions—choices about how they wish to allocate their scarce development resources. This enables the creation of "envelopes of resources," or "buckets." Existing projects are categorized into buckets; then managers determine whether actual spending is consistent with desired spending for each bucket. Finally, projects are prioritized within buckets to arrive at the ultimate portfolio of projects—one that mirrors management's strategy for the business.

An example: Traditionally, Honeywell management within business units had reviewed the breakdown of projects *at the end of each year*—asking where resources had been spent by project type, market, product line, and

---

* Note that "resources" includes dollars as well as people time, hence resource allocation is for both fiscal expenditures and person-power (person-days) allocation.

Figure 8.7: Use This Scorecard for Advanced-Technology Projects

1. Business Strategy Fit	Score = 0 (on 0 to 10 scale)	Score = 10 (on 0 to 10 scale)
Congruence	Only peripheral fit with our business strategies	Strong fit with several key elements of strategy
Impact	Minimal impact; no noticeable harm if program is dropped	Business unit future depends on this program
2. Strategic Leverage		
Propriety Position	Easily copied; no protection	Position protected (upstream & downstream) through a combination of patents, trade secrets, raw material access, etc.
Platform for Growth	Dead end; one-of-a-kind; one-off	Opens up many new-product possibilities in new technical & commercial fields
Durability (technical & marketing)	No distinctive advantage; quickly leapfrogged	Long life cycle with opportunity for incremental improvements
Synergy with Other Operations within the company	Limited to a single business unit	Could be applied widely across the company
3. Probability of Technical Success		
Technical Gap	Large gap between solution & current practice; must invent new science	Incremental improvement; easy to do
Program Complexity	Difficult to envision the solution; many hurdles along the way	Can see a solution; straightforward to do
Technology Skill Base	Technology new to company; almost no skills	Technology widely practiced within the company
Availability of People & Facilities	Must hire & build	People & facilities immediately available
4. Prob. of Commercial Success		
Market Need	Extensive market development required; no apparent market need	Product immediately responsive to a customer need; a large market exists
Market Maturity	Declining markets	Rapid growth markets
Competitive Intensity	High; many tough competitors in this field	Low; few competitors; not strong
Commercial Applications Skills	New to company; must develop these skills	Already in place
Commercial Assumptions	Low probability; very speculative assumptions	Highly predictable; high probability of occurring
Regulatory/Social/Political Impact	Negative	Positive impact on a high-profile issue
5. Reward		
Absolute Contribution to Profitability (5-year cumulative)	Less than $10M (estimate)	More than $250M (estimate)
Payback Period ("guesstimates")	Greater than 10 years	Less than 3 years
Time to Commercial Start-up	Greater than 7 years	Less than 1 year

Figure 8.8: Strategic Buckets "Mercedes Star" Method of Portfolio Management Ensures That Spending Mirrors the Strategic Priorities of the Business

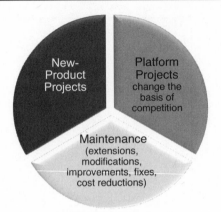

> The business's strategy dictates the split of resources into buckets
> Projects are rank-ordered within buckets
> Use different ranking criteria in each bucket!

so on. But that was like driving a car by looking through the rearview mirror. The information was backward-looking rather than forward-looking.

In the "new approach," the leadership team sits down *at the beginning of the year* and makes strategic choices about where the money will go for *the upcoming year*. As one executive stated, "If we don't make the decision, it will be made for us—and the default option is usually wrong!"

A rather simple breakdown is used at Honeywell: its "Mercedes star" method of allocating resources (Figure 8.8). The leadership team of the business begins with the business's strategy and uses the Mercedes emblem (the three-point star) to help divide up the resources. There are three buckets:

- Fundamental research and platform development projects (which promise to yield major breakthroughs and new technology platforms),
- New-product developments,
- Maintenance (product improvements and enhancements, fixes, cost reductions, and so on).

Management makes strategic choices and splits its development funds into these three buckets. Next, the projects are sorted into each of the three buckets and management ranks projects against each other within each bucket. In effect, three separate portfolios of projects are created and managed. The result: Followed with discipline, over time, the spending breakdowns across buckets and project types mirrors the business's strategic priorities.

Management does the same splitting exercise using other pie charts—by product lines, markets, and geography—as well.

Determining the size of the buckets: Sounds simple in theory. But how does one decide the size of these Strategic Buckets in the first place? Management typically uses a modified Delphi approach. This begins with a current-state assessment including:

- A historical review—where the money was spent for the last twelve to twenty-four months (typically a review of pie-chart splits across markets, business areas, project types, and perhaps geographies—see Figures 8.9 and 8.10).
- A results analysis of recent projects: How well have you done? Which types of spending and projects yielded the best results (the highest productivity)?
- A review of the current split in resources—the "what is."

The innovation strategy is also highlighted, along with a listing and quick review of major projects currently under way. These are the inputs to the decision-making session. Some companies even consider resource splits for best-in-class companies as an input.

Next comes the Delphi voting, in which senior managers simply write down what they believe the correct split of resources should be across several different dimensions.

Some examples: In one major tool manufacturer, one dozen key executives take part in the Strategic Buckets session. The current splits in resources, along with a list of current major projects, is presented; so are the overall business strategy and the strategies for each of the firm's four major product lines. Then the executives vote by allocating resources as percentages across product lines, across project types, and across geographic regions of the world. These votes are immediately displayed on a large-screen spreadsheet, are debated, and consensus is reached. The buckets are decided.

What dimensions to use for the buckets: What dimensions should be used in the Strategic Buckets splits? One R&D executive explained: "Whatever dimensions the leadership team of the business finds most relevant to describe their own strategy." Some common dimensions you might consider are:

- *Strategic goals:* Management splits resources across the specified strategic goals. For example, what percent should be spent on defending the base? On diversifying? On extending the base? and so on.
- *Types of projects:* Most firms have too many of the wrong kinds of projects, so decisions or splits should be made in terms of *types of projects* (as seen in Figure 8.8). Given its aggressive product-innovation strategic stance, at

EXFO Engineering, management targets 65 percent of R&D spending to genuine new products; another 10 percent to platform developments and research (technology development for the future); and the final 25 percent goes to incrementals (the "support-folio," namely, product modifications, fixes, and improvements). In this way, management tilts the portfolio in favor of bolder innovation projects.[19]

- *Across strategic arenas:* The most obvious spending split is across the strategic arenas. That is, as part of your strategy development exercise, you have assessed the attractiveness of each arena and defined the priorities of each. Now move to deployment—that is, decide how many resources each arena should receive.
- *Product lines:* Resources are split across product lines: For example, how much should you spend on Product Line A? On Product Line B? On C? A plot of product-line locations on the product life cycle curve is used to help determine this split.
- *Technologies or technology platforms:* Spending splits can be made across technology types (for example, base, key, pacing, and embryonic technologies) or across specific technology platforms: Platforms X, Y, and Z, and so on.
- *Familiarity Matrix:* What should the split of resources to different types of markets and to different technology types be in terms of their *familiarity to the business*? You can use the popular "familiarity matrix"—technology newness versus market newness—to help split resources.
- *Geography:* What proportion of resources should be spent on projects aimed largely at North America? At Latin America? At Europe? At Asia Pacific? Or at global?
- *By stage of development*: Some businesses distinguish between early stage projects and projects in Development and beyond. Two buckets are created, one for development projects, the other for early stage projects.

Gap analysis—adding up the projects: Following this splitting or voting exercise comes a gap analysis. Existing projects are categorized by bucket, and the total current spending by bucket is added up (the "what is"). Spending gaps are then identified between the "what should be" and "what is" for each bucket.

Finally, projects within each bucket are rank-ordered until you are out of resources. You can use either a scoring model (Project Attractiveness Scores) or financial criteria (the NPV and Productivity Index) to do this ranking within buckets.

Suggestion: Implement Strategic Buckets. This is an excellent method for ensuring that your new-product spending or deployment mirrors your business's strategic priorities. Even better, it's a way to set aside resources for more strategic and bolder innovations (so that all the resources aren't consumed by the smaller, shorter-term projects). Further, the method works, and it seems to suit management's style in most businesses!

Figure 8.9: Three Different Views of a Portfolio Are Revealed—by Project Types

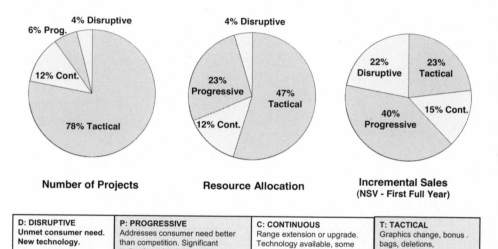

Number of Projects	Resource Allocation	Incremental Sales (NSV - First Full Year)

D: DISRUPTIVE Unmet consumer need. New technology.	P: PROGRESSIVE Addresses consumer need better than competition. Significant technology development.	C: CONTINUOUS Range extension or upgrade. Technology available, some development required.	T: TACTICAL Graphics change, bonus bags, deletions, seasonal.

Source: MARS Pet Foods.

By breaking the decision process into two levels—first decide the strategic breakdown of your resources via Strategic Buckets, and then decide which projects to do—your portfolio mix and balance of projects will ultimately reflect your business's priorities in terms of project types, markets, and product types. And via Strategic Buckets, you take steps to prevent the problem that many firms suffer from, namely, an overabundance of small, incremental, low-value projects, and a real lack of major innovations.

Strategic Views of Your Portfolio

Some firms have not adopted Strategic Buckets per se but use similar charts to portray their portfolio in a strategic way. For example, charts can show the mix and balance of projects in your portfolio—the "what is"—in a number of useful ways. These charts are helpful both at gate meetings and at portfolio reviews, and often move the leadership team toward a strategic buckets way of thinking.

There are numerous parameters, dimensions, or variables across which one might wish to view the balance of projects in a development portfolio:

Projects, resources, and sales: What is the breakdown of your projects by project type? And where are the resources going? Finally, again by project type, where are the sales coming from? Figure 8.9 shows a chart from the MARS Petcare (Pet Foods) business, showing three current views of the portfolio (the far right chart

Figure 8.10: These Pie Charts Show Actual Resource Allocation in the Portfolio by Project Type and Market Sector

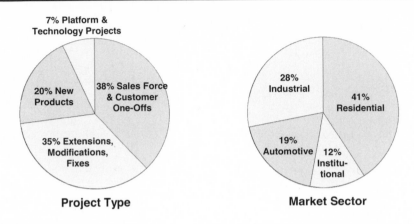

Project Type   **Market Sector**

Pie charts show different views of the portfolio, and point management towards Strategic Buckets thinking. Charts show resource breakdown by project type and market sector, year to date.

---

shows expected net incremental sales, the increase in sales, for year one, based on the data in each project's Business Case). Management reviews this and similar charts—breakdowns by product line and market segment—to gain a quick insight into the health of the current development portfolio.

Resource breakdown by project types: What is your spending on product innovation versus product renovation? And what should it be? Pie charts effectively capture the current spending split across project types (Figure 8.10, left pie). Pie charts that show the resource breakdown by project types are a particularly useful sanity check, as in Figure 8.10.

Markets, products, and technologies: These provide another set of dimensions across which managers seek balance. The question faced is: Do you have the appropriate split in R&D spending across your various product lines? Or across the markets or market segments in which you operate (see Figure 8.10, right pie)? Or across technologies? Pie charts are again appropriate for capturing and displaying data of this type.

Risk-reward bubble diagrams: About 44 percent of businesses employing a systematic portfolio-management method use the *risk-reward* bubble diagram in Figure 8.11, or one like it.[20] Here, the horizontal axis is some measure of the *reward* to the company, the vertical axis is a *success probability:*

Figure 8.11: This Popular Bubble Diagram Shows the Risk-Reward Profile of the Development Portfolio

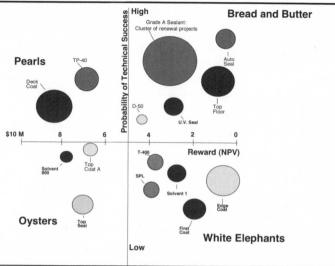

Projects are plotted as bubbles on this two-dimensional risk and reward grid. The bubble sizes denote the resources committed to each project. The shading shows the stage in the firm's *Stage-Gate* system (light = early stage).

- One approach is to use a *qualitative estimate* of reward, ranging from "modest" to "excellent."[21] The argument here is that too heavy an emphasis on financial numbers can do serious damage, notably in the early stages of a project. The other axis is the probability of overall success (probability of *commercial* success times probability of *technical* success).
- In contrast, other firms rely on very quantitative and financial gauges of reward, namely, the probability-adjusted NPV of the project. Here the probability of *technical* success is the vertical axis, as probability of commercial success has already been built into the NPV calculation.

A sample bubble diagram is shown in Figure 8.11 for a high-technology business unit of a major chemical company. Here the size of each bubble shows the annual resources committed to each project (dollars per year; it could also be people or work-months allocated to the project).

Given that this business unit is a "star business" seeking rapid growth, a quick review of the portfolio map in Figure 8.11 reveals many problems. There are too many White Elephant projects (it's time to do some serious project pruning!); too much money spent on Bread and Butter, low-value projects; not enough Pearls; and heavily underresourced Oysters.

One feature of this bubble diagram model is that it forces senior management to deal with the resource issue. Given finite resources, *the sum of the areas of the circles must be a constant*. That is, if you add one project to the diagram, you must subtract another; alternatively, you can shrink the size of several circles. The elegance here is that the model forces management to consider the resource implications of adding one more project to the list—that other projects must pay the price!

Also denoted in the bubble diagram is the product line that each project is associated with (via the cross-hatching, not shown). A final breakdown is timing (shown as shading). Thus, this apparently simple risk-reward diagram shows a lot more than simply risk and profitability data: It also conveys resource allocation, timing, and spending breakdowns across product lines.

Suggestion: Charts that display the current mix and balance of projects in the portfolio are popular at portfolio reviews and at gate meetings. This section has revealed a number of different displays and formats. Pie charts are quite popular (Figures 8.9 and 8.10), and lead nicely into Strategic Buckets. They are often used to display the current situation—the current breakdown in resources by:

- Project type: new products, improvements, sales force requests, platforms, and so on
- Market: market segment, market sector, or geographic market
- Product: product line or product category
- Technology: technology types or technology maturity (embryonic, pacing, base)
- Project size (by cumulative three-year sales)

Pick the dimensions that are most relevant to your business and your leadership team. Hint: Don't use too many different pie charts—they tend to overwhelm people at meetings. As one executive declared in frustration after acquiring portfolio management software, "We have a case of bubble-itis in our company!"

Consider one risk-reward model (as in Figure 8.11) with quantitative axes such as "probability of success" versus "reward" (which can be measured in terms of profitability, such as NPV, as in Figure 8.11; or cumulative three-year sales).

Develop a Strategic Product Road Map

The product road map is another strategically driven resource allocation method and can be used instead of (or along with) the Strategic Buckets approach. This top-down approach is designed to ensure that the list of projects—at least the major ones—contributes to or is essential for the realization of the business's strategy and goals.[22] A strategic product road map is an effective way to map out this series of initiatives in an attack plan.

> A strategic product road map establishes place marks for major projects envisioned well into the future.

What is a road map? It is simply management's view of how to get where it wants to go or to achieve its de-

Figure 8.12: The Product Roadmap Shows the Major Development Initiatives Envisioned Over a Five Year Period—New Products and Platforms

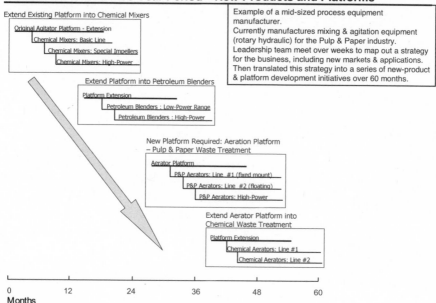

sired objective.[23] Note that there are different types of road maps: the product road map and the technology road map.

Your *strategic product road map* defines your *major* new-product and platform developments along a time line, often for five years into the future. The road map is a tentative plan, and provides "place marks"—tentative commitments of resources—for future projects. Five years is a long time to forecast, and thus the road map is updated annually: It's a "rolling plan," so that only the first year is ever implemented! An example is in Figure 8.12 for a process equipment manufacturer. Here the strategic product road map not only maps out the various major product developments and their timing, it also defines the platforms and platform extensions needed to develop these new products.

The *technology road map* is derived from the product road map. It lays out the technologies and technology platforms that are needed in order to implement (develop and source) the products and platforms in the product road map. The technology road map is a logical extension of the product road map and is closely linked to it.

Most often, the specification of projects on your product road map is left fairly general and high level. For example, designations such as "a low-carb beer for the Atkins diet market" or "ceramic-coated tooling for the aerospace industry" or "low-power petroleum blenders" as in Figure 8.12, are often the way these projects are shown on the product road map time line. That is, *place marks* for projects "yet to be well defined" are the norm: The road map is meant to be directional and strategic, but not provide detailed product definitions. As each project progresses through the idea-to-launch system, however, increasingly the project and product become specified and defined.

Creating your Strategic Product Road Map: The development of a product road map flows logically from your business's product innovation strategy. Delineating the major initiatives required as part of your product road map is a multifaceted task and includes the following:

- *Strategic assessment:* Often, the mere specification of a strategic arena as top priority leads logically to a list of those products and projects that are necessary in order to enter and win in that arena.
- *Portfolio review of existing products:* Here, you take a hard look at your current product offerings and decide which are tired and should be pruned or updated, and which should be replaced.
- *Competitive analysis:* Where are your competitors' products and product lines relative to yours? This exercise often points to the need for new products either immediately or in the foreseeable future.
- *Technology trend assessment:* Here you forecast technology and what new technologies, and hence new technology platform developments, will be required and their timing.
- *Market trends assessment:* Again, this is a forecasting exercise, and it looks at major market trends and shifts. In this exercise, often you are able to pinpoint specific initiatives that you must undertake in response to these evident market trends.

Suggestion: Strategic product road maps that lay out the major initiatives—major developments, products, and platforms—are also a powerful concept and can be used with or without Strategic Buckets above. Note that this road map should be strategic, with place marks defined for major projects, many of which might be bold innovations, and some of which are yet to be defined precisely. And the road map should be a time line for the longer term (not just a list of products and projects for this year).

How does one develop a Strategic Road Map? There is no science to this. Essentially it's a meeting over several days that involves a host of multifunctional players: product managers, market managers, technology mangers, source-of-supply managers, forecasters, strategy managers, and so on. The many and different inputs for developing your Strategic Road Map are highlighted above in the bulleted list. Once you have crafted your strategic product road map, be sure to go the next step and develop the technology road map, outlining what technologies are needed and when, in order to execute your product road map.

Figure 8.13: The Innovation Governance Processes—*Stage-Gate®* System, Portfolio Reviews, and Strategic Roadmapping—Are Integrated, with Each Decision Process Feeding the Others

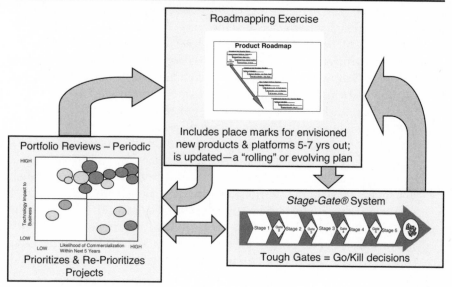

INTEGRATING THE GOVERNANCE ELEMENTS: GATING, PORTFOLIO REVIEWS, AND ROAD MAPS

Your product road map outlines which projects your business will probably undertake, and has a longer-term horizon; there are many "future projects" in your road map with tentative commitments earmarked for each. Meanwhile, your gating system manages your currently active projects, where Go/Kill decisions are made on an ongoing, real-time basis. And your portfolio reviews look at the entire portfolio of active and on-hold projects periodically. All three systems yield decisions on projects—but how do the three tie together?

Figure 8.13 shows the interrelations and interaction of the three decision systems to yield a more holistic picture of the innovation governance system:

- *Road maps:* Strategic product road maps are developed (at the top of Figure 8.13), providing a future view of the probable development portfolio. Methods for identifying road map candidate projects were outlined above: Some firms run the equivalent of a Gate 1 or "Gate 0" on these candidate projects before inserting them into the road map, using a nonfinancial approach such as a scorecard. From your product road maps, you develop your technology road map, which shows what technologies and capabilities are needed and when, in order to support the product road map.

- *Stage-Gate:* When the timing is right according to the road map, place-marked projects start out in your *Stage-Gate* system. They are screened at Gate 1 and start moving through the process, stage by stage, gate by gate (the bottom right of Figure 8.13). Gates are the quality control checkpoints: Some projects that looked great at the outset, and thus were included in the road map, will be spotted as duds at Gates 2 or 3, and are culled. Note: Just because a project is in the road map does not guarantee it will be done. So the *Stage-Gate* system acts as a check and balance on the visionary road map, and provides feedback: The road map is appropriately updated as active projects are killed. (Note that other projects are in your *Stage-Gate* system, too, not just those that came from the road map.)
- *Portfolio Review:* Once projects pass Gate 2* in the *Stage-Gate* system—when resource commitments become considerable, and when there is enough data to characterize the project—they "appear" in the development portfolio. Once "in the portfolio," the project, along with many others, is scrutinized at portfolio reviews (the left side of Figure 8.13). Although many companies consider the quarterly (or semiannual) portfolio review to be "a minor course correction," other firms make numerous Go/Kill decisions here. Thus, portfolio decisions impact both the gating system and the product road map, and updates are made to each.

And so the process continues—each decision process in Figure 8.13 feeding the others in a closed-loop system—with the various components of the governance process working in harmony.

DATA INTEGRITY

The best project-selection system in the world is worthless unless the data are sound.[24] As one executive cynically remarked about his firm's adoption of an elaborate financial evaluation tool, "They're trying to measure a soft banana with a micrometer," noting that the precision of the tool far exceeded the quality of the data on projects.

The lack of good, early information plagues many companies' new-product projects. Note that *on entering the development stage*, only one firm in five has good information on customer price sensitivity (what customers are prepared to pay for the new product); three-fourths of businesses lack data on customer reaction to the new product (for example, via a concept test); and almost two-thirds of firms do not have reliable data on market size and forecasted sales revenue from the new product.[25] Scott Edgett's APQC study of portfolio methods

---

* Gate 2 is the typical point where projects are placed "in the portfolio." Gate 1 is likely too early—not enough data. Gate 3, when full development really starts, is the point in some firms where the portfolio process kicks in.

reveals that the greatest challenge faced in portfolio management *was not the portfolio tool* or model—it was *the data integrity* (or rather, the lack of integrity)![26]

Fact-based decision-making in new-product development pays off! As evidence in Chapter 2 revealed, those businesses that devote more effort to the early phases of a project—for example, seeking and obtaining better market information, front-end loading their projects, and seeking sharp, early, fact-based product definition—are rewarded with much higher performance in innovation.

> The greatest challenge in project selection and portfolio management is not the selection tool, but getting better data integrity.

Clear Expectations

The first step to ensuring better data is to ensure that *information requirements are clear*. As one executive put it, "If the expectations are clear, there is a much better chance that project teams will deliver." But too often, project teams are uncertain about just what activities are expected and what information is required—what they should do and deliver—to enable the executives to make effective Go/Kill decisions. If senior management needs to know "expected sales" or the "target price" to plus-or-minus 10 percent, then make that requirement loud and clear to project teams!

One way to make expectations clear is *to install a robust idea-to-launch system*, and then *practice it*. At minimum, this process should specify:

- The stages, and in particular, *the best-practice activities within each stage* that project teams are expected to execute. Chapter 7, for example, outlined the recommended activities in Stages 1 and 2—the market studies, technical assessment, concept tests, and other key tasks as lead-up to building the Business Case. In your *Stage-Gate* process, these recommended or mandatory tasks should be a clear guide to project teams.
- The gates, and most important, the *information needs defined* for each of these Go/Kill decision points: What information does senior management need to see in order to make a timely and effective Go/Kill decision?

Project Team Accountability for Forecasts and Projections

A second key to data integrity is *instilling project team accountability*. This is a best practice that we saw in Chapters 3 and 5, and in Figures 3.6 and 5.7. In the *team accountability model*, project teams present forecasts or projections at early gates—for example, in the preliminary and full Business Cases presented at Gates 2 and 3. These projections typically include sales forecasts for the new product, costs, margins, a launch date, and so on.

On the basis of these and other data, senior management approves the project and commits the resources to move forward. These projections become the *success*

> Make project teams accountable for the projections they deliver. That way, projections are more realistic and accurate, and data integrity improves.

criteria against which the project is judged at subsequent gates, a concept introduced in Chapters 3 and 5. But most important, the *project team is now responsible for the achievement of these projections:* Following Launch, there is a Post-Launch Review (typically about one year after launch, that is, after a full year of operating results)—see Figure 5.7. Here, the project team presents the results it achieved—first-year sales, margins, costs, launch date—versus what was promised at Gates 3 and 5. One result of this accountability model is that the project team makes much more *professional and realistic estimates*—data integrity improves!

By contrast, in too many firms, there is a "launch and leave attitude"—that is, once the project nears launch, the project is handed off to the "commercialization folks," and the project team is no longer responsible for the project or accountable for achieving the numbers! In these poor-practice firms, winning is *getting your project approved*; and thus overzealous project teams are guilty of submitting optimistic projections, knowing well that they aren't really accountable for their achievement. Not surprisingly, data integrity is very poor and many projects are approved that should not be.

POPULARITY AND EFFECTIVENESS OF PORTFOLIO METHODS

Which methods are the most popular? And which work the best? In practice, not surprisingly, the *financial methods* dominate portfolio management, according to our portfolio best-practices study.[27] Financial methods include various profitability and return metrics, such as NPV, IRR, ECV, ROI, EVA, or Payback Period—metrics that are used to rate, rank-order, and ultimately select projects. A total of 77.3 percent of businesses use such a financial approach to select projects (see Figure 8.14). For 40.4 percent of businesses, this is the *dominant decision method.*

Other methods are also quite popular:

- *Strategic approaches:* Letting the strategy dictate the portfolio is a popular approach, and includes Strategic Buckets, Strategic Product Road Mapping, and other strategically driven methods. A total of 64.8 percent of businesses use a strategic approach; for 26.6 percent of businesses, this is the dominant method.
- *Bubble diagrams or portfolio maps:* 40.6 percent of businesses use portfolio maps, but only 8.3 percent use this as their dominant method. The most popular map is the risk-versus-reward map in Figure 8.11, but many variants of bubble diagrams are used.

Figure 8.14: Financial Models Are By Far the Most Popular Project Evaluation Tools... But Not the Most Effective

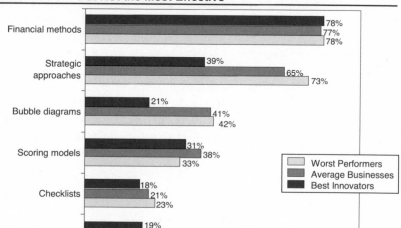

Percent of Businesses Using Each Method

- *Scoring or scorecard models:* Scaled ratings are obtained by using scorecards at gates and are added to yield a Project Attractiveness Score. These models are used by 37.9 percent of businesses; in 18.3 percent, this is the dominant decision method.
- *Checklists:* Projects are evaluated on a set of Yes/No questions. Each project must achieve either all Yes answers, or a certain number of Yes answers to proceed. Only 21 percent of businesses use checklists; and in only 2.7 percent is this the dominant method.

Popularity does *not necessarily equate to effectiveness*, however. When the performance of businesses' portfolios is rated on performance metrics, those businesses that rely heavily on financial tools as the dominant portfolio-selection model *fare the worst*. Financial tools tend to yield an unbalanced portfolio of lower-value projects and projects that lack strategic alignment. By contrast, strategic methods produce a strategically aligned and balanced portfolio. Moreover, they are highly rated by users in terms of "fits management's style" and "is understood by management."

> The most popular approaches, it turns out, are the least effective—but do use them. Just don't "bet the farm" based on these financial projections!

Interestingly, scorecard models are not nearly as popular but fare exceptionally well in use. They appear best for selecting high-value projects, and also yield a balanced portfolio. Scorecard models are also highly rated in terms of "fits management's style" as well as effectiveness (helps us make the right decision) and efficiency (does not waste time). Finally, businesses using bubble diagrams obtain a balanced and strategically aligned portfolio.[28]

It is ironic that the most rigorous techniques—the various financial tools— yield the worst results, not so much because the methods are flawed but simply because reliable financial data are often missing at the very point in a project where the key project-selection decisions are made. Often, reliable financial data—expected sales, pricing, margins, and costs—are difficult to estimate, in many cases because the project team simply has not done its homework. In other cases, it's a matter of an overzealous project leader making highly optimistic projections in order to secure support for the project.

RECOMMENDATIONS FOR PORTFOLIO MANAGEMENT

A number of tools and methods have been described that help you select development projects and visualize and manage your development portfolio. The recommendation is that you use a combination of approaches: *No one approach works perfectly, so triangulate!* Indeed, the best innovators use an average of 2.4 methods each, as they recognize that no one tool can do it all.

The recommendations are, for *bolder innovations* and *major new-product projects*:

- Use a financial analysis, namely, NPV (and the IRR and Payback Period) along with the Productivity Index, *but not at the early gates.* Too early a financial screen will kill all but the sure bets! However, a financial analysis is usually expected by Gate 3, and you always learn something from undertaking such an analysis. The NPV (a discounted cash flow method) is generally accepted as the most appropriate financial method to reflect value to the corporation. The Productivity Index, an extension of the NPV method, is best for ranking and prioritizing projects. For large but highly uncertain projects, consider using the expected commercial value (ECV), which builds in risk and probabilities.
- Use the scorecard (scoring model) method as well. Scorecards are well rated for effectiveness, efficiency, and their fit with management's style; they also yield robust portfolios, better than the financial models. But use *different scorecards* for different types of projects: Figure 8.6 for *genuine new products* and Figure 8.7 for *advanced-technology* or technology-platform projects.
- Introduce a few well-chosen success criteria—for example, first-year sales, launch date, and a profitability metric—by Gate 3. Use these success criteria

both at successive gates as Go/Kill criteria, and also to hold the project team accountable for key results and hence to improve data integrity.

For *lower-risk and smaller development projects*—such as product improvements, fixes, or extensions—*other project-selection methods* are more appropriate and practical. More on these projects in the next chapter.

Portfolio management is not just about tactical project selection—you must also consider strategic issues. From strategy all else flows, so use Strategic Buckets and Strategic Road Maps to translate strategy into project-investment decisions. Finally, the many charts in this chapter—the pie charts and bubble diagrams— provide useful ways for management to view the firm's development portfolios and are sensible additions to both gate meetings and portfolio reviews.

Data reliability is also a challenge. All these methods are only as good as the data upon which they are based. Securing more reliable data should be a goal, and indeed is a key outcome of an effective idea-to-launch system outlined in Chapter 5. So practice your *Stage-Gate* system with discipline! Additionally, make project teams accountable for the projections (and promises) they make at the critical Gates 3 and 5. Hold a Post-Launch Review, where promised versus actual results is the topic.

9

MAKING THE GATES WORK— GATES WITH TEETH

You gotta know when to hold 'em,
Know when to fold 'em,
Know when to walk away,
Know when to run.

—Kenny Rogers, "The Gambler"

CHALLENGES AT THE GATES

The devil is in the details. Perhaps the greatest challenge that users of *Stage-Gate*® face is making the gates work.[1] *As go the gates, so goes the process*! In a robust gating system, poor projects are spotted early and killed; and projects in trouble are also detected, then sent back for rework or redirect—and put back on course. But it seems that as quality-control checkpoints, the gates aren't too effective in too many companies and allow a lot of poor projects to proceed.

This chapter delves into the details of making the gates work. The previous chapter introduced many of the tools that are used in portfolio and project selection; in the current chapter, we take these selection tools, along with other concepts and approaches, and show how they can be effectively used at gate meetings to make better Go/Kill decisions.

Gates are rated one of the weakest areas in product development, with only 33 percent of firms having tough, rigorous gates throughout the idea-to-launch process.[2] And we saw in the previous chapter that most firms have too many projects and too many minor projects in their development pipelines. Finally, only 56 percent of development projects meet their sales targets (44 percent do not), which means that gates aren't doing their job: Too many bad projects and too many projects in trouble are sliding through!

GATE DEFINITIONS

Gates

"Gates" are project-review and decision meetings—the vital Go/Kill decision points in the *Stage-Gate®* idea-to-launch system. At gates, projects are evaluated by management; projects are approved and prioritized, resources are allocated to projects; and poor projects are killed before additional resources are wasted.

Gatekeepers

"Gatekeepers" are a management team of decision-makers and resource owners responsible for selecting the best project for development, and then ensuring that these projects receive committed resources—the gatekeepers thus facilitate the rapid commercialization of selected projects.

Gatekeeping

"Gatekeeping" is the set of management practices, behaviors, procedures, and rules of engagement that govern decision-making at the gates. These practices are designed to enable project teams to move good projects forward rapidly and effectively through to launch. Note that the emphasis here is on enabling and facilitating projects—not just on judging and critiquing.

Getting on the Same Page—Some Definitions

"Gates" are meetings between the project team and senior management designed to assess the quality of the project, make the Go/Kill and prioritization decision, and approve the needed resources for the next stage (see box entitled "Gate Definitions"):

- Gates are defined throughout the idea-to-launch process. Typically, there are about five gates for a major project, from the Idea Screen through the Go to Launch decision point, as shown in Figure 4.10.
- Gates focus on one project at a time. By contrast, portfolio reviews consider the entire set of projects. Gates tend to provide a much more in-depth assessment of the individual project than portfolio reviews.
- Gates have defined decision-makers: the gatekeepers (see box).
- Effective gates utilize the various tools seen in the previous chapter to sharpen the decision-making: NPV, Productivity Index, Payback Period, ECV, scorecards, and success criteria.

Gates with No Teeth

Although your company might have installed a *Stage-Gate* system, the gates are often either *non-existent* or *lack teeth*.[3] The result is that projects are rarely killed at gates. Rather, as one senior manager exclaimed, "Projects are like express trains, speeding down the track, slowing down at the occasional station [gate], but never stopping until they reach their ultimate destination, the marketplace." In short, the gates have no teeth: Once a project is approved, it never gets killed.

The reason: Management does not know how to say "no," that is, *drown some puppies!* Thus, even though gate meetings are held with the best of intentions— to provide a critical evaluation of the project and make a Go/Kill decision—the Kill option is rarely exercised. And like the addictive poker player who does not know when to fold his hand and walk away, there are many good (and not so good) reasons for continuing to push the project onward—see the box "Seven Reasons We Can't Kill Projects."

Even worse, in many firms we have investigated, there was never an intention to kill a project once under way. After the initial Go decision, the gates amount to little more than a project review meeting or a milestone checkpoint, but not a serious Go/Kill decision meeting.

An example: In one major high-tech communications equipment manufacturer, once a project passes Gate 1 (the Idea Screen), it is placed into the business's product road map. This means that the estimated sales and profits from the new project are now integrated into the business unit's financial forecast. Once into the financial plan of the business, of course, the project is locked in: There is no way that the project can be removed from the road map or killed. In effect, all gates after Gate 1 are merely rubber stamps. Somehow, management in this firm missed the point that the idea-to-launch process is a funnel, not a tunnel; and that gates after Gate 1 are also Go/Kill points: This should *not be* a one-gate, five-stage process!

In too many firms, like this example, after the initial Go decision, the gates amount to little more than a project update meeting, a project review meeting, or a milestone checkpoint: Is the project on time and on budget? But rarely is the issue of "should we continue investing in this project?" ever discussed. Thus, instead of the well-defined funnel that is so often used to depict the new-product process, one ends up with a tunnel where everything that enters comes out the other end, good projects and bad. Yet management is deluded into believing that the firm has a functioning *Stage-Gate* system.

> Gates are investment-decision or Go/Kill meetings. Because this is an options model, early decisions to move forward can be reversed at later gates, based on new information.

The point needs to be made: Gates are *investment-decision or Go/Kill meetings*. Like any

SEVEN REASONS WE CAN'T KILL PROJECTS

1. Momentum:
   - People and enthusiasm
   - We've already spent $XX—can't quit now
2. Difficult to say "no":
   - Nobody likes to "drown puppies"—a difficult and unpleasant task
3. Political reasons:
   - Executive pet projects
   - Executives saving face
4. The project team won't let go—too determined:
   - "Victory is just around the corner"
   - Stopping now is an admission of defeat
   - It's not career-enhancing
5. It's in the plan:
   - The project is already "in" the business's product road map
   - It's built into this year's financial plan—we can't take it out now
6. Incomplete or unreliable data:
   - It's difficult to make tough decisions when data are speculative, not fact-based
7. No method for killing projects:
   - No clear Go/Kill criteria among the gatekeepers
   - No "vote" taken at gate meetings—it's not really an investment-decision meeting

investment meeting, the most current information is reviewed, an assessment is undertaken, and a Go or Kill decision is made. Because this is an *options model*—that is, the decision to fully invest is made via a series of Go/Kill decisions—early decisions to move forward can be reversed at later gates: Often, projects look good and are approved at Gates 1 and 2 based on very limited information; but by the time they reach Gate 3, and with the benefit of more complete information, the evaluators determine that the project has turned sour and must be killed. That Kill decision must be made!

Hollow Decisions at Gates

A closely connected problem is *hollow gates*. Here, the gate meeting is held and a Go decision is made, *but resources are not committed*. Somehow, management fails to understand that approval decisions are rather meaningless *unless a check is cut*: The project leader and team must leave the gate meeting with the resources they need to progress their project. Instead, projects are approved, but resources are not—*a hollow Go decision*, and one that usually leads to too many projects in the pipeline, and projects taking far too long to get to market. And lacking the resources to get the project done, the project leader is set up for failure!

The Ugly Results

Gates without teeth usually means that there are too many projects in the development pipeline, many of them of limited value. And hollow gates—approving projects without committing resources—means that there is no limit to the number of projects that can be approved! Note, however, that approving too many projects for the limited resources triggers many ailments.[4] First, project team members are spread too thinly over too many projects. Multitasking is a good thing up to a point; but too much multitasking leads to decreased productivity—switching from task to task, with the associated "start up" and "shut down" costs. With resources spread so thinly, many projects are in a queue, awaiting people to work on them; thus, projects start to take longer and longer. In some firms, the process is virtually gridlocked—nothing moves. Even worse, facing tough time lines and without the time to do the job right, some project team members cut corners in order to save time. Doing too many projects has a few other negative side effects, as covered in Chapter 3: Project team members become stressed and start blaming each other for missed milestones, which is not good for team morale. And finally, on occasion, "clever teams" simply *dumb down their projects*.

Suggestion: Take a look at your gates. Are they working well? Do you actually kill projects at your gate meetings, or are they like gates in most firms—an information update-and-review meeting? And do you really commit resources to teams at gates; or is your company guilty of hollow gates? If the answers to these questions signal problems, read on and see what can be done.

GATES WITH TEETH—LEARN TO DROWN SOME PUPPIES

If "gates without teeth" and "hollow gates" describe your company's gates, then it's time to start drowning some puppies and reallocating (and committing) resources to the deserving projects. Here are some ways. The box entitled "Requirements for Gates with Teeth" summarizes some best practices found in various firms as they attempt to sharpen their gate decisions. Some of these practices were highlighted in previous chapters, while others are outlined in the current chapter. I integrate them here in the sidebar.

Prune the Current Portfolio—Major Surgery

One way to kick-start the process is by undertaking a ruthless one-time pruning operation—a tough-minded project-by-project portfolio review:

REQUIREMENTS FOR GATES WITH TEETH

1. Clearly defined gates in the process:
   - Defined as Go/Kill decision points
   - Not just project review, milestone review, or status update meetings
   - Projects cannot continue unless a Go decision is made
2. Data integrity:
   - Quality information to make the Go/Kill decision
   - Reliable information—based on solid front-end homework
   - Specify what homework is required or desired in your *Stage-Gate* system
3. The right deliverables:
   - Relevant information presented to gatekeepers in a useful manner
   - Clear expectations re: deliverables for project teams
   - Use templates, guides, and so on
4. Project teams accountable for results:
   - Versus the data (forecast) they present at gates
   - Build in a formal Post-Launch Review
5. Visible Go/Kill and prioritization criteria:
   - Made operational via a scorecard and "success criteria"
   - And the Productivity Index
6. A resource allocation method at the gate:
   - Linked to portfolio management—the big picture
   - The right balance and mix of projects
   - Employ Strategic Buckets and Product Road Maps
   - Full portfolio review with senior management: two to four times per year

An example: One major chemical company was suffering from too many projects: over 1,000 active development initiatives in their pipeline. A thorough review of the list revealed that many were mediocre, of limited value to the company or lacking strategic impact. A brutal pruning exercise reduced the list to 250 projects. The result: Time-to-market was cut in half within one year; and project execution improved dramatically.

Pruning the portfolio means making difficult choices. A 75-percent pruning rate in this example is extreme; experience suggests that in the typical portfolio, roughly half the projects should be cut. Drowning puppies is unpleasant for most managements, however: All projects look good; all are worthy or needed; and no one likes to kill any of them. The other tough issue is this: Even if there is the will to kill, which projects should be killed or put on hold?

Do Fewer But Better Projects—a Decision-Factory Mentality

In the longer run, strive for better new-product focus. Project selection must occur in light of your resource constraints—ensuring that the right number of projects is undertaken for the limited development resources available. It is better to undertake four projects and do them properly, rather than try to do ten badly. Thus, embrace the funneling approach, and know that a certain percentage of projects should be cut at each gate, especially the earlier Gates 1, 2, and 3:

> *An example:*[5] A division of Cooper Standard Automotive faced a gridlocked product-development system back in 2000. A chart from that year showed fifty major projects under way, time-to-market was "infinite," and there were zero launches. At that low point, a tough-minded executive forced a *decision-factory mentality* into his gate meetings—kill the weaker projects. The result was that by 2007, the number of major projects was down to eight, time-to-market was reduced to 1.6 years, and major launches were up to five annually. Revenue from new products steadily increased from 2000, had risen more than tenfold by 2007, and continues to increase.

The Optimal Kill Rate

A frequent question at our portfolio management seminars is this: Is there an optimal attrition curve? Or what percentage of projects should be cut or killed at each gate? For example, in the venture capital business one rule is: Look at 100 opportunities, invest in ten, and one will be a big winner.

In the case of product innovation, I know of no such optimal or *magic curve*, although some folks have unsuccessfully tried to calculate the theoretical optimal kill rate at each gate. One rule of thumb is that the number of projects at each stage should be inversely proportional to the cost of the stage. But doing the math leads to an exceptionally steep attrition curve, so it's probably a poor rule.

Another view is to use the *average attrition curve*, shown in Figure 1.5, the theory being that the average decision-maker is optimal. This attrition curve translates into seven projects in Stage 1; five projects in Stage 2; four projects in Stage 3; and 1.5 launches—roughly a five-to-one attrition rate from Gate 1 to Gate 5. Note that this curve is for true product developments—innovations that tend to be riskier; more-predictable, lower-risk, and minor projects have a more gentle attrition rate than five-to-one. Further, the shape of the curve in Figure 1.5 is wrong—it should be much steeper in order to optimize spending, That is, the greatest cuts as a percent should come at the early gates—for example, go from seven projects to three to two when moving from Gate 1 into Development—

with very little attrition after Gate 3. EXFO Engineering likens their process to a "funnel leading to a tunnel"; and a major chemical company computes the percentage of projects killed after Gate 3—the percentage of "late kills"—as a negative metric.

Whatever the ideal kill rate at each gate might be, here are some good practices:

- Track the percentage of projects killed at each gate. The percentage should be highest at the early gates, but after Gate 3 (that is, Gates 4 and 5), the percentage of kills should tend to zero—a funnel leading to a tunnel.
- If the kill rate at the early gates is close to zero—with nothing being killed— then *you do have a problem*: gates with no teeth. It is highly unlikely that every project that starts out in your innovation process is a good one, and thus some that pass Gate 1 should be cut later on.
- The kill rate should be higher for venturesome projects (a steeper attrition curve) than for lower-risk, predictable, and short-term projects.
- The average attrition curve in Figure 1.5 is not a good benchmark. Your ideal curve should be steeper at the beginning, and become less steep as it approaches the final stages. Note that the area under the curve in Figure 1.5 is roughly proportional to spending, so it pays to cut projects early rather than later.

Build Clearly Defined Gates into Your Innovation Process
Gates must be built into your idea-to-launch system, as in a typical *Stage-Gate* process shown in Figure 4.10. But gates are not just project-review meetings or milestone checks. Rather, they are *Go/Kill meetings*: Gates are the occasion when senior management meets to decide whether the company should continue to invest in the project based on the latest information; or perhaps cut losses and get out of a bad project. Note that gates are also *a resource-commitment meeting*, where, in the event of a Go decision, the project leader and team receive a commitment of resources to pursue their project: Projects cannot just be approved without committing the resources, otherwise the result is hollow gates and too many projects!

> Gates are an irrevocable decision to commit resources to a project leader and team—to complete the next stage of their project.

Employ Visible Go/Kill and Prioritization Criteria
Use scorecards: A number of firms (for example, some divisions at J&J, P&G, Emerson Electric, and ITT Industries) use scorecards for early stage screening (for Gates 1, 2, and 3 in Figure 4.10); the project is scored by the gatekeepers right at the gate meeting on key criteria. The scorecard method was introduced in the previous chapter as a project evaluation tool. Recall that scorecards rely on qualitative factors, such as market attractiveness, leveraging core competencies, and

Figure 9.1: Display the Scorecard Scores at the Gate Meeting—These Charts Usually Lead to a Rich Discussion

Project: Monty-21

Project Attractiveness Score: 34.4 out of 60 or 57%	Decision: KILL

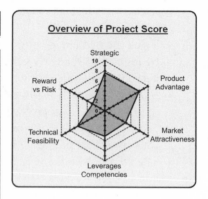

Evaluator	Strategic	Product Advantage	Market Attrac- tiveness	Leverage Compe- tencies	Technical Feasibil- ity	Reward vs. Risk	Score out of 60
JCC	0	10	4	7	7	10	38.0
MB	10	7	4	4	7	4	36.0
SJC	10	10	7	4	4	4	39.0
NCC	10	7	7	4	7	0	35.0
FK	7	7	4	4	7	0	29.0
FM	7	5	4	4	4	0	24.0
GRT	10	10	4	7	7	4	42.0
HH	7	7	4	7	7	0	32.0
Total:	61	63	38	41	50	22	275.0
Mean:	7.6	7.9	4.8	5.1	6.3	2.8	34.4
Team:	10.0	7.0	4.0	4.0	7.0	4.0	36.0
Std Dev:	3.42	1.89	1.39	1.55	1.39	3.54	

competitive advantage (rather than just on financial numbers such as NPV) to assess the relative attractiveness of a project at a gate.

Following the presentation of the project by the project team, the gatekeepers score the project on about six to ten such criteria on scales of 0–10. The scores are displayed on a big screen (see Figure 9.1), discussion and debate ensues, and a Go/Kill decision is made.

Use the right financial criteria: Most firms rely heavily on financial criteria to select development projects, as we saw in the previous chapter. Nonetheless, it's prudent to spell out what these criteria are—NPV (or ECV), IRR, and Payback Period— and what the hurdles are for different types of projects.

Employ success criteria: Another selection method introduced in the previous chapter, and employed with considerable success within gates at firms such as P&G, is the use of *success criteria:* "Specific success criteria for each gate relevant to that stage are defined for each project. These criteria, and targets to be achieved on them, are agreed to by the project team and management at each gate. These success criteria are then used to evaluate the project at successive gates." If the project's estimates fail on any agreed-to criterion at successive gates, the project could be killed. Note that success criteria can be used along with the scorecard method.

Try self-evaluation by the project team: Some companies encourage the project team to submit its own filled-in scorecard—a self-evaluation—prior to the gate meeting. The view is that the project team's judgment of the project's attractiveness is also important information for the gate-keepers. The gatekeepers also score the project as above, but *before seeing the project team's scores*. The two sets of scores are then displayed at the gate meeting, and differences in opinion between project team and gatekeepers are addressed.

> Build clearly defined gates into your innovation process. And use visible criteria— scorecards, success criteria, and financial hurdles—to help make the Go/Kill and prioritization decisions.

Alternatively, some companies encourage project teams to submit their evaluation regarding how solid or *reliable the information* is that is contained in the deliverables. That is, instead of rating the project on scorecard criteria, the project team self-rates the "integrity of information" contained in each of the deliverables.

Display in-process metrics at gates: In-process metrics are also considered important by some management groups, and hence are displayed at gates. In-process metrics capture how well the project is being executed, and whether it is on course and on target. Poor performance on these metrics is not usually a Kill indicator, but a strong signal that the project and team could be in trouble, and that course corrections are needed:

> *An example:* A noted Austrian electronics firm, Omicron Electronics GmbH, has introduced insightful metrics at gates in their *Stage-Gate* process.[6] They call it their "360-degree feedback at each gate" (see Figure 9.2). Here, three vital metrics are rated and tracked during each stage: meeting project targets, team efficiency, and quality of execution during the stage. The summary 360-degree chart in Figure 9.2 provides the total view of the project on these metrics at each gate meeting and helps indicate whether the project is on track and on course.

Employ a Resource Allocation Method at Your Gates

Gates are held in real time: when a project completes one stage and requires resources to proceed to the next phase. Although the gate meeting is largely focused on one or a few projects, the decision to proceed *cannot be made in isolation.* To ensure effective resource allocation right at the gate meeting, consider displaying a list of active projects with their ratings or prioritization level, together with current resource commitments (by department or by person). Sometimes the new project "passes" the gate criteria, but when compared to the other active projects, does not look so strong. And often the entire resource pool is fully allocated to the existing projects, and then tough decisions must be made: where to find the resources for the project under review at the gate. Management cannot keep adding projects to the "active list" without dealing with the resource implications.

Figure 9.2: A Best Practice Is to Display a 360 Degree View of In-Process Metrics

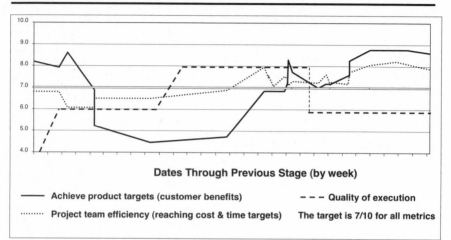

Dates Through Previous Stage (by week)

———— Achieve product targets (customer benefits)   – – – Quality of execution

.... Project team efficiency (reaching cost & time targets)   The target is 7/10 for all metrics

- A 360° evaluation by management, the project team, the project leader & the product manager (rating: 0 – 10, on the vertical axis).
- These rating data are summarized & shown at every gate meeting for the previous stage.

Implement a Formal Portfolio Management System

Your portfolio management system should be integrated into your gating process. Portfolio reviews are held periodically—typically two to four times per year— and are more holistic than gates, looking at the *entire set of projects* (but obviously less in-depth per project than gates do).[7] Portfolio reviews deal with issues such as achieving the right mix and balance of projects, project prioritization, and whether the portfolio is aligned with the business's strategy.

> *An example*: EXFO Engineering has implemented both *Stage-Gate* and Portfolio Management systems.[8] The gates make Go/Kill decisions on individual projects. But four times per year, the business leadership team, chaired by the CEO, evaluates, ranks, and prioritizes the complete slate of development projects during the Portfolio Review meeting. Any project at or beyond Gate 2 is included in this prioritization exercise.

Suggestion: Take steps to create gates with teeth. Try a one-time pruning exercise— a thorough portfolio review to dump weak projects. Then move to a decision factory mentality—gates where a certain percentage of projects do get killed. Employ clearly visible criteria at gates and build some portfolio thinking into the gate as well—comparing the new project to the list of active, existing projects to determine its priority. Ultimately, implement a formal portfolio management system with periodic (quarterly or semiannual) portfolio reviews of the entire set of active projects.

HOW EFFECTIVE GATES WORK

Now it's time to start thinking about how to use the various evaluation methods outlined in the previous chapter—scorecards, the Productivity Index, ECV—in a governance process for your business. In short, how do you integrate these models and tools into your *Stage-Gate* system to yield effective gates and gate decisions? For the rest of this chapter, we look at the design of gates: requirements, structure, criteria, gatekeepers, and protocol.

Requirements for Effective Gates

When designing your governance model for project evaluation and selection, and when electing the approach that best suits your business, be sure to consider these points:

Each decision point is only a tentative commitment in a sequential and conditional process. Each Go/Kill decision is only one in a sequence of such decisions. A Go decision is not an irreversible one, nor is it a decision to commit all the resources for the entire project. Rather, gate decisions can be viewed as a series of *options decisions*, beginning with a flickering green light at the Idea Screen, with progressively stronger commitments made to the project at each successive decision point. In effect, you buy discrete chunks of the project at each gate: The entire new-product project is incrementalized in order to reduce risk.

The gating procedure must maintain a reasonable balance between the errors of acceptance and errors of rejection. Too weak an evaluation procedure fails to weed out the obvious losers and misfits, resulting in misallocation of scarce resources and the start of a creeping commitment to the wrong projects. On the other hand, a too-rigid evaluation procedure results in many worthwhile projects—perhaps your next breakthrough product—being rejected. This is especially true at the very early gates, where the project is little more than an idea. Note that great ideas tend to be extremely fragile and vulnerable, and often too easy to kill.

Project evaluation is characterized by uncertainty of information and the absence of solid financial data. The initial decisions to move ahead with a project amount to decisions to invest that must be made in the *absence of reliable financial data*. The most accurate data in the project are not available until the end of the Development stage or even after Testing and Validation and as the product nears commercialization—information on manufacturing costs, capital requirements, and expected revenue. But at the early gates, data on projected sales, costs, and capital requirements are little more than educated guesses (if they exist at all).

This lack of reliable financial data throughout much of the new-product system emphasizes the *substantial differences* in the methods needed for new-product screening and pre-development gate evaluations versus those required for conventional commercial investment decisions.

Project evaluation involves multiple objectives and therefore multiple decision criteria. The criteria used in project Go/Kill decisions should reflect the business's overall objectives, and in particular its goals for its new-product efforts. Obvious new-product objectives are to contribute to business profitability and growth. But there could be other specific ones, including opening up new windows of opportunity, operating within acceptable risk boundaries, focusing on certain arenas of strategic thrust, or simply complementing existing products. Moreover, as was seen in Chapter 2, many qualitative characteristics of a new-product project—such as product advantage, market attractiveness, and leverage—are correlated with success and financial performance, and hence should be built in as goals or "desired characteristics" as part of the evaluation criteria.

The evaluation method must be realistic and easy to use. Project evaluation tools must be user-friendly. In short, they must be sufficiently simple and time-efficient that they can be used by a group of executives in a meeting setting. Data requirements, operational and computational procedures, and interpretation of results must all be straightforward.

At the same time, the evaluation method must be realistic. For example, it cannot entail so many simplifying assumptions that the result is no longer valid. Many mathematical and operations research evaluation tools fail on this point, largely because their simplifying assumptions render the method unrealistic, whereas some of the bubble diagram approaches introduced in the previous chapter are viewed as a little simplistic.

The Structure of Gates

A little structure at gate meetings goes a long way toward improving the effectiveness and efficiency of your business's decision-making. Well-designed gates and gate meetings have a common format, with three main components—see Figure 9.3:

1. *Deliverables:* Expectations must be made clear! Too often, project leaders do not understand the expectations of senior management, hence they arrive at gate meetings lacking much of the information that senior management needs in order to make a timely Go/Kill decision. So gates must define *visible deliverables in advance.* These are what the project leader and team must deliver to the gate—they are the results of actions in the preceding stage; these listed deliverables for a gate become the *objectives* of the project

Figure 9.3: All the Gates Have a Common Format

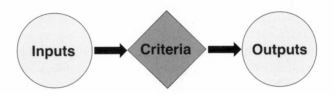

- **Inputs:** A prescribed list of "deliverables" that the Project Leader & Team must present to the Gate
- **Criteria:** A set of hurdles, criteria, or questions that the project is judged on
- **Outputs:** A decision: Go/Kill/Hold/Recycle
  If Go: approved Action Plan & resources committed

leader and team. A *standard menu of deliverables* is specified for each gate; also, at the preceding gate, both the path forward and the deliverables for the next gate are decided.

    An example: At Exxon Chemical, although each gate has a menu of standard required deliverables, the gatekeepers devote considerable attention at the end of each gate meeting to reaching consensus with the project team regarding just what will be delivered for the next gate. In this way, the expectations are made very clear for the project team.

2. *Criteria:* In order to make good decisions, your gatekeepers need decision criteria—criteria that are operational (meaning they are really used at gate meetings), visible, and clearly understood by all. These criteria are what the project is judged against in order to make the Go/Kill and prioritization decisions. These criteria are usually a standard set for each gate, but change somewhat from gate to gate. They include both financial and qualitative criteria, and are broken down into required (must-meet or knockout) characteristics versus desired characteristics useful for project prioritization (should-meet items).

3. *Outputs:* Too often, project review meetings end with a rather vague decision. Ask any three people who attended the meeting about what decisions were made, and you're likely to hear three different answers. Thus, gates must have clearly articulated outputs. Outputs are the results of the gate meeting and include a decision (Go/Kill/

> Gates have a common structure:
> - Inputs (deliverables)
> - Decision criteria
> - Outputs—Go/Kill/Hold/Recycle

Hold/Recycle) and a path forward. There are only four, sometimes five, possible decisions from a gate meeting; the decision cannot be to "defer the decision":

- *Go* means just that—the project is approved, and the resources are committed by the gatekeepers, both people and money, for the next stage; the Action Plan or "go forward plan" is approved, along with the time line and interim milestones; and the deliverables for the next gate are agreed to, along with a date for the next gate.
- *Conditional Go*—the project is approved, and resources committed as above, but subject to a condition being met within a specified time frame. Some companies allow this conditional go decision, as noted in Chapter 5; but there are risks, too—that the condition is never met and the project continues unchecked.*
- *Kill* means "terminate the project"—stop all work on it, and spend no more time or money here. And don't resurrect the project under a new name in a few months' time!
- *Hold* means that the project passes the gate criteria—it's an OK project— but that better projects are available or resources are not available for it. A Hold decision is a prioritization issue.
- *Recycle* is analogous to "rework" on a production line: Go back and do the stage over again, this time doing it right. Recycle signals that the project team has not delivered what was required of it.

Gates as Quality-Control Checkpoints

Gates are essentially the quality-control checkpoints in the innovation process, the occasion when you and your leadership team address two fundamental quality questions:

- Are you doing this project right?
- And are you doing the right project?

Thus "right projects right" becomes the motto for good gates. These two quality issues boil down to three main topics for the gate meeting:

Readiness Check:
- Have the steps in the previous stage been executed in a quality fashion?
- Have the project leader and team done their job well?
- Are the deliverables in good shape—is there data integrity?

---

* Most firms do not allow a Conditional Go decision—it's either Go Forward, Go Back, or Hold.

Figure 9.4: Gates Are a Three-Part Decision to Commit Resources

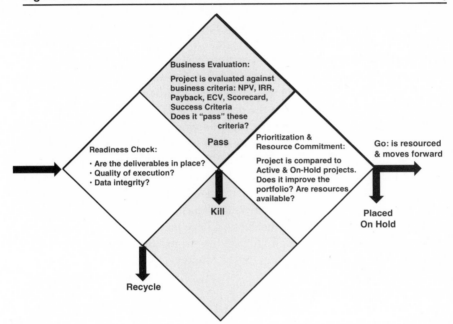

Business Evaluation:	• Is this a good investment?
	• Does the project (continue to) look like an attractive one from an economic and business standpoint?

Prioritization and Resource Commitment:	• How does the project compare to other active projects?
	• Are the proposed Action Plan and the resources requested reasonable and sound?
	• Do you have the resources available; or could they be found without damaging other active projects?

Note that these three topics are separate issues and should be debated separately. For example, often a project team does a superb job but has its project put on hold, simply because there are better projects to do. Unless the debate on "quality of execution" is separated from "business rationale," the team may have the impression that it is being chastised by senior management for the job it did. And morale suffers needlessly.

A Three-Part Diamond Decision
Gates can thus be viewed as a three-part diamond decision process—see Figure 9.4. The first part of the gate meeting is a "readiness check" and deals with the

deliverables: The focus is on the content of the deliverables, the quality of work underlying them, and data integrity. If the project fails on these readiness check criteria, the decision is not Kill, but rather Recycle—stop the meeting and instruct the project team to go back and do it right.

Next, the meeting shifts to the business evaluation—that is, is the project a worthy investment? Here the various models and tools introduced in the previous chapter are used: the financial tools, scorecards, and success criteria. If the project fails these business criteria, then the decision is Kill, as shown in Figure 9.4.

The final part of the gate meeting turns to approvals and resources. Recall that in the event of a Go decision, resources must be committed—no hollow gates allowed! But just because a project "passes" the business evaluation criteria, does not necessarily mean it moves forward! Here, the emphasis shifts to looking at this project in relationship to the other active projects—for example, how does the new project's NPV, Productivity Index, and scorecard score compare? Mix and balance could also be an issue: Do you have too many of this type of project in your portfolio? Discussion also focuses on the project team's proposed Action Plan and whether or not resources can be found.

Types of Gate Criteria

Readiness check: These address whether the project is even ready for the gate review and are usually handled in checklist format—one rating per required deliverable. Questions are: Are the deliverables in place? Based on good quality work? Data integrity satisfactory?

Business evaluation: Each gate has its own list of business evaluation criteria for use by the gatekeepers. These criteria are what the gate decision is based on and are both Go/Kill and project prioritization criteria. Business evaluation criteria are of several types:

- *Must-meet criteria:* These are preliminary Yes/No or knockout questions; a single No can signal a Kill decision. Checklists are the usual format for must-meet items.
- *Go/Kill criteria:* These are typically quantitative criteria. Failing to meet any one can signal a Kill decision. These usually include financial criteria and hurdles.
- *Should-meet or prioritization criteria:* These are highly desirable project characteristics, but a "No" on one question won't kill the project; rather, these questions are scored and a point count or project score is determined. Scorecards handle the should-meet questions well.

In the design of a gating scheme, the must-meet criteria or *checklist business questions* are efficient culling questions to ensure that the project meets minimum standards in terms of strategic alignment, company policies, feasibility, and so on. These questions are designed more to weed out obvious losers, "non-starters," and misfit projects rather than to give a strong green light. Examples include:

- Is the new project within the strategic mandate of your business?
- Is it consistent with your company policies on ethics, the environment, safety, and legal?
- Are there any showstoppers or killer variables (or the absence of these)?
- Are you capable of undertaking the project? Or is the project's scope just too big?

A No to these questions—for example, the lack of a strategic mandate or contravention of company ethics policies—is enough to kill the project.

Next are *Go/Kill criteria*, which typically are quantitative items that are compared to a minimum acceptable hurdle. Financial criteria are typical. Examples might be:

> Don't mix the various gate criteria—it gets confusing at the gate meeting. Rather, split them into logical categories:
> - Readiness check criteria (a checklist)
> - Must-meet—culling or knockout criteria
> - Go/Kill and prioritization—financial criteria, scorecard criteria, and success criteria

- Is the NPV (or ECV) positive (note that the NPV is calculated at the acceptable hurdle rate for this type of investment, thus a positive NPV signifies that the project clears the hurdle rate)?
- Is the Payback Period less than three years?
- Is the Internal Rate of Return (IRR) greater than 30 percent?

The Project Attractiveness Score based on the scorecard can also be a Go/Kill criterion: This score must clear a minimum hurdle (usually about sixty to sixty-five points out of a possible 100). Success criteria, if used, can be introduced here as well: Does the project meet or exceed the success criteria previously agreed to?

By contrast, the *should-meet criteria* capture the *relative attractiveness* of the project for purposes of prioritization. Example questions include:

- Is the market attractive—a large and growing one? How attractive?
- Is this familiar technology to us—do we have some of the technical skills in-house?
- Can the product utilize existing plant and production equipment/technology? How easily?
- Will the product have sustainable competitive advantage? How much?

These should-meet or "relative attractiveness" and prioritization questions are best handled in scorecard format, introduced in the previous chapter (see

Figures 8.6 and 8.7 for examples of excellent and proven scorecards). A *no* or *negative* answer to any one of these scorecard questions certainly won't kill the project. But *enough low scores* may indicate that the project is simply not attractive enough to pursue. The Project Attractiveness Score—the weighted or unweighted addition of the scorecard scores—is a key input to the Go/Kill decision and can also be used to judge the relative attractiveness of the new project versus existing projects right at the gate meeting.

Financial criteria are also used as relative prioritization criteria. Clearly, the NPV (or ECV), the IRR, and the Payback Period are Go/Kill criteria at gate meetings: These financial numbers must exceed a minimum hurdle, otherwise the project is dead. But converted into the Productivity Index, the NPV (or ECV) becomes a prioritization criterion and can be used to compare the new project to other projects in the pipeline and determine its relative attractiveness.

Suggestion: Most firms do not have a visible list of Go/Kill and prioritization criteria for selecting projects (other than financial criteria, which are probably not the best ones to use in any event, especially at early gates). If you lack visible criteria, develop a set. Consider using a set of must-meet questions in a checklist format as culling questions, followed by a short list of Go/Kill and a set of should-meet questions in a scorecard format to help determine relative project attractiveness. Be sure to use these criteria at your gate meeting, discussing each question and reaching closure on it. If you do this, chances are your gatekeeping group will make more-objective, more-reasoned, and better decisions.

TIPS AND HINTS IN GATE GOVERNANCE
Prioritizing Projects at Gates
When assessing the relative attractiveness of the new project versus active projects in the pipeline—for example by comparing the Productivity Index or scorecard score—only assess the new project's relative position. *Don't try to reprioritize all the other projects* in the pipeline. First, you don't have complete data on the other projects at this gate meeting; second, you don't have enough time; and most important, it's poor practice to prioritize another project when that team's members are not in the room to defend their project! The periodic reprioritization of projects takes place at portfolio reviews, not at gate meetings.

Consistent Gate Criteria from Gate to Gate
As much as possible, try to maintain consistency of gate criteria from gate to gate. This makes the gating system *easier to understand* for the gatekeepers; it also means that *projects at different stages can be compared* to each other. This is particularly important from Gate 2 onward, as typically here the project "enters the portfolio" and becomes part of the portfolio—it shows up in the rank-ordered lists, pie charts, and bubble diagrams shown at portfolio reviews.

The financial criteria must obviously change from gate to gate, especially at the early gates. For example, while it makes sense to look at NPV, IRR, and the Payback Period at Gate 3 (after all, a full Business Case is a deliverable to Gate 3), using such criteria at Gate 1, the Idea Screen, is not only impractical—the data are not available—it is also harmful. That's where the scorecard method proves its worth, because here many of the scorecard criteria can be applied from gate to gate. For example, consider the scorecard in Figure 8.6. Note that criteria such as strategic fit, product advantage, and leverages core competencies can be applied at Gate 1 almost as easily as at Gate 3 or 4. And most of the other criteria, such as market attractiveness and technical feasibility, can be estimated reasonably well even at early gates.

Solution: Keep the main criteria—the six factors in Figure 8.6—consistent from gate to gate. If necessary, modify the sub-questions for some of the factors. For example, the Financial Reward versus Risk factor essentially asks the question: Can you make money? At Gate 3, the sub-questions are very specific and based on hard data:

- The financial return (NPV, IRR, or ECV)
- The Payback Period
- The Productivity Index

At Gate 1, the fundamental question is still the same: Can you make money? But create a new list of feasible sub-questions that are much more qualitative, such as:

- What's the size of the prize (a qualitative scale from "modest" to "huge")?
- What are the odds you can make money here (from "really doubtful" to "easily")?
- How likely are the commercial assumptions (from "low probability" to "highly likely")?
- Would you invest your own money in this venture (from "not in a million years" to "here's my check")?

These questions rely on qualitative scales, but they can be addressed at Gate 1 even with limited information.

Lighten Up on the Early Gates

Senior management in some firms arrives at Gate 1, the Idea Screen, expecting a full Business Case and insists on employing tough financial criteria. Wrong! Gate 1 is only an idea screen . . . a flickering green light. Recall the options nature of *Stage-Gate*—the incremental spending model. You're *not betting the farm at Gate 1*, only a few pigs. So Gate 1 need not be a rigorous, tough gate.

> The best way to destroy true or bold innovation in your business is to have tough early gates and use rigorous financial criteria to make the early Go/Kill decisions.

Too tough a screen at Gate 1 kills all but the sure bets. Note that the most innovative ideas are often the most fragile ones, and a rigorous, financially based screen will kill them. By contrast, the "sure bets" are often the low-hanging-fruit projects . . . but not the best-tasting fruit.

Thus, be careful about what information you ask for (or expect) at Gate 1. The required deliverables should be kept consistent with the size of the investment made at each gate:

- Deliverable at Gate 1—a single idea sheet, no financials!
- Deliverables at Gate 2—a short list of market, technical, and business assessment items, based on preliminary investigation only.
- Deliverable at Gate 3—a full Business Case, complete with a DCF financial analysis.

Further, be careful about what criteria you use to make Go/Kill decisions at Gate 1. Don't use rigorous financial criteria too soon. First, you don't have the information to use financial criteria early on. Second, financial criteria will kill the most innovative ideas and concepts, and will ultimately drive you to a lackluster development portfolio. That is, using financial criteria too early will do damage and typically result in a lot of smaller, short-term, and predictable projects, but a dearth of bold innovations in your pipeline.

> *An example of how not to do it:* In one major conglomerate, senior managers in business units are understandably driven by financial numbers. And they carry this philosophy into the gate meetings, unfortunately. At Gate 1, the Idea Screen, some executives start demanding NPV estimates, full financial and risk assessments, and the like. For highly predictable projects, such numbers could be produced (although this is still too early!). But for more venturesome projects, these numbers simply aren't available at Gate 1—the project is little more than a gleam in someone's eye. And so it fails the gate meeting. Sadly, this firm has witnessed a number of potentially significant but ill-defined projects killed at early gates for the wrong reasons, only to be launched by competitors.

Different Criteria for Different Types of Projects

Would you use the same criteria to evaluate stocks, bonds, and real estate investments? Of course not! So it is in product innovation. Thus far, much of the discussion of selection criteria has focused on *innovative new products*; note that the financial and scorecard criteria outlined above (and in Figure 8.6) are for major, bold, and innovative product developments. But many development projects are smaller, lower-risk, and more predictable, and they merit somewhat simpler evaluation criteria. The scalable system portrayed in Figure 5.1 reveals three different versions of *Stage-Gate* that often correspond to three different Strategic Buckets of projects. Gate criteria for the *XPress* and *Lite* projects are usually much simpler than for major new-product projects. For example:

- For smaller, lower-risk projects—line extensions, updates, tweaks—the financial criteria that you use should be easier to compute and easier to use than the NPV. For example, use the Payback Period calculation. The advantage of a payback calculation is that the required estimates are less demanding: It's a simpler calculation, and you only have to forecast sales, costs, and earnings as far into the future as the payback year—perhaps only a few years forward—rather than the traditional five-year projections required in an NPV calculation.
- Scorecards can also be used for lower-risk projects. But the scorecard must be tailored to suit the size and nature of the project, and should be substantially different from Figure 8.6. For example, a major paper-products company employs a "Marketing Scorecard" for sales-initiated customer-request projects—a handful of simple questions that gauge the importance of the customer, impact on future business, cost-benefit of the project, and ease and speed of doing the project.

Another type of project is the technology development project. Here, traditional financial criteria are next to useless, because so little is known regarding the eventual commercial impact of the new technology or platform. Thus, the scorecard in Figure 8.7 is recommended for such technology or science projects—qualitative and strategic questions, with only "guesstimates" of the size of the prize.

Suggestion: Take note of the tips and hints above. First, don't try to reprioritize all your projects at your gate meetings—that's the role of a portfolio review. Next, try to design criteria that are fairly consistent from gate to gate: It's easier to follow this way, and projects can now be compared even though they are in different stages. The scorecard model works particularly well here. Next, lighten up on the early gates and avoid overuse of robust financial criteria too early—you'll kill your best potential projects! Finally, recognize that different categories or buckets of projects call for different evaluation criteria.

WHO ARE THE GATEKEEPERS?

Who are the people tending these critical gates—the gatekeepers who make the Go/Kill and resource allocation decisions and who are essential to making the new-product process work? Obviously, the choice of the gatekeepers is specific to each business and its organizational structure. But here are some rules of thumb:

- The first rule is simple: The gatekeepers at any gate must have the *authority to approve the resources* required for the next stage. That is, they are the *owners of the resources* required by the project team to move the project through the next stage.
- Since resources are required from different functions, the gatekeepers must *represent different functional areas*—R&D, Marketing, Engineering, Operations, and perhaps Sales, Purchasing, and Quality Assurance. There's not much sense having a gatekeeper group just from one functional area, such as Marketing or R&D!

The gatekeepers usually *change somewhat from gate to gate.* Typically Gate 1, the Idea Screen, is staffed by a small group, perhaps three or four people who are not the most senior in the organization. Here, the spending level is quite low. By Gate 3, however, where financial and resource commitments are substantial, gatekeepers typically include more senior people, for example, the leadership team of the business.

- Gatekeepers can also include people who will be *key to the project's success* at some future point. For example, for technology development projects, the gatekeepers at early gates are largely from the technology department, but many companies ensure that important people from the business units that will ultimately commercialize the technology attend these early gates, even though they are not committing their resources at these early stages.
- There should also be some *continuity of gatekeepers* from gate to gate. In short, the composition of the evaluation group should not change totally, requiring a total start-from-the-beginning justification of the project at each gate. For example, some members of the leadership team—the heads of Marketing and R&D, for example—might be at Gate 2, with the full leadership team at Gate 3 for major projects.
- Different types of projects have *different levels of gatekeepers*. Recall from Chapter 5 that *Stage-Gate* is scalable—there are Full, XPress, and Lite versions of the system, depending on project size and risk (Figure 5.1). In most firms, senior people only come to Gates 3, 4, and 5 for major projects; earlier gates and gates for minor projects are left to midlevel management people.

An example: In one major financial institution, there are two levels of gatekeepers from Gate 3 onward:

- A senior Gate 3 to 5 gatekeeping group for larger, riskier projects (total cost greater than $500,000). These are the senior VPs from the bank.

- A midlevel gatekeeping group—for lower-risk or smaller projects (this, coincidentally, is also the Gate 2 gatekeeping group for major projects).

HOW TO RUN GATES

Gates must be fair, and be perceived to be fair by the project team. They must also be transparent—there should be no room for politics and gamesmanship by gate-keepers. Gates must also be effective, yielding good decisions and sound resource allocations to the right projects. And gates must be efficient, yielding decisions in a timely fashion and not dragging on for the whole day. Thus, best-practice firms develop *professional gate protocols*, such as the following, a composite set of procedures borrowed from a handful of best-practices companies.

Gate Protocols

Gatekeepers must operate as an effective decision-making team. And all teams, even senior people, need *rules of engagement*. A sample list is provided in Table 9.1. It's critical that your gatekeeper group develop a similar list of behavior rules and then commit to abiding by them.

Gate meetings, although held when needed by project teams, are usually scheduled monthly for the leadership team of the business, often in conjunction with another executive meeting that day. Any project leader can "sign up" a project for a scheduled gate meeting with sufficient notice. Usually about sixty to ninety minutes of meeting time is allotted per major project (Gate 3 onward).

The material (deliverables) is delivered one week prior to the meeting. Teams are required to use a standard format for their deliverables (for example, templates) so that gatekeepers can compare projects more easily. When reading the advance material, if a gatekeeper has a major question or spots a showstopper, he or she should contact the gate facilitator or project team in advance—no surprise attacks at the gate meeting!

Hold the meeting! Cancellations or postponements are unacceptable unless the deliverables are not ready. And hold the meeting even if a Kill decision is imminent, in order to achieve closure, agree on lessons learned, and celebrate a correct Kill. Note: A correct Kill is deemed a success—*you just saved yourself a bag of money and heap of trouble!*

Video- and tele-conferencing are acceptable, but make sure you have the robust telecommunications facilities and that they work! The project team is present where geographically possible (or via video- or tele-conference). Usually the

> Learn from the best innovator companies. Develop a protocol for your gate meetings, including rules of engagement. And make sure there's a process manager in the room with the authority to facilitate the meeting and enforce discipline.

TABLE 9.1: A TYPICAL LIST OF GATEKEEPER RULES OF ENGAGEMENT

1. Gatekeepers must hold the gate meeting and be there
   - Postponed or canceled meetings are not an option
   - If you cannot attend, your vote is "Yes"
2. Gatekeepers must have received, read, and prepared for the meeting
   - Contact the gate facilitator or project team if there are showstoppers
   - No "surprise attacks" at the gate meeting
3. Gatekeepers cannot request information or answers beyond that specified in the deliverables
   - No playing "I gotcha"
   - Not a forum to demonstrate your machoism, political clout, or intellectual prowess
4. Gatekeepers cannot "beat up" the presenter
   - Give the Team an uninterrupted period to present
   - Q&A must be fair—not vicious
5. Gatekeepers must make their decision based on the criteria for that gate
   - Gatekeepers must review each criterion and reach a conclusion
   - A scoring sheet should be filled out by each gatekeeper at the gate meeting
6. Gatekeepers must be disciplined
   - No hidden agendas
   - No invisible criteria
7. Decisions must be based on facts and criteria—not emotion and gut feel
   - All projects must be treated fairly and consistently
   - Must pass through the gate—no special treatment for executive-sponsored or "pet" projects
   - All projects are subjected to the same criteria and with the same rigor
8. A decision must be made
   - Within that working day
   - If deliverables are there, you cannot defer the decision
   - Remember: This is a system built for speed—gatekeepers cannot create unnecessary delays
9. The project team must be informed of the decision
   - Immediately
   - Face-to-face (not by e-mail)
10. If the decision is Go, the gatekeepers support the agreed-upon Action Plan
    - Commit the resources (people and money)
    - Agree to release times for people on the project team
    - No one gatekeeper can override the Go decision or renege on agreed-upon resources
11. If the decision is Hold
    - The gatekeepers must try to find resources
    - Cannot remain on Hold for more than 3 months—up or out!
    - This puts pressure on gatekeepers to make tougher decisions (some real Kills) or commit more resources

team stays for the entire gate meeting, hears the full discussion, sees the scoring, and listens to the reasons underlying the decision (although some firms allow an in-camera private discussion by gatekeepers for which the project team is asked to leave the room for a few minutes).

A gate facilitator should be present—usually this is the *Stage-Gate* process manager. This person is analogous to the referee on a football field—not the biggest player on the field, but the guy with the whistle, and with ultimate control of the meeting.

A head gatekeeper is often nominated or designated, although this is optional. The head gatekeeper's role is to follow up with the project leader on loose ends, for example, making sure that the condition was met in the case of a Conditional Go decision.

The gate procedure is typically this: The project team has fifteen minutes to present, uninterrupted. Limit the number of PowerPoint slides to about ten or fifteen. Further, the team should not regurgitate the deliverables package but deal only with key issues—what the risks are and what decisions are requested by the project team—as well as new issues. Then follows a question-and-answer session, which the process manager moderates (the process manager ensures that the gatekeepers stay on topic and ask relevant and fair questions; the process manager must have the authority to call a time-out).

Once conversation has died down, the process manager takes gatekeepers through a list of criteria, starting with the readiness check questions, to determine whether the deliverables are in good shape. Use a checklist. Then follows the must-meet or knockout culling questions: Often simply showing these on the projector screen is sufficient, asking gatekeepers to reply by exception only.

The meeting now shifts to the Go/Kill and prioritization criteria. For example, the financial criteria are discussed, and the scorecard is handed out. The project is scored (gatekeepers are asked to keep their scores to themselves during this period of thoughtful reflection). The scorecards are collected and inputted immediately, and results are displayed on the projector screen, as in Figure 9.1. (If the project team has done a self-scoring, the results can now be displayed on a second screen next to the gatekeepers' scores.)

In the event of major differences of opinion between gatekeepers as in Figure 9.1, the process manager tries to get the differences on the table and move toward resolution. For example, the process manager identifies the high and low scorers and asks them to explain their positions. One by one, the process manager leads the gatekeepers through the scoring criteria, reaching an understanding and consensus on each.

Now for the decisions: First comes the Pass versus Kill decision, during which the process manager leads the gatekeepers through a review of the financial criteria—the NPV (or ECV), Payback, and IRR numbers versus the hurdles; the results of the sensitivity analysis; and the Project Attractiveness Score. A Pass versus Kill decision is made.

A Pass does not necessarily mean Go, however. It just means that the project meets minimum standards or hurdles, but it may not be the best project to do. Now *prioritization* and *resource commitment* become the topic. Often the process manager displays a list of active projects that shows their Project Attractiveness Scores, NPVs, and Productivity Indices. Gatekeepers then get a feel for how attractive this new project is relative to the others in the pipeline. Pie charts and a bubble diagram showing the current portfolio (previous chapter) are also displayed, so gatekeepers can see where the new project fits in, and whether it helps to balance (or unbalance) the portfolio. The project team's proposed Action Plan and resource needs are now reviewed. And issues of resource availability are discussed. The decision faced now is Go versus Hold, as shown in Figure 9.4.

The gate decision is now agreed: Go/Kill/Hold/Recycle. If Go, a project prioritization level is established and the Action Plan and deliverables for the next gate are agreed to. The resource commitments are made, and a date for the next gate is set. And the project team is informed in person—immediately (although usually the team is still in the room).

Hint: Decide in advance how consensus will be reached. This is not the Supreme Court and split decisions are not acceptable—it must be a unanimous Go or Kill. Some firms use the "majority rules" decision rule; in other firms, it's a democratic decision, except the boss or senior gatekeeper has 51 percent of the votes.

> *An example:* In one major bank, the senior executive at the gate meeting made the "split decision rule" very clear: "I let my executive team [at the gate meeting] make the decision. But if they cannot reach a decision within the hour, then I make the decision—this democracy quickly becomes a dictatorship."

I also include a tongue-in-cheek summary of ways to ruin gate meetings—each one is based on real-life experience. Avoid these behaviors at all costs—see the box entitled, "The Ten Best Ways to Ruin Gate Meetings."

Red Flags to Spot Projects in Trouble

What happens when a project gets into trouble within a stage—for example, it misses milestones, or its financial outlook changes? Do you wait until the next gate to address the problem and kill or redirect the project? Definitely not! But don't do what some firms mistakenly do, and that is to build in a host of additional gates within long stages. That becomes a bureaucratic nightmare.

The simple answer is to employ *red flags*. A red flag situation is much like a yellow flag at a NASCAR racetrack. When the yellow flag is dropped, everyone takes action—there is an emergency on the racetrack. All the race cars slow down; everyone proceeds with care.

Red flags work the same way. Whenever a project gets into trouble, the project leader is required to "throw out a red flag." The flag is picked up immediately by

THE TEN BEST WAYS TO RUIN GATE MEETINGS

10. Miss most meetings. When you do come, start reading the materials (deliverables) as the meeting starts.

9. Don't give the project team a chance to make its presentation. Attack with tough questions as soon as the team puts its first PPT slide up.

8. Always ask for information that has not been specifically requested; this way you keep the project team off balance.

7. Attack the team with vicious, rude questioning; make sure these junior people really live in fear of the executive gatekeepers.

6. Ignore the stated criteria at the gates. Make the decision from the gut. And ignore the facts—use your own opinion instead.

5. Dwell only on the financial projections. Spend at least 75 percent of the meeting arguing over numbers. The rest of the information doesn't matter.

4. Your role is that of a judge. Never offer any help or advice.

3. If in doubt, don't make a decision. Keep the project team waiting around for several weeks. It shows who's boss.

2. Don't prioritize projects. Just keep adding projects to the active list. There's lots of slack in the organization that needs cutting out.

1. Demand that the project team reduce the time lines and resources requested. And resources committed—they can be rescinded at any time.

the process manager, who meets with the team leader to discuss the seriousness of the situation; they alert the gatekeepers, and an emergency gate meeting may be scheduled. The notion here is not to wait out the situation but to take immediate action to correct the problem or to kill or redirect the project.

A red flag is triggered by any one of the following conditions:

- Technical roadblocks: whenever technical barriers are encountered that increase the development time and cost, or reduce the probability of technical success (versus the success probability estimate at the previous gate).
- Project schedule: if the project falls significantly (more than thirty days) behind the time line agreed to at the previous gate; or if two milestones in a row are missed.
- Product features and specifications: if the product design or product specifications are revised or relaxed, in a way that impacts negatively on meeting a customer need or on the product definition.

- Sales forecast: When there is a significant change in the projected product sales versus the sales estimates in the Business Case at the previous gate.
- Delivered cost: If there is a significant change in the expected product cost versus the cost in the Business Case at the previous gate.
- Resources: Whenever a major functional department fails to meet its ongoing resource commitments agreed to in the project's approved Action Plan.
- Business Case: If any change occurs that significantly impacts the Business Case and the financial outlook for the project versus the financial forecasts accepted at the previous gate.

Whenever any of the above occur, the project leader throws out a red flag. Action is taken.

Suggestion: The details of the governance system are fundamental to making *Stage-Gate* work. Be sure to define clearly *who the gatekeepers are*—the locus of decision-making. Note that gatekeepers change from gate to gate, and may be different people, depending on project type, magnitude, and risk level. Think through the *protocol for the gate meeting*, using the guidelines above borrowed from leading firms. Be sure to encourage the gatekeepers to develop *rules of engagement* to minimize bad behavior, and consider the use of *red flags* to spot projects in trouble and take the needed action.

WAYS TO ACCELERATE THE GATES

The protocols outlined above all help to make the gates more effective. But the need for speed and accelerated gates is still paramount, given the desire for fast Go/Kill decisions, combined with development teams working globally. If a project is held up awaiting a gate for three weeks, and this happens at all five gates, that's fifteen weeks, or almost four months of dead time—unacceptable in today's fast-paced world. We saw in Chapter 5 ways to remove waste and bureaucracy in the idea-to-launch system, and in particular, the concept of *leaning down the gates*. Using value-stream analysis, defining what information is really required to make the decision (keeping the deliverables lean), and creating clear expectations are but some of the ways that leading firms are accelerating gate decisions and removing non-value-added work. Here are other practices that firms employ to accelerate the gates:

Self-Managed Gates

In the case of smaller and lower-risk projects, some gates are now self-managed (for example, Gates 2 and 4 in Figure 4.10). In effect, the project team conducts its own review and makes its own Go/Kill decision. One major telecommunications firm has experimented with this approach (an alternative is simply to adopt a three-stage process, as in Figure 5.1).

Electronic Gates

The advent of global development teams and gatekeeping groups means that gate meetings in some companies have become electronic, global, and in some cases even virtual. A major paper company experimented with remote electronic gates: Here, the gate deliverables are distributed to gatekeepers automatically, electronically, and globally. Then, independently of each other, the gatekeepers score the project on an electronic scorecard, and also add comments. Subsequently, the global gatekeeping group assembles in a videoconference to debate the scores, resolve their differences, and make the Go/Kill decision. The use of extensive IT—for information dissemination, the scoring and integration of scorecard results, and the meeting itself—enables these electronic gates.

Virtual Gates

With virtual gates, there is no actual gate meeting; rather, gatekeepers simply review the deliverables and sign off on the Go/Kill decision, electronically and independently of each other. The goal here is to reduce absenteeism of key gatekeepers, to get input of people normally not at the gate meeting, and to speed up the decision process, especially in the case of remotely located gatekeepers. Although the advantages of virtual gates are obvious, the big negative is that because no meeting actually takes place, the gatekeepers do not have the opportunity to engage in back-and-forth discussion and the learning that ensues. Hence, they make the Go/Kill decision without benefit of full knowledge.

MAKE THE GATES WORK!

I began the chapter with the statement, "As go the gates, so goes the process." Although gates may represent only sixty minutes (times five) in a project's life, they are perhaps the most critical sixty-minute segments—and make all the difference between winning and losing at product innovation. The gates must work! And so it makes sense to spend a little time and effort getting the gates right.

By now, you realize that there's more to making the gates work than simply assembling a group of well-intentioned executives for a monthly meeting. There are many approaches, methods, tricks, and protocols that deliver better results, making the difference between the "normal" gate meeting—which is often inefficient and results in poor decisions (too many projects with an overabundance of weak, insignificant projects)—and meetings that are effective and efficient. The result is a stunning portfolio of high-value development projects.

10

DEVELOPMENT, TESTING, AND LAUNCH

I think all great innovations are built on rejections.
—Louise Nevelson (1900–1988), American artist

PARALLEL ACTIONS DURING STAGE 3: DEVELOPMENT

The project passes Gate 3 and is Go for Development. The front-end homework has been done and the product has been clearly defined: target market, product concept and positioning, benefits, and product requirements.

Stage 3, Development, begins and you implement your Development Plan as approved at Gate 3. That is, you translate your Business Case plans into *concrete deliverables*—a prototype product that has been partially validated with customers and also via extensive in-house tests. The deliverables and key tasks in Stage 3 are shown in Figure 10.1. Note that this chapter and Figures 10.1 and 10.2 are designed for *big development initiatives* or *bold innovations*—larger and higher-risk investments. Lower-risk and smaller projects may omit some of the actions outlined in the chapter.

> The dominant activity in Stage 3 is developing the product. But many other tasks occur in parallel during this stage.

The Development of the Product

The most visible activity in Stage 3 is the physical development of the prototype product (or creation of the service and its support, for example, the IT)—see Figure 10.1. Thus, the project team, largely the technical people, proceed to develop the product as per the Action Plan and as agreed in the product definition delivered to Gate 3. In-house, lab, and alpha tests are also conducted on the product to ensure that it works under controlled in-house conditions. The time lines and milestones guide the development activities, and multiple versions of the product as displayed to users in the iterative series of build-test-feedback-and-revise loops.

Figure 10.1: Multiple Parallel Tasks Are Part of Stage 3, Development

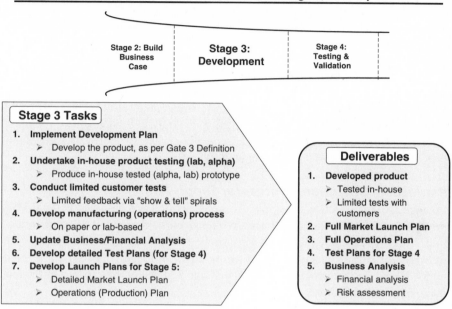

While the physical development and testing of the product proceeds, many other activities are concurrently being undertaken by other members of the project team. And there's a lot of work and many tasks here! Some of these are invariably overlooked until too late—hence the need for having a clearly defined Action Plan for Stage 3. Here are some typical activities that you should also build into Stage 3; not all will apply to you—your activities will depend on the nature of your projects and industry:[1]

Market Development

In Stage 3, you continue to monitor and research the market and the competitive situation to confirm product acceptance and a positive market situation. Early prototypes or lab samples are taken to a handful of trusted customers for initial reaction and feedback.

Also in Stage 3, the detailed Market Launch Plan comes together: This is a first cut at the full marketing plan, including pricing, distribution, promotion, sales force, and so on. Note that a tentative or "throwaway" market launch plan was delivered at the end of Stage 2, even before Development began! Obtain any legal approvals needed for your Marketing and Sales literature; and for technical products, develop plans for technical service and support to meet customer expectations. You should also be working with international affiliates on the above items to develop launch plans for these countries, securing volume and pricing commitments.

Also, if you have a commercial partner, design the launch plan elements with that partner—sorting out who does what, and getting commitments on both sides.

Finally, Stage 3 is the time to begin to identify appropriate test site customers for product testing in Stage 4 (including global sites).

IP and Product Regulatory Issues

This is the stage to finalize the details of the technology protection strategy (IP) and its implementation. Here, you begin to undertake full implementation of your technology protection strategy. And also, you will finalize and implement the plan for product regulatory issues (securing necessary approvals and resolution of regulatory issues—including global).

Production/Operations Process (or Supply Route)

In Stage 3, the production or supply process is defined and designed in detail (the process should be designed on paper, with process economics studied). Production costs and capital expenditures are spelled out, much more accurately than in Stage 2. Contact vendors to determine costs and lead times on equipment items. If you are in a process industry, in Stage 3, develop the process in the lab, using bench-scale pilots.

Stage 3 is the stage to define and resolve operations EH&S issues (environmental, health, and safety). If needed, develop and implement a plan to obtain manufacturing regulatory approvals.

Finally, Stage 3 sees the development of a detailed Operations and Supply Plan, along with quality assurance requirements and a Quality Assurance Plan. The facilities for production or operations trials in Stage 4 are designed. And consider ordering some long-lead-time equipment items for operations trials that will be required in the next stage.

Updated Business and Financial Analysis

With better data now available (based on a developed product and a defined production or supply process), you should redo your Stage 2 financial and business analysis:

- Determine the NPV, IRR, Payback Period, and Productivity Index, identifying your key financial assumptions.
- Perform a sensitivity analysis on key financial assumptions (for example, price, volume, costs).
- Assess the impact of the product on other products in your company (for example, cannibalization).
- Identify your pivotal business and financial risks.
- Prepare your Capital Appropriation Request (or CAPEX) for equipment required in Stage 4 (earlier, as noted above, especially if the equipment requires a long lead time).

Action Plans

This is the time to map out your plan for Stage 4, Testing and Validation (actions, resources, people, timing, schedule, and milestones). Some firms also develop a Discontinue Plan, an exit plan that deals with customers and their expectations, equipment purchased, and product inventory in-house or in the field in the event that the project is canceled in Stages 4 or 5.

Other plans developed here (and sometimes even earlier) are the Post-Launch Plan and the Life Cycle Plan:

- The Post-Launch Plan deals with issues that occur immediately after launch—what will be done, what needs to be measured, and what fixes or corrections are anticipated.
- The Life Cycle Plan moves well beyond the immediate launch phase and paints a picture through to product exit: new-product releases, continuous improvements, next-generation products, and even exit plans (see Chapter 5).

SEEK CUSTOMER INPUT THROUGHOUT THE DEVELOPMENT STAGE

As experienced project leaders will attest, even in the most astutely planned project, much can go wrong from this point on. A major challenge often faced in projects during Development is this: The product *definition isn't quite right; or things change*—user or customer requirements change over the course of Development.

The solution is *spiral or agile development*, a concept introduced in Chapters 2 and 5—see Figures 2.7 and 5.3. This means *seeking customer input and feedback at every step of the way throughout the entire Development stage* as the product takes shape. Seeking customer input and feedback is a vital and ongoing activity throughout Development, both to *ensure that the product is right* and also *to speed development toward a correctly defined target*. The original VoC research that was done prior to Development may not be enough to resolve all your design dilemmas; and technical problems may arise during the Development stage that necessitate a significant product design change.

> Sometimes the product definition is not right; and often customer requirements change. So build in the spirals—build-test-feedback-and-revise—here in the Development stage as well.

An example: In the development of a novel milk-packaging system using polyethylene plastic bags, DuPont of Canada's project team ran into a technical snag. The original concept was for milk to be packaged in one-quart plastic bags that would have a tear-off tab for easy opening and resealing. The pre-development market research tested and confirmed this product concept.

During development, however, technical difficulties arose that made the tear-off tab almost impossible to produce. Rather than merely assuming that a change in product design would be acceptable to the consumer, the project team quickly undertook a market study of users to determine the importance of the tear-off tab; it revealed that the tear-off tab was desirable but not essential, and that product acceptance by the consumer would not be significantly affected by its absence. The tab was removed from the design and the product went on to be a great commercial success in Canada.

Designing Customer Tests

Recall from Chapter 2 the argument that "Customers don't know what they're looking for until they see it." The message is simple: Get *something* in front of the customer as early as possible in Stage 3, Development, even if it's not the finished product. Only then will the customer have something to react to and be able to provide valuable feedback. So test, test, test with the customer throughout Development—and start early.

In-house product testing (or lab or alpha tests) is normally an integral facet of product development. But an in-house test only confirms that the product works properly under controlled or laboratory conditions. It says little about whether the product works under actual use conditions, and whether it delights the customer. Customers seem to have an innate ability to think of novel ways of finding product weaknesses, ways the design group could never have imagined. The "acid test" of the product design is with the customer.

Simple and Inexpensive Tests

These customer tests can be quite simple and inexpensive. Let's imagine that you are partway through the development of a fairly complex product—for example, a new lawn-and-garden tractor aimed at homeowners. Key components—the new automatic transmission and dashboard instrument panel—have already been designed, developed, and tested in-house. Both of these components are highly visible in the final product: They determine how the gear-shifting works and feels, and how the dashboard looks and functions. Here's what you can do to assess customer reaction:

1. Bring potential users (and your dealers) to the development site (or to a convenient location) to view and try out key components. You might mount the transmission on an existing tractor and display a mockup of the dashboard. Let customers look, touch, and try. Record their reactions and comments; then measure interest, liking, preference, and purchase intent much like in a concept test (and using the question format shown in Chapter 7 in Figure 7.6). Include probing questions, noting areas of particular likes and dislikes.
2. The same procedure can be used with focus groups of customers. Start with an introductory group session. Then move to the display area so customers

can touch and try. Finally, reconvene the group for a discussion of the merits and shortcomings of the tested components. The group session is more efficient than individual interviews (more inputs in a shorter period of time) and often leads to a more interesting and insightful discussion (the group members stimulate one another).

3. When the number of customers is small, try setting up a "user's panel"—an ongoing group of potential customers that acts as a sounding board or team of advisers during the development process. Whenever designs, design decisions, or components need to be checked, convene the customer panel—either physically or online—to get its reaction.

4. Customer partnerships are perhaps the most certain way of seeking continual and honest customer input during Development. Customer partnerships work particularly well when both the customer and the developer have something to gain from a cooperative development effort. Seeking customer input in such an arrangement is rendered quite straightforward: The customer's people become an integral part of your design team.

As you become more comfortable involving the customer in your Stage 3 development work, you can begin to accelerate the process. For example, in the case of software development, develop a small facet of the product in a few days—a rapid prototype of several screen displays. But don't keep it a secret: Show the screens to the customer and seek fast feedback as you proceed to the next step in development. The *ideal action is fast, highly iterative, and parallel:* A rapid or partial prototype is quickly fashioned, followed by immediate customer feedback, followed by development of another part of the product or a more complete prototype, and so on—a back-and-forth pattern, as illustrated in Figure 5.3.

The example is for software, and it's easy to visualize how one might bring facets of a partially completed software product to customers for reaction in a series of build-and-test. But this same procedure works for most industries: Don't wait until the very end of the Development stage before you expose your product to customers. Get something in front of them early: a rapid prototype, a lab sample or crude sample, or a rough working model.

Creating Unrealistic Customer Expectations

One concern often voiced is this: "What about creating unrealistic customer expectations?" This is a valid question: When undertaking these early build-and-test iterations, it must be made very clear to the customer exactly what stage of the development program you are in—that this is an early prototype test, and not a field trial or offer to sell. That's why several members of the project team should make the presentation to the customer, and you should not leave this test to the sales force! Another tip: Show your customer an outline of your idea-to-launch system and indicate exactly where the project is—in Stage 3, not Stage 5. Chances are your customer uses a similar new-product process and will understand immediately.

Suggestion: This spiral or rapid, iterative build-test-feedback-and-revise process is practiced by a minority of industries such as software producers, but the methodology has applicability to a much broader range of industries and settings. The point is: Break the development of the product into discrete chunks; rapidly develop partial prototypes, working models, lab samples, or parts of the product; then test these quickly with the customer. This iterative series of build-and-test steps will quickly move you down the field in Stage 3 to your goal of the right product, and in a much-collapsed time frame.

SHORTENING DEVELOPMENT TIMES

The second major challenge in the Development stage is to shorten development times. Not only do you realize your revenue sooner, you also minimize the chances that the development target has changed. Thus a *sense of urgency* is essential throughout Stage 3. This is one of the longest and potentially most troublesome stages of the project, but with the front-end homework done and with a fact-based product definition in place, many of the pitfalls and time wasters typical of the Development stage have been eliminated.

> Speed is everything! But not at the expense of quality of execution.

We saw in Chapter 2 five success drivers that are also *proven ways to reduce time-to-market*. Build these into your new-product system—this is the first way to reduce development time:

1. *Prioritize and focus:* The best way to slow projects down is to dissipate your limited resources and people across too many projects. By concentrating resources on the truly deserving projects, not only will the work be done better, it will be done faster.
2. *Do it right the first time:* Build quality of execution into every task and step of the project. The best way to save time is by avoiding having to recycle back and do it a second time.
3. *Front-end homework and definition:* Doing the front-end homework and getting clear project definition saves time downstream: It means clear product design targets and less recycling.
4. *Organize around a cross-functional team with empowerment:* Such a team is essential for timely development: It cuts down on "siloing" up and down the vertical organization and promotes parallel processing (rather than sequential problem solving).
5. *Parallel processing:* The relay race, sequential, or series approach to product development is dead. A more appropriate model is a *rugby game* or *parallel processing*. More work gets done in an elapsed period of time.

In addition, here are some "nuts-and-bolts" ways to reduce development time. Consider making them part of your methodology:

- *Use flow-charting:* Map out each task in a project, and then challenge the project team to figure out *how every task can be reduced in time*. Remove the time wasters! Wise shortcuts, or omitting the unnecessary, are obvious time savers.
- *Use planning tools:* Utilize critical path planning and project management time line software. Look for opportunities for undertaking tasks concurrently, or for beginning one task before another ends.
- *Add flexibility:* Overlap activities and stages; and bring long-lead-time activities forward into an earlier stage. These approaches were outlined in Chapter 5.
- *Regard deadlines as sacred:* Time-based innovation is impossible without a disciplined adherence to deadlines. "Sacred deadlines" means that a predetermined date is adhered to as a guideline for planning, with no excuses. Delays are dealt with via extra effort and resources, *not postponement*.
- *Have flexible funding:* Set aside envelopes of money (or resources) so that there's no waiting for a new budget year for money to start a promising project. Strategic Buckets are a useful concept here—buckets of money, not individual projects, are in the annual budget.
- *Move ahead anyway:* If gatekeepers cannot make timely decisions (for example, cannot arrange a time for a meeting, or don't show up to the meeting), the decision is an automatic Go. Make this a company rule.
- *Keep it simple:* Unbundle products and projects. For example, instead of tackling a project that requires three inventions, break it into three separate new-product projects. Project complexity doubles and triples development times, so work to reduce the complexity of projects.

Suggestion: When implementing your idea-to-launch system, *make every effort to reduce development times* of projects. The mere fact that you're now using a Stage-Gate® system that builds in quality of execution, homework, and early definition, cross-functional teams, parallel processing, and focus means automatic time reduction. But do more than this. Use the approaches outlined above during your implementation—flowcharting, planning tools, process flexibility, sacred deadlines, flexible funding, fast gate decisions, and complexity reduction. But be sensible, too: Often, the "quick fix" methods designed to speed things up—for example, cutting corners or omitting steps—yield precisely the opposite effect, and in many cases are very costly. Note that there is also a dark side to accelerated product development.[2]

A Solid Development Plan

In spite of these measures to reduce development time, there is still the commonly voiced complaint that the Development stage takes far longer than expected: The technical group is invariably accused of lacking a sense of time urgency. I hear this criticism often leveled at R&D or other technical people by marketing and management people. Part of the problem may be indeed that technical people have a longer-term orientation and don't exhibit quite the same degree of "hustle" and responsiveness that marketers and businesspeople do. But the problem may also be a management and planning one, for at the heart of every good development project is a *sound Development Plan*.

The physical development of the product must be driven by a well-crafted Development Plan. This is the Action Plan approved at Gate 3, which includes:

- A time-based display of activities, actions, and tasks. (Gantt charts, for example as in MS-Project, provide a time line and show activities along this line as bars, defining a start date and an end date for each activity; these charts are appropriate for relatively simple projects. Critical path plans are needed for more complex projects.)
- Resources required for each action or task, notably personnel, person-days, and dollars.
- Milestones to be achieved throughout the Development stage (and built into the time line). These milestones are measurable and definable points in the project where a review of the project can be conducted to determine if it is on track, on schedule, and on budget.

The time line or time schedule is a critical element in the plan. It must be aggressive, causing team members to stretch a bit. But it must also be realistic. Too often, a very compressed plan is put together in response to management's demands, and unrealistic completion times are assigned to tasks. But within weeks of implementation, the truth is known: The plan is pure fiction, and its credibility is lost. So be aggressive, but be realistic, too, in designing the time line.

Estimating Times and Work Effort

Another problem is the great difficulty estimating how long it will take to undertake certain tasks and how many person-days will be required. For example, some technical tasks may have an uncertain time frame—how long and how much work will it take to arrive at a technical solution? There are no easy answers to providing reliable time estimates here, other than four solid rules of thumb:

- The entire project team should develop the time line, as a team, working together (instead of the project leader developing the schedule alone; or each team member developing his or her part of the time line). This is one of the first agenda items of the newly formed project team: developing the detailed time line.
- The time estimates must be realistic and objective: Try to remove emotion and undue pressure by others from this estimation exercise.
- Use history as a guide. That is, how long have such tasks taken in the past? Smart companies keep a record of "estimated time" versus "what time was

really taken to accomplish the task." P&G finds that *profiling*—looking at historical time lines in previously completed but similar projects—provides a more accurate estimate of task times than teams' estimates.

- Apply a contingency factor. Invariably, activities take longer or involve more work than originally estimated. For some activities, there is a consistent pattern of underestimation of times. These data are collected at the Post-Launch Review.

Milestones—Critical Checkpoints

Milestones are those checkpoints along the way that you use to make sure you're on schedule and on budget. One rule that some firms employ is that if several milestones in a row are missed, the project should be *red flagged*: The project is clearly in trouble, and the project leader could call for a full review of the project. In this way, milestone points can be used to blow the whistle on projects that are heading off course before the problem becomes too serious.

To be effective, a milestone must be measurable and have a time frame attached. For example, in the development of a new software product, the statement "to have most of the code written and partially debugged" is a very poor milestone. Phrases such as "most of" and "partially" are not measurable. Rather, the milestone should be quantifiable: "To have 30,000 lines of code written and fully debugged by day 95 of the project" is better.

Milestone checkpoints are not to be confused with the periodic review meetings that technical managers often hold. These review meetings are usually scheduled on a calendar basis: Typical is the "monthly review of all projects." These meetings are more for information purposes than for control; but they do serve a useful role: Here senior technical people are able to review progress to date during this Development stage, and to provide insights, advice, and mentoring to technical people on the project team.

Practice Discipline

Project plans—time lines and milestone checkpoints—are meant to be followed. When a project falls way behind schedule, too often it is because the project team just went through the motions of developing an Action Plan complete with a time schedule simply to meet management's requirements that such a plan be prepared. Then it's business as usual, and the plan and time line are conveniently forgotten. Wrong! There must be constant self-discipline and accountability for these time schedules. Time lines are there for a purpose. One of the common traits I've observed among successful project leaders is a dedication to the plan and to the schedule:

> *An example:* A textbook case of a successful new product undertaken in DuPont's automotive paint refinish business was driven by a (then) relatively inexperienced project leader. One of her keys to success, she told me, was

her dedication to her schedule throughout the development phase of the project. She and her team used project management software to lay out the plan for the two-year development phase. Every Monday morning at 7:30, the entire team would meet to review progress: What did we accomplish last week; where are we on the time line; and what needs to be achieved by this time next week? Each Monday, the critical path plan was updated, and a new time schedule generated. "It was this discipline—this religious adherence to the time line—that drove the project so quickly and successfully," she explained. The project was one of the most successful and time-efficient that the business had ever experienced.

ON TO STAGE 4: TESTING AND VALIDATION

A prototype or sample product has been developed. Thanks to the ongoing in-house and customer testing that took place throughout Stage 3, the product has at least been partially proven even before it enters this Testing and Validation stage. The purpose of Stage 4 is to provide final and total validation of the entire project: the commercial product, its production, and its marketing. Typical activities in this stage include extended in-house product tests, customer field trials or usage tests, test markets, and trial, pilot production, or operations—see Figure 10.2.

> Stage 4 validates the product and its marketing and operations. Don't shortcut this stage.

Testing with Customers

Not only must the product work right in the Development Department, it must also work right when the customer uses, misuses, and abuses it. The product must also be acceptable to the customer (simply "working right" doesn't guarantee customer acceptance). Finally, the product must excite and indeed delight customers: They must find it not only acceptable, but actually *like it better* than what they're buying now. In short, customer reaction must be sufficiently positive so as to establish purchase intent.

For some products, the first time the customer can see and try the product is after the prototype or sample is completed. But this is risky! Don't wait until the product is fully developed before showing it to the customer. This grand unveiling could lead to some very unpleasant surprises rather late in the game. Use the *spiral development approach* to ensure acceptance all the way through Development.

One of the pitfalls here is the reluctance of the project team to unveil its "baby" too soon to customers, just in case the exposure is premature and might prompt a negative reaction:

An example: An optical firm was developing a new camera-microscope system for use in a lab. In the homework phase, team members had inter-

Figure 10.2: Stage 4—Testing and Validation—Is the Final Test of the Product, Operations, and Marketing Plans Prior to Full Commercialization

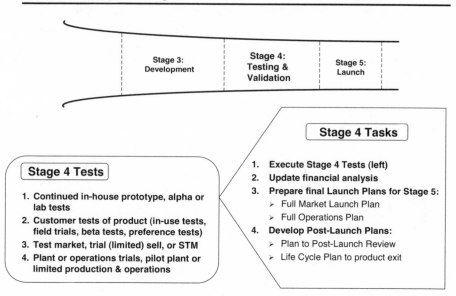

viewed lab users to solicit their inputs, and also brought in expert microscopists (users) to seek performance requirements. So far, so good. But no concept test presenting specs and performance characteristics of the proposed product was ever done. Here, the team leader argued that the customer would actually have to "experience the product in order to respond intelligently."

So he sought to develop a "working model." This was supposed to be a very crude but working version of the product, so that customers could have hands-on experience. The problem was that the so called "working model" ended up being almost the final prototype, and by this point, the project was into the millions of dollars. The project leader's reluctance to show early versions of the product or even product concepts to customers is understandable. But his arguments were faulty: Admittedly, a working model will yield better feedback, but concept tests and bringing customers in to see bits and pieces of the product as it takes shape also yield useful insights and solid feedback regarding product design; further, by deferring customer feedback and reaction to so late a point in the process, he placed the project and company in a needlessly high-risk situation.

Preference Tests

A *preference test*—in which customers, either individually or as a group, are exposed to the finished product and their interest, liking, preference, and purchase intent are measured—does several things. First, it provides a more accurate reading of likely market acceptance than the pre-development concept test or the customer tests done during Development. You now have the "commercial" or finished product to show the user. By contrast, in the concept test, customers saw only a *representation of the proposed product*—something fairly intangible. And even during Development, you only had pieces of the product, or a working model—but not the final product. During the Stage 4 preference tests, however, customers are exposed to *the real product*, one they can touch, taste, or try. Much more information is presented to them, and because they are better informed, their answers and reactions are likely to be better predictors of eventual market acceptance.

A preference test also provides clues to minor design improvements that can make the product even better. If the suggested design improvements turn out to be major, it's back to the drawing board for a total redesign and more customer tests, or perhaps a decision to move ahead on the development of release number two.

The final purpose of preference tests is to determine how and why the customer responds to the product. The words that customers use in their comments provide valuable hints about how the product should be communicated to the marketplace. The attributes or features that strike the customer first can be used in designing ads, brochures, Web pages, or sales presentations.

Once the preference testing is complete, what should you do with the data? Can market acceptance or market share be estimated from the data? Many of the same guidelines outlined in conducting a concept test in Chapter 7 also apply to the preference test:

- *Be careful not to "oversell" the product to the customer.* If you make too forceful or biased a presentation, what you're probably measuring is how good a salesperson you are, not whether the customer really likes the product.
- *Be sure that the customer is sufficiently well informed* about the product to be able to judge it. This is a particular problem with innovative products. If potential customers don't understand the product, its use, and its benefits, their responses won't mean very much. An information session held prior to the product test should give the customer relevant facts concerning the characteristics, use, and purpose of the product if these are not immediately apparent.
- *Be cautious in measuring price sensitivity* in customer preference tests. A common ploy is to ask an "intent to purchase question" about a product priced at, say, 99 cents. Then the question is repeated, and a price 5 cents higher is named. Not surprisingly, the proportion of "definitely would buy" responses goes down as the price goes up. This type of questioning is invalid, however. By quoting the first price as 99 cents, the interviewer has established a *reference price* in the buyer's mind that biases all subsequent price questions. If price sensitivity is an issue—that is, if you want to measure intent to purchase as a function of price—one price should be presented to one group of respondents, a second price to another group, and

so on. Even with these controls, however, measuring price sensitivity is tenuous at best.

- Don't take "preference" and "intent-to-purchase" data literally. A 52 percent preference level does not translate into 52 percent of market share. The concerns relating to concept-test results also apply here—these were outlined in Chapter 7. The results usually must be discounted to adjust for "yea saying," the lack of dollar commitment on the part of the buyer, and split purchases.

Extended Trials, Field Trials, or Beta Tests

Extended user trials (or beta tests or field trials) enable customers to use a product over a longer time period, usually on their own premises. Customers' reactions and intent are thus likely to be based on better information. Extended trials are particularly appropriate for complex products, for products that require a learning period, and when it takes time for the customer to discover the product's strengths and weaknesses. An extended trial may also uncover product deficiencies not apparent in a short customer test or a lab test.

The objectives of these customer tests usually include the following:

- To determine whether the product works well in actual use conditions (if not, what improvements are required)
- To gauge whether the product is acceptable to the customer (and why, or why not)
- To measure the customer's level of interest, liking, preference, and intent to purchase (and the reasons for these)
- To gauge price sensitivity—how preference and intent are affected by price
- To determine those benefits, attributes, and features of the product to which the customer responds most strongly (information useful in the design of the communications strategy for the product)

To undertake an extended trial, a sample of potential customers is identified and qualified (that is, they agree to participate). The product is then given or loaned to the customer, who proceeds to use it at home, in the office, or in the factory. A debriefing session is held with the user in which the usual questions—interest, liking, preference, and intent—are posed. Probing questions can be asked about the product's strengths and weaknesses, its ease of use, its frequency of use, and suggestions for improvement.

Skipping the extended field trials is tempting, but the results can be disastrous:

An example: One major marine-coating manufacturer was anxious to get the new product to market before competition, *at all costs!* The entire industry had been alerted to the fact that traditional ship-bottom coatings would no longer be accepted—they were toxic to plant life. Yet somehow, manufacturers had to figure out how to keep "things" from growing on ship bottoms, without using toxic materials.

The answer: very slippery paint. And so the company focused on a new generation of ship-bottom coatings based on silicone technology. In a rush, the company moved to *accelerated field trials*, testing the new coating on various steel plates that were dipped into seawater. No on-ship tests were undertaken, however. And the product was launched, with one of Europe's largest ship-owners being the first major customer.

All went well for the first year, until the developer began to get some complaints from the major user. "That slippery paint you sold us—guess what . . . it's slippery on both sides!" After one year of ocean duty, the paint was peeling off the ships. And that meant dry-docking the vessel, stripping off the paint, and repainting the ship. The costs were enormous, and the claims by customers began to mount.

The coating company survived, barely. But the damage was substantial to both its bottom line and its reputation.

When undertaking field trials or extended trials in the case of complex, technical, or B2B products, a little care taken at the beginning in the design of these trials can make the results so much more valid. Here are some tips:

1. *Pick the test sites carefully.* Convenience is a factor, but strive for representativeness, too. If you only pick "friendly customers," then you're likely to get positively biased responses and may be in for a shock after market launch.

2. *Get a written agreement with the customer in advance.* This agreement should specify, first of all, that this is a product test (many new products are placed with potential customers by aggressive salespeople, but the customer is not fully apprised that this is only a test!). Next, it should indicate something about the timing, test duration, test conditions, what will be measured, by whom, and how. How many times have we witnessed disputes over test results because a different testing procedure or metric was used? It could all have been avoided if these had been spelled out in advance.

3. *Be there!* Even if the tests are being done at midnight, be on-site. Unforeseen events have a habit of besetting otherwise straightforward product tests when the project leader isn't there to check up on things. Get your presence written into the agreement beforehand (item 2 above).

4. *Get the customer to sign off on the test results,* and most important, on the interpretation of these results—for example, that the test was a success or a failure. Two people can witness the same test and draw quite different conclusions from it. Get agreement, and get it in writing!

5. *Specify in advance what happens in the event of a successful test.* For example, if the beta tests are successful, is the customer expected to sign a purchase order and keep the new hardware or software? Or if the field trials are pos-

itive, does this automatically lead to commercial production runs by the customer?

A Final Note on Customer Tests: Not the Place to Cut Corners

User tests, both during Development and after the prototype or sample is ready, often prove critical to the success of the product. So don't cut corners here! Studies show that customer tests—whether they are performed or not, and how well they are executed—are significantly correlated with new-product success. Moreover, analyses of new-product failures reveal that in *half the failures, the customer test was poorly undertaken or skipped altogether.*[3]

Suggestion: Conducting customer tests is not a difficult step, nor is it unduly expensive. Given its pivotal role in identifying product deficiencies while there is still time to correct them, and in assessing likely market acceptance, build customer tests into your methodology, at minimum, following the Development stage, and ideally throughout Development via spirals. Remember: Check with the customer, and check again—to ensure there are no surprises!

The Final Trials

By now, the product has been tested with the customer and has been pronounced satisfactory. Minor design improvements have been incorporated. At the same time, the full Market Launch Plan is coming together. Finally, the time is ripe to test the product, its production, and the Launch Plan under commercial conditions. For the first time you pull together all the elements of the marketing mix—product, price, advertising, promotion, sales force, and so on—and test their combined effect. At the same time, you produce a limited quantity of the product in a trial operations or trial production run. The aim, of course, is to determine whether the strategy and programs will generate the sales and profits you expect. If the answer is no, then you can choose between modifying the strategy or killing the project. It's still not too late to turn back.

There are two possible ways to test the market launch strategy. Both are essentially experiments, and both cost less and are less risky than a full-blown launch. Each provides a fairly valid test of the launch strategy, while leaving time for course corrections to be made before the launch. And both are reasonably good predictors of eventual sales or market share.

The first is a *simulated test market,* a method that has gained popularity among consumer-goods producers. The second is a *full test market or trial sell,* which although more expensive, has wider applicability for different types of products. Let's look at each in more detail.

The Simulated Test Market

A simulated test market (STM) is a relatively inexpensive yet surprisingly useful method for predicting market share and sales from a *new consumer product.* Simulated test marketing refers to marketing research systems used to determine consumer reaction to product initiatives prior to their market entry. STM models are used to combine those consumer reactions (usually obtained in a simulated shopping experiment and experience) with marketing plan information to forecast the likely sales volume. More advanced STM systems can also identify the key drivers of volume, and so the product proposition (and its chances for success) can then be improved, all prior to market entry. There are a number of commercial versions of STM studies offered by various consulting or market research firms. Examples include BASES II, ASSESSOR, and Volumetric TEST.

Why have such techniques become so popular, particularly among consumer-goods producers? Cost is the big factor. Moreover, STMs are surprisingly predictive. Although the experiment is somewhat artificial—a simulated shopping experience—the results are very close to the market share finally achieved after launch. One major consumer-goods firm estimates that STMs provide an accuracy of plus or minus two share percentage points. Other reasons for using an STM include speed (it doesn't take as long to conduct as a full test market); the depth of data provided (segmentation data on triers and repurchasers); limited exposure (far less chance that a competitor will learn about your new product); and control. The one serious problem with an STM is its limited applicability—to relatively inexpensive consumer goods, the kinds of products found on supermarket shelves.

Test Markets or Trial Sells

Test markets (or trial sells) are the ultimate form of testing a new product and its marketing plan prior to committing to the full launch. Of the testing techniques, a test market comes closest to testing the full launch strategy before it actually takes place.

As in any experiment, there are subjects, treatments, and a control group. A representative sample of customers is chosen—they are the *subjects*. They are exposed to your new product and to the complete launch plan, which includes all the elements of the marketing mix. This is the *treatment*. (Several different treatments can be used on different groups to see which works best.) The *control group* is all people not exposed to the test market.

There are usually two reasons for conducting a test-market study. The most common objective is to determine (or verify) the expected sales of the new product. A reliable forecast of future sales is critical to the final Go/Kill decision at Gate 5. If the test market shows poor sales performance, the project can be killed, or perhaps recycled to an earlier stage for necessary revision of the product or its launch plan.

A second objective is to evaluate two (or more) alternative launch plans by testing two different treatments to see which gives better results. This type of test marketing is less common. For one thing, it's more expensive. Besides, the hope is that by the time you're ready to test market, strategy questions will have been resolved.

Test markets can be used for B2B products, in which case they're usually referred to as *trial sells*. A trial sell goes hand in hand with a trial production run of the product. If a limited quantity of the product can be produced, samples can be made available to a handful of company salespeople in one or two sales territories for trial sell. The elements of the trial sell are as close to those of the actual launch as possible: the price, the advertising literature, and sales presentation are identical. The only difference is that national advertising and promotion cannot be used for a single sales territory.

To Test or Not to Test?

A most important decision is whether to undertake a test market at all. One common school of thought argues that test markets aren't worth the time, trouble, and cost. Test markets are expensive, particularly in terms of competitive lead time. Moreover, a test market exposes your product to competitors, thus giving them time to respond. So if speed and the competitive situation are crucial factors, then consider omitting the test market—this may prove to be "intelligent corner cutting." But be aware of the risks, and try to *build other steps into your methodology* that address the customer acceptance issue much earlier in the process— for example, better front-end market research, constant customer spirals during Development, and well-executed beta or field trials.

Cost is another big factor. Test markets can cost hundreds of thousands, and sometimes even millions, of dollars. The value of the information generated by a test market must be weighed against the cost of conducting the test market. Another argument against test markets is that they exemplify the "horse and the barn door" situation. By the time the test market results are in, the development budget has been spent and the product is fully developed, the creative work has been done, the packaging costs incurred, and the plant tooled up, at least for limited production. What's left? It's almost too late in the game to make changes now—the time to have killed or modified the project was much earlier. This argument is persuasive in cases when expenditures up to the point of commercialization (for example, development) are particularly high in relation to launch costs.

Test markets or trial sells are not necessarily needless or wasteful. Give serious thought, however, to the pros and cons of undertaking such a test: Test markets should not be an automatic or routine part of every new product's plan. A test market is useful when *the uncertainties* and *the amounts at stake* are high:

1. *When there is still a high degree of uncertainty.* You may be very uncertain about the eventual sales of the new product as the Launch stage approaches. On the other hand, if you've built market studies into earlier stages of your project—a concept test in Stage 2, spirals during Development, and user and preference tests during Stage 4—then you should be fairly sure about market acceptance and hence may not need a test market.

2. *When the horse is still not completely out of the barn.* When there are many expenses yet to be incurred in the project before and during the full launch— for example, if a plant needs to be built or a production line retooled or set

up; or if an expensive global advertising and promotion campaign needs to be mounted.

Suggestion: If the risk remains high as the project approaches launch, consider building into your plan a final trial: a simulated test market or a full test market, accompanied by trial, limited production, or operations. An STM is recommended for consumer goods as a cost-effective predictor of market acceptance. For other types of goods, however, a full test market or trial sell is really the only method of accurately predicting the final sales results.

GO FOR LAUNCH

The final evaluation decision—Go to full production and full market launch—is largely *a readiness check:* that all is commercial ready and financially sound. Armed with the results of preference or end-user tests, test markets or trial sells, and pilot production runs, you can now make estimates of source-of-supply and marketing costs, sales volumes, final prices, and profit margins with a high degree of confidence. Before the product moves to full-scale commercialization, a thorough financial analysis is essential.

By now, the market and operations tests have yielded positive results. Armed with these results, the final NPV, IRR, and sensitivity analyses are now carried out. The expected return clearly exceeds the minimum acceptable level, even with pessimistic estimates of key variables. So the decision is Go for commercialization.

THE FINAL PLAY—STAGE 5: INTO THE MARKET
The Market Launch Plan

The marketplace is the battleground on which the new product's fortunes will be decided. Thus, the plan that guides the product's entry to the market is a pivotal facet of the new-product strategy. For the rest of this chapter, we look at *how to develop a Market Launch Plan* (MLP) for your new product.

First, what is a *marketing plan*? It's simply a plan of action for new-product introduction or market launch. It specifies three things:

- marketing objectives
- marketing strategies
- marketing programs

And the *marketing planning process* is a series of activities undertaken to arrive at the marketing plan—see Figure 10.3.

Too Little, Too Late

When does marketing planning begin? This section occurs rather late in the book because Launch is the final stage in *Stage-Gate*. However, this is not to imply that

Figure 10.3: Marketing Planning—Creating Your Market Launch Plan

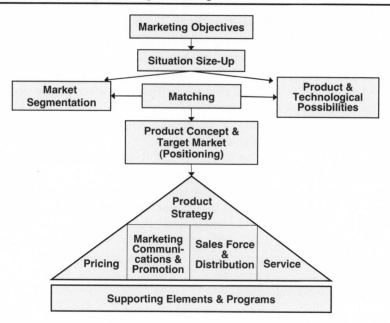

marketing planning should be the final step prior to launch. If you leave it to the end, you're likely to find you've done too little, too late.

Start early: Marketing planning is an ongoing activity that occurs formally and informally throughout much of the idea-to-launch system. Informally, it begins during the first few stages, right after the ideation or Discovery stage. By the time the project enters Stage 2, formal marketing planning is already under way as part of the development of the Business Case. The creation of a full market launch plan occurs simultaneously with product development in Stage 3 to emphasize that a formal MLP should be in place long before the product is ready for market introduction or even for a trial sell.

> Marketing planning is an integral part of your *Stage-Gate* system. Planning begins as early as Stage 2, with the delivery of a preliminary MLP, a component of the Business Case. The full marketing plan is crafted during the Development Stage and is refined in successive stages.

Suggestion: When in your idea-to-launch system does marketing planning begin? Does it begin, as in many firms, at the very end of the development project? Or do you start marketing planning in parallel with the development of the product? If it's a matter of "too little, too late," why not incorporate the marketing planning with the development activities in your *Stage-Gate* system?

An Iterative Process

The marketing planning process for a new product is iterative. The plan is not carved in marble at the early stages of *Stage-Gate*. Even the formal MLP that should be in place prior to Stage 4 (product testing and trials) is likely to be somewhat tentative. The first version of the formal plan will probably see changes before it is finally implemented in the Launch stage. In short, there will be many times when you will rethink and recast your marketing objectives, strategies, and programs before implementation.

Setting Marketing Objectives

Objectives are part of a marketing plan for good reason—otherwise, why bother going through the aggravation of setting objectives at all? First, *objectives provide decision criteria* that help when deciding among two or more alternatives in a plan. Second, a common and well-understood set of objectives for a new product *creates a sense of purpose*—a goal for the commercialization team to strive toward. Finally, marketing objectives become *a standard for measurement*, benchmarks against which to measure performance and help signal when course corrections are necessary.

Marketing objectives must be SMART:

- ✓ Specific
- ✓ Measurable (quantified)
- ✓ Action oriented
- ✓ Realistic, but a stretch
- ✓ Time bound (specify a time frame)

A typical objective might be expressed as: "to gain a leadership position in the market." This sounds laudable, but it's a poor objective. First, it is not useful as a decision criterion. Second, it isn't quantified. What does "leadership" mean? Does it mean "50 percent market share or better," or does it mean "the highest market share among competitors"? And what does "market" mean? The whole market? Or a specific and narrow segment of the market? Third, because the objective isn't quantified, it can't be measured. Finally, no time limit has been specified. Is the objective to be reached in Year 1 or in Year 10?

Suggestion: Review your firm's past marketing plans for new-product launches. Take a hard look at the "marketing objectives" section of the plan. Did the stated objectives establish good criteria for making decisions? Were they quantifiable and measurable? Did they specify a time frame? If not, strive for sharper objectives in future marketing plans using the SMART outline above as a guide.

The Situation Size-Up

The situation size-up is a key facet of marketing planning. A size-up is a *situational analysis*—it pulls together the relevant information and asks, "So what? What does

Figure 10.4: Undertake a Situation Analysis – Here Are Its Components

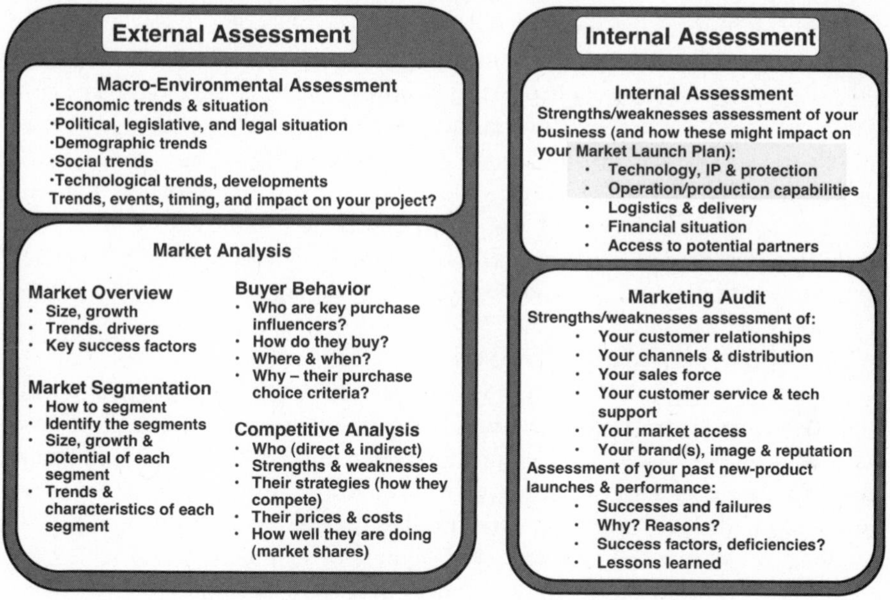

External Assessment

Macro-Environmental Assessment
- Economic trends & situation
- Political, legislative, and legal situation
- Demographic trends
- Social trends
- Technological trends, developments
Trends, events, timing, and impact on your project?

Market Analysis

Market Overview
- Size, growth
- Trends. drivers
- Key success factors

Market Segmentation
- How to segment
- Identify the segments
- Size, growth & potential of each segment
- Trends & characteristics of each segment

Buyer Behavior
- Who are key purchase influencers?
- How do they buy?
- Where & when?
- Why – their purchase choice criteria?

Competitive Analysis
- Who (direct & indirect)
- Strengths & weaknesses
- Their strategies (how they compete)
- Their prices & costs
- How well they are doing (market shares)

Internal Assessment

Internal Assessment
Strengths/weaknesses assessment of your business (and how these might impact on your Market Launch Plan):
- Technology, IP & protection
- Operation/production capabilities
- Logistics & delivery
- Financial situation
- Access to potential partners

Marketing Audit
Strengths/weaknesses assessment of:
- Your customer relationships
- Your channels & distribution
- Your sales force
- Your customer service & tech support
- Your market access
- Your brand(s), image & reputation
Assessment of your past new-product launches & performance:
- Successes and failures
- Why? Reasons?
- Success factors, deficiencies?
- Lessons learned

all this information mean to the development of your plan of action? What are the action implications?" Many situation size-ups are long, boring, and overly descriptive, and fail to answer the question "So what?" They begin with the heading: "Background," then move to "Description of the Market," and so on. They're full of information and long on description, but *short on action implications*. Make sure that your situation size-up includes the pertinent information, but always with the focus: "Here's what this means in terms of an action plan for our new product." The major areas—both internal and external—that should be covered in a situation size-up in a new-product marketing plan are shown in Figure 10.4.

Defining the Target Market

The importance of target-market definition is a key element of the product definition, a vital deliverable to Gate 3 (see Chapters 2 and 7). Clearly, one must have a precise definition of the target market before designing the product and before developing the launch plan. *From market segmentation, the rest of the launch strategy flows:* Segmentation is fundamental to effective marketing planning.

How is a target market selected or defined? The first step is *segmenting the market*—that is, identifying the segments. The second step is selecting the appropriate segment to be the *target market*.

Segmenting the Market

Market segmentation is a popular topic among marketing strategists, and too complex to be fully outlined in this chapter. Let's look at the highlights.

Market segmentation is the delineation of groups or clusters of people within a market such that there is relative homogeneity within each group and heterogeneity between groups. That is, the people (or firms) within one cluster or segment exhibit more or less the same buying characteristics and behavior, but they are quite different from the people or firms in other clusters or segments. The company that develops a strategy custom-tailored to a specific buyer or type of buyer is likely to be more successful than the firm that has only a single strategy in the marketplace. Henry Ford's remark, "You can have any color as long as it's black," may have worked for the Model T and in the early days of the automotive industry, but it fell flat once General Motors implemented a strategy of market segmentation in the 1920s: "A car for every purse and person."

Selecting the Right Target Market

A segmentation analysis should yield a number of potential market segments that could be targets for your product. At the same time, different versions of the product may be conceived to suit two or more segments. As Figure 10.3 illustrates, when one thinks of market segments, one also thinks immediately of how to target the segments—for example, what product benefits and features can be built into the product to suit it to a particular segment or segments. The next task is to select the appropriate target market from among these options.

What are the criteria for selecting the target market (and corresponding product concept) from among a list of options? Several straightforward criteria apply:

- *Segment attractiveness:* Which segment is the most attractive in terms of its market size, growth, and potential?
- *Competitive situation:* In which segment is the competition the least or the most vulnerable?
- *Fit:* Where is the best fit between the needs, wants, and preferences of each segment and the benefits, features, and technological possibilities of your product?
- *Ease of access:* Which of the segments is the easiest for your company to reach in its selling effort, distribution channels, and so on?
- *Relative advantage:* In which segment do you have the greatest advantage over competitors in terms of product features and benefits, as well as other facets of your entry strategy? Note that "fit" and "ease of access" are not enough; they suggest mere adequacy. You must also look for areas in which you have a strong likelihood of outdoing your competitors.
- *Profitability:* It all boils down to profits! In which segment are you most likely to meet your sales and profits objectives?

Product Strategy

The definition of the product strategy—exactly what the product will be—goes hand in hand with the selection of the target market. Target market definition and product strategy, together, are the leading edge of market strategy development and are front and center in the development of the marketing plan (see Figure 10.3).

What is meant by "product strategy"? For a new product, there can be several components to the term.

The product's positioning: Product positioning is a combination of market segmentation and product differentiation. "Positioning" in the marketplace means "how the product will be perceived by potential customers versus competitive products." It's the completion of the sentence: "Our product is the one that. . . ." The position is usually defined in terms of key underlying dimensions by which customers perceive and differentiate among competitive products.

Step 1 in defining the product strategy is the specification of the product's positioning—usually a sentence or two defining how the product will be positioned in the market and in customers' minds, relative to competitive products and in terms of benefits offered. If you can't write down a clear, concise, and meaningful positioning statement, chances are you're headed for trouble. A fuzzy positioning statement is usually an indication of fuzzy thinking—no product strategy or, at best, only a vague notion of strategy.

Product benefits and value proposition: The benefits that the product will deliver to the customer should be delineated. Remember: *A benefit is not a feature*, although the two can be closely connected. A feature is part of the product's design—a physical thing. A benefit is viewed from the customer's or user's perspective—some characteristic that is of value to the customer. The acid test of a benefit is this: "If the customer won't pay more for it, chances are it's not a benefit!"

Closely connected to product benefits is the *value proposition*: What is the product's value to the customer? This value proposition is usually a single and simple sentence that explains why the customer would buy this product versus another—what's the inducement?

Features and attributes: Step 3 is to translate the desired benefits and the value proposition into features, attributes, and product or performance requirements. This step is likely to result in a much longer list of items, and one that gets very close to defining the product specifications.

This three-step procedure—defining the position, outlining the benefits and value proposition, and itemizing the product features, attributes, and requirements—is a logical lead-in to the development of product specifications. This fourth and final facet of the product strategy is an exact definition of what the product will be and do, and something tangible the development group can work toward. In some projects, detailed product specs may not be possible at this point, and creative solutions by the development team may be required.

The Supporting Elements of the Market Launch Plan

By now the leading edge of the market launch plan has been developed—the target market and product strategy: The top of Figure 10.3 is in place. Now come the supporting strategies, the remaining blocks in the structure—see Figure 10.3. These are the *elements of the marketing mix* that will support the product launch. Let's have a quick look at the more critical ones.

Pricing Strategy

How does one go about pricing a new product? It is difficult to generalize, but there are some basic guidelines.

1. *What are the product's target market and positioning strategy?* Before you reach your pricing decision, both the target market and the product's positioning strategy must be specified. For example, if the product is aimed at a "niche" market, one with specialized needs, and if the positioning is a highly differentiated one, in essence you have a mini-monopoly situation: For that target market, you become the one and only product. A premium price strategy is likely the route to follow. Conversely, if the product is not well differentiated from competitive products, and if the target market is served by others, a competitive pricing policy is appropriate.

   Just in case you're tempted to enter the market on a "lowball" price basis (that is, using a low price as a means of gaining market share), remember that price is the easiest strategy for a competitor to counter, while a product advantage may take years to catch up with. Similarly, an advantage gained through a clever promotional program, a unique channel, a superior distribution effort, or branding may force the competitor to play catch-up for months or even years. In contrast, a price advantage is usually temporary: It can be countered tomorrow morning with a simple e-mail to all salespeople, dealers, and distributors, announcing a similar price cut.

   It does make sense, however, to use price as a leading weapon when you have a sustainable and real cost advantage: when your costs are truly lower than competitors' by virtue of product design or technology, or lower-cost production. Unfortunately, most firms are not in the position of being *best-cost producers*, especially in the case of a product new to the company.

2. *What are the other strategic issues?*
   a) *Skimming versus penetration:* One school of thought argues that a *penetration pricing strategy* that relies on low selling prices, high volumes, and low production costs is desirable. The profit per unit is low, but bigger profits come from volume. Usually, a larger investment in production facilities is required. The idea is to dominate the market through penetration pricing and reap the long-term rewards of *a leading market share.*

      The alternative to high volumes and low prices is a *skimming strategy*. The new product is aimed at the market segment for which the product has the most value, and which will pay a premium for it. Profit per unit is high, but volumes are lower. Investment in production facilities is also lower, so the risk is often lower. Although the product may never dominate the entire market, it may dominate the one segment and prove very profitable.

A combination of the two strategies is also possible. A skimming strategy is implemented to start with, attacking the high-value market segments. The initial risk is low. Once the product gains acceptance and the investment is partly paid back, then a penetration strategy is implemented: Increase production, drop prices, and strive for market dominance. Timing is critical. The shift must take place before competitors invest in the development and production of similar products.

b) *Overall business strategy:* The new product's pricing must be established in the light of your business's overall strategy. For example, senior management may have decided that a specific market or product category is top priority and will commit significant resources, at a loss if necessary, to gain a foothold in the market. Normal pricing practices may give way to larger issues.

3. *What is the product's value?* All new-product pricing boils down to *an assessment of the product's value or worth to the customer.* Value, like beauty, is in the eye of the beholder—the customer, in this case. Value is subjective; perceptions vary with the buyer. The price is objective, set by the seller. Ideally, the price accurately reflects the product's value.

Because two people can look at the same product and judge it to have a different value, the first question to ask is: value to whom? If you've done an effective job in defining the target market, that question will have been answered. The next question is: What is the product's value or worth? In assessing value to the customer, one usually looks at what the customer's options are. If similar products are available to the customer, then your product's value is simply the price of the alternative to the customer, plus or minus a bit, depending on the advantages of your product, service, delivery, reputation, brand image, and so forth, relative to the competitors'. In pricing in highly competitive markets characterized by relatively homogeneous products, start with competitive prices and work upward or downward from there.

If your product is significantly different from what is now on the market— a true innovation—it is often possible to *impute a value* by comparing the product's worth relative to the cost of the customer's "current solution"— whatever customers are doing or now using to solve their problem—an economic *value-in-use analysis.*

4. *If in doubt, research the customer:* Often, the only way to assess accurately the product's value to the customer is through market research. Pricing questions can be posed as part of the concept test or the product tests—see Figure 7.6. Tradeoff analysis (conjoint analysis) is another tool whereby different versions of the same product are presented to the respondent to measure

utility of different features versus price. Finally an STM or full test market or trial sell also can be used to test different pricing strategies.

5. *What is the contribution profit?* The place to start a pricing analysis is at the top line, not the bottom line, of a profit analysis. The first question to ask is: At what price might the product sell? Based on the assessment of the product's value to the customer, there will be a range of possible prices. Next, consider the *contribution profit per unit* at each possible price. Contribution profit is the selling price less variable costs per unit (direct labor, materials, sales commissions, and so on).

   This contribution profit at each proposed selling price is crucial: It tells you the relative volumes you must sell at each price in order to make the same annual profit. The contribution profit analysis thus gives significant clues as to the direction in which your pricing strategy should move.

6. *What about promotional pricing?* There can be a big difference between the ongoing or "normal" price and the introductory price of a new product. The pricing calculations, market research, and positioning strategy may all point to a premium price. But management may conclude that the price is too high to induce initial sales. If obtaining initial trials is a major challenge, don't sacrifice a well-conceived longer-term pricing strategy to do so. An introductory "promotional" price can be used to induce those first sales.

   Promotional pricing can take many forms. For consumer goods, it can be coupons, a cents-off deal, or a company rebate. For B2B goods, a simple explanation that an introductory price is being offered to the first customers to buy the product or beta-test customers will suffice.

Suggestion: Although pricing is one of the most critical decisions of the new-product's marketing strategy, all too often the pricing decision is handled in a sloppy fashion. Moreover, too often managers get locked into a "cost plus" mentality—prices are based on costs rather than on what the product is worth to the customer. In this section, six key points to remember have been highlighted. Use this list the next time you face a new-product pricing decision. The result will be a much more thoughtful approach to pricing, and usually a better decision.

Marketing Communications: Getting the Message Across

You've probably heard the saying that if you build a better mousetrap, the world will beat a path to your door. Many people took that seriously, as today there are *thousands of different types of mousetraps available*; most are commercial duds. Some are plain silly designs, but many are clever but just well hidden from the world. Not only must you have a superior product and compelling value proposition, you must *communicate it to the world*.

Steps in Developing Your Marketing Communications Plan

Normally, the marketing communications plan is developed by or with an advertising agency or an in-house advertising department. Thus, project team leaders are often tempted to wash their hands of the communications function—to subcontract this facet of the marketing plan and assume that "those advertising folks will handle it." This is wrong. An effective marketing communications program begins with the project leader and team. Whereas the details of the media plan and development of the "creative" (the artwork and copy) may be the task of others, the communications strategy itself is the project team's responsibility.

Before meeting with the advertising agency (the term "agency" is used to denote either an outside or in-company group), here's what to do:

1. *Specify the communications objectives:* Advertising can do many things. It creates awareness, knowledge, and understanding. It can shape attitudes and create a desire or a preference for a product. In the case of direct marketing, it can even create a sale. Advertising can do all these wonderful things—for a cost! Before talking to the agency, pin down *what you want your marketing communications to do for you and your new product*—and make these specific and quantifiable objectives.

   The role of advertising in the total selling effort must be decided before specifying detailed advertising objectives: How much of the communications job will advertising do, and how much will be done by the sales force or other mechanisms? For example, do you want your Web page to help create awareness and provide a minimal amount of product knowledge? Or will awareness be created via another medium and your Web page will provide detailed product information (some pharmaceutical companies use television or magazine ads to create awareness, and refer the target user to their Web page for much more in-depth product information)? Or will your Web page take the customer from awareness right through to purchase and be a direct selling tool?

2. *Specify the target market and positioning strategy:* Good advertising people will insist on knowing these in detail. Without a clear definition of the target market, how can they design a media plan? And without a positioning strategy, how will they know what the message is to be?

3. *Describe the target market:* Provide as much detail as possible on the target market and how it behaves: demographics, locations, occupations, and the like. Other types of segmentation may have been used, such as benefit, lifestyle, or volume segmentation. That's fine for most of the elements of the marketing strategy, such as product design, pricing, and so on. But remember, the advertising industry, and certainly the media plan facet, still relies heavily on traditional segmentation variables in the choice of appropriate media.

4. *Communicate the product to the agency:* The agency should study the product thoroughly before embarking on campaign development. You can help by providing as much detail as possible on how the product works, how it is used, and what its benefits, features, and attributes are.

With these four key steps in place, it's time to turn the advertising development over to the agency. The agency will devise a media plan—which media will be used, the frequency and timing of appearance, and the budget allocation—and the advertisements themselves. When the agency presents the results of its efforts, the project team must once again become engaged in development of the advertising plan.

5. *Review the plan and approve:* The review and approval of the proposed advertising and communications plan is next:

Review the media plan: The essential question is whether the proposed media plan will reach the target audience with the desired frequency. The plan should specify the *expected reach* and *frequency* of the campaign: how many potential customers the campaign will reach, who these people are, and how often they will receive a message.

First, look at each medium recommended by the agency, and in particular at the readership or viewership of that medium. Then compare that with the defined target audience and the communications objectives. Second, determine how often the target customer will be hit with a message.

Review the creative: Does the message back the product's position? Does it get across the product's benefits to the reader or viewer? An ad may be extremely creative and artistic, and may even win awards. The real purpose of an ad, however, is *effective communication of the product*. Don't feel shy about asking probing questions and critiquing the ad's potential effectiveness as a communication piece.

Run tests on the creative: If the communications budget is large enough, you may want to test the ads. For example, an STM above can be used to test an ad's effectiveness. The advertising agency will be able to design appropriate testing procedures.

Assess the worth of the objectives: Now comes the tough question. The proposed plan from the agency will include a budget. Review the advertising budget versus the original objectives. You can then decide whether to accept the costs as reasonable in light of the objectives, or to back off on some of the objectives—perhaps they were too ambitious to start with.

Build in measurement: The best way to know whether the advertising is achieving its objectives is to build in measurement. Decide with the agency how communications effectiveness will be measured. This may involve a market research study or measuring hits on a Web page, or it can be done as part of product registration and sale. Commercial services are an alternative to market research: Such services regularly measure viewership or readership of ads in various media.

Suggestion: You've probably heard someone remark that 50 percent of advertising dollars are wasted. The problem is that no one knows which 50 percent! It's true that advertising is still very much an art. Well-informed advertising decisions can be made, however. Use the steps outlined in this section; be tough on the advertising people, and see if you can't improve the effectiveness of this important element of the launch effort.

Sales Force and Distribution Decisions

For the majority of new products, sales force decisions will be straightforward: The product will be sold by your business's existing sales force or through your existing distribution system. At gates and in your project selection scorecard, several important questions will have been asked:

- Will the product be sold to a market you now serve?
- Will the product be sold to your existing customers?
- Will the product be sold by your sales force or via your present distribution system?

If the answers to those questions were "yes"—and they are for many new-product projects that pass the early gates—then the sales force plan boils down to tactical issues:

- Training the sales force (or distributors) in the selling of the new product.
- Providing the sales force with the appropriate selling aids.
- Developing a plan to devote sales force effort to the new product (for example, developing a call plan with the sales force to introduce the product).
- Motivating and providing incentives to the sales force (doing "internal marketing" to ensure that the sales force enthusiastically supports the new product, and providing the right incentives).

Don't underestimate this last item. In some companies, this internal marketing effort—getting the sales force and distributors on your side—is as critical (and almost as time-consuming) as the external marketing program!

For some new products, however, the use of the existing company sales force or distribution system may be inappropriate. If changes or additions to your sales force are to be made, two important questions must be answered:

- What is the nature of the selling job for the new product?
- Is the nature of the required selling job compatible with the talents, training, and operating methods of your current sales force (or distributors)?

In making sales force decisions for your new product—whether to use your existing sales force, hire a new sales force, work with a partner, or use a third party (a middleman)—the decision rests on a few critical factors:

- The fit between the nature of the selling job required for the new product and the skills and operating methods of your existing sales force—how they sell now.

- The degree of control over the selling effort that you need to exercise.
- And the relative costs of each option, and whether those costs are fixed or variable.

Other Supporting Strategies

The main elements of the launch are now in place: the product and target market definition, the pricing strategy, the marketing communications program, and the sales force and distribution effort. The remaining elements, not discussed in detail here, are physical distribution, customer service, and warranties. Each of these remaining elements is critical to the success of the new product, of course, and each must be built into your launch plan. Fortunately, most of the remaining elements are in place as ongoing programs in your company, and it's simply a matter of making use of what's already there for your new product.

The Final Step: The Financials

The financial forecasts are an integral part of any MLP. They cover two topics:

- What the plan will cost to implement (the budget)
- What the plan will achieve (sales and profits projections)

These *financials* are detailed profit-and-loss statements for the new product for Year 1, Year 2, Year 3, and so on—in essence, a *final financial plan* for the project.

The financial plan is important for several reasons. First, it serves as a *budget* for the new product—an itemized accounting of how much will be spent on Launch and where. Second, the financial plan is the *critical input for the final Go/Kill decisions* as the project moves closer and closer to full Launch and commercial production. The NPV, IRR, and Payback Period can all be computed from the financial plan. Finally, the financial plan provides *benchmarks*, which are critical to the control facet of the launch plan—making sure that the new product launch is on course.

In developing an MLP, and particularly for the first iteration, the financial plan is often the acid test. Any major discrepancies in strategic thinking are discovered and dealt with at this point. For example, the resulting sales and profits projections in the financial plan may be inconsistent with the sales and profit objectives that you defined at the beginning of the planning exercise. And the financials often reveal that the costs of implementing the plan are simply not warranted by the results the plan will achieve.

The existence of such discrepancies is no surprise. The marketing planning exercise is very much an iterative one. This was the first attempt—a roughed-out, tentative plan. Now, go back to the beginning of the planning exercise, and start again—the refining process. Rethink the objectives; redo the size-up; reformulate the launch programs; recalculate the financials. These iterations or recycles take time and effort, so it's important that you begin this marketing planning exercise early in the new-product process—ideally, before Gate 3.

As the product moves closer and closer to the Launch, and with each successive iteration and refinement, the launch plan starts to crystallize. And if the homework, tests, and trials have been properly executed, it should be a matter of clear sailing into a successful launch . . . with another big new-product winner on your hands!

11

IMPLEMENTING *STAGE-GATE®* IN YOUR BUSINESS

There is nothing more difficult to carry out, nor more doubtful of success, nor more dangerous to handle than to initiate a new order of things. For the reformer has enemies from all those who profit by the old order, and only lukewarm defenders in all those who would profit by the new order, this lukewarmness arising partly from their fear of their adversaries, who have the laws in their favor, and partly from the incredulity of mankind, who do not truly believe in anything new until they have had actual experience of it.

—Machiavelli, *The Prince*, 1532

LET'S GO DO IT

So when do we start? Let's do it!

You've just about finished reading this book; you've talked to a few of your colleagues; you've also read a few of the articles referenced here, and a few more. Your company has reengineered many of its processes and methods, and this *Stage-Gate approach* seems to tie in nicely. So you're convinced: The prospect of installing *Stage-Gate* with all its best practices in your company is increasingly appealing. Or perhaps you already have an idea-to-launch process, but it's dated—a little creaky and cumbersome, so it's time to redo, overhaul, or reinvent the system.

DESIGNING AND IMPLEMENTING *STAGE-GATE*
Tougher Than It Looks

You've seen the positive results in other firms. Now it's time to charge ahead in your company.

- If your current product-development process is more than three years old, or if it does not yield the results it should, or if it's missing some of the ingredients of a winning process described in the preceding chapters, then maybe it's time for a total process overhaul—a reinvention of your idea-to-launch system.
- And if you don't have a new-product process at all, or it's a causal or informal one, then now is the time to consider installing a professional system.

But recognize at the outset that the design (or reinvention) and implementation of a world-class *Stage-Gate* new-product system is certainly no easy task.

The development of new products is one of the most important endeavors of the modern corporation; it is also a most difficult task to perform successfully! Similarly, designing and implementing a *Stage-Gate* or new-product system is also the most difficult—conceptually and operationally—of any process-redesign tasks in your company. Don't assume that this is the typical "process reengineering task"—it isn't! So think before you act here, and don't underestimate the amount of work involved in the design and implementation of *Stage-Gate*.

> Don't underestimate the challenges of designing (or redesigning) and implementing an idea-to-launch system.

To help you, fortunately we have a *Stage-Gate system for designing and implementing a Stage-Gate system* (Figure 11.1)! After all, you're introducing a new concept into the company, so why not use a *Stage-Gate* approach to do it?

A Three-Stage Approach

The design (or reinvention) and implementation of *Stage-Gate* proceeds in three stages:

    Stage 1:—Laying the Foundation: An Innovation Performance Assessment
    Stage 2:—Designing (or redesigning) your *Stage-Gate* System
    Stage 3:—Implementing *Stage-Gate*—Change Management

I show these as three discrete stages in Figure 11.1. But as in any development initiative, the stages overlap. In fact, implementation has already begun in Stage 1—the mere fact that a team has been set up to look into ways to improve product innovation in your company has created certain expectations among potential user groups . . . the journey has begun!

STAGE 1: LAYING THE FOUNDATION, AN INNOVATION PERFORMANCE ASSESSMENT

"Understanding the problem is the first step to a solution." Stage 1 is a first and necessary step. Its purpose is to understand your current idea-to-launch process,

Figure 11.1: Here's a Typical *Stage-Gate* System for Designing and Implementing a *Stage-Gate®* System

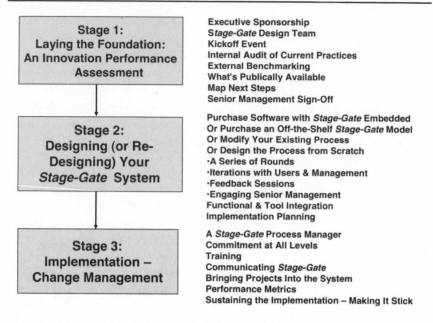

Stage 1: **Laying the Foundation:** **An Innovation Performance** **Assessment**	Executive Sponsorship S*tage-Gate* Design Team Kickoff Event Internal Audit of Current Practices External Benchmarking What's Publically Available Map Next Steps Senior Management Sign-Off
Stage 2: **Designing (or Re-** **Designing) Your** ***Stage-Gate* System**	Purchase Software with *Stage-Gate* Embedded Or Purchase an Off-the-Shelf *Stage-Gate* Model Or Modify Your Existing Process Or Design the Process from Scratch ·A Series of Rounds ·Iterations with Users & Management ·Feedback Sessions ·Engaging Senior Management Functional & Tool Integration Implementation Planning
Stage 3: **Implementation –** **Change Management**	A *Stage-Gate* Process Manager Commitment at All Levels Training Communicating *Stage-Gate* Bringing Projects Into the System Performance Metrics Sustaining the Implementation – Making It Stick

determine what needs fixing, and map out the requirements for the new system. This assessment step is often skipped over, with disastrous results. The usual situation is that all the people on the *Stage-Gate Team* think that they know what the problem is and what needs fixing, and want to forge ahead. Only later are they surprised to learn that they missed the mark—that others in the company had quite different views. So here are the key tasks in Stage 1:

1. Seek Senior Management Commitment

One key to the success at *Stage-Gate* is having senior management on board. If the executives of the business are not leading the charge here, expect a very tough and frustrating battle trying to move *Stage-Gate* forward. Thus, the very first step is to get the executive or leadership team of the company committed, and to single out one or two very senior people as *executive sponsors* of the effort. And make sure that your mandate from these sponsors is crystal clear—what it is that you and your team are expected to do, and what the deliverables are.

2. Assemble a Stage-Gate Design Team

You cannot design and implement *Stage-Gate* on your own. It requires a critical mass of people in conjunction with senior management support. Your executive sponsors should agree to a *Stage-Gate Design Team* and agree to release time for people to serve on this work group. (Sometimes this team is called the Design

Team, Reinvention Team, or Customization Team—I'll simply refer to it as "the team.")

Who should be on this team? The team must be carefully selected to include knowledgeable, bright, thoughtful, experienced, and influential people from the different functions involved in product development (and the different geographic areas, too). Additional members might include an executive sponsor (who represents senior management and lends credibility and authority to the team) and an outside expert, consultant, or facilitator (someone who has been through the exercise before). The team should be representative of your functional areas (Marketing, R&D, Sales, Operations, and so on), the various businesses or product areas, and geographic locations. There should also be a respected, passionate, and strong team leader.

How large should this team be? This team should not be a committee with a cast of thousands—rather this is a lean, action-oriented group. But there must be enough people to obtain diversity of opinion, function, and geography. The best teams that I've encountered operate with about five to ten people. Three or four is too few, not a broad enough perspective; more than ten is too many, so the group becomes unwieldy and it's almost impossible to schedule meetings.

What about time commitments by the team members? Anticipate a fairly intense effort, especially toward the beginning. Team members' calendars need to be freed up for key dates well in advance. There's a lot of work to be done, perhaps more than you expect. Once you're into Stage 2—the actual design of the system—the work can become quite heavy, depending on your approach here, with the team meeting off-site numerous times.

3. Hold a "Kickoff" Event

A kickoff workshop or conference is a good idea and achieves a number of goals. It helps to generate organizational buy-in right at the start. It is an excellent way to sound a "wake-up call" to the organization, creating awareness of need for improvement. Finally, by building in a "Problem Detection" session or presenting performance assessment results, the workshop helps to identify problems and key issues with current practice.

One serious trap that a well-intentioned team can fall into is the failure to keep the rest of the organization informed. In short, the team members become so focused on their own objective—to design and implement *Stage-Gate*—that they fail to take the extra time to communicate with others outside the team. And those in the company with a real interest in new products, but who aren't on the team, quickly view the team as "ivory tower" and distant. So six months later, when the new system is about to be launched, there already exists a significant constituency of naysayers.

The key rule here is: Keep your clients informed and involved! Don't forget: The rest of the folks in the organization are your customers or clients—the people who will ultimately use this *Stage-Gate* system. So before the team even starts out on its journey, it's best to have an information session—a new-products day or off-site kickoff event, which covers the following topics:

- ✓ Your business's new-product objectives versus your new-product performance (this often identifies a gap).
- ✓ Your current new-product practices (based on an internal study or audit, as outlined below).
- ✓ The need for a new way of handling new products.
- ✓ The concept of the *Stage-Gate* system and its positive impact at other firms (use the results presented in Chapter 4).
- ✓ An introduction of the team: its mandate and composition; and the role of other players present.

One activity I've often successfully built into this kickoff event is the Problem Detection session. Here, small work groups at the event break out, identify a list of key problems, and, most important, recommend potential solutions. They then reconvene and present their results to the other work groups. One result, invariably, is the recognition of the need for a better idea-to-launch system. Organizational buy-in has already begun!

4. Conduct an Internal Audit of Current Practices

Start doing the front-end homework, laying the foundation for the task ahead. Undertake an audit of *current new-product practices and deficiencies*—an innovation performance assessment—in your company. Besides the Problem Detection session outlined above, you have several other options here:

- Design and conduct *your own audit* within your business to determine the problems, barriers, pitfalls, and deficiencies that plague the way you approach new-product projects. You can do this via a survey, coupled with personal or group interviews. The list of problems identified provides an excellent incentive to get started on the design and implementation of a better new-product system; it also provides some guidelines and objectives for the team.
- Use the *Benchmarker*™ methodology (see Appendix A). The Product Development Institute (PDI) has developed *Benchmarker* in response to the repeated request by businesses, like yours, to undertake an internal audit of product development. *Benchmarker* is an efficient and proven way to conduct a thorough assessment and audit of *new-product practices and performance* in your business (your performance and practices are compared to numerous other firms via the PDI database).

- *Dissect a handful of your past projects* to determine success drivers and also things that are not working well. Select some projects that have been recently commercialized, and challenge each project team to undertake a retrospective flow-chart analysis—from idea to launch—as was laid out in Chapter 5. This postmortem provides many valuable insights into what's going wrong and what works in your current innovation process.

> Be sure to conduct an audit of current practices and performance—this identifies what works and what needs fixing, and is key to determining what is needed in a "new" or "reinvented" idea-to-launch system.

5. Benchmark Other Firms

Some teams benchmark other companies. This I recommend, as it allows you to see *Stage-Gate* in action and also to discuss with others some of the problems and pitfalls along the way. But a word of caution here: Benchmarking can take a lot of time; further, benchmarking is "field research" and best left to experienced field researchers, such as the PDI, PDMA, or APQC. Fortunately, there have been numerous benchmarking studies done by others. For example, our own research is published, and parts have been presented in earlier chapters. So has the PDMA's and APQC's. Therefore, though I suggest a few company visits for benchmarking, don't reinvent the wheel. Look to the literature (item 6 below), too!

6. Conduct a Thorough Literature Review

There have been countless studies over the last decades into new-product practices and performance. A number have been cited in earlier chapters. Go back and look at some of the findings in Chapters 2, 3, and 4. And read beyond the current book: I gave you many references to other researchers' studies in Chapters 2–4. My colleagues and I have also written several other books that may help: one called *Portfolio Management for New Products*,[1] which provides more insights into gate criteria and how to integrate portfolio methods into *Stage-Gate*; another book, *Product Leadership*,[2] aimed at the leadership team of the business, which provides guidance about the role of senior management as gatekeepers and strategists in the process; a book on breakthrough idea generation, which goes well beyond Chapter 6;[3] a book entitled *Lean, Rapid and Profitable New Product Development*,[4] which shows more ways to reduce waste and improve productivity in product innovation; and finally a recent book on crafting your business's product innovation and technology strategy.[5]

7. Look at What Is Publicly Available

Much has been written and much is available to help you in your design task. For example, *Stage-Gate Certified* software products highlighted in Chapter 5 often contain *fully developed Stage-Gate systems*. So all you need to do is a small amount of customization. If you have your own software platform, then consider purchasing an off-the-shelf *Stage-Gate* system, such as Navigator™, that you can customize and load into your existing software (see Appendix B).

If you're designing your own system rather than purchasing a system, be sure to Google "stage-gate" and get the many items available online. For example, Wikipedia has a fairly good description that provides a skeleton for your design effort. Further, some organizations have patterned their *Stage-Gate* system quite closely after previous editions of this book and have written articles outlining their process—see for example, TARGET, the U.S. Army's version of *Stage-Gate* for ground vehicle development.[6] This system is in the public domain, and it represents a very credible translation of this book into an operational *Stage-Gate* system. Finally, of course, there is this book: A number of teams tell me that they have simply taken Figures 4.10, 5.1, and 5.2, along with the contents of Chapters 4–10, and used this as the basis for their own *Stage-Gate* system. If that's your route, do a closer read of these chapters—much of what you need to craft your own process is in these chapters!

8. Map the Next Steps

Following these preliminaries—getting top management buy-in, selecting the team, undertaking a current-practices audit, and the kickoff event—the team is ready to move forward. But first it must propose a mandate and plan of action. The action plan deals with the next steps, namely, Stage 2 and the detailed design of the process (next section). Also, the team should be clear on its mandate or charter for the next stage and seek concurrence from senior management.

9. Secure Senior Management Sign-Off

Now it's time to go to a "gate"—to present the results and conclusions of Stage 1 in Figure 11.1 to the leadership team and to your executive sponsors. These deliverables include an identification of the problems and what needs fixing; the specs and requirements for the new process—what the system must be and do; the action plan for the next stage, including timing and resources required; and your mandate or charter for what lies ahead. The "gate" provides sign-off by senior management, and then it's "Go to the next stage."

STAGE 2: DESIGNING (OR REDESIGNING) YOUR *STAGE-GATE* SYSTEM

Now for the design of the system. The vital thing to remember is *ownership*: If people have not had a hand in crafting the process, there's much less likelihood that they will willingly adopt it! Your team's most important goal is implementation of a world-class new-product system. But if your goal is merely to design "the perfect innovation process," you'll probably succeed at that goal but fail overall. From the minute your team meets to map out your new system, every effort must be made to ensure implementation. And that means you must involve and engage the user community—gatekeepers, project team leaders, and project team members—in the design of the new system.

Your Design Options in Stage 2

Most teams pursue one of the following routes in the design (or redesign and overhaul) of their idea-to-launch system:

1. *Purchase an off-the-shelf version of Stage-Gate:* Then use your own software to operate the system. Navigator™ is a comprehensive *Stage-Gate* system, complete with all the templates, scorecards, stage and gate instructions; and even learning or teaching modules—see Appendix B. Support software to operate Navigator can be anything from standard browsers (such as Microsoft Explorer™ and Mozilla™) through to sharing and workflow software such as Microsoft SharePoint™, Microsoft Project™, or Lotus Notes™.* You will likely have to customize Navigator somewhat to suit your own business, its governance, and organizational structure.

> Use what is publicly or commercially available when designing your new system— off-the-shelf models, software, and published versions of *Stage-Gate*. Learn from those who have gone before.

2. *Purchase commercial software that includes a fully mapped-out* Stage-Gate *system.* This option was highlighted above, and indeed is the route that many firms take. Again, the embedded *Stage-Gate* system includes all you need to get going quite quickly, much the same as in Navigator, except that the software does much more than simply provide an electronic *Stage-Gate* manual; the software is intended to *automate* your idea-to-launch system (see Chapter 5).

3. *Overhaul your existing idea-to-launch system:* If your audit and benchmarking (above) reveal that your current idea-to-launch process is pretty good, then perhaps the "design stage" is merely a matter of improving and updating your current process. Some design modifications that teams electing this route typically incorporate are:

   - Reviewing the success drivers in Chapters 2 and 3 (such as VoC, front-end loading, fact-based product definition, effective project teams), and taking steps to build in these missing success drivers.
   - Incorporating the spirals and a Post-Launch Review.
   - Sharpening the gate deliverables packages—to create leaner and more-focused templates.

---

* Microsoft Explorer, Microsoft SharePoint, and Microsoft Project are the trademarks of Microsoft Corporation. Lotus Notes is the trademark of IBM Corporation; and Mozilla is a trademark of the Mozilla Foundation.

- Redoing and sharpening the gate criteria, complete with operational scorecards.
- Piggybacking portfolio management on top of your existing idea-to-launch system.
- Refining the roles and responsibilities of key people: project team members, project leader, process manager, and gatekeepers.
- Bolting on a front-end or ideation stage.

4. *Design your* Stage-Gate *system from scratch:* Often, this is the route if you have no idea-to-launch system in place, or if it is only a high-level or informal model. More on this challenging route below.

Designing Stage-Gate *from Scratch*

This is the most challenging route, and indeed was the standard way I operated when first designing and installing *Stage-Gate*. Even today, many teams opt for this route, simply because they feel they can do a better job than purchasing an existing model and believe that a customized idea-to-launch system is the only one that will work for them. (Experience dictates that you should be careful about both assumptions, as often neither is true!)

Usually this design work proceeds in a series of two-day off-site meetings attended by the team over two to four months. I call these "design rounds" because each meeting is usually followed by a period of sharing and seeking feedback from users and senior management (much like the spirals in *Stage-Gate*).

Round 1 usually gets agreement on the specifications and requirements for the new idea-to-launch system, maps out a conceptual model (a flow diagram like Figure 4.10), and provides a skeleton overview of each of the stages and gates. Then feedback is sought from your clients and management.

Round 2 digests the feedback and makes the needed changes. Round 2 also goes into more depth on the detailed design of the stages and gates. Then follows another period of sharing and feedback. Between meetings, team members work on individual components of the system, such as creating detailed deliverables templates and gate scorecards.

Round 3 (and 4, if needed) finalizes the design of the system and deals with the "other topics": roles and responsibilities of key people; rules of engagement for gatekeepers (try to get the gatekeepers to develop their own rules); alternate versions of *Stage-Gate* for lower-risk projects; red flags; illustrations and examples; and needed learning or teaching modules in the system.

The final *Stage-Gate* system that the team develops by the end of Round 3 or 4 usually includes most or all of the following topics:

- *An overview of the idea-to-launch system:* This is usually in the form of flow charts, as in Figures 4.10 and 5.1, with brief sketches of each stage and gate.
- *Stage descriptions:* Specifically, the purpose of each stage, and what activities are required in each stage. Often a description of each activity is developed

to provide the project team with a flavor for what is expected, and to incorporate current best practices. Some teams develop activity worksheets and illustrations or examples.

- *Deliverables:* What deliverables are the result or endpoint of each stage, and what will be delivered to each gate? In what level of detail? Some teams develop guides and templates for many of the deliverables, complete with field and page limits.

- *Gate descriptions:* What are the gate criteria, for example, as outlined in Chapters 8 and 9? How will projects be prioritized? And how do gates mesh with quarterly reviews of projects, project milestones, and annual budget setting? Finally, how do you begin to integrate portfolio management into your idea-to-launch system?

- *Gate procedures:* Who are the gatekeepers for each gate? How is the meeting run—for example, is there a referee or a facilitator present? What method should gatekeepers use to score the project against the criteria? How are Go/Kill decisions made? Should the project team be present for the entire meeting?

- *Organizational:* What should the composition of cross-functional project teams be? Where in the system should the project team be formed—at Gate 2? Or is that too early or late? Who does the work on the project prior to this point? Who should the project team leader be? Is it the same leader from beginning to end of the project? How much empowerment should the team be given? How should team members be relieved of their normal duties? Who does the annual performance evaluation of each team member? And how are team members given incentives, recognized, and rewarded?

- *What's "in" the process?* Which projects does this new system handle? All projects or just some types? And what about process developments (when the project may result in an improved manufacturing process)? Or platform projects and technology development projects—how are they handled (see Chapter 5)? And what about small projects—extensions, fixes, and modifications? Do they go through the full five-stage process, or should you perhaps have a three- and two-stage version of the process for low-risk projects, as in Figure 5.1? What about overlapping activities within stages, or overlapping entire stages? So how much flexibility is there?

- *How much flexibility across Business Units?* A debate always rages around how much each business unit can tailor the *Stage-Gate* system to its own needs versus the desire for a consistent, cross-business (and international) system with integrity. Most major firms develop a "corporate version" of *Stage-Gate*, with input from multiple business units. But they also allow some local customization to suit each business and geography. The various "custom" models, however, must have the same stages, gates, nomenclature, purposes, end-points, and deliverables, and major gate criteria across all businesses and globally.

Remember: Throughout the design rounds, as the idea-to-launch system takes shape, there is *constant information flow between team members and the various constituents in the organization*: senior management, potential gatekeepers, team leaders, and members. The goal here is to seek both feedback as well as buy-in. After this series of design rounds, potential users of the process—both team members and senior management—should have seen the new system several times and have provided feedback each time.

Functional Integration and Integration with Other Processes and Tools

When designing the process, be sure to deal with the issue of integration across functions and with other processes in your business. Each functional area usually has its own processes or systems—for example, a manufacturing sign-off that OKs production start-up, or the Finance Department's CAPEX or capital approval procedure. Thus, identify the *relevant existing processes* in your business that *Stage-Gate* must interface with, and ensure that you *dovetail* Stage-Gate *appropriately* with these processes.

Additionally, there are effective tools that your business has in place that apply to product development. Examples might be DFSS (Design for Six Sigma), Taguchi Methods (to improve product quality), project management techniques (such as project management software), or a partnering vetting-and-legal procedure. Don't discard or ignore these successful tools; rather, build them into your *Stage-Gate* system. They're useful tools; they work for you; and they will help in the installation and use of *Stage-Gate*.

Implementation Planning

At some point during Stage 2, an Implementation Plan must be developed for Stage 3. The implementation tasks are outlined in the next section below, but note that the implementation planning should be part of the design stage. Don't become so focused on designing the "perfect idea-to-launch" system that you forget about its implementation!

STAGE 3: IMPLEMENTING *STAGE-GATE*—CHANGE MANAGEMENT

Implementation is by far the longest, most difficult, and most expensive stage. It is about *change management*. This stage consists of a set of events and activities designed to inform people about the new or revised idea-to-launch system and train them in its use; to seek buy-in and commitment from the organization; and to bring projects—both new and existing—into the new system. The implementation stage normally is kicked off at some event or company conference whereby senior management indicates its commitment, and an overview of the system is presented. But each company's implementation plan must be designed to suit its

Figure 11.2: Different Implementation Strategies Exist for Different Types of Businesses

Directive and Focused
 	
• Philosophy:
  ✓ Just "do it"—executive edict
  ✓ No pilots
  ✓ Limited involvement by all
  ✓ Limited training & communications
 	
• Results:
  ✓ Immediate
  ✓ May not be sustained
	Participative and Integrated
	
	• Philosophy:
	  ✓ Balance of best practices & internal input
	  ✓ Most complex & coordinated strategy to implement
	  ✓ Considerable cooperation & effort by all
	
	• Results:
	  ✓ Long term sustainability
	  ✓ Most effective results
	  ✓ Integrated across the organization

No Implementation Strategy Required
 	
• Philosophy:
  ✓ Does not really qualify as a project
  ✓ Must be simple to do
  ✓ Must recognize small wins
 	
• Results:
  ✓ Good foundation for the future
  ✓ But little perceived short term value
	Broad Consultation
	
	• Philosophy:
	  ✓ Requires a non-threatening approach
	  ✓ Must rely on "made here" approach to appeal to the unofficial leaders
	  ✓ Relies on "grass roots" to push acceptance up to senior leadership
	  ✓ Also on "pain" factor experienced by staff in order to embrace change
	• Results:
	  ✓ Limited results
	  ✓ Due to difficulties encountered without leadership support

Vertical axis: **Importance of the Mandate** (Low to High)
Horizontal axis: **Degree of Change Needed Within Your Organization** (Low to High)

own culture and needs. The mechanics—the design of your new system—are relatively easy; but the behavioral side—getting commitment and change in behavior—isn't!

Note that there are different challenges and needs within companies, and the two-by-two chart in Figure 11.2 helps guide the implementation planning effort. In some organizations, the mandate to design and implement a new idea-to-launch system is strong and visible, with senior management driving the charge forward. This "mandate importance" is the vertical axis of the chart. Questions include:

- How significant and visible is your mandate?
- How important is your mandate to the company?
- Is your mandate linked to the business's strategy or to key business performance metrics?

The horizontal axis in Figure 11.2 captures how much organization change is required:

- How far-reaching is the change needed?
- Who is affected? What is affected?
- What is the magnitude of the impact?

The upper-right quadrant in Figure 11.2 represents the hardest work. Here are some of the organizational change tasks often found in an implementation plan for firms in the upper right quadrant. (Businesses in other quadrants can make use of some of these implementation change tasks, but likely not all will be needed):

1. Install a Stage-Gate Process Manager

No system, no matter how good, ever implemented itself. It needs someone to make it happen—that's the role of the process manager. To my knowledge, there has *never been a successful installation of* Stage-Gate *without a process manager in place!* And for larger companies, this is a full-time position.

> Put a process manager in place—a dedicated champion to drive the implementation of *Stage-Gate.*

Sadly, many companies miss this important point. They spend considerable time and money designing the system, and then drop the ball when it comes to putting a process manager in place. Too often, the new system is designed and is in the implementation stage for several years, but is led by a steering committee and is limping along. But it was only when a *dedicated champion* was appointed to devote his or her energies to the new idea-to-launch system that it really took hold.

Here is a quick list of some of the responsibilities that this process manager, or "keeper of the process," is charged with:

✓ leads the implementation effort of *Stage-Gate*
✓ is responsible for maintaining, updating, and improving the system
✓ provides for training for all, and also trains new employees
✓ uses portfolio management techniques to provide information for portfolio analysis and gate meetings
✓ tracks each new-product project through the process, and measures performance and ultimate success
✓ facilitates and referees the gate meetings
✓ acts as a coach and resource to project teams
✓ oversees the IT support system for product development
✓ seeks out and disseminates new tools for product development and project management

Ideally, the process manager should have been part of the team right from the beginning of the *Stage-Gate* design initiative.

2. Secure Commitment and Buy-In at All Levels

In order to achieve the needed organizational change, everyone must be committed! No new order of things will be successfully internalized in an organization unless there is commitment and buy-in from those at the top, from those at the middle level, and from the practitioners who must use the new system. If those at the top—senior management—don't commit to this new-product system, then very quickly the word spreads through the organization that the system isn't for real, that the most senior people don't support it! Moreover, top management has the authority to commit the vital resources, without which the new system will barely limp along.

Top management commitment alone isn't enough, however. Sure, the CEO can place a blessing on the new system, say the right words at executive meetings, and even dictate the implementation of the new system and allocate people to do it. All these items are a step in the right direction. But alone they won't yield a successful new idea-to-launch system.

Managers at the next levels down in the organization must also be on board. These are the decision-makers for the majority of new-product projects—the business unit manager, the marketing and sales managers, the R&D or engineering manager, the manufacturing and QA managers, and so on. These are the people who *tend most of the gates or key decision points* in the process, not the CEO or executive vice presidents!

If these key people have not committed to the concept and procedures of *Stage-Gate*, then all is lost. For example, if they behave badly at gate meetings—are poorly prepared, fail to use the stated gate criteria, shoot from the hip, let half-baked projects slip through gates with half the deliverables missing (or worse yet, let projects simply slide around gates), ask inane questions, seek irrelevant information, or kill projects for the wrong reasons—then even the best-designed system will quickly break down and fall into disuse. Unfortunately, I have seen all of these abuses within supposedly well-managed firms.

Fact: The *greatest change in behavior* is required not at the project leader and team level, but at *the decision-making level.* Managers who tend the gates face the greatest learning challenge. Thus, the buy-in of these managers is critical to the success of the *Stage-Gate* implementation.

Management commitment alone is not enough. The senior executives can say all the right things and even commit people and money. But that is no guarantee of success. The next level down—the people that tend the gates—can run sharp, disciplined gate meetings. But there's more to success than this. Implementation really happens in the trenches. Implementation means ordinary project team members and leaders buying into the system: R&D people, engineers, marketing people, and manufacturing folks—*the practitioners* in the organization—will ultimately make it happen. If they are not committed to making this new-product system work—if they see it as useless, bureaucratic, or another "flavor of the month" from management upstairs—then the process is doomed to failure. They'll simply pretend to be using the process: They'll go through the motions and say the right words, but in reality, it's business as usual.

Here are some of the ways that teams have used to get people "on board" and create the necessary organizational change:

Sell everyone on the need for product innovation! Surprising as this seems, not everyone in the organization is as convinced as you are of the need for new products. The "champions of the new system" by definition are the most supportive of a strong new-product effort; the rest of the organization is often not quite as convinced that new products are top priority. The implication here is that not only must you sell the concept of *Stage-Gate*, you must first promote the notion that "new products are vital for the health, prosperity, and even survival of your organization." There is much evidence available to support this view. Use it.

Suggestion: Use industry data to make your case for the need for new products; for example, some of the data from Chapter 1—about how new products have a major impact on company fortunes—on sales, profits, and even share prices!

Look at your own track record. What percentage of sales come from new products? What is your objective? What has been your growth driver? Compare your performance—profits, growth, and so forth—to that of competitors or other business units in your corporation.

Once convinced that new products are essential, the next question is: How do we get more winners? And that's where the idea-to-launch system is proposed as one solution—use the diamond in Figure 1.2 to make the point.

Use facts to underpin the potential benefits of Stage-Gate: There are many skeptics in any organization. As the quotation from *The Prince* that opens this chapter suggests, this skepticism arises from the "incredulity of mankind, who do not truly believe in anything new until they have had actual experience of it." If your colleagues don't have direct experience, then bring experiences in from other organizations where *Stage-Gate* has been used with success. That is, don't promise imaginary benefits based on speculation and hearsay; deal with facts and solid evidence.

To substantiate the need for a formal idea-to-launch system, take apart any unsuccessful project. At the root of its problems, you'll probably find serious process deficiencies: poor quality of execution; certain key activities not done at all or done too late; poor or nonexistent gates or decision points; and so on. If you can't provide the evidence from your own company, then at least rely on research studies done in others. Use the results from studies outlined in Chapters 2 and 3, where the overriding conclusion was that most firms' product-development processes are in serious trouble and that success and failure depends to a large extent on how well the process is executed. And show the data on how formal stage-and-gate systems improve performance (provided in Chapter 4) to give you the ammunition to prove your point.

Deal with the barriers and preconceptions: The initial reaction to an idea-to-launch system by some in your organization may be less than positive. Common views are, first, that any system is unnecessarily bureaucratic; and second, that it will now take longer to develop and launch new products. Both preconceptions are usually wrong! Nonetheless, there is a real danger that your system is indeed bureaucratic, and that it does extend the time-to-market. So *every effort must be taken to minimize bureaucracy, and to accelerate products to market.* Recall the ways to remove waste (Chapter 5) and to achieve speed (Chapter 10): Make sure that you build at least some of these best practices into your system.

Buy-in starts top down: Encourage and train senior people to start "talking the talk and walking the walk" of *Stage-Gate.* They must "model the way" and set the example for others. If they use the language of the system, ask the right questions (for example, ask about what stage or gate this project is in), and refer to gate criteria (even in casual conversation or ordinary meetings), then the rest of the organization gets the message.

Get the commitment to Stage-Gate *written into the business's mission and strategic plan:* This is not a major item, but it's another move that several companies have found useful to focus the spotlight on the new system.

If not in the business plan, then at least get the implementation and use of *Stage-Gate* built into people's KPIs (key performance indicators). For example, "successfully leading a project this year through the new system" could be a KPI for a project leader; and having "50 percent of all development projects operating within the new system by year end" might be a KPI for members of the business's leadership team.

Use pilots and get some quick wins: Identify a handful of projects, and use these as test or demonstration cases of "how to do it." Make sure that these projects are really well run: Select good potential projects—ones destined for success; choose pilot projects with able leaders and proficient teams; provide good mentoring and facilitation; and commit the right resources. Throughout their development, hold these projects up as shining examples to the rest of the organization: They are both illustrations of the use of the new system and proof that it works!

Getting organization buy-in and commitment is a prerequisite for successful implementation of the new system. This involves effective change management: changing attitudes, values, and actions. These requirements lead us into the next two critical items: communications and training.

3. Communicating Your Stage-Gate System

Effective communications and presentation of your new idea-to-launch system are cornerstones of its success. I've witnessed numerous instances when initial attempts to implement a well-designed system were *dealt fatal blows by poor communications vehicles:* The written documentation or electronic manual was too wordy; it was complex, hard to follow, and not user-friendly; and it simply turned the reader or audience off before the end of the first screen or page.

Remember: First impressions are lasting ones, and the initial documentation or presentation sets the stage for all that is to follow. Here are some actions you can take:

Design a promotional brochure or internal Web page: Virtually every company with a successful new-product system has not forgotten this "internal marketing" facet. They have designed simple, appealing introduction communication pieces for their system. Most have been professionally designed, with quality equal to a company sales brochure. The argument here is that in any organization, internal marketing is every bit as important as external marketing, so do it professionally.

Produce a user's quick guide—online: A user's guide is also needed. This is not so much for promotional purposes, but more to lay out the highlights of the new process for users. For example, the guide outlines the stages, gates, stage activities, gate criteria, and gatekeepers. But keep this guide short. This is not the place to overwhelm the reader with thirty pages of deliverables templates and forms!

The quick guide is the introduction—the teaser. It is a simple road map, intended only to provide an overview of the system and is not a substitute for the detailed and operational instruction manual.

Design a user-friendly online user's manual: The description of the idea-to-launch system delivered by the typical design team at the end of Stage 2 (Figure 11.1) tends to be simply that: a detailed description. But it's usually *not a very good user's manual*—it never was intended to be; rather, it is a working document.

The point here is, don't assume the working document that your team develops is the user's manual. It probably isn't! And if you try to make it the user's manual, experience suggests that you'll fail! So engage someone to translate your working document into an *operations manual* that will serve users well. Make sure it is easy to follow, easy to use, and an enabler—helping the project team members understand the new system, what tasks they are responsible for, and even help in the execution of tasks (via examples, worksheets, or drop-down "help" screens). Gate deliverable requirements should be spelled out, usually in the form of templates (with guidelines and examples) so that expectations are clear. And scorecards should be embedded so that project teams (and gatekeepers) understand how the project will be evaluated.

> Professional communications pieces—a Web page, a quick guide, and an online or electronic user's manual—are keys to getting others to understand and buy into the new system.

Develop a professional live presentation package: During the first year of implementation, your team will be presenting your new system to audiences throughout the corporation. The problem is that most people are not very good at making such formal presentations. So get some professional help and develop tools—from a PowerPoint presentation to a video show—that will heighten the professionalism and effectiveness of your presentation.

Remember the purpose of these presentations: The *official purpose* is instructional and informational—to teach people about this new process. But let's not kid ourselves: The *real purpose* is effecting change—to get organizational buy-in! If you don't secure buy-in, then the instructional facet of these presentations is wasted.

Come up with a good name for the process: Would a rose by any other name still be a rose? Maybe, and then maybe not! Many of those involved in *Stage-Gate* implementations concur that even seemingly trivial issues—the name you put on your process—are important:

- One German company called its process "The Project Controlling Process"— a turn-off, and not a good name.
- The U.S. Army's name for its *Stage-Gate* system is TARGET (an acronym for Tank Automotive Research, Development and Engineering Center Gated Evaluation Track), a good name, easy to say and remember, and it even sounds military.
- P&G's is called SIMPL (an acronym for Successful Initiative Management and Product Launch model), a name also intended to connote a much simpler and easier-to-use system when compared to the company's previous, somewhat bureaucratic Product Delivery Process.

4. Provide Training

The need for training and facilitation cannot be understated. Yet many companies confess to weaknesses in their initial training attempts: They simply underestimate the training needs of users. Training is important for two reasons:

> Provide training for both practitioners and gatekeepers. This is typically two days for project team members and a one to two-day boot camp for gatekeepers.

a) *We dislike the unknown.* We tend to have a negative predisposition toward things we don't understand. So if your audience—the intended users—doesn't understand the system, or has misperceptions about it, then watch out: You're in for an uphill battle trying to get implementation. If nothing else, training creates familiarity and a sense of comfort about unfamiliar things.

b) *People don't know how to use the system.* Your new system requires many people—project team leaders and members, and gatekeepers—to do new and different things, or to do old things in a new way. Without instruction, guidance, and facilitation, there is a high likelihood that people will simply get it wrong: They'll do a poor job on these new tasks. Learning by doing is great in theory, but the problem here is that you may not have this luxury. Stage-Gate *must work reasonably well the first time;* if it doesn't, users will become frustrated, and the system will be blamed. Training provides people with the necessary skills and knowledge to carry out these new tasks that *Stage-Gate* demands of them.

Those who have been through the implementation of an idea-to-launch system agree that training is important. But what topics should be covered in the training program? Three areas are common:

- *Soft skills: Stage-Gate* demands certain "people skills" or "soft skills" that may be new to some participants. These are often part of project management skills training and include: team leadership, interpersonal skills, time management, meeting management, conflict resolution, how to be a team member, and so on.
- *Hard skills: Stage-Gate* also requires certain people to undertake (or at least oversee) tasks they haven't done before. Hard skills topics include: financial and business analysis, risk assessment, VoC work and market information gathering, competitive analysis, robust design, project management (including the use of software for project management), designing and conducting field tests, and designing a professional market launch plan.
- *The use of* Stage-Gate: Users must be trained in the use of the new system. Specific topics here might include: the system—how it works, expectations at each gate (deliverables), gate criteria, the details of each stage, how a gate meeting works, and so on.

Most companies provide training to project team members (practitioners) as well as to gatekeepers. An intense one-day gatekeeper boot camp is common among some firms, where gatekeepers learn about the new system, their role, and how gates work, and even undertake some mock gate meetings. In some instances, even peripheral people—not normally on project teams or at gate meetings—are given a half-day information session on *Stage-Gate*.

5. Bringing Projects into Stage-Gate

How does one bring current projects into the system? The use of *piloting* (above) is one technique to gain organizational commitment. This is a gradual approach to bringing projects on board, in which only a few hand-selected projects are initially introduced to the new system. Some people find this approach takes too long, however. On the other hand, you can begin piloting projects as you are designing the process (in Stage 2 above), especially if the project leaders are also on the design team.

Other companies simply announce a start date: *All projects are "in the system,"* and leaders of ongoing projects must declare where they are in the process—what stage or gate—by that date. Moreover, all ongoing projects must clear one gate within, say, three months of the starting date. This gate may be the next gate, or if the project is not far enough into the stage, then the preceding gate.

Another route is to announce that all *new projects* starting today are "in the system." This is not a good tactic, as it takes forever to get projects into the meaty part of *Stage-Gate* (Stages 3 and 4) and years to be completely through the system—you wait a long time for results!

One of my favorite approaches is the use of "welcome gates." Project team members attend a two-day training session on *Stage-Gate*. At the end of the session—the final task—the concept of welcome gates is announced. Before departing, each project team must declare where its project is in the new system—in which stage and heading toward which gate. Next, the team must declare when it expects to be through that gate (usually a time limit of "next two months" is defined). But here's the difference: The "welcome gate" is positioned as a non-threatening gate, where projects *are not required* to have all the deliverables completed. That is, for this entry gate, the rules are relaxed a little. But once past this entry gate, the project must adhere to the principles of the new process.

> Try "welcome gates" to get projects into the system quickly, yet not intimidate project teams.

6. Metrics—How Well Are You Doing?

Is it too early to start thinking about new-product metrics? Certainly not! I strongly subscribe to the view that "you cannot manage what you cannot measure" and "what gets measured gets done." Some firms have made the mistake of not implementing measurement of their new-product system until too late.

The kinds of metrics various firms use to capture *system performance* fall into one of two broad categories:

1. *Post-process metrics:* These answer the question: "How well are you doing at product innovation?" They are "post-process" in the sense that they can only be measured after launch. These include both short-term metrics (measured immediately after launch: for example, "on-time performance") as well as longer-term metrics (measured a year or so after launch to determine, for example, "success rates of launched products"). Table 11.1 provides some commonly used post-process metrics.

   Data on these post-process metrics are gathered on individual projects but are most often reported in aggregate: For example, percentage of sales achieved by new products launched in the last three years; or the average slip rate (an on-time performance metric).

   These post-process metrics are very important measures. The trouble is, if these are the only metrics you employ, you might have to wait years to find out how well the new system is performing—and that's too long a period to wait to take corrective action. So most companies use *in-process* metrics, too.

2. *In-process metrics:* These answer the question: "Is your new system really working?" These in-process metrics can be measured almost immediately and capture how well new-product projects are unfolding—for example, whether they are on time at gates, and whether deliverables to gates are in good shape. Obviously, achieving high scores on these metrics is not the ultimate goal; but they are immediately measurable and they are *intermediate*

TABLE 11.1: POST-PROCESS METRICS—HOW WELL ARE YOU DOING AT PRODUCT INNOVATION?

These metrics are typically measured for individual projects and then aggregated or averaged to yield metrics for the entire business:

Short Term (measured immediately):
1. Timeliness:
   - Cycle time (months)—from Gate 3 to Launch (not too useful; must be a relative measure)
   - On-time launch (actual versus scheduled launch date—the variance in months)
   - The "slip rate" (time slippage as a percent of scheduled time; defined in Figure 1.3)
2. Development and Capital Costs:
   - On-budget projects (the dollar variance, or as a percent of the budgeted amount)

Longer term (measured much later; e.g., 1–2 years into launch, based on latest expected results):
1. Financial:
   - Profitability (NPV, IRR, Payback Period)
     - versus projections made at Gates 3 and 5, for example, recovered NPV (NPV actual/NPV forecast, across all approved projects)
     - versus your hurdle rate
   - Sales (units, dollars, market share) versus estimates at Gate 3
2. Success Rates:
   - Percent of products launched (passed Gate 5) that became commercial successes (you must define "commercial success")
   - Percent of approved Development projects (passed Gate 3) that became commercial successes
   - Attrition curves (numbers of projects per stage in the process: the "kill" rate—see Figure 1.5)
3. Percent of Your Business's Annual Sales Generated by New Products (you must define "new product"—use a tough definition so as not to count minor developments that aren't really "new products"—see Chapter 1; also you must define the time horizon: e.g., launched in last 3 years)
4. Percent of Sales Growth (or Profits Growth) Generated by New Products (similar to item 3 above)

metrics that serve as indicators (or early warning signals) of ultimate results. Table 11.2 provides some good examples of in-process metrics.

One major chemical company uses its "red-green" chart as a visual metric to spot projects in trouble, or problematic stages (Figure 11.3). Here, the various gates in its *Stage-Gate* process are shown across the top of the grid,

TABLE 11.2: IN-PROCESS METRICS—IS THE PROCESS WORKING?

Subjective metrics:
1. Quality of gate meetings (and deliverables):
   - Rating cards filled out at gate meetings (how effective was the gate meeting?). Sample questions are:
     - Were the deliverables in good shape? The result of quality work?
     - Were gatekeepers prepared?
     - Were good questions asked—relevant, on target, on topic?
     - Was a Go/Kill decision made? Resources committed? Communicated to all?
     - Was the decision the "expected decision"?
     - Efficient meeting?
     - Effective meeting?
2. Degree of "deviation from the system's rules":
   - Degree of change in Product Specs after Gate 3
   - Number of Design Change Requests
   - Number of canceled gate meetings due to "no-shows" by gatekeepers
3. Proportion of projects "really in" the system:
   - A judgment call by the process manager (via his or her project-by-project review)

Objective metrics:
4. On-time performance of projects in the development pipeline:
   - On-time gates (percent of projects at each gate that are on time; that is, when scheduled—for example, the red-green chart in Figure 11.3)
   - Average time variance (actual arrival date at gates versus scheduled date, in months or as a percent of schedule time)
5. On-budget performance:
   - Percent of projects that are on budget in each stage
   - Average variance in budgets per stage (actual versus budgeted, by stage—dollar amount, or as a percent of budgeted amount)

with the projects listed down the side. Inside each cell is the expected date for the gate meeting—when the project should have reached that review point. The actual date—when it really arrived—is also shown. When a project is "on time," color the box green; when it is late, color the box red.

Reading across the rows, one can spot projects that are clearly in trouble— those that are missing key gate-review dates. Reading down the columns shows the gates that are missed, suggesting that the previous stage is very much in trouble. For example, in the grid in Figure 11.3, projects Beta and Gamma are clearly off course; Stage 2, the Feasibility Stage, appears to be the most problematic stage in the process.

SUSTAINING THE IMPLEMENTATION EFFORT—MAKING IT STICK

Implementation does not end after a few months of intense activity—training, communications, bringing projects in, and so on. It's sometimes years before any new system really becomes part of the culture and "way of doing things" in the company. Change management is a process that is ongoing. Here are some of the *longer-term initiatives* that really make *Stage-Gate* stick.

Get the Gates Working

I said before that "as go the gates, so goes the process." Gates are often problematic for some months after the beginning of implementation in the typical *Stage-Gate* start-up. Thus, it's imperative that the process manager attend gates and develop and test rigorous protocols for the gates, work out the kinks, and get concurrence from the gatekeepers as to the best way to run gates. In Chapter 9, I gave many hints as to how to run gates and to make them work. But these "suggestions" were a collection from many companies, and your company may need to tailor these. Bottom line: The process manager should attend and facilitate (with a strong controlling role) every gate meeting, enforcing discipline and working toward an agreed-to procedure. One tactic is to hold "chalk talks" with the gatekeepers at the end of each gate meeting to do *a post-meeting review* (like the coach in the locker room at the blackboard): How well did we do? What can we do better at the next gate meeting?

Coach Your Project Teams

Even with training and a superb electronic user's manual (complete with illustrations, examples, and drop-down help screens), some project teams continue to get it wrong—they just can't change from the old ways of doing things. So the process manager becomes their coach. (Remember: process managers facilitate the gate meetings and thus control the agenda; they can remove a project team from the agenda if they think the team isn't ready.) Especially during the first year, the process manger should meet with project teams prior to a gate meeting and review their work and deliverables, making suggestions before they present to senior management. In this coaching role, the process manager often spots work that is deficient or not done, which for sure will be flagged by the gatekeepers. Or the project team may be preparing an "information dump" as their deliverables package, which is certain to overwhelm the gatekeepers. By now, the process manager is the most knowledgeable person regarding expectations at gates, what specific project teams are doing, and how to execute difficult tasks, and soon becomes the "resource person" and coach to whom project leaders turn.

Seek Continuous Improvement of Your Stage-Gate System

In spite of all the hard work and attempts to design "the perfect idea-to-launch process," it won't be! There are always things wrong with the process. Examples are:

- The gate deliverables templates are confusing or don't deliver what the gate-keepers want in the way they want to see it.
- Some activities that were recommended or mandated in the stages of the system should not have been; and others were mistakenly omitted and should be included.
- Ways of executing these activities—for example, guidelines and work-sheets—don't seem to work well.
- The gate meetings are cumbersome and need a rethink.
- The metrics are not operational (hard to measure) or not very revealing.

Thus, about four-to-six months into implementation, the process manager should reconvene the design team and *conduct a review and audit of the system's*

Figure 11.3: The Red-Green Chart Shows Time Slippage at Gates

	Gate 2	Gate 3	Gate 4	Gate 5	Post-Launch Review
Project Alpha	Aug 1/09 Sept 1/09	Dec 1/09 Feb 1/10	Sept 1/10 Sept 1/10	Dec 1/10	
Project Beta	Jul 1/09 Sept 1/09	Aug 1/09 Nov 1/09	Dec 1/09 Feb 1/10	Mar 1/10 Jun 1/10	Jun 1/11
Project Gamma	Feb 1/09 Apr 1/09	Jun 1/09 Aug 1/09	Dec 1/09 Feb 1/10	Jun 1/10 Jul 1/10	Jul 1/10
Project Delta	Jun 1/09 Jun 1/09	Jul 1/09 Nov 1/09	Feb 1/10 Mar 1/10	Jul 1/10 Aug 1/10	Aug 1/10
Project Echo	Sept 1/09 Sep 1/09	Nov 1/09 Dec 1/09	Aug 1/10 Sept 1/10	Dec 1/10	
Project Foxtrot	Sept 1/10 Sept 1/10	Oct 1/10 Dec 1/10	Apr 1/11		

In this grayscale chart, the dark cells are "red" and denote "late performance"
The light-gray cell are "green" and denote "on-time performance" (within one month)

performance and practices. This usually involves group meetings with project teams and the gatekeepers to determine what works, what doesn't, and what needs fixing.

Train New Employees

People come and go with increasing frequency these days. So it's not surprising that eighteen to twenty-four months into implementation, someone wakes up to the fact that one-third of the gatekeepers have never been on the formal training session and that many project team members are new. Thus, it's not surprising that some of the principles and practices that were understood back at the beginning are getting increasingly fuzzy. The process manager must ensure that new participants—both gatekeepers and team members—receive the necessary training, even if it has to be one-on-one. And arrange for an annual training session— an update for most people, but invaluable to new people.

TEN WAYS TO FAIL!

I wrap up this section with a tongue-in-cheek exposé of the top ten ways that people manage to ruin the implementation of *Stage-Gate*. Before you chuckle here, remember: These are all true—someone, somewhere did each one, and wished they had not!

10. Design the *Stage-Gate* process on your own, in your own office, and in a vacuum. You know best—teams are a waste of time!

9. Don't do any homework or auditing (Stage 1 above). You already know what the problem is in your company, so jump immediately to a solution. In fact, if you're really clever, you'll have a solution before you even know what the problem is!

8. Don't bother looking at other companies' *Stage-Gate* designs—their stages and gates, criteria and deliverables, activities, team structures, how they implemented, challenges, and so on. You have nothing to learn here.

7. If you do assemble a team, meet over several months in private. Then present "your grand design" and assume everyone in the company will applaud— even though they have not been involved in the design.

6. Don't seek outside help: Just read the book and design your process based on the generic one. Piece of cake! If you do seek help, hire a general or process consultant who knows nothing about product innovation management.

5. Don't waste time testing and seeking feedback from others in the company as your team designs your idea-to-launch system. After all, you're the design team and you're the experts—what do these "outsiders" know? Your design is likely to be near perfect!

4. When others do have questions or criticisms, treat these people as "cynics" and "negative thinkers." Refuse to deal with these objections, and never, never modify your new system . . . it's "your baby" and cast in marble.

3. Don't provide training—most of this "*Stage-Gate* stuff" is obvious. Anyone ought to be able to do it, just by reading the user's manual.

2. Speaking of manuals, make sure the *Stage-Gate* user's manual is heavy reading, dull, and full of checklists and forms. If in doubt, overwhelm the reader and user.

1. Don't bother installing a process manager—the system is so good, it will automatically implement itself.

After you're well into implementation, revisit this list above, and see how many misdeeds you're guilty of!

MOVING FORWARD

In Chapter 1, I challenged you and your business to focus on *bold innovation*—not just more of the same old vanilla development efforts that plague so many businesses these days. As a guide, I introduced the *Innovation Diamond* and the four key vectors that lead to superb performance in product innovation and will generate bold innovations for your business (Figure 1.2):

1. Crafting an *innovation strategy* that focuses your business on the right strategic arenas that will be your engines of growth.
2. Fostering a *climate, culture, and organization* that promotes bolder innovation.
3. Generating *big ideas* and driving these big concepts to market quickly via an idea-to-launch system, such as *Stage-Gate*.
4. Making the *right investment decisions* via building robust business cases and employing effective portfolio management to pick the winners.

We now come full circle. Two of the vectors in the Innovation Diamond are beyond the scope of this book, namely, innovation strategy and climate and culture, but I've given you good sources for these topics.[7] The critical topics of generating blockbuster ideas, building a solid business case, picking the winners, and designing and executing a world-class idea-to-launch system have been outlined here in sufficient detail that you and your colleagues should be able to move forward. This may be the end of the book, but for many readers, it's just the beginning of implementation . . . the next steps are yours.

APPENDIX A
The Benchmarker™ Audit Tool

A reliable, comprehensive evaluation of your product innovation performance can save you time and money by helping you to better understand which specific aspects of your innovation effort are working and which areas require attention. Benchmarker™, created by the Product Development Institute, is a reliable and trusted assessment tool designed specifically for product innovation. It is powered by the world's largest and most comprehensive innovation database. The audit model provides an executive *report card* detailing how your product innovation performance and practices compare with industry norms and with the best-performing companies.

Benchmarker involves seeking inputs from experts within your business on your new-product practices and performance (via an online questionnaire). It then evaluates your new-product development process and practices, relative to industry best practices, benchmarking these against hundreds of other businesses' and over 2,500 product launches, including the top-performing 20 percent. The audit model evaluates your new-product practices in ten critical areas, ranging from your development teams and resources, creativity, and ideation through to your development process, portfolio management, and product innovation strategy, along with the details of how you execute individual development projects. In the more comprehensive version of Benchmarker, personal and group interviews supplement the detailed survey questionnaire and provide more insight and qualitative conclusions as well.

By viewing your performance and practices versus the best businesses and the average or norm, you can spot what needs fixing, and thus Benchmarker is an excellent tool to build into Stage 1 (Figure 11.1) of your *Stage-Gate* design and implementation initiative.

For more information, see www.stage-gate.com.

357

APPENDIX B

The Navigator™ Stage-Gate *System*

SG Navigator™ is the official and operational *Stage-Gate* system—essentially "*Stage-Gate* in a box," ready to implement. It is designed to help organizations navigate the vulnerable and risky process of screening, selecting, and developing new products with greater ease, confidence, efficiency, and success. SG Navigator is the fastest and most economical way for your organization to get *Stage-Gate* up and running.

SG Navigator is a comprehensive, official interpretation of the world-class *Stage-Gate*® product-innovation business process—a road map for new-product success. It contains the required beliefs, goals, principles, measurements, and behaviors to achieve fast and successful product innovation.

SG Navigator is a practical, ready-to-use *operations guide*, integrating all best practices into detailed, cross-functional activities and requirements for each stage and gate for both the five-stage (high-risk) and three-stage (low-risk) *Stage-Gate* systems. Its content is the result of more than twenty years of empirical research, consulting engagements, and implementation experience with thousands of companies.

This off-the-shelf system contains:

- more than fifty ready-to-use templates (worksheets and deliverables) to guide each function through the activities required to complete each stage, ensuring appropriate effort and alignment from stage to stage and across functions,
- with clearly defined procedures, roles and responsibilities to ensure high-quality gates, seven research-based scorecards, gate presentations, and best-in-class gatekeeper rules of engagement,
- ten proprietary methods, guides, and illustrations designed to simplify complex tasks and challenges such as creating sharp, early product definitions,
- a do-it-yourself guide and sample project plan to enable quick and successful customization and implementation in your business.

The system is delivered in two popular formats, Web and Microsoft Word, to enable easy navigation for all your functional people involved in your product innovation system.

Source: www.stage-gate.com.

NOTES

CHAPTER 1: THE INNOVATION CHALLENGE

1. This first section is taken from an article by the author: R. G. Cooper, "The Innovation Dilemma: How to Innovate When the Market Is Mature," *Journal of Product Innovation Management* (hereafter *JPIM*) 28, no. 7 (December 2011).

2. R. G. Cooper, "Your NPD Portfolio May Be Harmful to Your Business's Health," PDMA *Visions Magazine* (hereafter *Visions*) 29, no. 2 (April 2005): 22–26.

3. R. G. Cooper, "New Products: What Separates the Winners from the Losers," chap. 1 in *The PDMA Handbook of New Product Development,* 2nd edition, ed. K. B. Kahn (New York: John Wiley & Sons, 2004).

4. Source of new-product sales data: M. Adams and D. Boike, "PDMA Foundation CPAS Study Reveals New Results," *Visions* 28, no. 3 (July 2004): 26–29; and *The PDMA Foundation's 2004 Comparative Performance Assessment Study (CPAS)* (Chicago: Product Development and Management Association, 2004). For mid-1990s data, see A. Griffin, *Drivers of NPD Success: The 1997 PDMA Report* (Chicago: PDMA, 1997).

5. R. G. Cooper and S. J. Edgett, "Maximizing Productivity in Product Innovation," *Research Technology Management* 51, no. 2 (March–April 2008): 47–58; also, Cooper, endnote 2.

6. I. Abel, "From Technology Imitation to Market Dominance: The Case of the iPod," *Competitiveness Review, An International Business Journal* 18, no. 3 (2008): 257–274.

7. A. G. Lafley and R. Charan, *The Game-Changer* (New York: Crown Business, Random House, 2008).

8. B. Kirk, "Creating an Environment for Effective Innovation," Proceedings of the Third International Stage-Gate Conference, Clearwater Beach, FL, February 2009.

9. The research underpinning the Innovation Diamond and the four vectors is based on a number of studies over the years: See, for example, R. G. Cooper and S. J. Edgett, "Maximizing Productivity in Product Innovation," endnote 5. Also see our major benchmarking study done with the APQC (American Productivity and Quality Center): R. G. Cooper, S. J. Edgett, and E. J. Kleinschmidt, "Benchmarking Best NPD Practices—Part 1: Culture, Climate, Teams and Senior Management's Role," *Research-Technology Management* 47, no. 1 (January–February 2004): 31–43; R. G. Cooper, S. J. Edgett, and E. J. Kleinschmidt, "Benchmarking Best NPD Practices—Part 2: Strategy, Resources and Portfolio Management Practices," *Research-Technology Management* 47, no. 3 (May–June 2004): 50–60; and R. G. Cooper, S. J. Edgett, and E. J. Kleinschmidt, "Benchmarking Best NPD Practices—Part 3: The NPD Process and Decisive Idea-to-Launch

Activities," *Research-Technology Management* 47, no. 6 (January–February 2005): 43–55. The roots of the Innovation Diamond and success vectors can be traced to earlier and pioneering work; see R. G. Cooper and E. J. Kleinschmidt, "Winning Businesses in Product Development: The Critical Success Factors," *Research-Technology Management* 50, no. 3 (May–June 1997): 52–66; and R. G. Cooper and E. J. Kleinschmidt, "Benchmarking the Firm's Critical Success Factors in New Product Development," *JPIM* 12, no. 5 (November 1995): 374–391.

10. For more on this important topic of developing an innovation strategy for your business, see R. G. Cooper and S. J. Edgett, *Product Innovation and Technology Strategy* (Ancaster, ON: Product Development Institute, www.stage-gate.com, 2009).

11. R. G. Cooper and S. J. Edgett, *Generating Breakthrough New Product Ideas: Feeding the Innovation Funnel* (Ancaster, ON: Product Development Institute, www.stage-gate.com, 2007); also R. G. Cooper and S. J. Edgett, "Ideation for Product Innovation: What Are the Best Sources?" *Visions* 32, no. 1 (March 2008): 12–17.

12. Adams and Boike, endnote 4.

13. "P&G Looks to Future with Major Ad Investments," *Toronto Globe and Mail,* September 6, 2010.

14. Our APQC benchmarking study, endnote 9. The new-product performance of businesses was gauged on ten metrics (such as: percentage of projects meeting sales and profit objectives; percentage of sales from new products; ROI on R&D spending; new-product profits relative to competitors; and time-to-market and slip-rate), which were then used to identify the top 20 percent of businesses—the "Best Innovators."

15. Cooper and Edgett, endnote 5.

16. Arthur D. Little, "How Companies Use Innovation to Improve Profitability and Growth," an Innovation Excellence Study, 2005.

17. R. M. Wolfe, *U.S. Businesses Report 2008 Worldwide R&D Expense of $330 Billion: Findings from New NSF Survey* (Arlington, VA: National Science Foundation, Division of Science Resources Statistics, NSF 10–322, May 2010).

18. "Obama to Raise R&D Spending to 3% of GDP," *Lab Manager Magazine,* October 15, 2009.

19. These are rough estimates and are based on the APQC benchmarking study, endnote 9.

20. Cited in C. F. von Braun, *The Innovation War* (Upper Saddle River, NJ: Prentice Hall, 1997).

21. Success rates from our APQC benchmarking study, endnote 9; also A. Griffin, *Drivers of NPD Success,* endnote 4.

22. Figure 1.5 is a composite chart based on a number of studies of the attrition rate of new products: Booz Allen Hamilton, *New Product Management for the 1980s* (New York: Booz Allen Hamilton, 1982); A. L. Page, "PDMA New Product Development Survey: Performance and Best Practices," PDMA Conference, Chicago, PDMA, November 13, 1991; A. Griffin, *Drivers of NPD Success,* endnote 4; and our own APQC study, cited in endnote 9.

23. Our APQC benchmarking study, endnote 9.

24. The original typology of new products was developed by Booz Allen Hamilton, endnote 22; the "all industry" data in Figure 1.5 are from the PDMA best-practices study, endnote 4.

25. The PDMA article that provides citations and a review of research into product innovation management is W. Biemans, A. Griffin, and R. Moenaert, "Twenty Years of

the *Journal of Product Innovation Management:* History, Participants, and Knowledge Stock and Flows," *Journal of Product Innovation Management* 24 (2007): 193–213.

26. According to the PDMA best-practices studies; see Adams and Boike, "PDMA Foundation CPAS Study Reveals New Trends," and Griffin, *Drivers of NPD Success,* endnote 4. See also J. Grölund, D. Rönneberg, and J. Frishammar, "Open Innovation and the Stage-Gate Process: A Revised Model for New Product Development," *California Management Review* 5, no. 3 (Spring 2010): 106–131.

CHAPTER 2: WHY NEW PRODUCTS WIN

1. See endnote 9 in chap. 1 for a summary of the benchmarking studies, the source of many of the bar charts in this chapter. The large-sample studies of new-product successes and failures (for example, the NewProd studies) are summarized in a number of sources, for example: R. G. Cooper, "The Stage-Gate® Product Innovation System: From Idea to Launch," in *Encyclopedia of Technology and Innovation Management,* ed. V. K. Narayanan and G. O'Connor (Chichester, West Sussex, UK: John Wiley & Sons, 2010), chap. 24, 157–167; R. G. Cooper, "New Products: What Separates the Winners from the Losers," in *PDMA Handbook for New Product Development,* 2nd edition, ed. K. B. Kahn (New York: John Wiley & Sons, 2004), chap. 1, 3–28; R. G. Cooper, "Stage-Gate® New Product Development Processes: A Game Plan from Idea to Launch," in *The Portable MBA in Project Management,* ed. E. Verzuk (Hoboken, NJ: John Wiley & Sons, 2004), chap. 11, 309–346; R. G. Cooper, "New Product Development," in *International Encyclopedia of Business and Management: Encyclopedia of Marketing,* 1st edition, ed. M. J. Baker (London: International Thomson Business Press, 1999), 342–355; and R. G. Cooper, "The Invisible Success Factors in Product Innovation," *JPIM* 16, no. 2 (April 1999): 115–133.

2. Reasons for failure are based on research summarized in Cooper, "New Products," endnote 1 above.

3. This section on reasons for new-product failure is updated from a section that first appeared in R. G. Cooper and S. J. Edgett, *Lean, Rapid and Profitable New Product Development* (Ancaster, ON: Product Development Institute, 2005), www.stage-gate.com.

4. Some of these success factors are reported in various publications. See endnote 1 above.

5. The research studies that identified these factors and results are summarized in endnote 1 above.

6. Parts of this section are paraphrased from Cooper, *PDMA Handbook,* endnote 1 above.

7. See endnote 14 in chap. 1.

8. R. G. Cooper and A. Dreher, "Voice of Customer Methods: What Is the Best Source of New Product Ideas?" *Marketing Management Magazine* (Winter 2010), extended online version at: http://www.marketingpower.com/ResourceLibrary/Publications/Marketing Management/2010/4/38–48_Xtended version3.pdf.

9. For Toyota's seven principles, see: J. Morgan, "Applying Lean Principles to Product Development," report from SAE International Society of Mechanical Engineers, 2005, www.sae.org.

10. Havelock and Elder, as cited in E. M. Rogers, "The R&D/Marketing Interface in the Technological Innovation Process," in M. M. Saghafi and A. K. Gupta, eds., *Managing the R&D/Marketing Interface for Process Success: The Telecommunications Focus,* vol. 1, *Advances in Telecommunications Management* (Greenwich, CT: JAI Press, 1990).

11. Parts of this section are based on an article by the author: R. G. Cooper and S. J. Edgett, "The Dark Side of Time and Time Metrics in Product Innovation," *Visions* 26, no. 22 (April–May 2002): 14–16.

12. Quoted in T. J. Peters, *Thriving on Chaos* (New York: Harper & Row, 1988).

CHAPTER 3: DRIVERS OF SUCCESS—WHY THE BEST INNOVATORS EXCEL

1. See endnote 9 in chap. 1 for a summary of the benchmarking studies, the source of the bar charts in this chapter. See endnote 1 in chap. 2 for the NewProd studies of individual new products, successes versus failures.

2. Ibid.

3. S. Osborne, "Make More and Better Product Decisions for Greater Impact," *Proceedings, PDMA Product & Service Innovation Conference, Atlanta: "Compete to Win"* (Mount Laurel, NJ: Product Development and Management Association, 2006).

4. R. G. Cooper, "Your NPD Portfolio May Be Harmful to Your Business's Health," *Visions* 29, no. 2 (April 2005): 22–26.

5. A. J. Campbell and R. G. Cooper, "Do Customer Partnerships Improve Success Rates?" *Industrial Marketing Management* 28, no. 5 (1999): 507–519.

6. M. E. Porter, *Competitive Advantage: Creating and Sustaining Superior Performance* (New York: Free Press, 1985).

7. G. Day, *Analysis for Strategic Marketing Decisions* (St. Paul, MN: West Publishing, 1986).

8. See APQC study and success-failure products studies, endnote 1.

9. T. J. Peters, *Thriving on Chaos* (New York: Harper & Row, 1988).

10. Source of P&G quotation: M. Mills, "Implementing a Stage-Gate Process at P&G," Proceedings, First Annual Stage-Gate Summit, St. Petersburg Beach, FL, 2007.

11. Peters, endnote 9, p. 302.

12. See drivers of new-product development success in endnote 1, chap. 2.

13. For best practices and remedies, see M. J. Baker, ed., *International Encyclopedia of Business and Management: Encyclopedia of Marketing, First Edition* (London: International Thomson Business Press, 1999); K. B. Kahn, ed., *The PDMA Handbook of New Product Development,* 2nd edition (New York: John Wiley & Sons, 2004); H. Levine, ed., *Project Portfolio Management: A Practical Guide to Selecting Projects, Managing Portfolios, and Maximizing Benefits* (San Francisco: Jossey-Bass Business and Management, John Wiley & Sons Imprint, 2005); V. K. Narayanan and G. O'Connor, eds., *Encyclopedia of Technology and Innovation Management* (Chichester, West Sussex, UK: John Wiley & Sons, 2010); and B. L. Bayus, ed., *Wiley International Encyclopedia of Marketing: Product Innovation and Management,* vol. 5 (West Sussex, U.K.: Wiley, December 2010), http://onlinelibrary.wiley.com.

14. Parts of this section are taken from R. G. Cooper and S. J. Edgett, "Overcoming the Crunch in Resources for New Product Development," *Research-Technology Management* 46, no. 3 (May–June 2003): 48–58.

15. Most of the conclusions regarding new-product problems and failure causes are based on several benchmarking studies (see endnote 1 above); but an additional and rich source of information, particularly the anecdotal information that leads to more insight into the problem and possible solutions, is the result of "problem detection sessions" held in over 300 businesses by the Product Development Institute Inc. over ten years.

16. APQC and previous benchmarking studies, endnote 9 in chap. 1.

17. R. G. Cooper, S. J. Edgett, and E. J. Kleinschmidt, *New Product Development Best Practices Study: What Distinguishes the Top Performers* (Houston, TX: American Productivity and Quality Center, 2003). See also endnote 9 in chap. 1.

18. "Overcoming the Crunch in Resources," see endnote 14.

19. Ibid.

20. A number of studies have been undertaken to determine the drivers of sales revenue from new products. See summary in: R. G. Cooper, "A *Stage-Gate*® Idea-to-Launch Framework for Driving New Products to Market," chap. 7.1 in *Project Portfolio Management*, ed. H. Levine (San Francisco: Jossey-Bass, 2005), 309–346; and earlier studies: R. G. Cooper, "Benchmarking New Product Performance: Results of the Best Practices Study," *European Management Journal* 16, no. 1 (1998): 1–7; also R. G. Cooper and E. J. Kleinschmidt, "Winning Businesses in Product Development: Critical Success Factors," *Research-Technology Management* 39, no. 4 (July–August 1996): 18–29.

21. R. G. Cooper, S. J. Edgett, and E. J. Kleinschmidt, "New Problems, New Solutions: Making Portfolio Management More Effective," *Research-Technology Management* 43, no. 2 (2000): 18–33.

22. This resource capacity analysis is taken from R. G. Cooper, "The Invisible Success Factors in Product Innovation," *JPIM* 16, no. 2 (April 1999): 115–133.

23. APQC benchmarking study, see endnote 9 in chap. 1.

24. The name "Stage-Gate" first appeared in print in R. G. Cooper, "The New Product Process: A Decision Guide for Managers," *Journal of Marketing Management* 3, no. 3 (1988): 238–255.

25. Adapted from R. G. Cooper, "The Stage-Gate Idea-to-Launch Process—Update, What's New and NexGen Systems," *JPIM* 25, no. 3 (May 2008): 213–232.

26. First-generation new-product processes were described in Booz Allen Hamilton, *New Product Management for the 1980s* (New York: Booz Allen Hamilton, 1982).

27. M. Mills, "Implementing a Stage-Gate® Process at Procter & Gamble," Proceedings, American Manufacturing Excellence "Focus on Global Excellence" Conference, Cincinnati, OH, 2004.

28. The impacts of implementing a stage-and-gate process have been reported in numerous publications over the years. See, for example, R. G. Cooper, "The Stage-Gate® Product Innovation System: From Idea to Launch," in *Encyclopedia of Technology and Innovation Management*, ed. Narayanan and O'Connor, chap. 24, 157–167 (2010); and as early as R. G. Cooper and E. J. Kleinschmidt, "New Product Processes at Leading Industrial Firms," *Industrial Marketing Management* 10, no. 2 (May 1991): 137–147.

29. M. Mills, "Implementing a Stage-Gate Process at P&G," endnote 10.

30. See endnote 28.

31. T. Agan, *Renovating Innovation: Why the Best CPG Companies Derive over Six Times More Revenue from New Products vs. the Rest* (n.p.: A. C. Nielsen, 2010).

CHAPTER 4: THE *STAGE-GATE*® IDEA-TO-LAUNCH SYSTEM

1. A quotation describing the quality process, which has equal applicability to the new-product process. See T. H. Berry, *Managing the Total Quality Transformation* (New York: McGraw-Hill, 1991).

2. Section taken from R. G. Cooper, "The Stage-Gate Idea-to-Launch Process—Update, What's New and NexGen Systems," *JPIM* 25, no. 3 (May 2008): 213–232.

3. R. G. Cooper, "New Products: What Separates the Winners from the Losers," in *PDMA Handbook for New Product Development*, 2nd edition, ed. K. B. Kahn (New York: John Wiley & Sons, 2004), chap. 1, 3–28.

4. This chapter is taken from many sources. See endnote 1 in chap. 2; also Cooper, endnote 2 above; also R. G. Cooper, "Stage-Gate Idea-to-Launch System," *Wiley International Encyclopedia of Marketing: Product Innovation and Management*, vol. 5, ed. B. L. Bayus (West Sussex, U.K.: Wiley, December 2010).

5. M. Mills, "Implementing a Stage-Gate® Process at Procter & Gamble," Proceedings, First International Stage-Gate Conference, St. Petersburg Beach, FL, February 2007.

6. NPD 2.0 is described in R. D. Ledford, "NPD 2.0: Raising Emerson's NPD Process to the Next Level," *Innovations* (St. Louis, MO: Emerson Electric, 2006), 4–7.

7. R. G. Cooper, S. J. Edgett, and E. J. Kleinschmidt, *New Product Development Best Practices Study: What Distinguishes the Top Performers* (Houston, TX: American Productivity and Quality Center, 2002); and R. G. Cooper, S. J. Edgett, and E. J. Kleinschmidt, "Benchmarking Best NPD Practices—Part 3: The NPD Process and Decisive Idea-to-Launch Activities," *Research-Technology Management* 47, no. 6 (January–February 2005): 43–55.

8. "Stage-Gate" is a term coined by the author—see endnote 24 in chap. 3. Second-generation processes are what many companies began to implement toward the end of the 1980s; the third-generation processes of the late 1990s have improved time efficiencies. For background on the evolution, see R. G. Cooper, "Third-Generation New Product Processes," *JPIM* 11, no. 1 (1994): 3–14.

9. D. Arra, "How ITT Drives Value-Creation with Value Based Product Development," Proceedings, Stage-Gate Summit 2010, Clearwater Beach, FL, 2010.

10. R. G. Cooper and A. Dreher, "Voice of Customer Methods Versus the Rest: What Is the Best Source of New-Product Ideas?" *Marketing Management Magazine,* Winter 2010, online extended version, http://www.marketingpower.com/ResourceLibrary/Publications/MarketingManagement/2010/4/38–48_Xtended version3.pdf.

11. EXFO Engineering is a medium-sized manufacturer of fiber-optic test equipment, with remarkably sound new-product methods; the firm has won the PDMA's "outstanding corporate innovator" award based on its portfolio management and stage-and-gate practices.

12. Ledford, endnote 6.

13. This section taken from Cooper, endnote 2.

14. T. Leavitt, "Marketing Myopia," *Harvard Business Review* (July–August 1960): 45–56.

15. G. Belair, "Beyond Gates: Building the Right NPD Organization," Proceedings, First International Stage-Gate Conference, St. Petersburg Beach, FL, 2007.

CHAPTER 5: NEXT-GENERATION *STAGE-GATE*®—HOW
COMPANIES HAVE EVOLVED AND ACCELERATED THE SYSTEM

1. Much of this chapter is adapted or taken from articles by the author: R. G. Cooper, "The Stage-Gate Idea-to-Launch Process—Update, What's New and NexGen Systems," *JPIM* 25, no. 3 (May 2008): 213–232; also: R. G. Cooper, "How Companies Are Re-inventing Their Idea-to-Launch Methodologies," *Research-Technology Management* 52, no. 2 (March–April 2009): 47–57.

2. R. G. Cooper and S. J. Edgett, *Lean, Rapid and Profitable New Product Development* (Ancaster, ON: Product Development Institute, www.stage-gate.com, 2005); also R. G. Cooper, "Formula for Success," *Marketing Management Magazine* (American Marketing Association) (March–April 2006): 21–24.

3. Section taken from Cooper, *JPIM* (2008), endnote 1.

4. Cooper, endnote 5.

5. L.Y. Cohen, P. W. Kamienski, and R. L. Espino, "Gate System Focuses Industrial Basic Research," *Research-Technology Management* (July–August 1998): 34–37.

6. R. G. Cooper, "Managing Technology Development Projects—Different Than Traditional Development Projects," *Research-Technology Management* (November–December 2006): 23–31.

7. K. B. Kahn, ed., *The PDMA Handbook of New Product Development*, 2nd edition (New York: John Wiley & Sons, 2005): 599.

8. Spiral development is described in: R. G. Cooper and S. J. Edgett, "Maximizing Productivity in Product Innovation," *Research Technology Management* (March–April 2008): 47–58.

9. Section taken from R. G. Cooper, "NexGen Stage-Gate®—What Leading Companies Are Doing to Re-Invent Their NPD Processes," *Visions* 32, no. 3 (September 2008): 6–10.

10. Section taken from Cooper, *JPIM* (2008), endnote 1.

11. J. Morgan, "Applying Lean Principles to Product Development," report from SAE International Society of Mechanical Engineers, www.shop.sae.org, 2005.

12. Ibid.

13. G. Belair, "Beyond Gates: Building the Right NPD Organization," Proceedings, First International Stage-Gate Conference, St. Petersburg Beach, FL, 2007.

14. R. Arra, "Value Based Product Development (VBPD): ITT's Initiative to Improve Product Generation," Proceedings, First International Stage-Gate Conference, St. Petersburg Beach, FL, 2007.

15. C. Fiore, *Accelerated Product Development* (New York: Productivity Production Press, 2005).

16. Cooper, endnote 2.

17. Cooper and Edgett, endnote 2.

18. R. D. Ledford, "NPD 2.0: Raising Emerson's NPD Process to the Next Level," *Innovations* (St. Louis, MO: Emerson Electric, 2006): 4–7.

19. R. G. Cooper and M. Mills, "Succeeding at New Products the P&G Way: A Key Element Is Using the Innovation Diamond," *Visions* 29, no. 4 (October 2005): 9–13.

20. S. Bull, "Innovating for Success: How EXFO's NPDS Delivers Winning New Products," Proceedings, First International Stage-Gate Conference, St. Petersburg Beach, FL, 2007.

21. H. Chesbrough, "'Open Innovation' Myths, Realities, and Opportunities," *Visions* 30, no. 2 (April 2006): 13–15; and H. Chesbrough, *Open Innovation: The New Imperative for Creating and Profiting from Technology* (Cambridge: Harvard Business School Press, 2003).

22. M. Docherty, "Primer On 'Open Innovation': Principles and Practice," *Visions* 30, no. 2 (April 2006).

23. R. G. Cooper and S. J. Edgett, *Generating Breakthrough New Product Ideas: Feeding the Innovation Funnel* (Ancaster, ON: Product Development Institute, www.stage -gate.com, 2007), chap. 5; also J. Grölund, D. Rönneberg, and J. Frishammar, "Open

Innovation and the Stage-Gate Process: A Revised Model for New Product Development," *California Management Review* 5, no. 3 (Spring 2010): 106–131.

24. Docherty, endnote 22.

25. Cooper and Edgett, endnote 2; section taken from Cooper, *JPIM* (2008), endnote 1.

26. Some of these "new activities" are based on C. Gagnon, "Open Innovation and Innovation Management Processes: Boosting the Impact of Innovation," Proceedings, Stage-Gate Summit 2010, Clearwater Beach, FL, 2010.

27. Ibid.

28. Adapted and modified from the Saab Aerospace PLC model, company brochure.

29. Section taken from R. G. Cooper, *Winning at New Products: Pathways to Profitable Innovation* (Microsoft Corporation white paper, 2005), www.microsoft.com. Also available on www.stage-gate.com.

30. *SG-Navigator*™ is a standard best-in-class *Stage-Gate*® framework, available from Stage Gate International at www.stage-gate.com.

31. *Business Week* editorial staff, "Six Sigma: So Yesterday? In an Innovation Economy, It's No Longer a Cure-All," *Business Week*, IN (Inside Innovation), section 11 (June 11, 2007).

32. Ibid.

33. B. Wood, "At 3M, a Struggle Between Efficiency and Creativity," *Business Week*, IN (Inside Innovation), sections 8–10 (June 11, 2007).

34. S. Edgett, *Portfolio Management: Optimizing for Success* (Houston, TX: APQC—American Productivity & Quality Center, 2007).

35. Evaluations of software are available from Stage-Gate International at www.stage-gate.com.

36. M. Mills, "Implementing a Stage-Gate Process at Procter & Gamble," Proceedings, Focus on Global Excellence Conference (Cincinnati, OH: Association for Manufacturing Excellence, 2004).

37. R. G. Cooper and M. Mills, "Succeeding at New Products the P&G Way: A Key Element Is Using the Innovation Diamond," *Visions* 29, no. 4 (October 2005): 9–13.

CHAPTER 6: DISCOVERY—THE QUEST FOR BREAKTHROUGH IDEAS

1. Arthur D. Little, "How Companies Use Innovation to Improve Profitability and Growth," an Innovation Excellence study, 2005, http://www.adl.com/reports.html ?view=53.

2. See benchmarking study, endnote 9 in chap. 1.

3. A guide to the development of product innovation and technology strategy is R. G. Cooper and S. J. Edgett, *Product Innovation and Technology Strategy* (Ancaster, ON: Product Development Institute, www.stage-gate.com, 2009). See also R. G. Cooper and S. J. Edgett, "Developing a Product Innovation and Technology Strategy for Your Business," *Research-Technology Management* 53, no. 3 (May–June 2010): 33–40.

4. J. Erler, "A Brilliant New Product Idea Generation Program," Proceedings, Second International Stage-Gate Conference, St. Petersburg Beach, FL, 2008.

5. R. G. Cooper and S. J. Edgett, "Ideation for Product Innovation: What Are the Best Sources?" *Visions* 32, no. 1 (March 2008): 12–17.

6. Parts of this chapter are taken from three sources: R. G. Cooper and S. J. Edgett, *Generating Breakthrough New Product Ideas: Feeding the Innovation Funnel* (Ancaster,

ON: Product Development Institute, www.stage-gate.com, 2007); also ibid.; and R. G. Cooper and A. Dreher, "Voice-of-Customer Methods Versus the Rest: What Is the Best Source of New-Product Ideas?" *Marketing Management Magazine* (Winter 2010), extended online version at http://www.marketingpower.com/ResourceLibrary/Publications/ MarketingManagement/2010/4/38–48_Xtended version3.pdf.

7. Example provided by Five I's Consulting Group, Dornbirn, Austria.

8. For more information on the use of lead users in idea generation, see E. A. Von Hippel, "Lead Users: A Source of Novel Product Concepts," *Management Science* 32, no. 7 (1986): 791–806. See also C. Herstatt and E. A. Von Hippel, "From Experience: Developing New Product Concepts via the Lead User Method: A Case Study in a 'Low Tech' Field," *JPIM* 9 (1992): 213–221; and G. L. Urban and E. A. Von Hippel, "Lead User Analyses for the Development of New Industrial Products," *Management Science* 34, no. 5 (May 1988): 569–582. See also E. A. Von Hippel, *The Sources of Innovation* (New York: Oxford University Press, 1988).

9. Adapted from E. A. Von Hippel, S. Thomke, and M. Sonnack, "Creating Breakthroughs at 3M," *Harvard Business Review* (September–October 1999): 47–57.

10. C. J. Beale, "On-Line Communities Shake Up NPD—an Introduction to the Value of This New Tool," *Visions* 32, no. 4 (December 2008): 14–18.

11. O. Gadiesh and J. L. Gilbert, "How to Map Your Industry's Profit Pool," *Harvard Business Review* (May–June 1998): 3–11.

12. G. Hamel and C. K. Prahalad, *Competing for the Future* (Cambridge: Harvard Business School Press, April 1996).

13. C. M. Christensen, *The Innovator's Dilemma* (New York: HarperCollins, 2000). Also see R. N. Foster, *Innovation: The Attacker's Advantage* (Summit Books, 1988).

14. Foster, endnote 13.

15. G. Day and P. Shoemaker, "Scanning the Periphery," *Harvard Business Review* 84, no. 2 (November 2005): 135–148.

16. Ibid.

17. Questions adapted from ibid.

18. Parts of this section on scenarios are taken from P. Schwartz, "The Official Future, Self-Delusion and Value of Scenarios," *Financial Times,* Mastering Risk section, May 2, 2000.

19. K. Hardy, "Maximizing Return on Investment: Rust-Oleum's 'Focused' Idea Generation Program," Proceedings, Stage-Gate Summit 2010, Clearwater Beach, FL, 2010.

20. H. Chesbrough, "Open Innovation: The New Imperative for Creating and Profiting from Technology" (Cambridge: Harvard Business School Press, 2003); and H. Chesbrough, "'Open Innovation' Myths, Realities, and Opportunities," *Visions* 30, no. 2 (April 2006): 18–19; also see M. Docherty, "Primer on 'Open Innovation': Principles and Practice," *Visions* 30, no. 2 (April 2006): 13–17.

21. Parts of this section are taken from "The Love-In: The Move Toward Open Innovation Is Beginning to Transform Entire Industries," *Economist* print edition, special section on innovation, October 11, 2007.

22. Ibid.

23. These examples are from P. Boutin, "Crowdsourcing: Consumers as Creators," *Business Week,* July 13, 2006.

24. L. Huston and N. Sakkab, "Connect and Develop: Inside Procter & Gamble's New Model For Innovation," *Harvard Business Review* 84, no. 3 (March 2006).

25. Source of example is HYVE AG, Germany; see also R. G. Cooper and A. Dreher, "Voice-of-Customer Methods Versus the Rest," endnote 6.

26. For more on how to implement open innovation, see R. G. Cooper and S. J. Edgett, *Generating Breakthrough New Product Ideas: Feeding the Innovation Funnel* (Ancaster, ON: Product Development Institute Inc., www.stage-gate.com, 2005), chap. 5.

27. Adapted from Falco-Archer, *Patent Mining*, 2005, www.falcoarcher.com.

28. D. H. Pink, *Drive: The Surprising Truth About What Motivates Us* (New York: Riverhead Books/Penguin, 2009).

29. M. Maley, "Driving Global Innovation: Kellogg Company's Secret Ingredient—People!" Proceedings, Stage-Gate Summit 2010, Clearwater Beach, FL, 2010.

CHAPTER 7: THE FRONT-END WORK—
FROM DISCOVERY TO DEVELOPMENT

1. A. J. Campbell and R. G. Cooper, "Do Customer Partnerships Improve Success Rates?" *Industrial Marketing Management* 28, no. 5 (1999): 507–519.

2. Parts of this section on VoC are based on the work of Abbie Griffin, professor at the University of Illinois and former editor of the *Journal of Product Innovation Management*.

CHAPTER 8: PICKING THE WINNERS—
INVESTING IN THE RIGHT PROJECTS

1. This chapter draws on many sources, articles, and books by the author and co-workers. R. G. Cooper, *Product Leadership: Pathways to Profitable Innovation*, 2nd edition (New York: Perseus Publishing, 2005); R. G. Cooper, "Portfolio Management for Product Innovation," Chapter 7.2 in *Project Portfolio Management: A Practical Guide to Selecting Projects, Managing Portfolios, and Maximizing Benefits*, ed. H. Levine (San Francisco: Jossey-Bass Business & Management, John Wiley & Sons Imprint, 2005); R. G. Cooper and S. J. Edgett, "Ten Ways to Make Better Portfolio and Project Selection Decisions," *Visions* 30, no. 3 (June 2006): 11–15; see also R. G. Cooper, S. J. Edgett, and E. J. Kleinschmidt, "Benchmarking Best NPD Practices—Part 2: Strategy, Resources and Portfolio Management Practices," *Research-Technology Management* 47, no. 3 (May–June 2004): 50–60; R. G. Cooper, S. J. Edgett, and E. J. Kleinschmidt, "Portfolio Management: Fundamental to New Product Success," in *The PDMA Toolbox for New Product Development*, ed. P. Beliveau, A. Griffin, and S. Somermeyer (New York: John Wiley & Sons, 2002): 331–364. Portfolio management is described in greater detail in R. G. Cooper, S. J. Edgett, and E. J. Kleinschmidt, *Portfolio Management for New Products*, 2nd edition (New York: Perseus Publishing, 2002).

2. Parts of this section are taken from an article by the author and co-worker: R. G. Cooper and S. J. Edgett, "Overcoming the Crunch in Resources for New Product Development," *Research-Technology Management* 46, no. 3 (2003): 48–58.

3. Cooper, Edgett, and Kleinschmidt, "Benchmarking Best NPD Practices," endnote 1.

4. Portfolio management was originally defined in R. G. Cooper, S. J. Edgett, and E. J. Kleinschmidt, "Portfolio Management in New Product Development: Lessons from the Leaders—Part I," *Research-Technology Management* (September–October 1997): 16–28; also Part II (November–December 1997): 43–57.

5. Parts of this section are taken from R. G. Cooper, "Maximizing the Value of Your New Product Portfolio: Methods, Metrics and Scorecards," *Current Issues in Technology*

Management, Stevens Institute of Technology: Stevens Alliance for Technology Management, vol. 7, iss. 1 (Winter 2003): 1.

6. NPV is explained in Investopedia, www.investopedia.com.

7. T. Faulkner, "Applying 'Options Thinking' to R&D Valuation," *Research-Technology Management* (May–June 1995): 50–57.

8. For more information on the Productivity Index, see *Portfolio Management for New Products* and "Ten Ways to Make Better Portfolio and Project Selection Decisions," both in endnote 1.

9. Options pricing theory uses the Black-Scholes options pricing formula, a direct result of work by Robert Merton as well as Black and Scholes. In 1997, Scholes and Merton won the Nobel Prize in economics for this work (Black had died).

10. A summary of these success drivers is in the PDMA handbook: R. G. Cooper, "New Products: What Separates the Winners from the Losers," in *PDMA Handbook for New Product Development*, 2nd edition, ed. K. B. Kahn (New York: John Wiley & Sons, 2004), chap. 1, 3–28.

11. An example of a rigorous scoring model, research-based, is in R. G. Cooper, "The NewProd System: The Industry Experience," *JPIM* 9 (1992): 113–127.

12. Results from different portfolio methods, and management's ratings of these methods, are given in *Portfolio Management for New Products*, chap. 6, in endnote 1.

13. The "success criteria" method is explained more in "Ten Ways to Make Better Portfolio and Project Selection Decisions" in endnote 1.

14. The practical use of success criteria is explained in R. G. Cooper and M. Mills, "Succeeding at New Products the P&G Way: A Key Element Is Using the 'Innovation Diamond,'" *Visions* 29, no. 4 (October 2005): 9–13.

15. W. E. Souder, "A System for Using R&D Project Evaluation Methods," *Research Management* 21 (September 1978): 21–37.

16. G. L. Lillien and P. Kotler, *Marketing Decision Making: A Model-Building Approach* (New York: Harper & Row, 1983); see also W. E. Souder and T. Mandakovic, "R&D Project Selection Models," *Research Management* 29, no. 4 (1986): 36–42; F. Zahedi, "The Analytic Hierarchy Process—a Survey of the Method and Its Applications," *Interfaces* 16, no. 4 (1986); 96–108. The software *Expert Choice* is found at www.expert choice.com.

17. Stage-Gate for advanced technology and technology platforms is described in R. G. Cooper, "Managing Technology Development Projects—Different Than Traditional Development Projects," *Research-Technology Management* 49, no. 6 (November–December 2006): 23–31.

18. Celanese Corporation (formerly Hoechst Chemical), as described in *Portfolio Management for New Products*, endnote 1.

19. S. Bull, "Innovating for Success: How EXFO's NPDS Delivers Winning Products," Proceedings, First International Stage-Gate Conference, St. Petersburg Beach, FL, February 2007.

20. Portfolio management practices and performance studies are summarized in *Portfolio Management for New Products*, endnote 1.

21. Bubble diagrams with "value" measured *qualitatively* are recommended in P. Roussel, K. N. Saad, and T. J. Erickson, *Third Generation R&D, Managing the Link to Corporate Strategy* (Cambridge: Harvard Business School Press & Arthur D. Little, 1991).

22. *Portfolio Management for New Products*, endnote 1.

23. For more on road mapping, see R. R. Cosner, E. J. Hynds, A. R. Fusfeld, C. V. Loweth, C. Scouten, and R. Albright, "Integrating Roadmapping into Technical Planning," *Research-Technology Management* (November–December 2007): 31–48; also T. Talonen and K. Hakkarainen, "Strategies for Driving R&D and Technology Development," *Research-Technology Management* (September–October 2008): 54–60; and P. Groenveld, "Roadmapping Integrates Business and Technology," *Research-Technology Management* (November–December 2007): 49–58. Some of this section on road mapping is taken from Alcatel-Lucent Technologies. See R. E. Albright, "Roadmaps and Roadmapping: Linking Business Strategy and Technology Planning," Proceedings, Portfolio Management for New Product Development, Fort Lauderdale, FL, Institute for International Research and Product Development & Management Association, January 2001; see also M. H. Meyer and A. P. Lehnerd, *The Power of Platforms* (New York: Free Press, 1997).

24. This section is based on "Ten Ways to Make Better Portfolio and Project Selection Decisions" in endnote 1.

25. Source of information deficiencies is R. G. Cooper, S. J. Edgett, and E. J. Kleinschmidt, "Benchmarking Best NPD Practices—Part 3: The NPD Process and Decisive Idea-to-Launch Activities," *Research-Technology Management* 47, no. 6 (January–February 2005): 43–55.

26. S. J. Edgett (subject matter expert), *Portfolio Management: Optimizing for Success* (Houston, TX: APQC, American Productivity & Quality Center, 2007).

27. Portfolio management practices and performance studies are summarized in *Portfolio Management for New Products*, endnote 1.

28. Ibid.

CHAPTER 9: MAKING THE GATES WORK—GATES WITH TEETH

1. Sections in this chapter are from several sources by the author. See R. G. Cooper, "The Stage-Gate Idea-to-Launch Process—Update, What's New and NexGen Systems," *JPIM* 25, no. 3 (May 2008): 213–232; R. G. Cooper, "NexGen Stage-Gate®—What Leading Companies Are Doing to Re-Invent Their NPD Processes," *Visions* 32, no. 3 (September 2008): 6–10; R. G. Cooper, "Effective Gating: Make Product Innovation More Productive by Using Gates with Teeth," *Marketing Management Magazine* (March–April 2009): 12–17; and R. G. Cooper, "How Companies Are Re-inventing Their Idea-to-Launch Methodologies," *Research-Technology Management* 52, no. 2 (March–April 2009): 47–57.

2. See APQC benchmarking study, endnote 9 in chap. 1; in particular, R. G. Cooper, S. J. Edgett, and E. J. Kleinschmidt, "Benchmarking Best NPD Practices—Part 3: The NPD Process and Key Idea-to-Launch Activities," *Research-Technology Management* 47, no. 6 (2005): 43–55.

3. The term "gates with teeth" comes from S. Jenner, "'Gates with Teeth': Implementing a Centre of Excellence for Investment Decisions," Proceedings, First International Stage-Gate Conference, St. Petersburg Beach, FL, February 2007. Jenner is an auditor of IT project proposals in the government of the United Kingdom (Criminal Justice Information Technology). The U.K. government has implemented its version of *Stage-Gate* called "Gateways" for government-funded internal initiatives. See also R. G.

Cooper, "Effective Gating: Make Product Innovation More Productive by Using Gates with Teeth," *Marketing Management Magazine* (March–April 2009): 12–17.

4. The effects of cycle-time reduction and resource deficiencies are outlined in R. G. Cooper and S. J. Edgett, "The Dark Side of Time and Time Metrics in Product Innovation," *Visions* 26, no. 22 (April–May 2002): 14–16; and R. G. Cooper and S. J. Edgett, "Overcoming the Crunch in Resources for New Product Development," *Research-Technology Management* 46, no. 3 (May–June 2003): 48–58.

5. S. Osborne, "Make More and Better Product Decisions for Greater Impact," PDMA Product and Service Conference "Compete to Win," Atlanta, GA, October 2006.

6. Five I's Innovation Management, Austria, a firm specializing in the design and installation of *Stage-Gate* in Europe.

7. See S. J. Edgett (subject matter expert), *Portfolio Management: Optimizing for Success* (Houston: APQC, American Productivity & Quality Center, 2007).

8. See S. Bull, "Innovating for Success: How EXFO's NPDS Delivers Winning Products," Proceedings, First International Stage-Gate Conference, St. Petersburg Beach, FL, February 2007.

CHAPTER 10: DEVELOPMENT, TESTING, AND LAUNCH

1. Some of this section is taken from the Navigator™ *Stage-Gate* system, available at www.stage-gate.com.

2. R. G. Cooper and S. J. Edgett, "The Dark Side of Time and Time Metrics in Product Innovation," *Visions* 26, no. 22 (April–May 2002): 14–16.

3. See NewProd studies, endnote 1, chap. 2.

CHAPTER 11: IMPLEMENTING *STAGE-GATE*® IN YOUR BUSINESS

1. R. G. Cooper, S. J. Edgett, and E. J. Kleinschmidt, *Portfolio Management for New Products,* 2nd edition (New York: Perseus Publishing, 2002).

2. R. G. Cooper, *Product Leadership: Pathways to Profitable Innovation*, 2nd edition (New York: Perseus Publishing, 2005).

3. R. G. Cooper and S. J. Edgett, *Generating Breakthrough New Product Ideas: Feeding the Innovation Funnel* (Ancaster, ON: Product Development Institute Inc., www.stage -gate.com, 2007).

4. R. G. Cooper and S. J. Edgett, *Lean, Rapid and Profitable New Product Development* (Ancaster, ON: Product Development Institute, www.stage-gate.com, 2005).

5. R. G. Cooper and S. J. Edgett, *Product Innovation and Technology Strategy* (Ancaster, ON: Product Development Institute, www.stage-gate.com, 2009).

6. H. Molitoris, "TARDEC Is Right on TARGET," *U.S. Army TARDEC Accelerate Magazine* (Summer 2010): 24–29.

7. For more on developing an innovation strategy for your business, see R. G. Cooper and S. J. Edgett, "Developing a Product Innovation and Technology Strategy for Your Business," *Research-Technology Management* 53, no. 3 (May–June 2010): 33–40; see also endnote 2 above.

INDEX